THE MUSLIM STRUGGLE
FOR CIVIL RIGHTS
IN SPAIN

Sussex Studies in Spanish History

General Editor: Nigel Townson, Universidad Complutense, Madrid
Consultant Editor: José Álvarez-Junco, Universidad Complutense, Madrid
Advisory Editors: Pamela Radcliff, University of California, San Diego
Tim Rees, University of Exeter

José Álvarez-Junco, *The Emergence of Mass Politics in Spain: Populist Demagoguery and Republican Culture, 1890–1910*

Tom Buchanan, *The Impact on the Spanish Civil War on Britain: War, Loss and Memory*

Andrew Dowling, *Catalonia since the Spanish Civil War: Reconstructing the Nation**

Hugo García, *The Truth about Spain!: Mobilizing British Public Opinion, 1936–1939*

Irene González González, *Spanish Education in Morocco, 1912–1956: Cultural Interactions in a Colonial Context*

Patricia Hertel, *The Crescent Remembered: Islam and Nationalism on the Iberian Peninsula*

David Messenger, *L'Espagne Républicaine: French Policy and Spanish Republicanism in Liberated France*

Javier Moreno-Luzón, *Modernizing the Nation: Spain during the Reign of Alfonso XIII, 1902–1931*

Inbal Ofer, *Señoritas in Blue: The Making of a Female Political Elite in Franco's Spain*

Mario Ojeda Revah, *Mexico and the Spanish Civil War: Domestic Politics and the Republican Cause*

Elizabeth Roberts, *"Freedom, Faction, Fame and Blood": British Soldiers of Conscience in Greece, Spain and Finland*

Silvina Schammah Gesser, *Madrid's Forgotten Avant-Garde: Between Essentialism and Modernity*

Manuel Álvarez Tardío and Fernando del Rey Reguillo (eds.), *The Spanish Second Republic Revisited*

Nigel Townson, *The Crisis of Democracy in Spain: Centrist Politics under the Second Republic, 1931–1936*

Nigel Townson (ed.), *Is Spain Different?: A Comparative Look at the 19th and 20th Centuries*

* Published in association with the Cañada Blanch Centre for Contemporary Spanish Studies and the Catalan Observatory, London School of Economics

THE MUSLIM STRUGGLE
FOR CIVIL RIGHTS
IN SPAIN

Promoting Democracy Through
Migrant Engagement, 1985–2010

AITANA GUIA

sussex
ACADEMIC
PRESS
Brighton • Chicago • Toronto

2014

Copyright © Aitana Guia, 2014.

The right of Aitana Guia to be identified as Author of this work has been
asserted in accordance with the Copyright, Designs and Patents Act 1988.

2 4 6 8 10 9 7 5 3 1

First published in 2014 by
SUSSEX ACADEMIC PRESS
PO Box 139
Eastbourne BN24 9BP

and in the United States of America by
SUSSEX ACADEMIC PRESS
Independent Publishers Group
814 N. Franklin Street, Chicago, IL 60610

and in Canada by
SUSSEX ACADEMIC PRESS (CANADA)
1108 / 115 Antibes Drive, Toronto, Ontario M2R 2Y9

British Library Cataloguing in Publication Data
A CIP catalogue record for this book is available from the British Library.

Library of Congress Cataloging-in-Publication Data
Applied for.

Paperback ISBN 978-1-84519-581-6

Typeset & designed by Sussex Academic Press, Brighton & Eastbourne.

Printed on acid-free paper.

Printed by Edwards Brothers Malloy

Contents

Preface by Series Editor, Tim Rees   vii
Acknowledgements   ix
List of Abbreviations   x

Introduction   1
The Migrant Experience and the Transition to Democracy in Spain   1
Democracy, Inclusion, and Citizenship   3
Repositioning Democratization in Spain   6
Islam and Democratization in Spain   8

 1 **The Fight for Citizenship and Inclusion in a Borderland City:**   10
   Melilla, 1985–1988
   A Critical Borderland City   10
   The 1985 Immigration Act   13
   Muslim Melillans   15
   Muslim Women Activists   18
   Spanish Nativism   22
   In the Shadow of Morocco, but a Long Way from Spain   26
   From Constitutional Patriotism to Sedition   28
   Repercussions   37

 2 **The Struggle for Voice, Status, and Rights in Mainland Spain,**   41
   1989–2005
   Finding an Independent Voice   42
   "I could only think about papers"   46
   Racism and Migrant Rights   52
   When "Exceptional" Becomes "Ordinary"   58
   The World Upside Down   59
   Twisting the Government's Arm   63
   Achievements and New Challenges   70

 3 **Religious Pluralism, Secularism, and Women's Rights,**   74
   1968–2010
   From State Catholicism to Religious Pluralism   75
   The Construction of Spanish Islam   78
   "Worthless piece of paper"   83
   Conflicts over Women's Rights   87
   The Public Practice of Islam in Spain   95

4 Mosque Building, Catalan Nationalism, and Spain's Politics   101
  of Belonging, 1990–2010
    Mosque Building and Nativist Resistance in Spain   103
    Barcelona and the Mosque that was Never Built   106
    A Path towards Peace or "Ravalistan"?   109
    Muslim Immigrants on Catalonia's Nationalist Fault Lines   111
    The Spectrum of Possibilities for Muslims in Catalonia   116
    Osona: the Rise of the PxC and the Collapse of *Convivencia*   122
    Interculturalism   127

5 Reclaiming Islamic Spain: from the Córdoba Mosque to the   130
  Festival of Moors and Christians, 1965-2010
    Islam in Spain's Memory Debates   131
    The Córdoba Mosque-Cathedral and the Limits of *Convivencia*   135
    The Festival of Moors and Christians   139
    Interpreting the Festival of Moors and Christians   142
    "Mooricization"   146
    The Festival of Moors and Christians in Democratic Times   149
    "We are not fanatics"   151
    Dynamics and Alternatives   155

Conclusion   161

Notes   167
Bibliography   204
Index   228

Series Editor's Preface by Tim Rees

Modern Spain is rightly celebrated as an example of a successful 'transition' from dictatorship to democracy. The creation of a democratic constitution, liberal institutions and the extension of the rights of citizenship during the 1970s are usually seen as the principal achievements of this process of political change. Recent debates now often focus upon the extent to which this transformation did not just begin after the death of General Franco in 1975 but whether it also had important roots in developments taking place within Spanish society, and even within the regime's own organisations, during the final years of dictatorial rule. In contrast, a consensus has largely reigned that the transition ended with the failed military coup of February 1981. After this attempt to set back the political clock, Spain became a liberal democracy on a par with its counterparts in the European Union. Nevertheless, questions concerning political participation and civil rights were not all resolved at this point and some of the most fundamental difficult questions about the nature of citizenship have only really been raised subsequently.

In *The Muslim Struggle for Civil Rights in Spain*, Aitana Guia draws attention to one of the most significant of these attempts to establish and define civil rights in post-democratic Spain. As she makes clear this has by no means been a conflict peculiar to Spain; indeed one of the many strengths of her study is the way she draws careful comparisons with parallel situations in other countries of Europe and North America. What does set Spain somewhat apart is the Iberian Peninsula's long and much studied history as host to previous Muslim societies and forms of Islamic rule. This study demonstrates the ways in which this past, both real and imagined, resonates with the reality of a much more recent Muslim presence in modern Spain. By 2005 approximately one million people in Spain had an affinity with Islam, rising to 1.7 million in 2014 (3.6 percent of the population). Their origins are diverse. Some are Spanish converts but most have been immigrants drawn from different parts of the world, including the religiously devout but also the secular. They are part of a pattern of recent immigration that has brought labour and cultural diversity to a country that had a declining and aging population. Nor have communities developed evenly across Spain, with Madrid, Catalonia, Murcia and Almeria having the largest proportions of Muslims. Whatever their backgrounds, physical appearance, dress, cultures and customs have made them highly visible.

Guia locates the origins of contemporary conflicts about the position of Muslims in Spain within the so-called 'enclave' of Melilla, itself a remnant of Spanish colonial rule in North Africa and a borderland with modern Morocco. As she shows, many of the goals for the struggle for Muslim rights were first established here, along with the terms in which debates about the nature of Spanish citizenship and Spanishness have subsequently been conducted in mainland Spain. The book charts the development of organised campaigns since 1985 to give Muslims equal status as citizens, and for recognition of religious and cultural rights. Divisions among campaigners, and particularly the position of women, are dealt with sensitively. Using a rich variety of sources, particularly interviews, Guia offers fascinating insights into the experience of Muslims in contemporary Spain and the ups and downs of their struggle to gain a voice, to establish places of worship and to have their cultural interests acknowledged.

Reactions to the Muslim minority have been predictably mixed within Spain. In particular, demands for equality have often clashed with 'nativist' assumptions that Spanish identity and citizenship are to be equated predominantly with a white-European and culturally Catholic (if not practicing) background to which Muslims, by their very nature, cannot be fully admitted. The sense that Islam is itself antithetical to democracy and opposed to liberal secular rights, particularly for women, provides fuel for these views and also means that they have often had a currency across other political divisions in Spain, despite clear differences between successive conservative and socialist governments in their responses to demands for equality. Spanish Muslims have also had to negotiate existing fault lines between Spanish and regional identities, and religious and secular attitudes. As Guia demonstrates clearly, this has been particularly acute in Catalonia where Muslims have often found themselves trapped between Castilian/Catalan linguistic and regionalist conflicts. Similar problems have accompanied the demand for religious pluralism, sometimes unsettling both committed Catholics and convinced secularists alike. Overt hostility to Muslims has been fairly muted in Spain, at least in comparison with some other European countries, with only a nationalist fringe adopting openly anti-Islamic agendas.

The central argument of this book is positive, suggesting that campaigns for Muslim civil rights have strengthened rather than weakened democracy in Spain. The cause of Muslim civil rights has gained ground with many achievements, though these do not as yet amount to full equality in either law or practice. Although these are issues of minority rights, they also touch strongly upon more general questions about citizenship, integration, multiculturalism, religious pluralism and secularism, Spanish and regional identities. They are also a reminder that democracy in Spain was not just achieved in the 1970s in Spain but has been continually developed, and fought for, ever since.

Acknowledgements

I owe a huge debt of gratitude to Adrian Shubert, Antonio Cazorla-Sánchez, Roberto Perin, Pamela Beth Radcliff, Margot Irvine, Sandra Parmegiani, Suzanne Langlois, Tom Cohen, Jonathan Edmonton, the late Varpu Lindström, and the professors and graduate students of the York University Migration History Workshop, for their insightful comments and generous assistance. Field research in Spain would have been impossible without the hospitality of the Escutia and Cubí-Fernández families. Ryan Perks edited and made the manuscript much more readable. I am especially grateful to my partner, Ivano Stocco, for the constructive criticism, moral support, and the best cover I could have hoped for. My daughters Oriana and Miranda, finally, were a constant source of motivation.

List of Abbreviations

ACESOP   *Associació Cultural Educativa i Social Operativa de Dones Pakistaneses* (Cultural, Educational, Social, and Operational Association of Pakistani Women).

AEME   *Asociación de Emigrantes Marroquíes en España* (Association of Moroccan Emigrants in Spain).

APWC   *Associació de Treballadors Pakistanesos de Catalunya* (Association of Pakistani Workers in Catalonia).

ATIME   *Asociación de Trabajadores Inmigrantes Marroquíes en España* (Association of Moroccan Immigrant Workers in Spain).

CGT   *Confederación General del Trabajo* (General Confederation of Labour).

CCIC   *Consell Cultural Islàmic de Catalunya* (Islamic Cultural Council of Catalonia).

CIE   *Comisión Islámica de España* (Islamic Commission of Spain).

EEC   European Economic Community.

ETA   *Euskadi Ta Askatasuna* (Euskadi and Freedom).

EU   European Union.

FEERI   *Federación Española de Entidades Religiosas Islámicas* (Spanish Federation of Islamic Religious Entities).

HOAC   *Hermandad Obrera de Acción Católica* (Workers' Brotherhood of Catholic Action).

ICCV   *Centro Cultural Islámico de Valencia* (Islamic Cultural Centre of Valencia).

JOC   *Juventud Obrera Cristiana* (Christian Worker Youth).

MMPAS   *Escola d'Adults Miquel Martí i Pol* (Miquel Martí i Pol Adult School).

NGO   Non-Governmental Organization.

OCMP   *Comité Organizador del Pueblo Musulmán* (Organizing Committee of the Muslim People).

PCL   *Plataforma per la Llengua* (Platform for the Catalan Language).

PP   *Partido Popular* (Popular Party).

PSC   *Partit dels Socialistes de Catalunya* (Socialists' Party of Catalonia).

PSOE   *Partido Socialista Obrero Español* (Spanish Socialist Workers' Party).

PSUC   *Partit Socialista Unificat de Catalunya* (Unified Socialist Party of Catalonia).

PxC   *Plataforma per Catalunya* (Platform for Catalonia).

UCIDE   *Unión de Comunidades Islámicas de España* (Union of Islamic Communities of Spain).

UGT   *Unión General de Trabajadores* (General Union of Workers).

Introduction

The Migrant Experience and the Transition to Democracy in Spain

In 1977 Ahmed Karrouch, a Moroccan of Amazigh[1] origin, arrived in Vic, a small city in the heart of Catalonia. It was his second attempt to immigrate to Spain. A year earlier, Spanish authorities had deported him because he lacked status. This time, however, he found work in a metal factory, a position he would maintain for more than thirty years. With the help of his boss and friends he stayed clear of police, and eventually obtained residency and work permits. His wife and three children had remained with his parents and siblings in a small village near the Moroccan city of Nador. But eight years after his departure, Karrouch would use the newly passed 1985 Immigration Act to reunite his family of five in Spain. We know this because one of his daughters, Laila, would go on to become a writer, the first Amazigh to pen a memoir in Catalan about growing up as a young Muslim immigrant in Spain.[2]

For many years, the Karrouchs, a large family, managed to survive on Ahmad's wages; occasionally, this was supplemented by the piecework that Ahmed's wife Fadma would do from home. Ahmed had been reluctant at first to let his wife leave the house to find work because he wanted her to "maintain traditions". However, he eventually relented: one could not work full time and do all the shopping and errands for a family of five. It was time for the Karrouchs to adapt to their new reality. Accordingly, all members of the family made a concerted effort to excel at school or work, and to learn both Spanish and Catalan.[3] It was not easy to overcome the isolation that came with being only the third Moroccan – and first Amazigh – family to settle in Vic. But the Karrouchs's tenacity, hard work, and capacity, coupled with larger, structural changes, were crucial to their success.

Ahmed Karrouch had arrived in Spain at a crucial moment in the country's history. Francisco Franco had died in 1975 and, two years earlier, the Basque separatist group Euskadi Ta Askatasuna (ETA) had assassinated Luis Carrero Blanco, the dictator's self-appointed successor. Spain's second post-Franco government, headed by King Juan Carlos I and the centrist Prime Minister Adolfo Suárez, held a national referendum to reform Franco's legal system and institute democracy after decades of authoritarian rule. In June 1977, on the eve of the first democratic elections, Spaniards took to the streets across the country. In 1978 the country ratified a progressive constitution that established a system of parliamentary democracy based on the rule of law as well as polit-ical, social, and economic rights. This new constitution aimed to "protect all

Spaniards and all the peoples of Spain in the exercise of human rights, their cultures and traditions, languages and institutions".[4]

Just as the authors of the first constitutions of revolutionary France could not imagine extending 'universal rights' to the colonial subjects of the French Empire, Spanish legislators did not have families like the Karrouchs in mind when they drafted the Constitution of 1978. Although the document would have a clear, if unintended, spill-over effect for immigrants to Spain, it was primarily concerned with the various regional nationalist movements, as well as the multitude of different cultures native to the Iberian Peninsula.

Nonetheless, the constitution maintained the right of foreigners to "enjoy the public freedoms guaranteed by the present Title [of fundamental rights], under the terms to be laid down by treaties and the law".[5] It thus set in motion a series of developments that would culminate in 1985 with the Law on the Rights and Freedoms of Foreigners in Spain. Moreover, the new constitution promised religious pluralism, removed Catholicism as the country's official religion, and eventually obliged the government to sign independent agreements with minority denominations and religions throughout the country. The new constitution thus conceded to the Karrouchs and similar immigrant families the legal right to practice Islam in Spain – no small matter given the country's longstanding prohibition on Islam and Judaism.

Indeed, one of the most remarkable aspects of the Constitution of 1978 was its abolition of the Francoist insistence on cultural and national uniformity. So while Article 2 stated that the "Constitution is based on the indissoluble unity of the Spanish Nation, the common and indivisible country of all Spaniards", it also stated that it "recognises and guarantees the right to autonomy of the nationalities and regions of which it is composed and the solidarity amongst them all". It also privileged cultural pluralism and claimed that "[t]he wealth of the different language modalities of Spain is a cultural heritage which shall be the object of special respect and protection".[6] Such measures were unprecedented, and they would affect the Karrouchs doubly: because they were immigrants, and because they had settled in newly autonomous Catalonia.

The Constitution of 1978 divided Spain into seventeen "autonomous communities" and, later on, two autonomous cities, Ceuta and Melilla (both part of mainland Africa). The new democracy demonstrated great flexibility in its ability to decentralize and manage regional nationalism.[7] It also made it possible for thousands of migrants like Ahmed Karrouch and his family to partake, as active agents, in Spain's newfound commitment to liberal democracy, cultural diversity, and religious pluralism.

Ahmed Karrouch's arrival in the late 1970s coincided with the end of the mass emigration of Spaniards to northern Europe and Latin America, and the beginning of international immigration to Spain. The country was now an economically developed democracy; it had benefited greatly from the so-called "economic miracle" of the 1960s and seventies, and it was on the verge of joining both the European Economic Community (EEC) and the North Atlantic Treaty Organization (NATO).

Migration to Southern Europe had followed a different pattern than the rest of the continent. The colonial and east–west migrations so typical of postwar Western Europe were non-existent in Spain. On the contrary, Portuguese, Italians, Greeks, and Spaniards themselves formed the initial contingent of migrant workers sent to reconstruct Western Europe after World War II. However, as the oil crisis of 1973 hit Europe and labour recruitment campaigns in industrialized countries subsequently waned, migration to Southern Europe gathered pace. Net exporters of labour for decades, Spain and its Mediterranean counterparts were ill-equipped to deal with the influx of immigration (indeed, Spain would only approve an Immigration Act in 1985). Like the Italian, Portuguese, and Greek governments, Spanish lawmakers dealt with millions of irregular migrants by frequent general amnesties of undocumented residents.[8]

Subsequent migration to Spain, largely of Latin Americans and Africans, was quick and considerable compared to other countries in the European Union (EU). In 1985, immigrants comprised a mere 0.63 percent of the Spanish population; by 2005, the country's 5 million immigrants accounted for fully 10.8 percent of the population. By comparison, in 2005 the percentage of immigrants in France was 10.2, in Germany 12.3.[9] As of 2011, Spain's 5.7 million immigrants represented 12.2 percent of the population, of which 2.4 percent were EU citizens. In terms of nationality, Romanians made up the largest immigrant community in Spain, followed by Moroccans, Britons, Ecuadorians, and Colombians.[10]

The tools that researchers have used to quantify the number of Muslim immigrants in Europe are necessarily inadequate. While it is possible to find data on the overall number of citizens from Muslim-majority countries living in Spain, it is virtually impossible to differentiate between devout Muslims and nonbelievers. This data also excludes converts, practicing naturalized Muslims and their Spanish-born children, and practicing undocumented residents. In 2011, immigrants in Spain from countries with strong Islamic traditions, including Morocco, Pakistan, Senegal, Algeria, and Nigeria, accounted for 986,000 persons, yet the number of practicing Muslims amongst this group is unknown.[11] The Union of Islamic Communities of Spain (UCIDE) puts the number of Muslims at 1.5 million, 70 percent of whom reside in just four regions: Catalonia (387,582), Madrid (241,372), Andalusia (235,098), and Valencia (157,992). As a Moroccan, Ahmed Karrouch is part of the secong largest but oldest immigrant community in Spain, one largely concentrated in Madrid, Catalonia, Almería, and Murcia.[12]

Democracy, Inclusion, and Citizenship

Democracy and democratization are multifaceted concepts that can range from the extension of universal suffrage to the transition from an authoritarian regime, from a more democratic form of government to the "gradual development towards the perhaps never fully achievable ideal of democracy". According to this last definition – one employed throughout this study – the process of democratization "does not end with the transition to democratic government and therefore applies even to countries [such as Spain] regularly recognized as democracies".[13]

The two core principles on which most definitions of democracy rest are people power and political equality. Scholars who emphasize popular control argue that 'the people', as the source of political authority, are granted the freedom to elect a government that is responsive to their views and amenable to the public interest. Citizens are also entitled to take active part in the common affairs of society at every level. Critics of 'vote-centric' democratic theories, however, point out that a system based on the numerical supremacy of votes cannot achieve legitimacy since minorities, by their very relationship to the majority, may be excluded from the exercise of real power within the system. Other scholars emphasize the second principle and argue that all citizens are entitled to a voice and that all persons should be given equal consideration in the formulation and delivery of public policy. As constitutive elements of democracy, equality and inclusion are, however, contentious. If democracy is merely understood as the presence of effective rules for political competition among rival elites, then they are not relevant. Nonetheless, Robert Dahl, among others, has argued that contestation among rival groups and individual equality are separate but equally necessary criteria for democracy. Democracy can therefore be viewed as a competition for public power under roughly equal conditions.[14]

In the present context inclusion refers to opportunities for electoral participation, to acts of political participation, and to the state's responsiveness to such acts. Inclusion thus depends on the existence of formally recognized opportunities for participation in the process of making collectively binding decisions. The right to vote is at the heart of democratic inclusion and is thus one of the primary criteria for deciding whether or not a political system is inclusive. The exclusion of a rapidly expanding migrant population that is unable, permanently or for long periods of time, to access citizenship thus diminishes the inclusiveness of Spanish democracy in this respect. As this study will attempt to show, the Muslim struggle for civil rights that began in Ceuta and Melilla in 1985 made the young Spanish democracy more inclusive by enfranchising thousands of Muslim residents, ending nativist[15] rule in those cities, and questioning Spain's first Immigration Act (see Chapter 1).

A second way to think about inclusion is to look at acts of political participation. This study employs a 'thick' conception of citizenship premised on citizenship as the result of activity from below, as opposed to a 'thin' conception of citizenship as an official status granted from above. 'Thick' citizenship implies that individuals come together in civil society to demand new rights or the implementation of existing ones.[16] More than a fixed concept, citizenship can thus be seen as a dynamic historical process, the outcome of legal, political, and symbolic battles waged over time. As Pamela Beth Radcliff argues, the Spanish transition to democracy was a moment in which different modes of citizenship became openly contested. The major line of division ran between the proponents of the "citizen movement", a form of grass-roots participatory democracy based in the communitarian tradition, and political elites, who envisioned a more rights-based representative democracy in which citizenship was a more abstract and disembodied category, one that would be protected, not empowered.[17]

Instead of viewing democratic citizenship merely as a legal status granted by the Constitution of 1978, this study looks at the construction of democratic citizenship as a grassroots development shaped by the limitations to citizenship imposed by the Constitution and immigration laws. Even though the concept of citizenship maintains a pretense of universal inclusion, it has always been qualified by membership in a particular polity and also by particular characteristics that exclude or marginalize certain groups, whether by age, gender, sexuality, religious affiliation, or ethno-cultural membership.

In post-Francoist Spain, the tension between inclusion and exclusion has revolved around the status of immigrant communities on the mainland and ethno-cultural minorities in Ceuta and Melilla. As Radcliff asserts, "Not only can ordinary people be agents in the process of becoming citizens, but furthermore, their actions help define what constitutes democratic practice and participation in any specific context".[18] The fight for status undertaken by millions of undocumented migrants in Spain since 1985, their organizing and network efforts, as well as their struggles to find a voice in Spanish politics and society thus exemplify Geoff Eley's notion of democracy and democratization as products of struggle and popular pressure (see Chapter 2).[19] Undocumented migrants deprived of citizenship rights are paradoxically the heirs of the "citizenship movement" prevalent amongst Spaniards at the transition to democracy, and which has since been deactivated.

Another aspect of political participation that has shaped the features of democratic citizenship is religious activism by self-identified Muslims, both converts to Islam and immigrants from Muslim-majority countries. While the democratizing impact of socio-political activism of Muslim Melillans and undocumented migrants in mainland Spain has been overlooked but not fundamentally challenged, religious activism is often suspected of undermining democratic values and of reversing the hard-won separation of church and state. Chapter 3 counters this view by arguing that Spanish Muslims' fight to have Islam officially recognized as an integral and historically significant religion in Spain, their struggle to ensure the public practice of Islam in a condition of equality with that of Catholicism, and their attempts to adapt the tenants of Islam to Spain's constitutional framework – particularly in relation to women's rights – have actually contributed to the normalization of religious pluralism in Spain.

The responsiveness of public discourse and public policy to the interest of minorities and disempowered groups comprises a third crucial characteristic of an inclusive democracy. Chapter 4 explores the anti-mosque backlash in Catalonia during the 1990s and connects it to an increasingly ethnically based and exclusionary nationalism. Particularly regarding sites of prayer in Catalonia, both public discourse and public policy have departed from inclusivity and equality. Moreover, in a pluralistic society such as Spain, the virtue of public discourse is not just the willingness of all involved to participate in politics, but also the willingness to listen and take seriously a range of views with which one may disagree. Political debates that aim to achieve consensus or are premised on persuasion rather than power, manipulation or coercion are also a sign of inclusivity.[20] Will Kymlicka and Wayne Norman argue that democracy not only depends on the justice of its institutions or foundational documents, but also on "the virtues, identities, and practices of its citizens, including their ability to co-operate, deliberate, and feel solidarity with those who belong to different ethnic and religious groups".[21] Controversies over the construction of mosques, as well as an unwillingness to engage in a conversation over the derogatory narrative and rituals of the Festival of Moors and Christians (discussed in Chapter 5) exemplify the reluctance of ethnic Spaniards to engage with ethnic and religious minorities' demands.

Repositioning Democratization in Spain

According to the dominant narrative of twentieth-century Spanish political history, the transition to democracy commenced in June 1977, less than two years after Franco's death, with the country's first free elections, and it was cemented shortly thereafter, in December 1978, when a majority of Spaniards ratified a democratic constitution. Often employed in studies of Spain's democratic transition, this rather narrow timeline ignores the fact that becoming a democratic citizen takes time and education. Historians such as Antonio Cazorla-Sánchez and Pamela Beth Radcliff dispute the standard timeline and argue that 1978 marked not the start of democracy in Spain but the pinnacle of a process that had begun much earlier. The Constitution of 1978 was the result of Spaniards' presence in the streets, as well as in grassroots political organizations, during the preceding decades.[22]

While there is disagreement over when, exactly, the process of democratization began, it is generally agreed that 1982 marked its conclusion; by that time, most of the institutional framework was firmly in place, Spaniards had elected a new Socialist-led government, and an attempt at a military *coup d'état* in February 1981 had ended in abject failure.[23] Yet while the decentralized structure of Spain was nearly complete, the electoral and party system was fully functional, and elites and political parties deactivated the "citizenship movement" of workers, students, and ordinary Spaniards in favour of a pragmatic and representative approach to policy making, this study argues that the debate over democracy and democratic citizenship did not end in 1982.

Any narrative that limits Spain's democratic transition to the period 1975–1982 hinders our understanding of the democratization process in Spain in at least two ways. First, it does not differentiate clearly between the transition, consolidation, and deepening phases of Spain's democratization process.[24] This is important because many of the factors that might assist in the maintenance or strengthening of democracy are not necessarily the same as those that bring it about in the first place. Democratic consolidation, like democracy itself, is an amorphous concept; it can range from the existence of free and fair electoral procedures to a broader expansion of participation as well as the reduction in social and economic inequality necessary to ensure this. In this study, democratic consolidation is understood as the processes by which democratic political institutions are anchored and stabilized. It is similar to what Víctor M. Pérez-Díaz calls "institutionalization", the stage at which a democratic regime becomes "legitimate in the eyes of most of the population most of the time, and the basic rules of the political game not only prevail de facto but have been internalized by both politicians and society".[25] Democratic deepening is understood as the processes that reinforce and embed democratic practices in society and thus close the "gap between formal legal rights in the civil and political arena, and the practical possibility of practicing those rights".[26]

The typical timeframe also hinders our understanding of democratization in post-Francoist Spain because it tends to overlook, as a result of its very limited chronological framework, the contributions of immigrants and religious minorities in Spain. Two of the key elements of the consolidation of democracy in Spain, the 1985 Immigration Law that determined the status and fundamental rights of non-Spaniards, and the 1992 Agreement of Cooperation between the government and the Islamic Commission of Spain (CIE), which legalized and protected the practice of Islam in the country, are often omitted from a narrative that assigns all credit to the peaceful accomplishments of ethnic Spaniards during the period 1975–1982.

Often, the process of democratization manages to institutionalize a democratic regime but fails to incorporate ethnic or religious minorities. Patrick Heller concludes in his study of India and South Africa that "even as formal constitutional democracy has been consolidated, there is little evidence of an increased capacity of subordinate groups to have an effective role in shaping public policy".[27] What has been overlooked in the study of democratization in Spain is the struggles of disenfranchised minorities for rights, status, and a voice, as well as their impact on the democratization process and the evolving definition of citizenship.

Incorporating the struggles of immigrant and religious minorities into the history of Spain's transition to democracy allows us to recognize that the debate over democratic citizenship did not subside in 1982. On the contrary, it was forcefully resumed in 1985 by the struggle of 20,000 Muslim Melillans for Spanish citizenship (see Chapter 1). It continued to reverberate throughout mainland Spain until regular venues for accessing status were put in place in 2003 (see Chapter 2). And from its socio-political origins, it grew to include the demand for religious and cultural rights as part of the struggle for visibility and legitimacy that began in 1992 and continues to this day. All of this is part of what Spanish Muslims call the country's unfinished "religious transition", from Catholicism as a state religion to state neutrality and parity among confessions (see Chapters 3–5).

Islam and Democratization in Spain

The resurgence of religion as a factor in international politics since the Iranian revolution of 1979, and especially since the events of 11 September 2001, has contributed to the debate over whether certain forms of religion are incompatible with democracy. As a result, the role of religion – and especially Islam – in the process of democratization and the maintenance of social cohesion has been questioned by many. For example, Ernst Gellner and Samuel P. Huntington, among others, have argued that Islam is incompatible with civil society and western democracy. By contrast, scholars such as Fred Halliday, Hugh Goddard, and John Esposito have called attention to the variety of Muslim responses to the discourse on and practice of democracy, ranging from the belief that democracy is incompatible with Islam, to the belief that it is an essential component of the faith.[28] While the scholarly consensus largely rejects reductionist theses concerning Islam and democracy, arguments claiming that Islam is a threat to democratic values, popularized by Oriana Fallaci, Bat Ye'or or Bruce Bawer, among others, remain highly influential.[29]

In Europe, many politicians and intellectuals have argued that Muslims are essentially incapable of embracing democratic politics since Europe's tradition of secularism clashes at the most fundamental level with the trenchant religiosity of Muslim migrants.[30] Muslims will hijack Europe and transform it into 'Eurabia', goes the standard argument, if Europeans do not defend Enlightenment values, in particular the rights of women and sexual minorities.[31] Other public intellectuals have contended that Muslims can be accommodated in Europe provided they adhere to the civic code and values that lie at the heart of the European social and political system.[32] Still others have questioned whether strict secularism is suitable for Europe, highlighting the need to make accommodations without losing the core values inherited from the Enlightenment tradition.[33]

A few scholars have attempted to move beyond the question of whether assimilation is desirable, or even possible, and have looked instead at how Muslims have adapted religious and cultural practices to fit the European context. Indeed, some go as far as to refer to Islam in Europe as a distinct syncretic practice: Euro-Islam.[34] Rather than following this approach, this study analyzes the ways in which Muslims in Spain have interacted with the various social and political segments of Spanish society. In so doing, it focuses not only on the way European culture has influenced the incorporation of Muslim immigrants to their host society, but also how Muslims have affected and transformed this new environment – not to mention themselves – in the process.

This study focuses on Muslim migrants because, more than any other group of newcomers, they stand out as religiously, culturally, linguistically, and ethnically different, at least according to 'native'[35] perceptions. Their status as visible minorities has meant that they have had to confront formidable barriers in their struggle for recognition and survival. The starkness and extremity of their struggle, as well the solutions they have adopted, could well serve as an important paradigm for understanding the struggles undergone by minorities throughout modern Europe. The choice of Muslims is also connected to Spanish history and the historical narratives Spaniards have used – and continue to use – to legitimize their national and cultural identity. As Mary Elizabeth Perry argues, the various medieval kingdoms of the Iberian Peninsula were unified only by constructing a Christian identity that "required a common enemy more than a tradition of peaceful coexistence". This common enemy was found in Spain's defeated Islamic kingdoms, in the forcefully converted Muslim populations known as *Moriscos*, in Muslim pirates, and in Ottoman Turks. Eloy Martín Corrales has likewise argued that Maurophobia, or the fear of Moors, has been a constant and mutable feature of modern Spanish identity, one that continues to inform public discourse and historical narratives.[36]

Of course, the choice of Muslim migrants (as well as native converts to Islam) as an object of study is not meant to suggest that they represent a unified, homogenous bloc. In reality, Spanish Muslims have been marked by a considerable degree of ethnic, ideological, denominational, gender, and generational diversity. Some Muslims are now naturalized citizens, while others remain undocumented and itinerant. Some are devout, some are not. Therefore, unless otherwise stated, when this book talks about 'Muslims', it refers to culturally Islamic persons, both believers and nonbelievers.

This book looks at an aspect of the consolidation and deepening of democracy in Spain that has otherwise been overlooked. Its core argument is that by fighting for religious and cultural rights, status and citizenship, Muslim immigrants and converts have contributed, *sine qua non*, to Spain's transition to democracy in the post-Franco era. They have catalyzed a set of laws aimed at minorities, enshrined the protection of religious pluralism at the regional and national levels, and initiated a vibrant and healthy conversation among the country's intellectual and political elites on the rich historical and cultural legacy of Islam in Spain. Together, Muslims and non-Muslims have learned to be citizens of a heterogeneous society, and today Spain is more solidly democratic as a result.

1

The Fight for Citizenship and Inclusion in a Borderland City

Melilla, 1985–1988

The North African cities of Ceuta and Melilla, conquered by Portugal and Spain in 1415 and 1497, respectively, differed from the general trend in the fight for autonomy and decentralization that would engulf Spain during the country's transition to democracy after 1975. Even though the 1978 Spanish Constitution allowed Ceuta and Melilla to become Autonomous Communities, local authorities in both cities preferred to remain as close to the mainland as possible. Lingering memories of the chaotic decolonization of the Spanish Sahara in the mid-1970s led ethnic Europeans in Ceuta and Melilla to opt for the safety of centralization over the uncertainty of autonomy; if centralization was no longer an option, then being part of the mainland province of Málaga, located in the newly created Autonomous Community of Andalusia, was viewed by most as the next best thing. It was not until 1995, at the end of the fourth mandate of the Socialist Prime Minister Felipe González, that both cities applied for, and obtained, autonomy.[1]

While colonial legacies and the fears of their ethnic European inhabitants ensured that Ceuta and Melilla would be the last Spanish regions to gain autonomy, their borderland status and mixed populations placed them at the forefront of growing tensions between immigrants and ethnic Spaniards during this period. The Muslim struggle for legal status and civil rights in Spain thus began in the unsuspecting and often overlooked city of Melilla in the 1980s.[2]

A Critical Borderland City

Melilla is a mid-sized Spanish city located on the Mediterranean coast of North Africa, at the northeast edge of the Moroccan Rif Mountains. Prior to the 1497 conquest of the city by Spain's Catholic Monarchs, Queen Isabella I of Castile and King Ferdinand II of Aragon, Melilla was part of the Kingdom of Fez. Although bordering Imazighen tribes and Moroccan authorities have repeatedly threatened the sovereignty of the enclave, Melilla has remained a Spanish military outpost since its conquest. By 1900, long after the shock of the Melilla War (1859–1860) – pretentiously called the 'War of Africa' by many Spaniards – had worn off, Melilla had 8,956 inhabitants. A dynamic city eager to receive economic migrants from mainland Spain, Melilla had reached a population of 39,852 by 1910. By 1920, the city's population grew to 50,170, peaking at 81,182 in 1950. Most European descendants came from the Spanish provinces of Madrid, Málaga, Barcelona, Seville, the city of Ceuta, and other Andalusian provinces.[3]

Between 1936 and 1975, Melilla enjoyed a prominent position within the national-historical narrative promoted by the regime of General Francisco Franco. Franco and his military retinue launched their 1936 rebellion in Melilla, and the city continues to honour this past. Indeed, it was the last Spanish city to remove commemorative statues of Franco from public spaces in accordance with the 2007 Historical Memory Act aimed at the removal of divisive symbols pertaining to the dictatorship. Melilla's city hall argued that the statues paid tribute to Franco-the-military-leader, not the dictator, since he had protected Melilla during the Second Moroccan War (1920–26). His role in these events was arguably overstated.[4]

In addition to being an important military hub, Melilla's free port was integral to the transport of both legal and illicit goods, and its economy was dependent on trade with the surrounding Moroccan territory, as well as on investments and tax breaks from Spain. By 1975, however, Melilla's economic splendor was behind it and its free port status was threatened by Spain's application to join the customs union of the European Economic Community (EEC). The new democratic Spanish government thus proclaimed its intention to promote development in the area as a way to counter Moroccan claims over the enclave.[5]

Indeed, the Moroccan government has, since the country gained independence in 1956, regularly called for the decolonization and return of Ceuta and Melilla to Morocco in its appeals to the United Nations General Assembly, yet these enclaves have never been included in the UN decolonization list.[6] Spain has repeatedly denied Moroccan demands, arguing that it has a long-standing claim to sovereignty dating back to 1497, while simultaneously calling for the decolonization of British Gibraltar, part of the United Kingdom since 1714. Spain has held on to Ceuta and Melilla, despite the high economic cost – particularly in the case of the latter city, which is more isolated from the Spanish mainland, and thus more difficult to defend – for the same reasons it has kept the Canary Islands: Spain has controlled them for nearly five hundred years; they have been populated mostly by ethnic Spaniards; and there was no significant military uprising that would have made keeping them too economically or politically costly for the new democracy.

Ceuta and Melilla transitioned to a pluralistic party system by adopting the same political agents as mainland Spain. Between 1979 and 1983, the city was controlled by the centrist Union of the Democratic Centre (UCD), the same party that ruled in Madrid and which controlled the majority of local governments.[7] By 1985, the two main parties were the Spanish Socialist Workers' Party (PSOE) and the Popular Alliance Party (Alianza Popular), but various smaller local parties, such as the right-wing Nationalist Party of Melilla, also existed. As elsewhere in Spain, the PSOE won the 1982 national elections by a landslide and all elected representatives from Melilla, a congressperson and two senators, were Socialist. However, most Muslim Melillans, as non-citizen residents, were disenfranchised, and only a handful were members of a political party.

The census of 1985 put the population of Melilla at 52,388–2,827 of which were of Moroccan descent. But because the border that divided Melilla and Morocco was porous, the number of undocumented residents was unknown. Some Muslim leaders claimed that 27,000 undocumented residents lived in Melilla. A 1986 census indicated they were 17,824, that is, 25.3 percent of Melilla's official residents in 1985. Undocumented Muslim residents were either Moroccan citizens, stateless, or held a colonial document called a Statistics Card (31.1 percent), which was used for little more than identification. Muslim Melillans called the card a *"chapa de perro"*, a dog tag.[8] Regardless of their numbers, undocumented residents of Melilla had none of the democratic guarantees enshrined in the 1978 Constitution.

Before the 1980s, undocumented residents were barred from purchasing real estate or renting apartments, travelling to mainland Spain, receiving unemployment benefits, and accessing the nearest hospital in Málaga without special travel authorization from the government delegate.[9] Neighbourhoods were segregated, with European descendants living in the modernist-style downtown or in newly constructed suburbs, while African descendants lived in shanty towns with no running water or sewage.[10]

Muslim Melillans crossed the border between Morocco and Spain on a daily basis. This made Melilla into a borderland, an area marked by the constant wrangling and negotiations inherent in all cross-border travel. The concept of a borderland, as distinct from a colonial enclave, defines an area horizontally according to its geographical proximity to the surrounding hinterland, rather than defining it vertically in relation to the power differential vis-à-vis the former colonial metropolis. In his study of borderland identities in Italy, for example, David H. Kaplan argues that the emergence of multidimensional identities in border areas is less likely in those border regions where coexisting nationalities representing different ethnic, linguistic, and religious groups occupy conflicting positions. In Melilla, cross-border identifications were discouraged by authorities on both sides of the border. Muslim Melillans thus found their identities both marked by the state's borders and limited by its practice of territorial exclusion and demands of exclusive loyalty.[11]

To the governments of both Spain and Morocco, as well as to nationalists in both countries, national identity was a singular and exclusive concept: Muslim Melillans were either Spanish or Moroccan – they could not be both. While unconditional loyalty to a single national identity is a defining character of modern nationalism the world over, by the 1980s much of the developed world was grappling with more fluid concepts of identity. Globalization and the increasingly vociferous claims of identity politics reduced national identities to one more affiliation among many others, and not necessarily the defining one.

Borderlands such as Melilla, where ethnic, religious, and culturally diverse populations lived together in close quarters, were particularly ill-suited to a rigid and restrictive definition of national identity. While Melillans of European descent had no qualms about considering themselves exclusively Spanish, Melillans of African descent had to juggle with competing and often conflicting identifications. With the explosion of regional nationalisms across Spain following Franco's death, the notion that identities could be hyphenated, as they were in many other countries, was still a rarity.[12]

The 1985 Immigration Act

With the onset of the so-called 'economic miracle' of the 1960s and seventies, Spain shifted from being a country of emigrants (primarily to South America and other, more economically prosperous European countries) to one of immigrants (largely from North Africa and Latin America). As Northern European countries began to close their doors to large-scale immigration following the onset of the oil crisis of 1973–74, Southern Europe became a more attractive destination for prospective migrants. As a reflection of this new reality, the 1978 Constitution protected the rights of aliens by granting them the same public freedoms as Spaniards "under the terms to be laid down by treaties and the law".[13]

Yet politicians engaged in the transition to democracy simply did not place the development of immigration policy at the top of the government's agenda during this period. It was not until 1981 that the UCD government proposed an immigration act, which it ultimately failed to pass. The new Socialist government elected a year later was impelled to harmonize immigration policy after the approval of the Asylum Act of 1984 and two rulings by Spain's Constitutional Court stating that aliens in Spain should be entitled to fundamental rights, due process of law, and the protection of the courts. These measures were finally approved by the Socialist-dominated Congress during the last stages of the country's planned entry into the EEC, in 1986.[14]

The Act made it mandatory for foreigners who were resident in Spain to obtain work and residency permits. It developed provisions to grant foreigners the fundamental rights enshrined under the Spanish Constitution. It also developed a constitutional right to enfranchise foreigners who were citizens of countries that bestowed similar voting rights on Spaniards. The Act, however, restricted the right to join a union, to assemble freely, and to associate freely to legal residents. The 1985 Act also increased border policing capabilities and attempted to restrict the numbers of immigrants who were permitted to enter the country.

Foreigners complained that the Act made it difficult to obtain the required work and residency permits, and that they could attain permanent residency status only after a long and convoluted process. Critics claimed it was directed more at policing than integrating foreigners. Petitioned by NGOs, Joaquín Ruiz-Giménez, the Spanish Ombudsman, appealed certain articles of the Act to the Constitutional Court, even though all political parties had endorsed it. Ruiz-Giménez asked that the Act be reformed so that, "rather than make foreigners expellable, it made them integratable".[15]

The Act cited Spain's colonial past and offered "preferential treatment" to Latin Americans, Portuguese, Filipinos, Andorrans, Equatorial Guineans, Sephardi Jews, and Gibraltarians who "identified with or had a cultural affinity to" Spain. Residency and work permits were expedited for these immigrants, as was the mandatory waiting period – shortened from ten years to two – otherwise required before applying for citizenship.[16]

Although Spain held the disputed territory of Western Sahara until 1975 and parts of northern Morocco until 1956, the Immigration Act denied preferential treatment to immigrants from these territories. While, as we saw, it made a point to include Sephardi Jews, whose ancestors had been expelled from Spain in 1492, it ignored Muslims and *Moriscos* (converted Muslims) who were expelled in successive waves between 1492 and 1614. Centuries of autocratic rule and religious homogeneity in Spain contributed to designate those perceived not to share Spain's culture and identity, as did the fear of a growing population of Muslims who would gain Spanish citizenship quickly if granted preferential rights. Cool relations between Spain and Morocco, meanwhile, revived the historic rivalry between Christian Spain and Muslim North Africa, further fuelling Muslims' exclusion.

However, of the groups that had maintained longstanding cultural and historical ties to Spain, perhaps the most blatant form of exclusion was visited upon those Muslims who were born in, or were long-time residents of, Ceuta and Melilla. Under the Immigration Act, these individuals were automatically considered foreigners, and thus were forced to apply for residency and work permits. These approximately 20,000 undocumented residents differed from other immigrants in that they did not need to be smuggled into Spain; the border had been permeable before the 1980s, and many people from Melilla's hinterland could simply relocate to the city at will. Melilla-based journalist and writer Ricardo Crespo suggested this exceptional borderland situation could be used to solve the problem created by the Immigration Act:

> Let's be honest, the fight in Melilla is not about residency, it is about naturalization. The Immigration Act is too narrow for Muslim Melillans. After many years of extraordinary abuse, we should compensate them with an Exceptional Law that takes into account the full extent and complexity of

their situation. Otherwise, the Immigration Act is almost entirely anti-Muslim, and on some points probably unconstitutional as well.[17]

Similarly, a press statement by Muslim leaders explained why the Immigration Act was not fair to Muslims in Ceuta and Melilla in the following terms: "The Immigration Act caters perfectly to the Christian community. It grants residency status to, and 'integrates' (so they say), Muslims in Melilla, but as 'extended foreigners.' In other words, it legalizes political and legal inequality . . . [It institutionalizes] the exploitation of already exploited people".[18]

The Spanish ombudsman also advocated special legal provisions for Muslim Melillans outside of the Immigration Act. In December 1985 *El País*, Spain's leading pro-democracy newspaper, urged the government to exempt from the Act at the very least holders of the colonial Statistics Card. If the government did not exempt card holders, the paper argued, these people risked losing *arraigo* (rootedness, or seniority rights in legal terms), and might have to wait ten more years to apply for citizenship.[19] This was the first time that the legal concept of *arraigo* had been proposed as a solution for Muslims in Ceuta and Melilla, but it was going to take two more years of tension for Madrid to grasp its usefulness and put it into effect.

The concept of *arraigo*, though not mentioned in the Immigration Act, would become increasingly germane to the resolution of conflicts over official status in Spain. The concrete legal definition of *arraigo* tends to vary. It was alternatively defined by various Spanish governments as one's having lived a period of time in the country, maintaining a link with citizens or permanent residents, or knowledge of the host society. Yet its essence has remained the same: a way to subvert the tenuous claim to the national soil of Muslim Melillans and undocumented immigrants in mainland Spain.

Arraigo appeals to the "territorializing, often arborescent conceptions of nation and culture . . . [that] are associated with a powerful sedentarism in our thinking", explains Liisa Malkki. *Arraigo* also highlights "powerful metaphoric practices that so commonly link people to place" and are "deployed to understand and act upon the categorically aberrant condition of people whose claims on, and ties to, national soils are regarded as tenuous, spurious, or nonexistent". This was certainly the case for Muslim Melillans.[20]

Muslim Melillans

In May 1985, *El País* published "Legalize Melilla", an article written by Aomar Mohamedi Duddu,[21] a Spanish Muslim, economist, employee of the Melilla city hall, PSOE member, and leader of Melilla's undocumented Muslim residents. Duddu was a charismatic and imposing figure in Melilla city politics, one who scorned dissent and traveled the slums of the city in a Mercedes Benz that local Muslim businessmen had given him as a gift for his involvement in the community. He was, in many ways, a prototypical "ethnic entrepreneur", and both friends and foes alike struggled to discern where his true allegiances lay.[22] Duddu used his Spanish citizenship and exceptional education – he was one of the few Muslim Melillans with a Spanish university degree obtained thanks to a Moroccan scholarship – to mediate between Muslims and European descendants,[23] and to reap personal advantages in his community. Melilla was hardly the only place where an authoritarian and egotistic leader was able to create a mass movement and, paradoxically, open spaces in which democratic practices, values, and ideals could grow.[24]

A month before publishing his opinion piece, Duddu had founded Terra Omnium [every man's land], whose mandate was to defend human rights, campaign to grant citizenship to nearly 20,000 undocumented Muslim Melillans, and promote *convivencia*, that is, peaceful coexistence between peoples with different religion and ethnicity. Crespo claimed that Terra Omnium "made Melilla a little more the land of its inhabitants".[25] The organization was at the core of the fight against the Spanish government's efforts to apply the Immigration Act to Muslim Melillans. Contrary to the provisions of the Act, Terra Omnium argued that undocumented Melillans could not be considered foreigners because they were either born in Melilla or had been long-time residents there. According to this argument, Muslim Melillans were every bit as Spanish as their Christian neighbours.

Civic organizations in Melilla were not that different from those of mainland Spain: many small political parties, remnants of the political effervescence of the transition to democracy, were still active, as were religious, cultural, athletic, and educational associations. These organizations were, however, dominated by European descendants, and the involvement of Muslim Melillans in their activities was a rarity. When the Muslim Association, the leading Muslim organization in Melilla – indeed, the first of its kind in Spain, founded in 1968 – joined forces with Terra Omnium to create the Organizing Committee for the Muslim People (OCMP), it helped to create public space for Muslims, thus diversifying Melilla's civil society.

The OCMP, a federation of the secular Terra Omnium and the religious Muslim Association, was a united front with a mixed leadership. Duddu, its most visible spokesperson, was supported by the vice-president of Terra Omnium, Abdelkader Mohamed Alí, and a handful of other 'lieutenants,' as European descendants called them. Sid Driss Abdelkader, Melilla's most prominent and widely respected Islamic leader, was heavily involved as well. Even though Muslim Melillans had concerns and demands about the public practice of Islam – for example, there was no Muslim cemetery in the city – their fight was for political rights rather than religious accommodation.

The creation of the OCMP and the publication of "Legalize Melilla" marked the beginning of a Gandhian-style campaign of civil disobedience that included *hartals* (shutdowns of workplaces, offices, schools, and shops), rallies, hunger strikes, and a refusal to apply for the mandatory foreigners' permit. These actions were highly effective, as was demonstrated by the closing of 90 percent of the 446 stalls in Melilla's six local markets on 7 December 1985, which effectively shut down the city's food supply.[26] Activists also wore white clothing and hung white sheets from their windows and balconies in what they called a "white protest".

The OCMP operated on two levels: in large assemblies with lively and at times tense debates involving thousands of people (who usually gathered at the central mosque or at a local high school amphitheatre), and in a small leadership committee that met frequently and informally at members' houses. Both levels served as "schools of democracy", even though they often were unable to counter the personal aspirations of Duddu.

While the fight to oppose the Immigration Act was largely centred in Melilla, the Muslims of Ceuta often joined their Melillan counterparts. Muslim leaders in both communities agreed that Spanish Muslims had a moral claim. To this end, they appealed, by way of a series of press releases, to King Juan Carlos I, and they considered bringing their cause to the United Nations, as well as to other Arab countries. They called on the Spanish government to grant citizenship to everyone who was born in Ceuta and Melilla or had lived there for more than ten years, the period of time foreign residents had to wait to apply for citizenship elsewhere in Spain.[27]

Two weeks after the publication of "Legalize Melilla", an editorial in *El País* echoed Duddu's concerns. Melilla, the article claimed, was subject to "an authentic religious and racial 'apartheid'". Some Muslim Melillan activists agreed and claimed that "Franco is not yet dead in Melilla," and "democracy has not arrived here yet". Nonetheless, while Duddu and other Muslim Melillans obtained some support from left-wing organizations, intellectuals, and NGOs on the mainland, the Melilla branch of the PSOE expelled Duddu and the city hall fired him soon after the publication of "Legalize Melilla".[28]

Political parties are indispensable in the implementation and achievement of democratization. The party system in Melilla was competitive and democratic; electoral rules were stable and mainstream political actors accorded legitimacy to official parties and the party system. Yet for the most part, parties were not well rooted in Melillan society. Since they tended to reflect the concerns of European descendants with Spanish citizenship, they left 3,000 Spaniards of African descent and around 18,000 undocumented Muslim residents without representation. The "politics of presence", to borrow a phrase from Anne Phillips, was thus completely absent for Melilla's underrepresented Muslims.

According to the more narrow definition of democratic consolidation, one that emphasizes electoral procedures and outcomes, Melilla was already a fully functional democracy. But if democratic consolidation requires the substantial expansion of participation and a necessary reduction in social and economic inequality to guarantee the participation of minorities, then Melilla was a problematic case indeed. While the city had begun the transition to democracy by the 1980s, the process of democratization was not nearly complete.

After being expelled from the PSOE, Duddu considered running for the June 1986 general election with his recently created Party of Melillan Democrats, a decision he ultimately rejected since only about 3,000 Muslim Melillans had the right to vote. The Party of Melillan Democrats had the potential to contribute to democratic consolidation by offering political representation to Muslim Melillans, instilling democratic values in its members as a result, and organizing opposition to discrimination. It would also have increased the legitimacy of the party system in the eyes of many Muslim Melillans. This was ultimately a missed opportunity, however: polarization between communities and the demands of the civil rights struggle sidetracked Duddu's efforts.

The majority of Muslim Melillans supported Spanish sovereignty over the city; how they negotiated their identity on a personal level was an entirely different matter. When pressed on this point, Duddu claimed in an interview from 1986 that he was "Hispano-Moroccan".[29] Abdelkader Mohamed Alí, in line with sociologist Zygmunt Bauman's concept of fluid modernity, claimed that multiple identities were indeed compatible and that most Muslim Melillans considered themselves a mixture of Muslim, Melillan, Rifian, and Berber/Amazigh. Some also added Spanish and Moroccan to this formula.[30] Muslim Melillans rejected what they saw as a static and homogeneous conception of national identity, one that led to the dichotomy of 'us' and 'them'. They fought to obtain Spanish citizenship, but also to include their hyphenated identities in what it meant to be Spanish. Their understanding of hybridity, similar to South Asian, West Indian, and African immigrants in Britain, embodied both inclusion and social cohesion.[31]

Muslim Women Activists

Muslim women participated in the assemblies and rallies of the OCMP, albeit in a segregated fashion, but none of them became a leader of the movement. Terra Omnium's leadership, too, was entirely male. Male leaders spoke on behalf of female participants and male policemen negotiated with them, even during women-only protests. The media interviewed only males. *El País* noticed this, and in March 1986 sent a female journalist to investigate. Karmentxu Marín, who in 1976 had been one of the founding journalists of *El País*, reported on the plight and invisibility of women in the movement. Marín, too, was a rare voice in a male-dominated public arena. Muslim women's involvement in the struggle for citizenship in Melilla sparked the creation of the first Muslim women's organization in Spain, the Committee of Muslim Women. Female activism was thus not only about fighting for citizenship; it also placed gender inequality itself at the centre of the struggle for political representation.

The Committee of Muslim Women held its first protest on 25 January 1986. Hundreds of Melillan women gathered in the city's main square, the Plaza de España, and marched around a monument that, ironically, honoured the heroes of various Spanish colonial campaigns. They carried white flags and wore white armbands and headscarves in clear emulation of the Argentine mothers of the Plaza de Mayo. "We are not foreigners, we have lived almost our entire lives in Melilla", one elderly protester exclaimed.[32]

The women's march came after months of protests, by which time both the municipal and national administrations had lost patience. On the day of the march, police prevented a gathering of women from moving from Cañada de la Muerte, on the outskirts of town, to the Plaza de España. They arrested male leaders from Terra Omnium that were acting as spokesmen for the female protesters and warned its secretary that they would take further action if the women did not disband. Failing to comply, riot police attacked 200 women with batons, but some managed to reassemble in small groups and march downtown anyway, avoiding road blocks along the way. At Plaza de España, where the group had now swelled to 300 participants and thousands of onlookers, riot police used batons and fired tear gas and rubber bullets. Twelve women and three police officers were injured. One police officer was stabbed.[33]

As the Moroccan media broadcast news of the police action word spread immediately. Duddu called it criminal and improper for a democracy. The PSOE Director General for Domestic Policy, Rafael de Francisco, pointed out that the demonstration was unauthorized and claimed that police had no choice but to use force in order to restore public order. The protest was a public relations nightmare. According to the local newspaper, *Melilla Hoy*, "the event was filled with insults . . . violence, and hatred . . . Something important is being broken: Melilla's peace, calm, and the possibility of bringing the sides together".[34]

Isabel de Torre, a lawyer known for working pro-bono for Muslim Melillans, accused Duddu of "cowardly manipulating" Muslim women. She was upset that Duddu had not warned women about riot police baton charges, nor had he provided them with the training necessary for such a risky protest. The Committee of Muslim Women was quick to respond in a press release, titled "We think, too". It is "indignant and repulsive", claimed the Committee, "that Ms. Isabel de Torre, with her qualifications, says categorically that Muslim women cannot think for themselves. She looks down on and humiliates us". The release went on to say, "the Committee of Muslim Women acts within the Muslim community, but is entirely autonomous in its decision-making and how it dialogues with male Muslim brothers . . . No one manipulates us, we would not permit it". Mimuntz Mohamed, one of the protest organizers, said that women had not been adequately informed of the risks involved and agreed that the charge of manipulation was, in part, true.[35] It is difficult to ascertain how independent the Committee was, but there is plenty of evidence to suggest that its members supported their male counterparts, even if it entailed physical risks.

Arkia Mimoun Mohamed was a forty-two-year-old widow with ten children, aged seven to twenty-five, all of whom lived under one roof. She had promised her husband, twenty-five years her senior, that she would never remarry and would dress in white in remembrance of him until her death. A long-time resident of the oldest Muslim neighbourhood, Cañada de la Muerte, Mimoun Mohamed participated in the women's protest and became the spokeswoman of the "Mothers of the Plaza de España". "As a girl, I studied at the mosque and our own Muslim leaders told us not to speak out, otherwise they [ethnic Europeans] would throw us out of our homes, they would take our papers", said Mimoun Mohamed. She said she was routinely called a *mora* (Moor). "Our children have studied a bit and now we know things shouldn't be this way".[36]

Mimoun Mohamed married her mother's cousin when she was thirteen, yet her seven daughters did not repeat her life's path. Indeed, the family survived thanks to the wages of the two eldest daughters, who cleaned ships and offices.[37] It was common for female residents of Cañada de la Muerte to work as domestic servants or cleaners while their male counterparts were unemployed. "I like that my girls grow up free, so they have good self-esteem. If a girl dresses like a Muslim, they [ethnic Europeans] provoke her more".[38] Mimoun Mohamed was no liberal – she believed it was sinful for women to smoke, that women were inferior beings and were possessions to be transferred from fathers to husbands – but, in the context of Melilla, she was prepared to bend her views on gender.

Melillan women were divided by ethnicity and religion. Muslim women and those of European-descent lived in separate societies in which gender roles were prescribed by tradition, religion, class, and citizenship. Most Muslim women in Melilla were illiterate, though a small percentage had completed high school, and a few had studied at university. In the 1980s, segregation was still strong and intermarriage a rarity. For example, Muslim women delivered their babies in segregated rooms at local health clinics. While Marín reported finding Muslim prostitutes "married", as part of common-law relationships, to Spanish soldiers, that was the extent of intermarriage.[39]

Despite geographic segregation and the barriers of class and citizenship, young Muslim women negotiated their religion and gender differently than their mothers had. This was at least partially a result of the fact that they could look at alternative gender roles amongst women of European-descent, women who, thanks to the emergence of a feminist movement during the transition to democracy, enjoyed a growing influence over public life. Karima Aomar Tufali, a student of fine arts and a sculptor, was a member of the women's organizing committee. She believed that "Islam restricts freedom for women across the board and makes it so that even women support male dominance". She fasted during Ramadan out of respect for her father, a Quranic teacher, but "once in a while I have a beer or a ham sandwich". "To be a belittled Moor and a woman is difficult enough. But to be a belittled Moor to Spaniards and a woman to belittled Moorish men"[40] is impossible, she claimed. In other words, young Muslim women faced a complex set of oppressions: economic exploitation and religious and racial discrimination from European descendants, and gender discrimination from fellow Muslims.[41]

Although in Duddu's words, women were "a strong pillar in the Muslim fight", no efforts were made to erase traditional practices of gender segregation. Most protests were organized in a segregated manner, a pattern that would repeat itself on the mainland. When a group of males launched a hunger strike, the three women that joined them said that "the number of women on hunger strike would grow if a [separate] place was found for them". During assemblies at Leopoldo Queipo High School, women sat in the balcony and men, with a few "more progressive women", sat in the orchestra section, reproducing traditional gender segregation even though there was no official seating policy. The sole assembly led and attended exclusively by women occurred in 1987, a time when most male leaders were in either prison or exile.[42]

Ethnic Europeans used the discriminatory treatment of Muslim women by Muslim men to attack Muslim activists and question their attachment to democratic values. The Pro Melilla Association and the Nationalist Party of Melilla, both extreme-right groups, issued a press release which raised this point: "[The men] separate the women from them and put them at the back during meetings . . . some leaders . . . want to put them back in veils; but we will free Muslim Melillan women and their sound of freedom will echo throughout Melilla". These groups did not explain how they planned to liberate Muslim women, but at least they mentioned that "we must admit that a decent salary for Muslim domestic servants is needed". Indeed, a fair salary would have gone a long way towards helping Muslim women liberate themselves.[43]

The sociologist Jasmin Zine has called narrow perceptions of Muslim women as victims of an autocratic religion that undermines their individual rights, "gendered Islamophobia". If Islamophobia is "fear or hatred of Islam and its adherents that translates into individual, ideological and systemic forms of oppression and discrimination", then gendered Islamophobia "can be understood as specific forms of ethno-religious and racialized discrimination levelled at Muslim women that proceed from historically contextualized negative stereotypes that inform individual and systemic forms of oppression".[44] In Melilla, neither the Pro Melilla Association nor the Nationalist Party of Melilla was known for its feminist stance. Yet the objectification of Muslim women was not the sole prerogative of the extreme right.

Spanish Nativism

The early 1980s was a difficult period for Melillan ethnic Europeans. The post-World War II wave of decolonization rendered European control of contested African territories anachronistic. The United Nations Declaration on the Granting of Independence to Colonial Countries and Peoples, adopted by the General Assembly in 1960, together with Moroccan calls for the return of Ceuta and Melilla, made Spanish control of these cities problematic. Memories of decolonization in the Spanish Sahara were bitter. While Spanish authorities in the late Franco years had promised a peaceful transfer of power, premised on the right to self-determination for the native populations of the region, Morocco and Mauritania claimed traditional ties to the territory and, as Franco was dying, both countries participated in the division and occupation of the former Spanish colony. The 1975 Green March, which saw hundreds of thousands of unarmed Moroccan civilians, inspired by King Hassan II and protected by Moroccan troops, occupy the Spanish Sahara was particularly frightening for European descendants in Ceuta and Melilla. They feared they would not be able to resist a similar move against their cities and dreaded the possibility that their own government, weakened during the transition to democracy, would be reluctant to use force to defend them.

Their greatest fear was thus Morocco. After negotiations in 1984 between Spain and Britain over the future of British-held Gibraltar, Hassan II warned that "[w]hen Spain recuperates Gibraltar, I believe she will find it difficult to maintain her sovereignty over both sides of the Strait [of Gibraltar]". This was a restatement of what was known in Morocco as the "Hassan II's doctrine", the idea that the resolution of the issue of Spanish-controlled Ceuta and Melilla was linked to the resolution of the Gibraltar question.[45] To compound nativist fears, Spain's agreement to join NATO in 1986 excluded the two cities from its mandate to protect Spanish territory. Morocco was, after all, a strategic ally to the United States. Worse still, Spain had announced its intention to reduce its military presence in North Africa and some Spaniards, such as writer Juan Goytisolo, as well as the Communist Party of Spain, favoured ceding Ceuta and Melilla to Morocco. Economic uncertainties overlapped with military threats. Both cities were apprehensive about Spain's impending incorporation into the EEC and the consequences this could entail for their economies.[46]

Yet perhaps the greatest immediate threat in the eyes of local nativists[47] was the rising number of Muslims in Melilla. According to the then PSOE mayor of Melilla, Gonzalo Hernández, this growth was a "crucial problem for the city's future". Hernández favoured a firm implementation of the Immigration Act to reduce the proportion of Muslims in Melilla. Juan Díez Cortina, leader of the Nationalist Party of Melilla, echoed this view when he warned that "Melilla could die due to excessive Moroccanization". Some nativists believed an increase in the number of Muslims would lead to the election of a Muslim mayor, a sign that would surely signal the loss of

Melilla's European character.[48] Duddu's "Legalize Melilla" article raised many questions, among them the nature of the city itself. Duddu challenged what he called Melilla's official historical narrative.

> Melilla is a beautiful Spanish city with a strong military and administrative character, which is poorly connected to the Spanish peninsula due to its distance and because successive national governments have forsaken it. Melilla is home to 55,000 Spaniards and thousands of Muslims, who live in Melilla because its port welcomes trade and because it is a model of ethnic and cultural (Christian, Muslim, Jewish, Hindu) integration. The integrity of Melilla is threatened only by sporadic customs inspections and, above all, the so-called March of the Turtle (named in contrast to the rapid Western Saharan Green March) – the slow, continuous invasion of Melilla by undocumented Moroccans who tilt the demographic balance in their favour.[49]

Duddu's ironic explanation highlighted how nativists' sense of victimization could result in discrimination towards Muslims. Duddu believed that considering Melilla a model of integration was a parody and belied the divide between the communities. The metaphor of the turtle's march shows that nativists feared they were becoming outnumbered and that Morocco was poised to take over Melilla. As the daily traffic of thousands of domestic servants and other itinerant workers between Melilla, Ceuta, and their respective hinterlands attested, both cities relied on cheap labour and the purchasing power of Muslim residents and neighbouring Moroccan towns.[50]

Yet nativists rejected any suggestion that Muslims could be their equals as citizens. Nativist rejection was even stronger for those Muslim Melillans who had become Spanish citizens. According to Duddu, when "a Muslim with a Spanish National Identity card keeps his Moroccan citizenship, he is (we are) considered doubly dangerous, a fearsome fifth column, radio-controlled and financed by Hassan II or Libyan leader Muammar Gaddafi, who should be neutralized immediately".[51] In the nativist imagination, ethnicity and descent determined national loyalties. Indeed, nativism was premised more on ethnic loyalty than national identity or identification. As such, if a European descendant sided with Muslim Melillans, he or she was branded an 'other'. For example, when journalist Ricardo Crespo, a Spaniard of European descent, attended a local soccer game, nativists in the crowd shouted, "A Moor has come", "It smells of Moor here", and "That Moor sickens me". Crespo had to be escorted out by police.[52]

Though Muslims came increasingly to champion democratic politics in the struggle for inclusion and civil rights, nativists considered Muslims uneducated enemies of democracy with "fanatic" mentalities that belonged to "our 1940s [the period of early Francoist rule]".[53] Nativist reactions to Muslim activism were premised on a descriptive understanding of democracy. According to this view, democratic practices were reduced to the narrow space provided by electoral politics, established political parties, and associations such as trade unions, all of which were controlled by European descendants. When Muslims created their own organizations, these were perceived as authoritarian in nature and as a front for Moroccan interests in Melilla. Nativists felt justified in this position by their feeling of European superiority, ethnic solidarity, claims of victimization towards mainland Spain, and a rhetorical embrace of ethnic and cultural integration while simultaneously recycling old orientalist stereotypes concerning the inability of Muslims to practice, or even to understand, democracy.

The gap between the two communities was not merely a matter of perception; nativists also feared losing their privileges and entitlements if forced to share power and resources with their Muslim neighbours. Civil servants and law enforcement officials sustained the status quo of discrimination against Muslim Melillans as well. Often, when Muslims qualified for citizenship, they faced hostile bureaucrats and lawyers who discouraged them from applying. After the publication of Duddu's article, nativists – one of them a police officer – attacked local Muslims. The justice system did not prosecute the aggressors, and a campaign of solidarity was mounted to protect the police officer, who had been threatened with disciplinary action. El País argued that the judiciary did not adequately protect Muslims and that defence lawyers contributed to Muslims' social ostracism by refusing to represent them.[54]

Nativists held control of local authorities and elected representatives to Spain's Senate and Congress. The June 1986 general election was in many ways a test run for how much Melilla's European descendants would support inclusion of their Muslim neighbours. The results were not auspicious. Because nativists largely felt let down by the Socialist government in Madrid, which they claimed had favored local Muslims, they shifted allegiance to the conservative Popular Coalition. The party went on to win all three Congress and Senate seats.

As other colonial settler populations before them, nativists also felt victimized and feared being ostracised and abandoned by mainland Spaniards. Editorials in El País confirmed this apprehension by comparing local nativists to other European colonialists, and even South African racists. "Political discrimination coloured by racism, the worst traditions of religious fundamentalism, abuse of the most basic respect for human dignity" was not the image the country wanted to promote, bombastically editorialized El País. Nativists' protests, it continued, "recalled the historical short-sightedness and political insensitivity that many European nations often displayed when they had been forced to live together with other peoples". Moreover, the PSOE's initial support and acquiescence in nativism recalled the socialism and "pacification" campaigns of Guy Mollet, the French Prime Minister during the Algerian War of Independence.[55] Some ordinary Spaniards also found Melillan nativists distasteful. In Galicia, for example, an article entitled "Antipatriotic and Suicidal" argued that nativist protests were "shameful and dangerous to our country".

[The protesters] called "patriotic" an egoism that pretends to speak for Spain, but instead dirtied our flag to cover the disgraceful marginalization and exploitation of a minority. They said that they acted for the "benefit" and "integration" of Muslims, when really they want to continue to discriminate against them, even to expel them.[56]

In addition to their association with the ills of colonialism, nativists also provided a reminder of the historical mistakes Spanish society would have to leave behind in the transition to democracy. According to *El País*, Nativists held "despicable views of religious intolerance and ethnic discrimination that recalled the sad days of Spain's past". Nativism exhumed Spain's "historical nightmare, the expulsion of Spanish Jews by the Catholic Kings and of the Moriscos by the Austrian [Habsburg] monarchs". Nativist protests were a "remnant of [the days of] old Christianity and blood purity [*limpieza de sangre y de cristianismo viejo*], which the Spanish government seems tempted to re-enact in Melilla". The government, *El País* maintained, had to stand up against the ancient privileges of "old Christians," those with "Castilian ancestry and a pink complexion . . . Racism does not only occur in [Apartheid] South Africa".[57] Despite these exaggerated comparisons, the point remained that its treatment of minorities was a test for Spain's fragile decade-old democratic institutions, culture, and constitution.

Neither nativists nor Muslim Melillans had much experience with democratic practices in 1985. A mere ten years since Franco's death, eight since the first democratic elections, and seven since the approval of the Spanish Constitution, Melilla's parties and organizations lacked the presence of a 'democratic memory', established democratic practices, or an internal hierarchy in the structure of political organizations that would help them navigate entrenched ethno-cultural conflicts. Moreover, Melilla's borderland status, coupled with its ethno-cultural diversity, made democratization more challenging and messy than elsewhere in Spain. As Renske Doorenspleet argues, democratic consolidation is "probably only threatened by civil society when the active dominant coalition is anti-democratic".[58] While nativists in Melilla genuinely supported the rule of law and the establishment of new democratic institutions, their descriptive understanding of democracy, combined with their adoption of passive citizenship, rendered them oblivious to both the exclusionary nature of their positions as well as the democratizing efforts of their Muslim neighbours.

To make matters more complicated, nativists and Muslim Melillans had adopted different civic virtues. According to William Galston, responsible citizenship requires the presence of certain civic virtues, three of which are particularly relevant to this study: "general" virtues such as courage, law-abidingness, and loyalty; "social virtues" such as independence and open-mindedness; and "political virtues" such as the capacity to discern and respect the rights of others and a willingness to engage in public discourse with others. Both Muslim Melillans and nativists were loyal to Spain, at least initially. Yet while nativists were law-abiding, Muslims opted for peaceful disobedience to some of the laws they considered unjust. It thus took greater courage for Muslims to demand change than for nativists to uphold the status quo. Muslims were also more responsible citizens in terms of the social and political virtues they exhibited – for instance, by initiating a public debate about the fairness of the Immigration Act.[59] Though they lacked citizenship, Muslim Melillans, paradoxically, were more responsible and active citizens than many nativists; they acted as democratic citizens before nativists and mainstream Spanish society acknowledged them as such. The irony, lost to most participants, was that once Muslim Melillans obtained citizenship, they tended to assume the passive understanding of citizenship already adopted by the majority of their fellow Spaniards.

In the Shadow of Morocco, but a Long Way from Spain

The geostrategic position of Melilla, specifically the sovereignty battles fought between Spain and Morocco for the enclave, did not leave Muslim Melillans untouched. Their religion and ethnicity made them suspect in the eyes of many European descendants in the area. In addressing Spain's historic attachments to the region and Morocco's desire to move in on Ceuta and Melilla, Duddu attempted to assuage these fears by insisting that "Melilla has a place and that place is and will always be the Spanish state".[60]

Geostrategic considerations also encouraged Madrid to treat Muslims, particularly those in Ceuta and Melilla, with fairness in order to safeguard relations with Morocco and its common Western allies. Hassan II expressed a similar desire to preserve the rights and identities of Moroccans living in Spain, especially in the country's North African enclaves. To this end, Moroccan Prime Minister Mohammed Karim Lamrani told the Spanish ambassador in Rabat that "[Morocco] hopes the Spanish government will put the necessary mechanisms in place to ensure that nothing disturbs the understanding between our countries". The Spanish ambassador reassured him that Spain was not planning to expel Moroccan residents from the country.[61]

The Moroccan nationalist Istiqlal (Independence) Party was, however, eager to exploit conflicts between nativists and Muslim Melillans in an attempt to weaken Lamrani's government and increase the party's popular support. In December 1985, the party called for Ceuta and Melilla's immediate and unconditional surrender. The following February it organized a rally in Nador, the Moroccan city closest to Melilla, to denounce police action against Muslim women in Melilla. While many Muslim Melillans expressed appreciation for Istiqlal's rally, which "supports the fight against injustice", they wanted nothing to do with the party or Moroccan political infighting. When Muslim Melillans negotiated an agreement with the Spanish government, Istiqlal's newspaper, *Al Alam*, said that "Spain wants to integrate Moroccans [sic] in Ceuta and Melilla to consolidate its occupation of the cities".[62] In response, Istiqlal encouraged Moroccans to consider Muslim Melillans apostates if they became Spanish citizens, and to forbid them burial in Morocco, a significant gesture given the fact that Melilla did not have a Muslim cemetery at the time.

In its outraged criticism of Spain, however, Istiqlal failed to note something that was on the mind of every nativist in the area: neither the police abuse of Muslim women in Melilla, nor police, judicial, or bureaucratic harassment of Muslim Melillans could be compared with the treatment Moroccans had received from their own government just two years earlier, during the January 1984 bread riots in Nador and Tetouan, during which hundreds of Moroccans were gunned down from government helicopters[63]

But Moroccans were not the only ones divided by Melillan politics. Spain's Socialist government had initially championed the nativist position indirectly through their government delegate in Melilla. Indeed, "Delegate, the people are with you", became a common chorus in nativist marches. But as Muslims organized and mounted a credible campaign against the Immigration Act, the PSOE Minister of Interior, José Barrionuevo, ordered his government delegate to tone down his pro-nativist stance because it conflicted with Spain's international image and desire to join the EEC. "The Immigration Act does not say anywhere that it wants to slander the Muslim community", said the Minister; rather, "it aims to integrate the community into the social fabric of the city".[64]

In order to de-activate the conflict in Melilla, Barrionuevo offered to grant legal status, though not citizenship, to Ceuta and Melilla's undocumented residents and pledged to improve their social and economic standing. He agreed to pave roads, increase the sewage network, add lighting in Muslim neighbourhoods, and put money into healthcare and education. But by then it was too late for social improvements alone. Barrionuevo also offered assistance to Muslims residents who wished to relocate to mainland Spain, thereby addressing the fear that European descendants were being outnumbered by Muslims. Citizenship was to be granted only in gradual intervals in order to minimize the impact on Ceuta and Melilla. Barrionuevo played both sides of the fence: he tried to appease Muslims and nativists and preserve the integrity of the Immigration Act. It did not work.[65]

Madrid was undermined by its own representatives on the ground. An editorial in *El País* blamed strained community relations on the "slowness and arrogance" of the Socialist government delegate and mayor. Local authorities, who believed Duddu was "deceptive", did not yet understand that Muslim activism was a mass movement that extended far beyond its leaders. To *El País*, behind Muslim activism was a "feeling that Muslims were victimized and targets of injustices, were subject to racist prejudices and patriotic emotions". It was inconceivable that the Spanish government would "not accept Muslim Melillans as Spaniards, reject their claims, and then send police forces after them when they demanded their right".[66]

From Constitutional Patriotism to Sedition

When the Immigration Act was passed, the demands of Muslim Melillans turned from social to political demands, and contrary to the Act's aim to preserve the status quo, Muslims in Ceuta and Melilla used it to challenge nativist tutelage in their cities. The OCMP organized its first protest on the initial deadline set by the Immigration Act for 31 October 1985. Hundreds of Muslim Melillans clashed with police, two "Moroccans", as the local press called them, were arrested, and at midnight, Muslim women protested with pots and pans in an Argentinean-style *cacerolada*. The protesters said that they were tired of being viewed as "foreigners in our own land". Most Muslim Melillans refused to apply for foreigner permits as the act specified, preferring instead to risk deportation to Morocco.[67]

As the details of the Immigration Act spread and large numbers of Muslims grew interested in the movement, broader non-violent community actions were planned. Antonio Moreno, the delegate of the Socialist national government, was weary of Muslims' political activism and refused to issue permits to gather in stadiums, bullrings, and auditoriums. When, in spite of this prohibition, gatherings took place on private property owned by Muslims, Moreno cautioned attendees that their meetings could entail negative consequences. Try as he might, Moreno could not dissuade the protesters, and soon hundreds of people were gathering daily on the large patio of the main mosque in town. This should not be taken as a sign of the religious nature of these protests, however; this location became a meeting point for Muslim protesters because other secular alternatives had been denied to them. From the beginning Muslim activism in Melilla was socio-political, rather than religious in nature. Indeed, once educational authorities had reconsidered, Muslim Melillans would hold their largest assemblies at the Leopoldo Queipo High School.[68]

The OCMP called for the first large-scale protest ever organized by Muslims in Melilla to occur on 23 November 1985. After their lack of success with Melillan authorities, the protesters' goal was to attract Madrid's attention. In a press release, Moreno advised Muslim Melillans not to participate. "It is the view of this government delegation", he wrote, "that those who plan to attend the protest against the Immigration Act organized for the 23rd have been misinformed by persons who wish to distort the government of Spain's true intentions and to confuse and terrorize a group that deserves all of our respect and consideration". Moreno implied that he championed the cause of undocumented Muslims, yet his previous actions contradicted this stance. His statement also revealed the national government's anxiety on the issue.[69]

Yasmina Ahmad, a female protester, disagreed with Moreno's analysis. "I thought today's protest was correct", she told *Melilla Hoy*,

> because the fact that there are Muslims who were born in Melilla but aren't Spanish isn't right. They can't go on living as foreigners. They're Spanish. I

have Spanish citizenship, but I have siblings who were born here who do not have it. This can't be. I don't understand it. Some are not eligible to have it, but most do and they don't get it because they don't have documents. I got my citizenship because I found a lawyer and paid for it.[70]

The OCMP directed its message to people like Yasmina in their newspaper advertisement for the rally: "Beyond race and belief, good MELILLANS stand with Muslims in their LEGAL PROTEST . . . because we are all Melillans". Here organizers were re-appropriating the title of Melillan, which nativists continued to apply only to themselves.[71]

It is common, in Spain as elsewhere, for authorities to downplay the importance of a protest while organizers exaggerate it. Whereas according to Moreno, 4,000 people participated in the protest, the organizers said it was closer to 22,000. *Melilla Hoy* reported 7,000. The significance of the march, however, went far beyond these contradictory numbers. "For the first time in Melilla's history, Muslims protested, legally and in large number", said *Melilla Hoy*. The most popular slogan of the day, chanted in both Spanish and Cherja, a Tamazight dialect, was "We are Melillans". Yet *Melilla Hoy* echoed a nativist worry when it claimed that "The protest lacked Spanish flags and more voices to clarify that, beyond the fact that 'we are Melillans', the protesters want to be Spanish, though Aomar [Duddu] mentioned this a few times in his final speech". At the end of the protest, participants cheered for King Juan Carlos I, and called for citizenship for Muslim Melillans. The protest was also notable because it included, "unusually, a large number of women and children who chanted alongside the men from the back of the march".[72]

In response to the protest, all of Melilla's political parties, from the PSOE to the extreme-right Nationalist Party of Melilla, organized a counter-demonstration to be held two weeks later, on 6 December (Constitution Day). The parties, with support from business associations and educational authorities, called for a strict application of the Immigration Act, which could entail deportation for thousands of undocumented residents. Their slogan was, "For the Constitution and human rights, we say yes to the Immigration Act".[73] The nativist march was framed as a defence of Spanish sovereignty over Ceuta and Melilla and triggered unprecedented consensus among European descendants. "If 4,000 Moroccans took to the streets to call us racists and slave drivers, and if now 20,000 Spaniards don't take to the streets, we might as well leave for Málaga [in mainland Spain]", said a spokesman of the counter-demonstration.[74]

On Constitution Day, thousands took to the streets of Melilla. The counter-protest was the largest demonstration in the city's history, attended by 35,000 to 40,000 people according to Moreno, and 42,000 according to city hall. Attendees used the march to reaffirm the Spanish character of Melilla. "We're here, dear fatherland", "Melilla for Spaniards alone", and "This is the real Spanish protest", read some of the banners. Mayor Hernández called it "a success; the entire population participated" – minus, of course, the approximately 21,000 Muslims whom he did not consider Melillans.[75]

Though Julio Bassets, Melilla's PSOE senator, said the march stood for "community harmony and peace", Duddu called it "fascist nostalgia of the old [Franco] regime" and denounced Melilla's political parties and elected officials for their partisanship.[76] The Spanish flag, Duddu said, "is for everyone, not only for one of the two communities. The Constitution Day protest was not about rights, it was to repress the Muslim community".[77] The OCMP and the Workers' Commissions, the Communist-affiliated Spanish trade union, criticized the counter-march as well: "the Constitution should not be used as a tool to pit communities against each other . . . Human rights should not be invoked in the abstract or by those who deny them to other persons; who employ cheap labour and receive social security benefits when others do not; who want to ensure their supply of servants at low cost".[78]

Muslim leaders, as well as those – such as the Workers' Commissions – who were said to support the "Moroccan" enemy, received reprisals and threats. For example, the city hall punished Duddu, employed as manager of three local markets, by asking him to open the markets every day at dawn, before simply rescinding his contract. By contrast, the Workers' Commissions, which was the only organization with both Muslim and European members to support the Muslim protest, dismissed a high-ranking secretary because he aligned himself with nativists and replaced him with Abdelkader Mohamed Alí, the Muslim vice-president of Terra Omnium, who had been born in Melilla but did not have Spanish citizenship at the time. Mohamed Alí, who was to become the first Muslim to be elected to the European Parliament in 1996, had been active in Melilla's associational milieu since he joined a local branch of scouts as a teenager, where he was the only member of African descent. For Mohamed Alí, being active in associations and unions was the only way to fight discrimination against Muslim Melillans. Associations acted as "schools of democracy" for him, but also as spaces in which he could counter stereotypes about Muslim Melillans and build bridges with European descendants.[79]

As the second, 31 January 1986, deadline to complete immigration forms approached, the OCMP ratcheted up its protest. Thousands of homes in Muslim neighbourhoods were draped in white, a colour symbolizing "peace, law, and justice". The OCMP asked residents to wear a white armband to "protest a law that wants to inflict damage on a community which, for its nature and rootedness, can never be considered foreign". Forty Muslims went on hunger strike and the OCMP encouraged people to join them in a Ramadan-like fast for three days. As a result of this agitation, the government postponed yet again the deadline to submit applications for work and residency permits. However, the protesters did not let up: they wanted exemption from the Immigration Act, not more time to comply with it.[80]

The Spanish government eventually became more amenable to the demands of Muslim Melillans. De Francisco announced that the Ministries of Justice and the Interior would grant Spanish citizenship to Muslims with ten or more years of residency in Ceuta and Melilla. He said the Ministry of Interior "would be generous", and that the Immigration Act would only "apply to foreigners of any denomination who could not prove their *arraigo*". In this regard, De Francisco had conceded to the demands of Muslim protesters. "In some sense", he said, "Duddu was right".[81]

Representatives of the Muslim communities in Ceuta and Melilla and the Spanish Ministry of Interior formed a Joint Commission on 10 February 1986 to seek ways to legalize Muslim residents. It was the result of a strategy, successfully adopted by Muslim Melillans, of bypassing local nativist authorities and negotiating directly with Madrid. *El País* said the agreement reached between Muslim Melillans and the national government closed "the dark tunnel of damages, discrimination, and delays that were directed at the community of Moroccans and Muslims who were long-time residents [of Ceuta and Melilla]".[82] Thanks to the agreement, the OCMP prepared 5,000 citizenship applications in a matter of weeks. This contrasted sharply with the 1,500 permit applications that had been processed in the preceding seven months. Approximately 10,000 Melillans, nevertheless, remained undocumented – a challenge for nativists and the national government alike.[83]

Melilla's elected representatives were not invited to join the Joint Commission and complained that they had been excluded from this process. The president of the conservative Popular Coalition in Melilla, Luis Fernández, said the agreement was unconstitutional. "Muslim leaders can say whatever they want, but criteria for what constitutes *arraigo* for residents of Ceuta and Melilla should be determined by the representatives of the Spanish people: parties and institutions", argued Fernández. The then president of the People's Union of Melilla, and later president-mayor of the city, Juan José Imbroda, agreed that the arrangement "was a humiliating and shameful action [*bajada de pantalones*] by the government of Spain . . . the total and complete abandonment of Melilla by the government and measures should be taken. We've been had".[84] The widening gap between the national government and local nativists was highlighted by the April 1986 protest organized by local nativists – and then promptly cancelled – to oppose the visit of Minister of Interior Barrionuevo. The leader of the Nationalist Party of Melilla, Manuel Díez Cortina, was subsequently arrested and accused of plotting an attack on the government delegate.[85]

In an effort to win over nativists and address their sense of victimization, the Spanish government introduced an investment plan for Ceuta and Melilla. Between 1986 and 1988, the cities would be allotted 15 billion pesetas [$260 million today] "to create a socioeconomic climate to help with the integration of Muslims". Moreover, a portion of the 15 billion pesetas earmarked for infrastructure improvement and socioeconomic development was redirected at strengthening the border-fence between Morocco and Melilla in an attempt to placate growing nativist opposition to the

Socialist government. The ban on travel to mainland Spain was also lifted for Muslim residents, which was supposed to be a win-win situation for both Muslims and nativists. It permitted Muslims to obtain employment in other parts of Spain and reduced the ratio of Muslims to nativists in the city. But Muslim Melillans were not keen to leave. After all, why sever ties with relatives who lived nearby, and why leave when Melilla was set to reap European-level benefits on African soil?[86]

The Melilla city hall, the police, and the judiciary stepped up harassment of Muslims. In 1986, Melilla had just one judge, José María Treviño, the father-in-law of Luis Fernández, president of the Popular Coalition. Muslim Melillans complained to the Ministries of Justice and the Interior, as well as the General Council of Judicial Power, that Treviño stalled both their applications for citizenship and reports that they had filed against police officers and elected officials. In his usual bombastic rhetoric, Duddu called Treviño "a Christian defender . . . [who] wanted to vanquish all Muslim protesters". Madrid agreed to review police actions and send civil servants to Melilla's courts in order to process applications for citizenship. The General Council of Judicial Power, meanwhile, launched an investigation into Melilla's judiciary.[87]

Duddu believed, not unreasonably, that an informal coalition comprised of Treviño, Hernández, and the police were aiming to undermine Muslim activism and the agreement between Muslim activists and the national government. The PSOE national government, moreover, seemed to agree with him when, in June 1986, it asked that Mayor Hernández, also a Socialist, step down because the courts found that he had improperly dismissed Duddu the previous November, had subsequently refused to reinstate him, and was reluctant to provide Muslim residents with access to medical care and other services. Madrid also reassured Muslim activists that it intended to honour the government's agreement and that any delays in processing citizenship applications were merely administrative, not political. All the same, the agreement died.[88] Progress was too slow, harassment of Muslims on the ground too stern, and the gulf between nativists and the national government too wide.

In the June 1986 general elections in which the PSOE lost all of its seats in Melilla, most Muslim Melillans were disenfranchised. Since they were excluded from the electoral party system, the OCMP encouraged its supporters with Spanish citizenship to abstain from voting and to vote instead in an unofficial parallel election held in the city's four mosques. According to *El País*, this parallel election constituted another blow to government-Muslim relations. The gap between communities deepened further when the vice-president of Terra Omnium resigned from the executive of the Worker's Commissions. Mohamed Alí wanted a new union for Muslim Melillans alone. "The Muslim Melillans are severing their last links to any kind of Spanish institution or organization and are creating the conditions so that their movement can become the proper liberation struggle of an oppressed minority", wrote *El País*. Duddu concurred, promising that "if they force us to be foreigners in our own land, we will not recognize current institutions".[89] In the official election, a conservative representative was elected to Congress with 9,069 votes; Duddu received 9,400 votes in the parallel unofficial election. Had Muslim Melillans had voting rights, Duddu would likely have won a seat in the Spanish Congress – a point not lost on nativists.[90]

The national government, however, had not yet decided whether to side with Muslim Melillans or continue to appease nativists. On the one hand, Madrid removed the administrative barriers that Muslims had complained about and appointed a special judge to review citizenship applications. On the other, the government, in a nod to nativists, replaced government delegate Moreno with a Melilla-born former police commissioner and bodyguard of Prime Minister Felipe González, Manuel Céspedes, who lacked the political experience required for the job. *El País* was unconvinced by the government's double strategy of granting citizenship to Muslims and appointing a law-and-order government delegate for nativists: "The government is alternating between contradictory decisions due to overlapping and opposing demands, in each instance attending to the side that yells loudest and highlighting the absence of any real state policy".[91]

Melillan nativists also managed to send representatives to the Muslim-Madrid Joint Commission, despite express wishes to the contrary by Muslim Melillans. As a result, Duddu withdrew from the Joint Commission and instead accepted a role as a consultant on ethnic minorities in the Ministry of Interior, a position from which he later resigned. By November 1986, one year after the first Muslim march, the conflict had reached a stalemate.[92]

Once the political space for Muslim Melillans narrowed to the point of non-existence, some activists turned to Morocco for support. Duddu and many other Muslim Melillans came to see themselves as more Moroccan than Spanish. Increasingly, Muslims demanded cultural as well as legal rights, and asked that their religion and languages – Arabic and Cherja – be officially recognized.[93] On 22 November 1986, to mark the first anniversary of the Muslim rally in Melilla, thousands of Muslims marched "against the Immigration Act [and] for our Muslim and Arab character, human rights, and survival". Marching in the name of their "Arab character", when most were in fact Imazighen, was a nod to Morocco.[94] Posters featuring Hassan II and the slogan "Our sovereignty is indivisible: God, fatherland, and king / Melilla is Morocco / For the unity of Morocco" appeared in public spaces in Melilla. City hall said the posters were "threats to Melilla's Spanishness" and called for the prosecution of those responsible for putting them up. To some, it appeared that Madrid was losing Melilla.[95]

Duddu's embrace of a Moroccan annexation of Melilla exacerbated divisions within the Muslim community. While most Muslims Melillans stood behind Duddu and rebuffed negotiations with Madrid, in Ceuta a sizeable majority led by Ahmed Subaire argued for ongoing dialogue, as did an important minority in Melilla led by religious leader Driss Abdelkader and younger activists, such as Abderramán Mohamed.[96] Duddu had not only abandoned hope that he would reach an agreement with the Spanish government; he was now actively discouraging others from trying to reach one as well.

The Ministry of Interior downplayed support for Morocco among Muslim Melillans. In a press release, the Ministry interpreted the OCMP's new demands as merely Duddu's attempt to "maintain and create excuses to exercise his leadership and fuel his spurious economic interests". The ministry was hinting at the fact that Duddu had replaced his paycheque from the Spanish Ministry of Interior with unspecified financial support from the Moroccan government.[97]

El País argued that Duddu's demagoguery indicated a "growing situation of social and political degradation". The newspaper linked Duddu's change of allegiance to visits he had made to Morocco in August and October 1986. "It is clear the Muslim leader's strategy is to create the conditions necessary to abandon [the Ministry of Interior] with a stink and then return home a strengthened leader by saying that Madrid had made it impossible for him to do otherwise". *El País* blamed the government's ineptitude and its failure to address underlying injustices for causing Muslims to turn to Morocco rather than to Spain. The newspaper stressed that by permitting reprimanded and relocated police officers to return to Melilla, and by processing citizenship applications slowly (418 applications in 1986, with 15,000 residents still undocumented), local Melillan authorities and the Spanish government were encouraging conflict.[98]

Rabat welcomed the pro-Moroccan stance of Melillan activists, which helped legitimize Morocco's claim to the enclaves, and applauded Duddu's resignation from the Ministry of Interior. To Morocco, Duddu was now a patriotic citizen. He had studied on a Moroccan scholarship in Spain, had travelled on a Moroccan passport, and had done his military service in the Moroccan city of Nador; Duddu was simply returning his loyalty where it belonged.[99]

When Duddu returned to Melilla after a second trip to Morocco in January 1987, he announced at a large assembly that Muslim Melillans would gain rights only after "both cities were decolonized" and Melilla was made a part of "Moroccan territory". Duddu said that he was now completely and unambiguously Moroccan and that Muslims who were opposed to Morocco were traitors and "puppet collaborators" with Madrid.[100] Duddu's unequivocally pro-Moroccan position made him an easy target for nativists, who lobbied to revoke his Spanish citizenship. Other Muslim activists, such as Ahmed Moh, called him "an authentic dictator".[101]

Duddu's transformation from Spanish Melillan in 1985 ("I never use the term Moroccan nationalized in Spain", he claimed: "Muslim Spaniard is better"), to Hispano-Moroccan in 1986 ("We're tired of having to confirm our Spanishness by opposing our neighbouring country"), to solely Moroccan in 1987 was perhaps indicative of the mood and the pressures felt by many Muslim Melillans. Duddu had tried a constitutional patriotism *à la* Jürgen Habermas when he said that Muslim Melillans "want to abide by the Spanish Constitution, ensure justice, liberty, equality, and harmonious relations between the communities in Melilla. We want a new consciousness for Melilla", but with little success. He concluded that only Morocco could ensure the preservation of Muslim Melillans' identity and rights. For those who had suspected Duddu's intentions all along, his support of Morocco merely confirmed their worst fears.[102]

According to Mohamed Alí, vice president of Terra Omnium, the question of rights and citizenship took precedence over definitions of identity amongst Muslim Melillans. Terra Omnium decided to make a legal claim to Spanish citizenship, which its members viewed as independent of individuals' multiple identities and identifications. Mohamed Alí argued that Muslim Melillans should be entitled to Spanish citizenship without having to adopt and embrace Spanish identity, which for many Muslims – and ethnic Spaniards, too – was synonymous with Christianity. Most Muslim Melillans did not want to join Morocco because they rightly saw it as an underdeveloped and authoritarian state, and Spanish citizenship was one way they could ensure a democratic and prosperous future for themselves. For Terra Omnium's supporters, Muslim Melillans were merely constitutional patriots who aspired to enjoy the rights and responsibilities that came with Spanish citizenship. Granting citizenship to Muslim Melillans, argued Mohamed Alí, would be a first step towards widening the breadth of Spanish identity and tackling segregation and discrimination. Citizenship would be a path by which Muslim Melillans could begin to feel Spanish.[103]

Tensions between pro-Morocco and pro-Spain Muslims, and between Spanish and Moroccan border authorities, peaked in late January 1987. Duddu had fled to Nador in "self-exile" because he did not feel safe "either in Melilla or the occupied territories [sic]". His departure weakened his influence over his supporters in Melilla (for instance, a call to shut down Muslim businesses was unsuccessful for the first time in two years). Duddu and his supporters were not, however, prepared to give up. From Nador, Duddu spoke of the need for a violent anti-colonial liberation struggle. Government delegate Céspedes called Duddu "a coward . . . [who] from Nador, with a border in between, barks orders to escalate violence. The worst is he's using young kids [to do this work]".[104]

Indeed, February 1987 saw the outbreak of violence in the city. Three Muslim Melillans were injured by gunfire, a fourth one, forty-one-year-old father of four and resident Mohamed Hammu, was killed, and one Melillan nativist was stabbed. Seventeen police officers were injured in rioting that resulted in cars burnt, homes pillaged, and Molotov cocktails thrown. Thirty-two Muslims – all of the leadership except Duddu and the president of Terra Omnium, Halifa Mohamed, who were in Morocco – were arrested and charged with instigating a revolt. Abdelkader, the religious leader, was among them. Mohamed Alí was arrested at gunpoint in a crowded fast food restaurant on a Saturday evening. The police who participated in his arrest included disciplined officers who had returned to Melilla from the mainland. Céspedes led anti-riot units through the streets, something unsuitable for a bureaucrat representing the national government but keeping with his former job as a police officer. Violence, said *El País*, deepened the "process of gangrene . . . [and benefited] the [Moroccan] annexationist position".[105]

Most protesters were charged and freed. Abdelkader, who was infirm, was placed under house arrest, and nine others were imprisoned on the mainland and charged with sedition, a crime that carried up to twenty years in prison. Judge Treviño called for the arrest of Duddu, claiming that "he, along with his supporters from the Coordinating Committee of the Moroccan [sic] Peoples of Melilla and the Terra Omnium association, had launched a subversive movement against Spanish sovereignty in Melilla". The rioters, said Treviño, were Muslims, and the victims, whose homes and cars had been burnt, were "Spaniards".[106]

With most male leaders in prison, the soft-spoken Karima Tufali, the wife of Mohamed Alí, took over the role of spokesperson for those Muslim Melillans who still met daily at the main mosque, organized business closures, and demanded the release of political prisoners. Tufali allied herself with Abdelkader, who was still under house arrest but favoured negotiations with Madrid. In prison, detainees were divided between Duddu's supporters and supporters of negotiations with Spain. Those who supported the latter position sent a letter to Céspedes blaming Duddu for the riot. In Morocco, Duddu advocated unity, but attacked religious leader Abdelkader as "a sell-out to all Muslims. He has betrayed us". Duddu also accused Madrid of using force to extract statements from prisoners who opposed him.[107]

Darío Fernández, renowned for defending victims of state terrorism in the so-called "Almería Case", represented prisoners who wished to negotiate.[108] Dris Benyelloun, a Moroccan attorney living in Madrid, defended Duddu's supporters. The old-fashioned Spanish criminal code defined sedition as rebellion or incitement to rebellion. Article 225 required authorities to warn protesters twice – by waving a Spanish flag during the day or sounding a drum, trumpet, or other instrument at night – to retreat and disband before they could take action against them. Fernández claimed in court that no warnings were given. He also argued that the climate of violence had influenced the Melillan judge's decision to indict the Muslim protesters for sedition.[109]

Because Duddu refused to surrender to Spanish police and continued to be active from Nador, many Muslim Melillans believed that he had put his personal safety before community aims. Abdelkader called him a "traitor . . . [who] has tricked the Muslim people. The community was never ruled democratically because he was the only one who was allowed to speak. We're tired of this. We don't need leaders. When we get identification cards, no one will talk or think anymore. We only want our rights".[110]

The majority of prisoners were offended by the charges of sedition and planned to rally with nativists as soon as they were freed. They told Alex Grijelmo, an *El País* reporter, that they opposed Duddu because of "his personality . . . his initiatives, because he reneged on our legitimate original demands. We embrace the [Spanish] Constitution and wish to normalize our situation as citizens and Muslim Melillans". In other words, the prisoners were repeating what they had always said: "We want to be Spanish with full rights". As nativists and pro-Spain Muslims continued to oppose Duddu and Morocco as common foes, they drew closer together.[111]

It was at this point that Madrid ruled to exclude long-term Muslim residents of Ceuta and Melilla from the Immigration Act and create a new temporary residency permit for most of them. The prisoners were freed, pending trial, on 21 February 1987, and were subsequently acquitted. Pro-Spain Mohamed Alí and Ahmed Moh stepped down from their positions as vice president of Terra Omnium and general secretary of the Party of Melillan Democrats, respectively, and Duddu's support collapsed.[112]

Repercussions

The struggle mounted by Muslim Melillans was, after demonstrations by "*sans papiers*" in France in the 1970s, one of the largest mass civil rights movements in Europe.[113] The conflict in Melilla was not a cultural conflict between people with different religions; rather, it was a political conflict over access to citizenship, power, and resources. The long-term struggle to improve living conditions and end discrimination against Muslim Melillans remained, but Muslim activists could say they had won the short-term battle for citizenship. In three years, the number of legal Muslim Spaniards in Melilla quadrupled. In 1988, 6,500 Muslim Melillans had acquired Spanish citizenship, 5,000 were on their way to becoming citizens, and 1,500 had obtained provisional identification cards.[114] The struggle of Muslim Melillans for citizenship had resulted in the enfranchisement of no less than 38 percent of the city's population. As Adam Przeworski argues, people have historically conquered the right to vote by demanding, and eventually enforcing, concessions from the ruling elites.[115] In Melilla, this burden and its inherent risks – and, ultimately, its long-term success – were shouldered by Muslim residents.

The struggle in Melilla speaks to the greatest challenge to enfranchisement that democracies currently face: the exclusion of undocumented residents and most legal residents lacking citizenship from electoral politics. With voting rights, Muslims Melillans were now a force to contend with in local elections. For example, in 1996 Mohamed Alí, now a member of the United Left Party, became the first Muslim deputy elected to the European Parliament, and three years later, Mustafa Hamed Moh Mohamed Aberchán, a leader of the Coalition for Melilla, a PSOE splinter group, became the first Muslim mayor of Melilla. Aberchán received Spanish citizenship in 1987 when he was twenty-seven years old as a direct result of the fight by Muslim Melillans. Muslim candidates won further elections in 1995, 1996, and 1999.[116]

The Muslim struggle in Melilla not only achieved citizenship for thousands of undocumented residents and encouraged their political participation, but to some extent also reinforced civil society. From only two organizations in 1985 – the religious Muslim Association and the political Terra Omnium – the number of political organizations representative of Muslim interests in Melilla had grown to four by 1988: the Muslim Association, the only one that survived the troubles unscathed; the re-founded (on a pro-Spain basis) Terra Omnium; the newly created Averroes Association; and Neópolis, a mixed Muslim-Christian organization.[117] The days of Duddu – and Muslim unity – were over. Mohamed Alí explained how Muslims pushed the limits of a newly created political space for all Melillan residents, regardless of their ethnic origin and religious affiliation, in the following terms:

> We have created Neópolis, an association for Muslims and Christians, as a vanguard of ideas. The mass movement is over and we have to prioritize coherent and sensible plans, such as research on education for Muslim Melillans, on social problems, housing, and employment for Muslims. We need to produce documents, reports. This has never been done. We have to offer alternatives, as a way to incorporate Muslims [into Melillan society].[118]

The leadership and internal dynamics among Muslim Melillans were also democratized during the struggle for citizenship. By the end of this struggle, the excessive power of the populist Duddu was widely questioned, his authoritarian style in mass assemblies no longer acceptable, and the willingness of the Muslim community to follow his political manoeuvrings exhausted. Duddu remained in Morocco, swore formal allegiance to Hassan II in March 1987, and was eventually given a government job in Rabat. Nativists continued to lobby Madrid to repeal his Spanish citizenship, but since Duddu kept a low profile, the government did nothing. It was only when he became a governor in Morocco that Duddu formally lost his Spanish citizenship. Mohamed Alí said that in retrospect, Duddu "was necessary, he brought us recognition. He played an important part, but leaders are products of masses and unfortunately he grew vain". Autonomous, democratically organized movements can help to keep in check the aspirations of personal power so common to political leaders like Duddu. The lack of political experience of Muslim Melillans at the time allowed their movement to become disproportionately focused on the figure of Duddu, but it nevertheless set a precedent in democratic practices and trained a new set of leaders that would take over the fight for human rights and equality.[119]

Duddu's charisma had been necessary to gather support among Muslim Melillans and to sustain their struggle for two years. His 1987 turn to Morocco and escape from Melilla, at a crucial moment of state and nativist repression, were also needed to strengthen Muslim Melillans' allegiance to Spain and to sever the community's ties with the Moroccan monarchy. Either way, Duddu was a crucial player until the end. Eventually, nativists were sufficiently appeased by Duddu's departure, Muslim disunity, and the restoration of law and order that they could rediscover their Muslim neighbours as equal citizens. Old animosities ebbed and nativist discourse softened. Slowly, they began to accept that Muslim Melillans were not Moroccans, but fellow Spaniards.

Juan Goytisolo once described nativism in Spain as "a sacrosanct ethnic union against the Moor".[120] As the 2001 riots against Moroccan greenhouse workers in the Andalusian town of El Ejido or the 1999 xenophobic outburst against Muslim immigrants in the Catalan town of Terrassa demonstrate, the 1980s would not be the last time that Spanish nativists rose up against outsiders of a different faith. However, Melilla provided an example of how Muslim activism could successfully challenge the legitimacy of Spanish nativism and, by forcing the inclusion of a discriminated minority into the political body, achieve democratic ends.

The end of the conflict, with a rapprochement between nativists and Muslims in their opposition to Morocco and Duddu, set the stage for the slow growth of interpersonal trust. In the Melilla borderland, where 'bonded solidarity' premised on a sense of common nationhood and cultural identity could not be taken for granted, the Muslim struggle forced nativists and Muslims to create new ways of communicating with each other, as well as personal and institutional bridges that increased the city's social capital and helped generate the necessary consensus for inclusive governance. The best symbolic example of this cooperation was when Eid al-Adha, the Islamic Festival of Sacrifice, was incorporated as a statutory holiday in 2009. Melilla was the first city in Spain to incorporate an Islamic holiday into an official calendar otherwise populated by Catholic and nationalist holidays. The Muslim struggle also brought material gains to all inhabitants in the form of significant funds allocated by Madrid for socio-economic development and border control. The goal of narrowing economic inequality, erasing symbolic borders and geographical segregation between communities, all preconditions for the growth of social cohesion, has also been a legacy of the struggle. For example, Mohamed Ali and Karima Tufali were eventually able to open a clothing store on the main commercial avenue, something unthinkable in the 1980s.

Muslim Melillans were also pioneers in fighting a bottom-up campaign to question and enlarge the meaning of Spanish identity along the lines of Habermas's constitutional patriotism. They claimed that what united Melillans was not their cultural and religious identity, but rather their identification with Spain, its democratic institutions, and its rights and responsibilities. The degree to which one identified with its various identities – European, Amazigh, Moroccan, or Spanish, to name just a few of the possibilities available to them – was now a private affair, with little-to-no public significance.

The struggle would reverberate throughout Spain in later years in more ways than one. Most crucially, the concept of *arraigo* would resurface, in 1991 and then again in 2001, to justify granting status to a large number of undocumented residents on the Spanish mainland. Muslim Melillans were also pioneers in creating organizations led by minority members themselves and in popularizing a strategy of mass mobilization based on large-scale rallies and hunger strikes that would be replicated in migrant activism across mainland Spain.

Muslim Melillans successfully challenged unfair immigration laws and institutional discrimination against Muslims. While they were not successful in acquiring the status of "cultural affinity" with Spain for former Spanish colonial Muslim subjects and descendants of Muslims expelled from Spain, they nevertheless won democratic rights for Muslims in the borderland cities of Ceuta and Melilla and commenced the long fight to improve Spanish immigration laws. The challenge, a precedent for others, had been laid down.

2

The Struggle for Voice, Rights, and Status in Mainland Spain, 1989–2005

Social protest in Spain changed drastically after Franco's death in November 1975. In the decade that followed, public demonstrations would come to focus on blanket calls for democracy, the resolution of labour disputes, and the desire for regional autonomy, a goal that would be successfully realized in the 1980s with the institutionalization of a regional state structure. Community groups, trade unions, and political parties worked together during these years to forge a new democratic culture, and Madrid handled the attendant ideological conflicts, with one important exception – the Basque terrorist group ETA – more or less peacefully.[1]

Yet as democracy became institutionalized in Spain, and the political actors of the transition period were absorbed into various local, regional, and national administrative structures – or simply disappeared altogether – movements reflective of an entirely new set of concerns emerged. During this period, women's groups began to draw attention to issues such as domestic violence and gender disparities in the workplace; environmentalists pushed for the use of alternative sources of energy; and in the 2000s, marital rights were extended to gays and lesbians, though not without staunch opposition from the Catholic Church.[2] What, then, of the country's growing number of immigrants?

Some scholars have argued that the oldest Muslim immigrant group, Moroccans, has been integrated into Spanish society via the exclusion model theorized by Stephen Castles. They argue that Moroccan immigrants have been "incorporated into certain areas of society, such as the labour market . . . [yet] denied access to others, such as the welfare system, citizenship and political participation".[3] Without minimizing the significant levels of exclusion and discrimination faced by Moroccans in Spain, this view is overly static and neglects both the social and political agency of migrants. It overlooks the fact that, together with regional nationalist movements, immigrant communities in Spain have launched the largest and most widespread social protests the country has seen since the 1990s. Indeed, immigrant protests have encompassed the entire state, challenging

Spanish society's core understanding of human rights and status.[4]

Moreover, the various regularization processes have, despite their obvious limitations, provided opportunities for positive change; immigrants have been quick to recognize these openings, and have organized accordingly. Sidney Tarrow's theory of "political opportunity structure", which emphasizes how changes in the political environment affect the possibility for collective action, helps to explain how immigrant organizations used regularizations to increase their access to policy makers and strengthen links with influential allies.[5]

Finding an Independent Voice

Though immigrants have always sought a direct involvement – as opposed to participation through native representation – in the mainstream political process, this has been denied them by both opponents and supporters alike. In this sense, the Madrid organizing committee for the Year against Racism is a prime example of just the kind of well-meaning institution that became, inadvertently, part of the problem. As late as 1997, the committee had failed to incorporate immigrant organizations themselves into the group's activities. "The truth is I thought it was enough that immigrants were represented by non-governmental organizations that defend their rights and have a place on the committee", explained Jesús Pedroche, the committee's chair.[6] It was only after immigrant organizations began to complain of exclusion that Pedroche invited them to join. This type of goodwill, combined with the assumption that ethnic Spaniards could represent immigrants' interests better than immigrants themselves, was typical of the period.

To be sure, immigrants found allies at all levels of the Catholic Church – in the Episcopal Commission on Migration, the Diocesan Delegation for Immigrants, the Catholic charity Cáritas, and in local churches. A number of NGOs, including SOS Racismo and the Association for Human Rights, lobbied politicians on immigrants' behalf. And public intellectuals such as the writer Juan Goytisolo and the Arabist Bernabé López García championed the immigrant cause, publishing books and penning regular opinion pieces in the main national newspapers.[7]

Yet some NGOs that advocated for immigrant rights were nonetheless reluctant to work with immigrant organizations themselves, even though they allegedly spoke on their behalf. As Mohammed Chaib, founder of the Ibn Battuta Association and socialist member of the Catalan Parliament, explained, many organizations feared a loss of influence and power: "Some native organizations that work on the same social issues were upset that we, immigrants, were organizing ourselves. Rather than support us, they felt that we were stealing their customers". Yet as the comments of Abdelhamid Beyuki, president of the Moroccan Immigrant Association of Workers in Spain (ATIME), make clear, immigrants wanted to be "active and not passive subjects; we want to be part of [Spanish] society for good or ill. Often the goodwill, support and solidarity we get becomes a kind of charity, and no one likes charity".[8]

Beyuki, ATIME's first president, was born in the Moroccan city of Martil, near Tetouan. He came to Spain clandestinely by boat in 1984 when he was twenty-three years old and became a permanent resident in 1987. He had been politically active in Morocco, serving as chair of the Moroccan National Student Union while a law student at the University of Rabat. After the brutal repression that ended the 1984 bread riots, he left the country for good. "Morocco wasn't a good place for people who had opinions", he stated.[9]

As immigrants to Spain, paternalism and condescension became part of everyday life. According to Rashid Nini, a Moroccan journalist who published a journal about living illegally in Spain for two years, immigrants "must withstand the country's indulgent gaze. And I do mean indulgent, indulgent to the point of aggression. An abhorrent ignorance", he wrote. "People stare at you in the streets. You know exactly what's in their minds. To some you are disgusting and they distance themselves from you, leaving you with the impression that you are a danger on the loose, something from which they must be protected".[10]

Muslim immigrants in Spain, who at this time were mostly Moroccans, tried to obtain help from the Moroccan embassy and consulates in Spain. The primary concern for Moroccan officials, however, was not assistance for their citizens in Spain but rather the maintenance of friendly relations, trade deals, and diplomatic arrangements with Madrid. Abdellatif Filali, the Moroccan Minster of Foreign Affairs, once called for a moratorium on Spanish deportations of illegal immigrants, but this had little to do with the human suffering these measures entailed, and everything to do with the way these highly publicized police actions were damaging Morocco's reputation abroad.[11]

The Moroccan government seemed to favour instability and precarious-ness for its citizens in Spain over a content and secure diaspora that could potentially sever ties with Morocco. As in Spain during the 1950s and sixties, when hundreds of thousands of Spanish migrant workers left the country for greener pastures, the Moroccan economy depended heavily on financial remittances – hard currency from migrants overseas.[12] Of course, Morocco talked about the need to treat migrants with dignity, yet it did not offer its support when immigrants took it upon themselves to fight for status in Spain.

The Moroccan government also viewed labour activism with suspicion; in Morocco, similar liberties were not tolerated. Hamid, an undocumented agricultural worker who lived in a shantytown near Madrid in the early 1990s, had this to say about Moroccan authorities in Spain:

> They can go to hell . . . It's a shame that our main enemies are our own compatriots, the representatives who are supposed to defend us. Rather than protect our interests, the [Moroccan] embassy in Madrid, after burying us in

piles of documents, refuses to give us passports or to register us so that we can work. Then on top of this they send "informants" [*chivatos*] who, when they see that we are joining unions created democratically in Spain, rat us out to the Spanish police because they think we're acting politically against King Hassan.[13]

A fellow migrant shared a similar story: "I applied for a passport back in Morocco two years ago and they haven't given it to me. And so here I am, stuck between the [Spanish] Immigration Act and my own government. I'm forced to live like a beggar".[14]

The events of 1985–1987 in Melilla had revealed the Moroccan government's inconsistent support for local Muslims. When Muslim Melillans called for Spanish citizenship, Moroccan officials kept quiet, yet as the leadership in Melilla adopted a more pro-Moroccan stance, the government stepped in. When Melilla's Muslim leader, Aomar Duddu, stressed his Moroccan identity and turned to Morocco for help, Rabat commanded Muslims in Ceuta and Melilla to take action. Similarly, in mainland Spain Moroccan representatives were careful to support only those immigrant groups that put Moroccan state interests first. For example, ATIME, the largest immigrant group of the Moroccan diaspora, was deemed too independent and threatening to these interests, and thus received little help.

ATIME was formed in 1989, four years after the 1985 Immigration Act and two years after Muslim Melillans won Spanish citizenship for themselves. ATIME said that unlike other organizations for immigrants, which were mostly comprised of ethnic Spaniards, it was an "organization *of* immigrants . . . [not an] organization in solidarity with immigrants". It claimed that only ATIME and organizations like it could guarantee "the need for and right to self-representation . . . as a way to ensure the most representative and varied sort of citizen participation".[15] While ATIME agreed that organizations run by immigrants and native support groups shared similar goals, it argued that only the former could instil in migrants the values of active citizenship. Mohammed Chaib concurred, claiming that the most important feature of the Ibn Battuta Association was that it was an organization "conceived by immigrants for immigrants".[16]

ATIME opposed the Immigration Act, calling it "an excessively restrictive legal and juridical framework that harmed immigrants as citizens and human beings". The organization had a twofold mandate: to serve immigrants and to advocate for their rights. It started by helping undocumented migrants navigate Spain's circuitous immigration bureaucracy. It provided legal advice and information. It also monitored workplace conditions and kept an eye out for police harassment, human rights violations in internment centres, and irregular deportations. Eventually, ATIME also acted as a consultant to regional governments throughout Spain. In 1989, ATIME had around 500 members and offices in Madrid, Valencia, and the Basque territory. Though the majority of its members were male, ten Moroccan women who worked as domestic servants joined the original core of

ATIME. By 2001, at the height of migrant activism, it had 14,000 members and fifteen regional offices.[17] As the immigrant population grew, ATIME diversified and created sections to address social, educational, and cultural concerns.

ATIME and the Association of Moroccan Emigrants in Spain (AEME), which was older, vied for leadership of the Moroccan diaspora in Spain. The two organizations shared similar goals, but their political ideologies and strategies were distinct. While AEME tended to align itself with the United Left Party and its union affiliate, the Workers' Commissions, ATIME partnered with the PSOE and its union affiliate, the General Union of Workers (UGT). AEME supported small activist groups and extra-parliamentary acts of civil disobedience, while ATIME tended to protest through legal, institutional channels. In 1999, the Office of the Attorney General launched proceedings against the AEME leadership for its radical actions, and two years later the organization dissolved.[18] ATIME, on the contrary, burgeoned into a provider of immigrant services, as well as consultant to various levels of government. However, rather than divide the Moroccan community in Spain, the existence of two separate immigrant organizations helped to broaden the political networks to which immigrants could have access.

As ATIME's influence grew, official Moroccan representatives in Spain began to feel threatened. ATIME denounced irregularities in Moroccan embassies and consular offices in the Spanish media and gave voice to immigrant resentment. In April 1991 ATIME organized protests in front of the Moroccan embassy aimed at exposing corruption and bureaucratic inefficiency. Moroccan consular officials, working with embassy satellite organizations known as *amicales* (or *widadia* in Arabic), "will give you the right documents or a job offer only if you give them money", claimed Kemal Magrebi, an ATIME member. According to the group, the *amicales* were corrupt and nepotistic, one of the many issues faced by Moroccan immigrants in Spain.[19]

Another problem, revealed during the national regularization of 1991, pertained to Spanish immigration authorities' insistence that Moroccan nationals submit their applications to the Moroccan embassy in Madrid instead of the Immigration Institute, where all other immigrants were required to go. It is unusual that immigration authorities should rely on the diplomatic outposts of immigrants' country of origin to process their applications – a measure that reflected the lack of professionalism and experience of Spanish immigration authorities at the time.

ATIME continuously denounced the record of corruption and mismanagement among Moroccan consular bureaucrats. It called for equal treatment of foreigners, regardless of origin and organized protests to this end. To counter ATIME, Moroccan authorities encouraged the *amicales* to get more involved in the problems of immigrants, but this incitement to action backfired. Rather than align with the Moroccan government, as they had done in the past, the *amicales* joined ATIME and AEME in criticizing Moroccan consular officials.[20] As a result, Azeddine Guessous, the

Moroccan ambassador to Spain, was forced to quell a planned protest of Moroccan business organizations in the country with promises of a full investigation. ATIME continued to monitor matters and, in September 1991, assembled around 300 Moroccan immigrants outside the Moroccan embassy in Madrid. "The Embassy of Morocco is a real obstacle to our integration in Spain", said the ATIME president at the rally.[21]

Guessous, who had denied any corruption or wrongdoing, nonetheless replaced several consular officials within a month of the protest. Meanwhile, a judge had charged the Moroccan consul in Barcelona with counterfeiting thousands of documents in collusion with an *amicale* in exchange for payment, though these charges were dropped following diplomatic intervention.[22] Nonetheless, Madrid had learned an important lesson: in subsequent regularizations, Moroccan immigrants would apply directly to Spanish institutions, an ATIME and AEME demand from the very start.

In some cases, friendly relations between Spain and Morocco could work to the benefit of Moroccan migrants. For example, goodwill gestures of diplomacy led to two small regularizations in Spain, the first a result of Hassan II's visit to Spain in 1989 (when 1,500 Moroccans were regularized), the second a result of the Spanish prime minister's visit to Morocco in 1991 (with 2,000 Moroccan labourers obtaining residency status – though it should be noted that 7,000 had submitted applications). Moroccan immigrant groups blamed Moroccan authorities for the low rate of acceptance. Yet neither of these two measures helped matters much, as the estimated number of undocumented Moroccans in Spain remained at 40,000 as of July 1990.[23]

"I could only think about papers"

The growth in the number of undocumented workers increased social problems and human tragedies, undermining migrants' abilities to contribute to Spanish society. Living underground chips away at the humanity of an individual. "I could only think about papers", explained Algerian writer Lyes Belkacemi. "My head was unable to think about anything else . . . The uncertainty of not knowing when I could live as a person again was a source of constant suffering".[24] Nini concurred: "I was tired of being constantly on the alert. I wanted to leave home for once feeling calm, to be able to walk with someone without a police cruiser pulling up behind me, without having to explain myself or show identification. I was tired of hiding all the time like an idiot, tired of running."[25]

In *Cockroach*, by the Lebanese-Canadian writer Rawi Hage, the novel's protagonist, an Arab immigrant, imagines himself as a Kafkaesque cockroach. Similarly, Nini explained that at times he "felt as though he'd been turned into a rat . . . a frightened rat hiding from invisible cats". Belkacemi believed that he was "condemned to self-hatred as a beetle, to be and think like a shadow . . . I tiptoed around the world without making a noise". What these allegorical zoomorphs – cockroaches, rats, beetles, flies, and bumble-bees – have in common is that they live apart from human beings.[26]

Nini warned that if Spanish society could not, for its own sake, learn to treat immigrants with dignity, a tremendous opportunity would be lost. Many would detach themselves emotionally and be pushed into the world of petty crime. "I believed that . . . though I was here illegally, it did not mean I was a criminal. I was a problem that required a solution. I could easily become a criminal though. The chances were high".[27] Nini went on to explain that many of his acquaintances had become drug dealers, smugglers, and robbers, though some were also agricultural workers and street vendors. He admitted that he felt pulled towards crime because he did not know how to make a more legitimate life for himself in Spain: "How do I explain it? . . . I knew that it was easy to rob English people . . . The difficult part was admitting to myself that I was a thief inside . . . I'm not sure a real thief is inside of me. Anyway, I managed to control myself".[28]

Discrimination did not only reduce one's humanity; it was also economically costly and inefficient, particularly in cities, where it was virtually impossible for undocumented residents to go about their business in a regular way. "I avoid the Plaza de las Palmeras because the police are always there asking the darkies to show them papers", claimed Belkacemi. Ironically, these same documents – or lack thereof – were not an issue in rural settings; at least in Nini's experience, police were more lenient there: "As long as you're working in the fields, no one bothers you. The problems start when you go to the big cities. Your skin colour draws a lot of attention".[29] In the countryside, many immigrants learned that their labour could serve as a substitute for official documentation:

> When the police ask you for papers, all you need to do is show them your hands so that they know that you earn a living in the fields. Then they let you go. Here, on the [Iberian] peninsula, worn hands are the ID cards of Arab immigrants. And they are better than the blue document that will bestow on you the right to reside and work, but which is impossible to get.[30]

In his book *Ètica per una convivència* (Ethics for Coexistence), Mohammed Chaib called for a review of immigration law in order "to stabilize the lives of those who live among us already, alone or with their families, so that they can stop thinking about 'papers' all the time and become active participants in neighbourhood, city, even national projects". Chaib wanted to give immigrants the opportunity for self-realization as full citizens. "The day I come across immigrants in the streets and they do not talk about papers, but rather, for example, concerns of culture, I will say that we have achieved a great feat". According to Chaib, this was "about defending the concept of citizenship, that immigrants have the same opportunities, rights, and responsibilities as natives to develop as full human beings".[31]

The regularization of 1985–86 accepted 23,000 out of 44,000 applicants (see Table 1). Even though there had been three deadline extensions, many people did not fulfill all the requirements and thus remained undocumented. The mass regularization of undocumented residents occurred thanks to the propitious conjunction of both internal and external factors. Spain was due to join the Schengen Agreement in 1992, which called for signatories to eliminate borders with fellow EU member states and to reinforce borders with non-member states. The Spanish government planned to impose a visa requirement for Moroccans travelling to Spain. The writers Antonio Gala and Manuel Vázquez Montalbán argued that an amnesty for undocumented workers was a fair trade for the upcoming visa requirement, which would further strain relations with Arab countries (Spain had recently permitted the US military to use its airbases during the NATO bombing of Iraq). Immigrant groups denounced the visa requirement as well, arguing that it would increase their dependence on Moroccan officials and fuel illicit traffic across the Strait of Gibraltar.[32]

Table 1 Extraordinary Regularization Processes

Year	Number of Applications	Accepted Applications
1985–86	44,000	23,000
1989 Moroccans	N/A	1,500
1991 Moroccans	7,000	2,000
1991	130,000	110,000
1996	25,000	22,000
2000	244,327	152,207
2000 Appealed	57,616	36,013
2001 Ecuadorians	24,884	24,352
2001 *Arraigo* (rootedness)	338,680	157,883
2005 Normalization	691,655	578,375
Total	**1,513,032**	**1,107,330**

Source: Compiled by author using data from González Enríquez, "Undocumented Migration" and *El País*.

Perhaps the most important internal factor in the Spanish government's move towards amnesty was the sheer number of undocumented workers in the country. Sociologist Antonio Izquierdo estimated that in 1990 between 72,000 and 124,000 undocumented migrants were resident in Spain, and he was unequivocal in blaming the 1985–86 regularization process for failing to resolve this situation since "It did not address the desires of irregular [migrants] to remain permanently". It also failed to find efficient ways for migrants to re-apply for residency and work permits, which may account for the fact that only 39 percent of applicants accepted in 1985 were still legal in 1990.[33] Indeed, Madrid had actually tightened requirements for renewal.

For example, workers could not re-qualify for a work permit if they became unemployed. And women and children reunified with spouses and fathers in Spain were entitled to residency, but not work permits, which often led to irregular, under-the-table work arrangements.

A second internal factor was the rallying, during the late 1980s, of Spanish intellectuals and social justice organizations around the idea of a national amnesty for undocumented workers. The Catalan group *Cristianisme i Justicia* (Christianity and Justice) called on Madrid to "significantly rectify the Immigration Act of 1985, offer amnesty to humble foreign workers who have lived in Spain clandestinely for years, and to pardon persons who rot in prisons simply because they do not have a passport or fixed employment". As calls for an amnesty mounted, immigrants, too, launched a campaign for the "regularization and integration of immigrants".[34]

A third internal factor was a conversation in favour of amnesty within the ruling Socialist party. In December 1990, after the release of a government report entitled "The Situation of Foreigners in Spain: A Basic Understanding of Spanish Immigration Policy", the Congress agreed that a national regularization was needed in 1991. In April of that year, the Socialist contingent in Congress requested that the PSOE government rectify flaws that had emerged during the 1985 regularization, and offer legal status to migrants already in the country who could document their integration ("*inserción*") or prove their rootedness ("*arraigo*"). In 1987, as we saw in the previous chapter, the Spanish government had used the concept of *arraigo* to resolve tensions among nativists and Muslims in Melilla, and the term was now resurfacing in a similar context.

In addition, the Congress asked the government to modify existing asylum and refugee legislation, to create an Inter-Ministerial Commission on Migration, to establish migrant work quotas, and to approve a plan to promote immigrants' social integration. The country needed to establish an institutional framework for managing immigration flows and the integration of immigrant populations. The Inter-Ministerial Commission was duly created and one of its first initiatives was to push for reform of the 1985 Immigration Act. A quota system for migrant workers, as well as a plan to bolster immigrants' social integration, was also put in place in 1992 and 1994, respectively.[35]

For the Socialist government, immigration policy would assume a three pronged approach: the first secured borders and reduced illegal inflows, the second rationalized and made procedures more efficient for legal migration, and the third promoted integration. A broad regularization based on *arraigo*, the government felt, could simultaneously integrate immigrants, minimize criticism from NGOs over the detention and deportation of undocumented persons, beef up borders, and rationalize existing immigration bureaucracy.[36] All parties, except for the United Left Party – which claimed that *inserción* and *arraigo* were both vague and difficult to prove – voted in favour of the PSOE resolution.

José Luis Corcuera, the Minister of Interior, described the discourse over immigration policy during this period as "a dispassionate debate [undertaken] in a climate of consensus" (something that would certainly change over the following decade). This consensus was, however, utilitarian and ethnocentric. Migrants had to be both "needed and assimilable". Moreover, migrants were also considered a threat, with Corcuera reminding Spaniards that a "minority of [immigrants] partook in criminal behaviour". Visas and strengthened borders, as the argument went, were thus necessary measures of control.[37]

The Socialists instituted a national program of regularization between June and December 1991. The regularization applied to all immigrants who had arrived prior to 15 May 1991; who could show that they had guaranteed employment for the next six months; and who had worked for at least nine months of the preceding two years. Immigrant organizations, church groups, NGOs, and labour unions were satisfied with the decision, publicized it among their members and assisted immigrants with paperwork. Ángel Suquía, the cardinal-archbishop of Madrid-Alcalá and Spain's most important Catholic prelate, called on parishes to inform immigrants of the decision and on employers to furnish migrants with "all the documents they need to become legal".[38]

The regularization aimed to "put the ball in the court of society . . . The government has always been blamed for being inflexible. Now the citizenry has a chance to demonstrate its ability to welcome others", explained Fernando Puig de la Bellacasa, Director General for Domestic Policy. Official campaigns such as "Come to Light: Put it Right", addressed both native employers and undocumented labourers. However, this governmental washing of hands did not go uncriticized. José Carlos Rodríguez Soto, a Colombian missionary and member of the African migrant solidarity Karibú Association, complained that native Spaniards discriminated more fiercely in the labour market against Africans than against East Europeans or Latin Americans. "Why should the law be pushed down to the level of society when that same society discriminates, *de facto*, against specific groups of foreigners?" asked Rodríguez Soto. "If indeed 'the ball is in the court of society,' should not all the means available be provided so that society picks the ball up and plays the game cleanly?" Here Rodríguez Soto was criticizing the "Come to Light" campaign specifically: the government did not need to convince immigrants of the necessity of obtaining proper documentation, he argued; it needed to educate employers on the ills of hiring employees illegally and thus depriving them of full rights.[39]

Contrary to popular perceptions, Izquierdo's data showed that immigration in Spain was from the beginning highly feminized. In the 1985–86 regularization, 39 percent of the 44,000 immigrants who applied for status were women. Izquierdo explained that a demand for female domestic servants, especially from the Dominican Republic, the Philippines, Equatorial Guinea, Cape Verde, and Morocco, had always been high. North African women were also sponsored by male relatives in large numbers during the 1985–86 regularization. Numbers of female migrants were even larger when migrants from other EU countries were included: the share of French and German female immigrants to Spain made up 61 and 58 percent, respectively.[40]

In 1991, ATIME claimed that at least 57 percent of Moroccans living in Madrid were women, most of whom worked as domestic servants. Both married and single women took advantage of employment opportunities in Spain. A month before the 1991 regularization, female members of ATIME created Al Amal. Aicha Mellagi, its first president, explained that "it is easier for [Moroccan] women now to find work than it is for men . . . [but] this inversion causes many problems regarding gender roles". Indeed, women's new role as breadwinners was not without problems, particularly when men had to remain in Morocco with children or were unemployed in Spain. The Moroccan immigrant community at large looked on this situation with a certain level of disdain. Mellagi complained that her family criticized her for "being a bad mother" because she chose to work in Spain rather than be a stay-at-home mother.[41]

Al Amal set three goals for itself: to lobby, along with ATIME and other immigrant groups, for a large-scale amnesty; to improve working conditions for domestic workers, an issue that Spanish unions had been slow to embrace; and to eradicate "the prejudices of our own society, which disrespected working women and women who left for Europe". While the first two aims targeted Spanish society, the third targeted the Moroccan diaspora in Spain as well as Moroccan society itself. Women's position, argued Mellagi, had changed, for better or worse. "What was impossible for us in Morocco, has been made possible here in Spain", she said.[42]

Al Amal focussed its efforts on labour rights, in particular those of women in domestic service. In Madrid, for example, thirty Moroccan women occupied a church. They called for "a fair law to regularize domestic service". "Once employers had given the pre-contracts that were necessary for the regularization", Mellagi explained, "they refused to offer standard work contracts, which meant many female employees could not apply for social security, unemployment, or qualify for paid vacations". Often, domestic servants were forced to work as many as fourteen hours per day.[43]

Al Amal also advocated family reunification. "The Ministry of Foreign Affairs demands too many 'papers' for the special visa we need to bring our families over", Al Amal said. "Now that we are regularized workers, we pay the same taxes as Spaniards, but we do not have the same rights . . . I applied to bring my son over and they asked me for more documents than for a worker", claimed an East European migrant.[44]

It was common for female members of ATIME to be segregated from their male counterparts and to hold separate rallies at common protests. This began to change in 1992. At a large protest held in Madrid, women joined one of three marches, and a group of Moroccan domestic servants spoke up in the common gathering and denounced the fact that their pay was the lowest in the labour market.[45]

The 1991 regularization granted status to 110,000 people out of 130,000 applications (see Table 1). ATIME calculated that only 30 percent of the 130,000 North Africans in Spain had qualified for work and residency permits. The figure would have been higher had Madrid not required migrants to have a minimum six-month job contract, which created a black market in contract forgery, and had corruption in Moroccan consulates throughout Spain been tackled on time.[46]

At the end of the regularization, immigrant groups petitioned to extend deadlines: thousands of applicants had not had sufficient time to gather all required documents on account of the inefficiency of foreign bureaucracies. Demonstrations took place in Valencia, Madrid, and Saragossa in December 1991. Demonstrators pointed out that three extensions had been granted in 1985.

In Madrid, protests were segregated by gender. Fifty women, organized by Al Amal, gathered in the Plaza Tirso de Molina, and 300 men and a handful of Spanish women organized by ATIME, marched on the streets. AEME called the law "fascistic crap". It called for "papers for everyone", a slogan that would outlive the organization, as well as work and residency permits for five years rather than one.[47]

But the government in Madrid believed that the regularization criteria had been "generous and flexible". Immigrants with employment or real possibilities of obtaining it had qualified for status; only "criminals . . . [and] those who had refused to apply" were excluded, claimed the Director General for Domestic Policy, and they would be deported "by due process of law". In light of the barriers Moroccan immigrants had faced with Moroccan authorities in Spain to obtain the required documentation, the government's assessment was misleading. While the protests failed to have the regularization process extended, they were granted an extension – until March 1992 – to apply for family reunification.[48]

Racism and Migrant Rights

Migrant activism may have spiked with the onset of regularization processes, but it was not limited to these occasions alone. In between regularizations, migrant organizations deepened democratic practices by helping their members to become active citizens and by promoting the protection of vulnerable minorities. They lobbied governments to strengthened human rights legislation, monitored violations of human rights, advocated for labour rights in precarious sectors where immigrants were a majority, and initiated a conversation around concepts hitherto unfamiliar to Spaniards, such as white flight or racial profiling.

Just as Muslim Melillans had criticized the 1985 Immigration Act for discriminating against persons who lacked "cultural affinity to or identification with" Spain, Moroccan immigrants on the mainland fought for equality with other immigrants. One of the main battles of this period concerned the extension of the one-year work permit to five years. Madrid granted five-year permits only to so-called 'affinity groups', such as Latin Americans, Portuguese, Filipinos, Andorrans, Sephardic Jews, Gibraltarians, and Equatorial Guineans, but not to Moroccans. "We feel unprotected", said Beyuki, arguing that rhetorical statements against xenophobia and intolerance were not enough. The government needed to "undertake actions that enable us to defend ourselves . . . not even legal immigrants are equal in rights to the rest of the citizenry", Beyuki claimed.[49]

In addition to peaking during regularization periods, migrant mobilization and activism in Spain has followed the rhythm of xenophobic outbursts. At its first congress, held in Madrid in 1991, AEME petitioned the Spanish Congress to include racism as a crime for the first time in the country's criminal code. As tensions between visible migrant minorities and extreme-right groups grew, and police harassment of undocumented immigrants continued, AEME, together with SOS Racismo, an NGO of French origin that supports immigrants and fights racism, stepped up its lobbying efforts. Yet it was not until November 1992, following the brutal, racially motivated murder of Lucrecia Pérez, an undocumented Dominican migrant who had worked as a domestic servant, that public opinion came to reflect AEME's demands as well. (In the eyes of many Spaniards, Pérez's murder was all the more repugnant since it was committed by an off-duty Civil Guard linked to extreme-right groups – this just eleven years after another Civil Guard had attempted a *coup d'état*). The strong public outrage that followed the murder helped to place AEME's demands for increased migrant protection on the Congress agenda. By 1995, Congress had voted to modify the Spanish criminal code to include racism as a crime.[50]

Many ethnic Spaniards were not indifferent to racism and xenophobia. In the churches where immigrants protested, held hunger strikes, or sought asylum, parishioners brought "blankets, clothing, and food, and show[ed] interest in our demands", explained one protester in the Vallecas district of Madrid. At the same time, AEME was experiencing high levels of harassment. Extreme-right groups sent letters to AEME members calling them "treacherous Moors". As one correspondent put it, "It is intolerable that you come to Spain against the will of Spaniards and then have the audacity to issue us demands".[51]

Nonetheless, immigrants played a lead role in denouncing racial profiling during this period. "Being dark is reason enough [for the authorities] to stop you in front of everyone and to search your pockets", explained Nini. "Yesterday a cop car passed by me slowly. My appearance gave me away".[52] Significantly, racial profiling is not a recognized phenomenon in Spain; the term has no currency, in either Spanish or Catalan, technical or common speech, though the European Parliament has recently offered two awkward translations.[53] This begs the question: how can an issue be problematized if the language to describe it does not exist?

Racial profiling amounts to the daily harassment of immigrants. Some managed to face these frustrations with a sense of humour. For example,

Nini pointed to the absurdity of immigrants' position when he described the actions of a friend: "Abdelkader would laugh telling me that he had given the police different nationalities when he was stopped. He would say that he was Iraqi, then Palestinian, etc. He said he was a roving Arab League. The first thing he did in Spain was burn his passport. He disavowed his identity".[54] Yet others were unwilling to tolerate it. On 6 December 1992, Rosalind Williams, a naturalized Spanish citizen of African-American descent, arrived at a Valladolid railway station with her husband and son. After disembarking, a member of the National Police approached Williams and asked her to identify herself. When asked why he was performing an identity check on Williams, the officer responded that he was following an order from the Ministry of Interior to check the identity of persons who "looked like her", "persons of color" because "many of them are illegal immigrants". Williams decided to pursue the matter in the courts, and indeed her case went all the way to the Spanish Constitutional Court, where she was told that the police had acted appropriately. With help from the Open Society Foundation, Williams went to the United Nations Human Rights Committee, who ruled that Spanish laws should be changed and that the government of Spain should apologize to Williams. While Williams obtained a private apology, she was deprived of the public apology and public debate on racial profiling she had sought. Immigrants and ethno-cultural minorities continue to question the practice of racial profiling today, pointing out that it fails to identify lawbreakers effectively and often alienates the very same communities whose cooperation the police so desperately need.[55]

In the 1980s and nineties, white flight – another concept that does not quite translate into Spanish or Catalan, even if "*huida blanca*" can be found in specialized literature – was widespread in urban centres populated by immigrants. In the Raval neighbourhood of Barcelona and the Russafa neighbourhood of Valencia, as well as in smaller towns – for example the Sant Pere neighbourhood of Vic or the Barri de l'Erm neighbourhood of Manlleu – ethnic Spaniards whose families had lived for generations in these neighbourhoods left for other areas, only to regret having left once some of these neighbourhoods were eventually gentrified. To be sure, segregation by class and ethnicity was nothing new. In the 1960s, the writer Francisco Candel condemned the segregation of Andalusian migrants in Catalonia. It was not the Andalusians who wished to live in a "world apart", Candel argued, but ethnic Catalans, who, fearful of migrant numbers and lower socioeconomic status, tended to isolate themselves.[56]

The midsized agricultural town of El Ejido, in Andalusia, provides a blatant example of housing segregation. Here, white flight in some neighbourhoods combined with attempts to keep the downtown free of immigrants. Moroccan immigrants were forced to live in the greenhouses where they worked or in sheds attached to them. When a trickle of seasonal workers attempted to move downtown, mostly to the La Loma de la Mezquita neighbourhood, and to open small businesses, natives picked up and moved elsewhere. Property owners in the neighbouring city of Almería raised rents for immigrants as a tactic to keep them out of the downtown. In one 1999 protest, an immigrant complained that "[w]e're not asking for mansions or to be given homes for free. We work and want to be able to pay our rent. But a fair and just rent, the same it would cost any family. Anything else is discriminatory and abusive."[57]

A study of 1,300 immigrant households published in 1999 by Almería Acoge, a migrant advocacy group, showed that 60 percent did not have running water, electricity, or a toilet, and that 42 percent of these were inadequate sheds or cabins attached to greenhouses or other agricultural sites. In the Valencian region, it was easier for Nini to pretend that he was a student rather than an undocumented worker. "We had to make the landlord believe that we were students because otherwise, she wouldn't have allowed us to rent her place. As an undocumented worker, you're supposed to live in your shoes". Many wound up squatting in derelict buildings. Even with the proper documentation, it was difficult for visible minorities to find an apartment to rent. The European Monitoring Centre on Racism and Xenophobia (EUMC) report "Muslims in the European Union" corroborated that discrimination towards Moroccan immigrants in the workplace and in housing was rampant in Spain.[58]

White flight was a common phenomenon in Spanish schools as well. The Catalan-Amazigh writer Najat El Hachmi described her experience of this phenomenon as a teenager in the Catalan town of Vic:

> My school had constant problems of enrolment. In the end, most of us were foreigners, Moroccans, or other immigrants who had come a long time ago [from other parts of Spain]. What was scandalous was that the two other public schools in Vic were over-enrolled . . . Catalan parents did not want their children to go to the schools – mine and another one – which contained immigrants. The front pages of the daily papers in Vic reported a breakout of racism. Polemics piled on top of polemics, and we kids did not understand a thing about it. Of course, we understood it was a touchy subject . . . but those parents who complained didn't even know us.[59]

White flight, of course, drove a wedge between immigrants and natives. Opportunities for casual contact in supermarkets, stores, in public squares and parks, in schoolyards and restaurants diminished. When Chaib's parents met his in-laws, he explained, "it was the first time that my parents had spent an evening with [ethnic] Catalans in more than twenty years living in Catalonia". No wonder then, he later wrote, "the main task remaining for . . . immigration is for the separate communities to find ways to interact".[60]

Immigrant organizations also monitored conditions in detention centres and sought strategies for guaranteeing the rights of vulnerable minorities. ATIME's lawyer pointed to structural barriers faced by migrants in detention centres. Lawyers could only meet with clients for an hour a day.

Fernando Sales, president of the Association against Torture, viewed this as unconstitutional. In 1991, detainees went on hunger strikes to receive proper medical attention and the right to report abuses of human rights to judges. They also demanded that undocumented workers be released. Campaigns against internment centres for undocumented workers have been and are still a constant feature of human right activism in Europe.[61]

As in other parts of Europe, immigrant activism emerged first in urban settings. ATIME and AEME were strongest in Madrid, where they could find allies, group together in significant numbers, and meet in common spaces, such as centres of prayer or recreational sites. In cities, immigrants also tended to have more stable, less seasonal employment; they also tended to work shorter hours, which permitted them time to strategize, build the necessary trust among migrant members and other community members, and devote energy to organization building. For instance, Chaib explained that the creation of the Ibn Battuta Association in Barcelona "was a spontaneous idea that occurred to a group of friends while at university, and began with unorganized meetings . . . in the cafeteria".[62]

In rural contexts, the situation was the opposite: immigrants were forced to work long hours in contract or seasonal employment. They were itinerant. They might pick strawberries in Murcia or Huelva in the spring, and harvest plums or peaches in Lleida, several hundred kilometres away, during the summer. Weaker community ties and less stable work made it nearly impossible to organize sustainable political campaigns. Furthermore, rural workers faced heightened barriers to the granting of status. Because employers tended to offer short-term contracts or no contracts at all, it was difficult to become a legal resident. To qualify for a national regularization, for example, an agricultural migrant needed to have a documented job offer from multiple employers.

In June 1992, ATIME, now one of the most influential Muslim immigrant advocacy groups, threw its weight behind the protest of agricultural workers in Murcia who were agitating for better working conditions and easier access to the migrant workers quota. The Catholic Action Brotherhood of Workers (HOAC), the Workers' Commissions, the UGT, and Murcia Acoge, part of the Acoge Network, joined the battle. ATIME and the Acoge Network worked in tough circumstances, and they were routinely threatened by far-right groups. In 2000, the Almería Acoge offices in El Ejido were fire bombed during anti-immigrant rioting.[63]

In 1992, due to pressure from business associations, political parties, and immigrant organizations and their allies, the Spanish government approved a quota system for migrant workers. 20,000 new workers per year could be recruited into labour-seeking sectors such as agriculture, construction, and services, either in Spain or abroad. Even though the measure was largely welcomed by unions and public intellectuals, who praised the opening of safe channels for immigrants to obtain status in Spain, ATIME warned that a quota system could produce a large black market in the illicit trafficking of undocumented persons.[64]

Yet in spite of its overtures to immigrants, the government continued to hinder undocumented migrants' access to status. In 1993–94, many immigrants were forced to return to their countries of origin in order to obtain the visas that would qualify them for the work quota system. The visa requirement aimed to correct the fact that applicants had entered Spain illegally or had overstayed their tourist visas. Many who had secure work permits and could afford the trip travelled back, but those who could not were forced to remain in Spain undocumented. The government worsened this already impractical requirement a few years later when it required immigrants to apply for visas and then, with no guarantee that their applications had been accepted, return to their country of origin to await news from Spanish authorities. Again, most immigrants stayed put and remained undocumented.[65]

Many immigrants believed that this particular policy, at best, discouraged them from applying for status, and, at worst, provided cover for a generalized process of deportation. Immigrants pointed to the fact that while in 1993–94, 20,000 positions had been opened for migrant labourers under the quota system, only 8,000 positions were created in 1995, a clear modification of the system aimed at decreasing migrants' chances of obtaining status. In theory, the quota system was the most guaranteed and regular channel to legal status. In practice, however, immigrants were unsatisfied with it. The door to status was not opened wide enough.[66]

In 1994, immigrants and their supporters successfully pressured the government to enact a Plan for the Social Integration of Immigrants. The government conceded that the 1991 regularization and subsequent work quotas had been insufficient to raise immigrants' living conditions; reforms to health, housing, and education needed to accompany legal changes. The plan's goals were to open up public services to immigrants; fortify workplace rights in sectors where migrants were a majority, namely agriculture and domestic services; bump the length of work permits up to five years; and grant immigrants the right to vote in local elections. All of these were long-standing demands of ATIME and other immigrant organizations. While the plan was approved, its implementation was uneven. For instance, the right to vote in local elections would only be granted to some immigrants.[67]

The government's initiatives were welcomed, but with a degree of scepticism. "There is no feasible plan for health, education, or housing unless the one-year limit on residency permits, conditional on obtaining a work permit first, is not reformed", complained Beyuki. The spirit of "the plan is good, but its aims contradict its premises from the start. It focuses on already documented immigrants and overlooks the 300,000 illegal immigrants", said a member of the Karibú Association.[68]

Amid the wave of promised readjustments, the Socialist government created an advisory structure comprised of representatives from immigrant groups, their supporters, and other related public institutions. The Forum for Social Integration of Immigrants had a direct line to the government.

ATIME was made an immediate member and since 2000 it has held the vice-presidency of the Forum. The creation of this body signaled that immigrant organizations had become partners in policy making related to immigration and integration.[69]

When "Exceptional" Becomes "Ordinary"

In 1996, PSOE Prime Minister Felipe González was defeated and the conservative Popular Party (PP), headed by José María Aznar, came to power. Days before the Socialists stepped down, their interim government modified the regulations of the Immigration Act and approved an exceptional regularization process for undocumented immigrants. This prompted an editorial in *El País* to ask whether a national regularization every four or five years was indeed "special" or "exceptional" any more. The newspaper argued that unless the government could streamline administrative procedures, such regularizations would become the *de facto* norm.[70]

By 1996, it had become clear that immigration policy in Spain was managed by "exceptional" regularizations, rather than ordinary channels to obtain status. In the twenty years leading up to 2005, five such "exceptional" regularizations had taken place. By 1996 it was also evident that, with conservative politicians increasingly eager to garner electoral benefits from a law and order approach to immigration – one that minimized measures towards integration and granted limited rights to immigrants, the 1985 consensus on immigration policy had largely disappeared. The influence of immigrant organizations was also diminished when conservative parties were in government.

Immigrant groups, unions, and much of the liberal media praised the 1996 regularization. For the first time, immigrants were not required to prove employment to apply for legal status, a requirement that had fuelled a widespread black market in counterfeit job contracts.[71] However, applicants still had to demonstrate that they had worked or lived in Spain before January 1996. The Workers' Commissions submitted 3,000 applications for workers who were unable to obtain the required documentation on time, but could demonstrate *arraigo* and were thus, in the eyes of the union, worthy applicants. In the end, only 22,000 migrants, rather than the projected 60,000, met the criteria. The government offered no extensions, nor did it modify the criteria.[72]

Following the 1996 regularization, the PP temporarily cancelled the annual migrant workers quota system and narrowed, once again, ordinary routes to status. Henceforth, immigrants were required to file for a work permit, along with a job offer, with a regional Labour and Social Security Board; return to his or her country of origin for a visa; and return if and when the work permit was granted, which rarely happened since the boards generally prioritized employment for Spaniards.[73]

Immigrant groups had gained a measure of respectability and visibility in the late 1980s and early nineties, but they quickly lost traction after the PP gained power. By 1997, the Madrid organizing committee for the Year against Racism could overlook immigrants as serious policy partners; immigrants were back to being recipients of native benevolence, rather than active participants in decision-making. "It seems that the [Autonomous] Community of Madrid [also governed by the PP], by not including us, wants our organizations to wither. How can an organizing committee apparently opposed to racism be racist?" wondered a spokeswoman for Al Amal. Beyuki claimed that a year earlier, at initial meetings in Madrid to establish an immigration plan for the region, immigrant groups had similarly been rendered invisible. Only in the final consultation phase of the plan, by which point it had become difficult to make changes or offer meaningful input, were a coalition of immigrant groups included enthusiastically.[74] For many, this reeked of tokenism.

Setbacks, however, did not slow the work of activists. In 1998, immigrant groups advised the government that rather than a state secretary for migration, they needed a Ministry of Immigration that could unify procedures between the four separate Ministries of Foreign Affairs, Labour, Social Affairs, and of the Interior in charge of immigration matters at the time. In 2008, again under a Socialist government, the Ministry of Labour and Social Affairs, which had managed most immigration matters up to that point, became the Ministry of Labour and Immigration, thanks largely to the lobbying efforts of immigrants and their supporters.[75]

The World Upside Down

In 2000, the same immigrant organizations that had consistently opposed the provisions of the 1985 Immigration Act changed gears by welcoming a debate then taking place in Congress concerning the reform of the Act. For the first time, immigrant organizations were willing to accept the legal framework regulating immigrants and their social integration. It was a milestone in the fight for immigrant rights in Spain, a short period of time in which Spanish society demonstrated a marked openness vis-à-vis the fundamental rights of undocumented migrants and new residents.

Though a large number of immigrants were regularized in 1996, many more remained undocumented in 1998. The PP, perhaps because it lacked an absolute majority in Congress, had not significantly altered established immigration policy. Activists mobilized in an effort to influence the political process. Cáritas, the Episcopal Commission on Migration, and Manos Unidas launched a joint campaign for "a decent Act to defend migrant workers and to regularize illegal immigrants". The Catholic groups argued for legal equality between immigrants and citizens. They asked that the values of the United Nations Universal Declaration of Human Rights be enshrined in the proposed Act. They also called for easier access to health and education, and a more straightforward set of procedures for obtaining status. Simultaneously, immigrant groups, unions, and NGOs mounted a campaign for another round of regularizations. In April 1999, 1,000 protesters marched in Almería, not only to demand status, but also to end housing discrimination and segregation.[76]

In Madrid, all parties of the Congress eventually agreed on a draft Act to reform the original, but in the last stage of proceedings the PP changed its mind and decided not to support the joint agreement. The sticking point for the PP was a clause on equal rights: The PP did not believe that undocumented immigrants should be entitled to the same rights as full citizens. Specifically, the PP wanted the clause, "in conditions of equality with Spaniards", removed from the draft. Asked to clarify, the national delegate for immigration, Enrique Fernández-Miranda, said the PP would of course grant fundamental rights to undocumented immigrants, rights such as the right to life and physical integrity, but that is where things would end. *El País* retorted, with a healthy dose of sarcasm, that "It would be unthinkable otherwise!"[77]

The PP argued that the clause granting equal rights to undocumented residents would swell the numbers of illegal immigrants entering the country. Indeed, from 1998 to 2000, their numbers had grown, and immigration, along with unemployment and terrorism, had become one of the top worries for Spaniards.[78] By politicizing immigration, the PP hoped to put a conservative majority in Congress in the upcoming elections.

In broad strokes, the PP pushed for strengthened borders, more deportations, and limited rights for illegal residents, while the opposition pushed for more effective immigration policies and social integration. The opposition hoped to equate the rights of undocumented residents with those of legal residents and citizens, minus certain political rights that would be reserved for the latter. It also wanted to limit deportations to just convicted offenders and longer work and residency permits.[79]

Given the new political climate, immigrant groups, who had opposed the Immigration Act for fifteen years, now campaigned to defend the Congress's proposal. In Madrid, a coalition of over sixty organizations came together. "We call upon society to help us pressure the PP to respect the parliamentary consensus that has been built up over the last eighteen months, to take democracy seriously, and not mock Congress, society, and NGOs", said Beyuki. Protests to safeguard the Act swept across Spain and shadowed parliamentary proceedings. In Madrid, protesters gathered outside of the Senate and the headquarters of the PP. In a symbolic gesture, immigrant groups and unions boycotted the Forum for Social Integration of Immigrants.[80]

Activists pointed to the PP's change of heart midway through the parliamentary process as politick and hypocritical. "They only wanted the [Immigration] Act reformed because they thought it would never pass", claimed the Workers' Commissions. The UGT said it was "government filibustering" and that the PP "questioned constitutional precepts, wanted to limit fundamental rights, condemned thousands of immigrants to exploitation, even slavery, and contravened some laws of the European Union". Beyuki said the government "was opposed to the integration of immigrants and had made clear its position with its scandalous amendments [to the Congress draft act]".[81]

The PP did not take the criticism lying down. It vetoed the Congress proposal in the Senate and sent a unilaterally modified draft back to Congress, as required by Spanish law. Congress would not have it. In January 2000, Congress dismissed the PP-Senate modified draft and passed its original draft reform, titled the Act on Rights and Freedoms of Foreigners in Spain and their Social Integration. Except for "their Social Integration", the full title of the Act was the same as in 1985. The inclusion of this small clause was, however, a major advance for immigrants. Decades after Britain or France, Spain was acknowledging that it was more than a country of 'hosts and 'guests' – it would now be a permanent stop.

The January 2000 Immigration Act granted undocumented immigrants the right to assembly, to free association, to basic education, and to strike. It enshrined the concept of *arraigo*, which meant clearer procedures for migrants who had lived at least two years in Spain and had an offer of employment as an ordinary way to obtain status. It maintained the quota system, something the PP had tried to circumvent. Finally, it removed automatic detention and deportation for migrants found without documentation and eased regulations on family reunification.[82] *El País* welcomed these changes:

> The law aims clearly at integration. In addition to upholding the basic rights of undocumented migrants, it regularizes . . . and equalizes rights (except the right to vote) between documented immigrants and citizens. The law's intentions are honest and it takes good advantage of Spain's currently strong economy. This is how human rights are advanced. In times of economic growth, the benefits of the welfare state are extended to vulnerable groups and, in time, solidified into rights. We take our hats off to the Congress.[83]

While the 1985 Immigration Act made the right of immigrants to vote and run for office contingent on regulations in their countries of origin – basically, if a Spaniard could vote in a migrant's country of origin, the migrant could do the same in Spain – the January 2000 Act did away with this. It granted immigrants with status the right to vote in local elections regardless of whether or not Spaniards could vote in these individuals' country of origin, and it even encouraged undocumented immigrants to participate "in municipal debates and decision-making that are of a concern to them".[84]

The Act was "a huge symbolic victory . . . just and merited . . . a big success for Spanish society and not just for immigrants", said ATIME's spokesman. SOS Racismo said that the new Act represented a victory for activists. The UGT, more cuttingly, stated that parliamentary procedures had "revealed the true face of the [PP] government, which spurns democratic procedures, uses the politics of migration as an electoral ploy, and has no interest in ensuring the basic rights of working immigrants".[85]

Soon after the January 2000 Immigration Act came into effect, an anti-immigrant riot erupted in the town of El Ejido, a PP stronghold. For three days, ethnic Spaniards took to the streets in large numbers, burned the head-quarters of a migrant rights NGO, mobbed immigrants that were caught off guard, and barricaded the town to stop police from restoring order.[86] Immigrants were reminded that though they had achieved a degree of security in the national political arena, their status was still precarious on the ground.

The new Act would be implemented by a government that had not supported it and which had been unresponsive to the needs of immigrants. In Valencia, a broad coalition of immigrants and their supporters rallied to demand that Madrid implement the Act correctly, especially as it applied to housing, health, and education. Activists feared that unless they took action, particularly in PP strongholds such as Valencia, the Act would remain a bunch of talking points and little else.[87]

If activists did not pressure the government, they feared they would miss out on a crucial stipulation of the Act: yet another national regularization. That regularization would turn out to be the largest to date, and its criteria were broader than ever before. It did not ask for proof of employment. Undocumented immigrants who could show that they had been in Spain before June 1999, had registered with their municipality (padrón), and had applied for a residency or work permit – even if it had been rejected – were eligible for regularization. From March to July 2000, 244,327 migrants submitted applications for status, 152,207 of which were granted (see Table 1).[88]

With the regularization underway, Prime Minister Aznar announced during an official state visit to Morocco that he would change the January 2000 Immigration Act as soon as he could. The PP wanted what it called a "Counter-Reformation". Speculation raged as to the meaning of this charged reference: was it to the deviant nature of the Act, like the Protestant Reformation itself?

In fact, the PP hoped to rewind the January 2000 Act to its 1985 version. It aimed to eliminate the only two venues by which immigrants could obtain status: the quota system and arraigo. It wanted greater executive flexibility, rather than standardized criteria, to decide who could come or go, even if this meant that immigrants would be pushed back underground.[89] Immigrant groups, unions, NGOs, and Catholic groups took Aznar's comments seriously and once again mobilized against the government.

What was significant about the January 2000 Act was the sudden shift of allegiances. Immigrant groups that had previously spoken out against the 1985 Immigration Act suddenly rallied to support the 2000 act. Spanish intellectuals, too, vouched for the new Act. Eliseo Aja, Chair in Constitutional Law at the University of Barcelona, voiced the view that "a part of the indispensable social contract needed for a correct convivencia had been reached". For the first time, immigrants accepted the legal framework for immigration and had succeeded in placing social integration on the political agenda.[90]

The PP countered by saying that the January 2000 Immigration Act was incompatible with the recommendations of the 1999 Tampere meeting of the European Council; it claimed that the Act had sounded a clarion call for illegal migration, which would be pulled towards Spain by relaxed requirements for the granting of status. Opponents, of course, argued that the Act was fully compatible with the Tampere guidelines and that pull factors, if they existed more than anywhere else in Europe, were economic, not legal, in nature.[91]

Images of illegal migrants washing up on the shores of Spain in small, precarious boats were more widely publicized in the year 2000, helping to reinforce the narrative that illegal immigration was out of control. According to the Spanish National Institute of Statistics, however, only 4.9 percent of North Africans and 9 percent of sub-Saharan Africans had arrived illegally by boat. In 2000, the Spanish police and coastguard intercepted 750 boats, detained 12,000 individuals, rescued 1,000 castaways, and recovered fifty drowned bodies from the sea. The numbers of individuals lost during the treacherous crossing of the Mediterranean were unknown. Although these numbers were similar to previous years, their geographic distribution had shifted. While in southern Spain the number of migrants attempting to cross the Strait of Gibraltar declined thanks to the collaboration of Moroccan authorities, in the Canary Islands this figure grew from 2,410 in 2000 to 9,756 in 2002. The ATIME spokesman decried Aznar's efforts at scaremongering and to "raise the spectre of invasion . . . In two weeks he has set the cause of immigration back more than the Immigration Act managed to do in fifteen years".[92]

The January 2000 Immigration Act marked the end of a political consensus on immigration. The PP won subsequent national elections and put a conservative majority in Congress. It then moved swiftly to reform the Act, as it had promised. The PP Immigration Act, enacted less than a year later, in December 2000, revoked many of the changes that had just been won. Conservatives patted themselves on the back, even though the General Council on Judicial Power reminded them shortly after their electoral victory that "a return to the 1985 Act, which deprives foreigners of the right to assembly, to free association, to protest and strike, and to join a union, is highly worrisome".[93]

Twisting the Government's Arm

The first grassroots opposition to the PP government's new tone came from Andalusia, where the Moroccan Human Rights Association, the Andalusian Human Rights Association, eleven city halls, and 500 small groups signed a collective document. The "Manifesto of the Two Shores [of the Strait of

Gibraltar]" called on Madrid to retain the content of the January 2000 Immigration Act, keep venues open for legal immigration, and reduce the death toll in the Strait of Gibraltar.[94]

Opposition then spread to Almería in September 2000, where that year's regularization process had rejected the largest proportion of applications (19 percent of all rejections came from this province) and where rioting in El Ejido had only recently ended.[95] 200 immigrants occupied the Church of San José – which under the Francoist dictatorship had been associated with working class protests – and seventy-five went on a hunger strike. The protesters wanted their applications to be reconsidered. Madrid refused to speak to them. "The hunger strike is absurd", said the government delegate, Fernando Hermoso. "It doesn't resolve anything. The protesters asked me to communicate their petition to widen the process of regularization to the government, but the government of Spain does not act under that kind of pressure".[96]

The strike in Almería spread to other Andalusian cities, Ceuta, and the Canary Islands. Madrid responded by saying that the only action it deemed legitimate from immigrants was a legal one. The government suggested that the protesters hire lawyers and appeal decisions in court. In the end, the protests petered out and thousands of immigrants took the government's advice and appealed their rejections in court. This relieved matters temporarily, since the January 2000 Immigration Act specified that immigrants with pending appeals could remain in the country. The Almería legal aid system was overwhelmed. Farmers, too, complained that they did not have enough workers with the right documentation to meet their needs. There were 80,000 rejected applicants in the region of Almería alone; the government had little choice but to act.[97]

Though Hermoso stressed that "strikes and occupations were the worst kinds of pressure to put on this government", it was, in reality, those tactics that proved most effective. In Lleida, for example, twenty-nine migrants from the Ivory Coast were granted refugee status after camping out, in protest, in the city's main square. Shortly afterwards, 100 undocumented migrants pitched tents in the Plaça de Catalunya, in the heart of Barcelona. Thirty organizations and over 1,000 citizens came out to support them. The national government, the Catalan regional government, and the city of Barcelona intervened and pledged to find a solution. Two days later, Madrid agreed to review those applications that had been rejected during the 2000 regularization process because it did not want to deport tens of thousands of already "integrated" persons.[98]

When a small number of applicants were successful in appealing their rejections, activists pushed for yet another national regularization to accommodate applicants who were unable to meet the 2000 deadline. A coalition of 300 organizations argued that Madrid had not instructed regional delegations properly on the criteria for rejection. As a result, claimed the coalition, the 2000 regularization was applied unequally across Spain.

Statistical variances between regions revealed this to be true. In the provinces of Asturias and Girona, for instance, 98.2 and 82.2 percent of applicants, respectively, were successful, while in Barcelona the success rate was a mere 29.1 percent. Because Madrid had not specified the necessary documentation to prove residency, criteria in each province fluctuated widely, and in some cases hardened as the regularization progressed and more immigrants applied.[99] In some cases, NGOs took applications to neighbouring regions, where they were successful even though their home regions had rejected them. "The process was a mess", said SOS Racismo.[100] Among other consistent measures, Madrid needed a unified national database. ATIME claimed that the "situation was grievous" and that officials played favourites with different immigrant groups. Latin Americans, claimed ATIME's head, had a success rate of approximately 80 percent, while for Moroccans it was only 52 percent. The difference was due to "discrimination owing to religion and geographic origin".[101]

In response to this criticism, and perhaps to avoid yet another regularization, Madrid committed itself to a thorough review of rejected applications in 2000; as a result, 36,013 further applications were accepted (see Table 1), but not before rumours spread that yet another amnesty was in the works.[102]

Right after the PP succeeded in December 2000 in reforming the January 2000 Immigration Act, a tragic event helped to place the plight of undocumented workers squarely in the hearts and minds of Spaniards. On 3 January 2001, twelve undocumented Ecuadorians died in a van en route to work, struck by a train on an unmanned railway crossing near Lorca, Murcia. There were only two survivors: the driver, the sole legal immigrant in the van, and a thirteen-year-old, who under Spanish law should have been in school. The labourers were on their way to a broccoli farm whose owner had been condemned repeatedly for labour violations. The sister of one of the deceased blamed not the conductor of the train, but the untenable legal situation endured by her sister in Spain:

> The van left Lorca before dawn. You want to know why? Because no one had papers and because at night it's easy to hide. The driver took neither the safest nor shortest route. Why? Because it's dangerous to take the highways, where there are usually Civil Guards. So he took secondary, little used roads ... No, I'm serious. My sister Gladys was not only killed by the train.[103]

Word of the accident spread throughout Spain, particularly in agricultural regions. In Murcia, Rumiñahui, an organization for the region's predominantly indigenous Ecuadorian immigrants, led a march from Lorca to Murcia city, a distance of 70 kilometres. Rumiñahui, named after an Inca warrior who battled the Spanish in the sixteenth century, imported tactics, such as long marches, from indigenous struggles in the Americas. Because the accident had caused strong public outrage on both sides of the Atlantic, the Ecuadorian and Spanish governments negotiated the granting of status to 24,352 Ecuadorians on humanitarian grounds (see Table 1).[104]

The high failure rate of applicants in the 2000 regularization in Barcelona, combined with outrage at the Lorca tragedy, resulted in the most successful church occupations in Spain. In the Raval neighbourhood of downtown Barcelona, South Asian immigrants organized a protest at the Santa Maria del Pi church. The 2000 regularization had rejected Pakistanis at a high rate and many feared deportation. 300 undocumented migrants occupied the church and commenced an indefinite hunger strike. They risked immediate deportation under the provisions of the PP Immigration Act passed in December 2000. A Moroccan who participated in the strike explained that "it is the only means we have left to face the [PP] Immigration Act, which excludes us and condemns us to marginality".[105]

Due to support from the public, the Santa Maria del Pi protest lasted for forty-seven days, unlike similar occupation-style protests in Madrid, Totana, Jumilla, and Lorca, which burned out in less than a week. Two coalitions were crucial to the protest's longevity and success: Papers per Tothom (Papers for Everyone) and the Citizen Platform against the Immigration Act (later watered down to Platform of Citizens for Peaceful Coexistence).[106]

The protest was not limited to Santa Maria del Pi. The HOAC and Catholic Worker Youth (JOC) offered spaces for migrants to hold additional protests. A key figure was Josep Vidal Aunós, a priest who "followed the laws of the Gospels" over the country's laws and had a history of offering up his parish to all kinds of clandestine movements during the Franco years. It was in his church that the Catalan Workers' Commissions began to meet in 1964.[107]

In a country with deep Catholic roots, the symbolism of protest in a church, rather than a university or public square, did not go unnoticed. The idea of sanctuary, the right to protection from undue punishment in the sacred space of the church, went back to medieval times; in this way protesters drew from a very proud tradition. They also followed in the footsteps of similar sanctuary movements that had taken place throughout the western world in the late twentieth century.[108]

Catholic activists were joined by such organizations as SOS Racismo, Médecins sans Frontières, and the Barcelona Federation of Neighbourhood Associations. Activists called for "active resistance to the [PP] Immigration Act." A number of city halls disagreed with the Immigration Act and endorsed civil disobedience. On 31 January 2001, the Santa Coloma de Gramanet city hall motioned to grant non-status residents the same rights as status residents. The UGT and the Workers' Commissions, meanwhile, said that they would accept membership applications from non-status workers despite the fact that the PP immigration law forbade this.[109]

The Barcelona protest split into two broad camps: one, led by Papers per Tothom and the General Confederation of Labour (CGT), was radical and anarchist; the other, led by the Workers' Commissions and the UGT, with support from the Socialists' Party of Catalonia (PSC), the Republican Left of Catalonia, and the Catalan United Left Party, was a grouping of social democratic, socialist, and communist organizations. While the former supported hunger strikes and occupations, the latter backed away from direct action. "Other means of pressure need to be found", said Ghassam Saliba, the Lebanese-born representative of the Workers' Commissions for migrant workers.[110]

A week after the start of the hunger strike in Santa Maria del Pi, imitation protests spread to eight other churches in Barcelona and most public institutions, NGOs, and unions became involved. In Santa Maria del Pi, the archbishop of Barcelona, Ricard Maria Carles, held mass in solidarity with protesters and called upon authorities to assist immigrants.[111]

The authorities, however, were not forthcoming. They argued that the strategies used by immigrants were crude and disagreeable. Occupations, in their view, were not just ineffective, but presented public health risks as well. The government delegate called occupations "unacceptable social blackmail" and appealed to the moderate coalition to tone down radical actions. National and regional governments were particularly uneasy with Papers per Tothom, whose decision-making – done collectively at large public assemblies, usually in multiple languages, including Urdu, Spanish, Bengali, Tamazight, and Arabic – made it virtually impossible to negotiate with representatives. The government did not routinely deal with such unwieldy systems of organization.[112]

The use of hunger strikes, however, pressured negotiators to find quick solutions. Miren Santiago, a well-meaning but unsophisticated supporter of the protesters at Santa Maria del Pi, explained why protesters had opted for a hunger strike: "The Pakistanis, Indians, and others decided that the hunger strike was right for them. In the West we have one way of fighting, we have Marx, and in the East they have another, Gandhi".[113]

Although initially a handful of women had participated in the strike at Santa Maria del Pi, the protesters were largely men, as was the case throughout Barcelona. Women played key support roles as male strikers grew weak, sick, and tired. This gender division may have been as much social as practical. In churches, protesters were cramped into tight quarters. They slept together and shared limited bathrooms. It was tough enough to avoid conflict among men who spoke different languages and had different upbringings without the added dimension of gender tension.

Curiously enough, the nominal spokesperson for the largely Indian and Pakistani population of protesters was Norma Falconi, a small, soft-spoken, middle-aged Ecuadorian woman of indigenous descent. She was also an active member of the CGT. She made an unlikely choice for spokesperson, though she was well connected to both immigrant activists and their ethnic Spanish supporters. She kept a low profile in the mainstream press, revealing little about herself in order to avoid any cult of personality, and conveying only the decisions of protesters agreed upon in mass assemblies. "The organized undocumented immigrants must have their own identity, be their own protagonists", she said.[114]

One church that bucked the trend of male-centred activism was the Church of Sant Pau. There, protesters were women, both immigrants and ethnic Spaniards. They signed a manifesto in which they argued that "thousands of women work every day for women's autonomy, contribute their labour to the development of the country, and maintain the economic health of their families". Female immigrants had different needs, they argued. The women asked that "in the face of the [PP] Immigration Act, their specificity as women be taken into consideration". The lack of legal protections for undocumented female migrants opened them up to "sexual abuse and limited their ability to report on their abusers".[115] In effect, the difficulties they faced to access status were more complex than those of their male counterparts.

The PP Immigration Act stipulated that when an immigrant sponsored a spouse, the spouse was legal only in so far as he or she remained married to the legal immigrant. This meant that for many women, marriage was the only way that they could keep their legal status. Consequently, many women clung to abusive relationships more than they might have under other circumstances. The women of Sant Pau called for "residency and work permits independent of marital status", and that women be allowed to "keep residency and work permits in the case of separation or divorce". They spoke out against the general lack of gender sensitivity in immigration and refugee regulations. They also asked that "rape be included as a cause for political asylum" and that "women who had been forcibly married in their countries of origin be considered under humanitarian grounds". As mothers, the protesters called for "the right to natural child rearing" and "immediate family reunification". As workers, they called for permits for domestic servants and rights for women working in the underground economy, such as sex workers.[116]

Though Falconi admitted that women were more active in the Barcelona protests as nurturers and as maintainers of children and households, as support personnel, and as intermediaries between politicians, parishioners, and other immigrants, she argued that the Sant Pau protest represented a major achievement for women:

> We can't measure women's participation in the occupations by quantity, but rather by quality of participation. One church was dedicated solely to women, because women, who had specific demands, occupied it . . . Women immigrants who participated in the Barcelona occupations played an important political and organizational role: they held meetings, especially with women immigrants who could not participate in occupations because they were caring for their families. In Sant Pau, immigrant women participated directly in the occupation, with constant support from ethnic Spanish women. They organized meetings of 120 to 200 persons. They ensured that the most motivated women were given a place and opportunity to identify legal problems, problems of abuse, family reunification, sexual assault, and prostitution, and that actions could be taken to ensure the success of the occupations. When the women of Sant Pau ended their protest, they continued to meet and organize actions afterwards.[117]

Confronted with the Barcelona protests, Madrid agreed to allow NGOs and unions, comprised mostly of ethnic Spaniards, to revise and oversee the application review process, though ATIME was also given a role. The PP government said it would review rejected applications on "humanitarian grounds" and look for "exceptional circumstances". The PSOE, in opposition, campaigned for another regularization and to wave the visa requirement for migrants who already lived in Spain, a measure it had been reluctant to implement while in office.[118]

An agreement between activists and the national government was reached on 4 February 2001, though a final settlement, called the Barcelona Agreement, would not be signed for another month. The Barcelona Agreement stipulated that participants in the occupations would not be arrested and deported unless they had a criminal record. The agreement also stipulated that all previously rejected applications, not just those of hunger strike protesters, would be duly reviewed under provisions of the Immigration Act dealing with *arraigo* and humanitarian and exceptional circumstances. Women who had been victims of domestic violence or sexual abuse would be permitted to apply for status and the visa requirement would be waved for them.[119]

The Barcelona occupations marked a high-water mark in immigrant-led protest. For perhaps the first time, many ethnic Spaniards realized that immigrants were capable of speaking for themselves. On 11 February 2001, undocumented migrants from all over Spain gathered in Barcelona. They titled their gathering "Immigrants Speak", as though it had been a long time coming (as indeed it had). For the first time, immigrants had a collective voice all over Spain. Regardless of whether they were undocumented or had status, immigrants managed to make Spanish democracy more inclusive and plural.[120] The occupations also made South Asians, the most populous group in the Barcelona city centre, visible as never before. Numerous community organizations would emerge from the organizing efforts of this period and the Raval neighbourhood would become a priority site for revitalization projects.[121]

As protest in Barcelona waned, it spread to other cities. In Madrid, Valencia, Málaga, Murcia, Almería, and Lepe, immigrants occupied churches and universities. Protesters marched from Pinto and Alcalá de Henares to Madrid. The "roar of immigrants", as *El País* called it, would force Madrid to extend the Barcelona Agreement to other regions of the country and even widen the Agreement's initial provisions in some cities, such as Valencia. Eventually the government would agree to another national regularization, popularly known as "regularization by *arraigo*". The government used Article 31.4 of the PP Immigration Act to justify the "regularization for *arraigo*". The article stated that "A temporary residence permit could be granted in the case of exceptional humanitarian circumstances or when *arraigo* could be shown, if the circumstances fall within the regulations".[122] This would grant status to 157,883 immigrants (see Table 1), the largest number to date. Migrants who had been in the country before 23

January 2001, with an offer of employment rather than a signed contract or those who were related to legal residents or citizens of Spain were eligible to apply. A wide array of documents could be used to prove *arraigo*.

It had never been easier to obtain status in Spain. Yet immigrants and their supporters knew that their successes had not come easily. Without their organized efforts, such a broad regularization would never have occurred, contrary to what those who ascribe agency exclusively to native Spaniards believe. Pressure from trade unions, business organizations, and opposition parties alone would not have been enough to open the door so wide. Falconi concluded by saying that immigrant activism "had achieved a victory, the first of its kind for immigrants in Spain."[123]

Achievements and New Challenges

Lack of citizenship in Spain, a category rooted in land and tradition, raises immediate, visceral suspicions amongst many Spaniards. As Tony Judt put it in *Postwar*, his history of Europe after 1945, it was not long ago in European history that "cosmopolitan" was a term of slander.[124] Though scholars and human rights defenders have scrutinized and questioned the necessary link between citizenship and rights, Spanish regulations, like those in other European states, are based on a narrow view of rights for non-citizens (albeit with certain provisos for other citizens of the EU). Current understandings may change as states are forced to contend with fluid movements of people, diasporas, and transnational relationships, but for now, European thinking on migration is constrained by narrow and static views on human movement and settlement.[125]

Nonetheless, by 2001 immigrants in Spain had created migrant organizations and had their own voice in debates about immigration and social integration. Their efforts to defend a quota system for migrant workers as an ordinary way to obtain status and to streamline and ease immigration regulations had contributed to the post-Franco strengthening of Spain's institutional framework. Immigrant organizations had also established solidarity ties with NGOs and trade unions in the fight to obtain status and labour rights and had succeeded in introducing into the Immigration Law the idea of regularization by *arraigo*.

However, as a legal concept, *arraigo* was defined primarily by policy-makers, with little input from immigrants or their supporters. In 2001, for instance, the PP said *arraigo* meant that one had lived a minimum of three years in Spain, had employment, and could demonstrate "family ties with Spaniards and other legal foreign residents".[126] NGOs, churches, and immigrant sympathizers generally played an important role in nurturing roots, particularly when it came to providing documentary evidence for what was and remains a highly subjective concept.

Even though an individual's ability to obtain status would be contingent on the party in power – it was certainly easier under Socialist than it was under Conservative governments – the standard way to obtain status by *arraigo* eliminated the reasons for the outbreak of immigrant activism between 1985 and 2005. The last regularization in 2005, referred to as "normalization", granted status to 578,375 people (see Table 1). It was the largest regularization in Spain and was implemented with the understanding that it would be the last. Afterwards, *arraigo* functioned as an ordinary rather than extraordinary path to status, and as a deterrent against future exceptional regularizations.

Arraigo may have opened doors for some immigrants, but it did not change the outlook of many ethnic Spaniards. According to Lisa Malkii, the motherland was still the motherland, "a grand genealogical tree, rooted in the soil that nourishes it. By implication, it is impossible to be a part of more than one tree. Such a tree evokes both temporal continuity of essence and territorial rootedness". Yet immigrants themselves pushed for *arraigo*'s institutionalization and managed to keep it as "a mechanism of humanitarian flexibility" in the otherwise restrictive PP Immigration Act of December 2000.[127]

Even though a precarious consensus on the need for ordinary ways to obtain status had been achieved by 2001, this did not translate in a reduction of tensions related to immigration management. Since 2000, Spain has followed the trend identified by Stephen Castles and Mark J. Miller in other western countries as the politicization of immigration. Immigration has become a white-hot political issue that both major parties, the PP and the PSOE, have used as election ploys. After fifteen years of avoiding the flawed 1985 Immigration Act, the PP tackled it with urgency in 2000, and in 2004 the PSOE, back in office, did the same. Part of the pressure to reform the Act, however, also came from the European Union and legal challenges in courts of law.[128]

In 2004, immigrants attempted a second sanctuary-style protest in Barcelona. However, they were not successful, as they lacked support from the major political parties, including the PSOE – which was now in power both nationally, as well as in the region of Catalonia and the city of Barcelona – and from the same mainstream activists who had backed them in 2001. There were also tensions between older, more established immigrants and newcomers. Members of the Ibn Battuta Association, close to the PSC, made a point of discouraging activists from occupying the Cathedral of Santa Eulalia, an action they would have likely supported a few years earlier. Moreover, the terrorist train bombing of Madrid just a few months earlier cast a cloud of suspicion over Muslims everywhere.[129]

As far as the right to vote is concerned, Spain is still upholding many limitations for non-EU citizens to participate in elections. The PSOE signed a series of bilateral agreements with Latin American countries in 2009 that allow their nationals living in Spain to vote in local elections. Due to a clause in the Spanish constitution, the PSOE only offered these agreements to democratic countries that had friendly diplomatic relations with Spain. The new policy created a tiered immigration system. At the top were immigrants from countries which, according to the Immigration Act, enjoyed special cultural affinities with Spain and thus could access longer employment and residency permits; in the middle were immigrants from the same countries who could access longer employment and residency permits, but could not vote; and at the bottom were immigrants from largely Muslim countries who had neither affinity rights nor could vote. In other words, while it became easier to be Peruvian- or Colombian-Spanish, it became harder to be Moroccan- or Pakistani-Spanish.

While immigrants have created a robust network of representative organizations, the largest of these groups have been transformed from radical advocates of migrant rights to service providers dependent on public funds. According to sociologist Sonia Veredas Muñoz, immigrant organizations currently move between clientelism and cooption. She argues that immigrant civil society has been built "from above", which entails the "suppression of debate over the structural conditions in which civil and political rights are exercised by migrant populations". Sociologist Juan David Gómez-Quintero concurs; he argues that immigrant organizations, though central to the struggles for rights in Spain, have reproduced "an exotic, assistance-needing idea of immigration that may have hindered immigrants' efforts to obtain citizenship ... The logic of patronage, of cooption and dependency on grants to provide services, complicates the prospect of immigrants as citizens".[130] Indeed, since 2000, ATIME and the Ibn Battuta Association, now the recipients of government funding, have moved gradually from political protest to the provision of settlement services for immigrants. Groups that once challenged immigration policy and advocated radical forms of activism, such as AEME or Papers per Tothom, have since become irrelevant or defunct.

The transformation of immigrant organizations from radical critics of the Immigration Act to partners in policy making does not, however, remove these groups' ability to respond to the needs of immigrants "from below". While there is ample evidence to connect immigrant organizations to patronage and cooption by political parties and governments, one cannot but wonder, in light of the frequent corruption scandals witnessed in Spain, whether immigrant organizations are merely an example of adaptation to the prevailing political culture.

Finally, clientelism and cooption do not entirely negate the "developmental effect" that joining a migrant association has on individuals. Members learn democratic practices and are granted a space to deliberate and debate. A network of immigrant organizations also provides "social infrastructure" that reinforces the public sphere. And on an institutional level, associations can help to guide the voice of the citizenry towards participation in the formal political process, helping individuals to exert their rights within an institutional framework.[131]

While immigrant organizations may have at times upheld perceptions about immigrants as foreign, inarticulate, and in need of benevolence, they have also encouraged immigrants to think of themselves as engaged citizens.

They pushed steadily for democratic decision-making, manoeuvred a plurality of civil and governmental bodies, and forced the government to alter existing immigration policy for the better.[132]

3

Religious Pluralism, Secularism, and Women's Rights, 1968–2010

According to José Casanova, in recent decades European society has undergone a "progressive though highly uneven, secularization . . . An increasing majority of the European population has ceased participating in traditional religious practices, at least on a regular basis, even though they may still maintain relatively high levels of private individual religious beliefs".[1] In contemporary Europe, however, secularization does not necessarily equate with *laïcité*, a strict separation of state and church. Most European governments have either adopted neutrality in religious matters or maintain a national church, but they have not enforced a strict separation of the secular/public and religious/private spheres, as the 1905 law on the Separation of the Churches and the State did in France. While democratic Spain has no state religion, it falls short of *laïcité* or strict neutrality; public institutions in Spain have a constitutional obligation, for example, to maintain cooperation with the Catholic Church, among other confessions.

According to Casanova, secularism depends on "societal modernization as a process of functional differentiation and emancipation of the secular spheres – primarily the modern state, the capitalist market economy, and modern science – from the religious sphere, and the concomitant differentiation and specialization of religion within its own newly found religious sphere".[2] Yet as the Spanish case illustrates, the division between these spheres is not always complete, nor are these spheres mutually exclusive. Rather, the present chapter views this relationship as the constant shifting of two dominant outlooks, an unstable, dynamic interaction that often brings societal contradictions to the fore.

Contrary to common assumptions, which often assume that Muslim activism in Europe is at odds with democratic values, Muslim religious activism in Spain has widely embraced the constitutional framework set up in 1978. Spanish Muslims have endorsed the absence of an official state religion, and have demanded that public authorities support a plurality of religious communities in Spain. However, they have also demanded a genuine 'religious transition' in the country; the post-Franco transition to democracy, in their view, has left some issues unresolved. Of particular relevance for Muslims in Spain has been – and remains – the privileged position of the Catholic Church. The religious transition they advocate would assure absolute state neutrality in this regard – in other words, it would ensure that public authorities privilege no single confession over others. While the influential and active Catholic lobby has rebuffed Muslim attempts to achieve parity on this issue, adherents of both faiths share a desire to defend the role of religion in the public sphere and to limit a stricter implementation of *laïcité*.

Muslim efforts to dignify and institutionalize the practice of Islam in the country, as illustrated by the 1992 Agreement of Cooperation between the State and the Islamic Commission of Spain, have increased the presence of religion in the public sphere and the involvement of the state in protecting religious practices. Advocates of *laïcité* have not welcomed this; moreover, they have singled out Muslims in particular as harbingers of an unwelcomed resurgence of religion in Spain. Yet Muslims are not the main proponents of religion in the public sphere: this role has always been occupied by Catholic lobby groups and the Catholic Church.

Ana I. Planet argues that the Agreement of Cooperation moved Muslim Melillans away from the kinds of socio-political activism that defined their struggle for political rights in the 1980s (discussed in Chapter 1) to a more religious form of activism.[3] In mainland Spain, similarly, the Agreement fuelled religious activism by providing incentives for Muslims to organize along religions rather than ethno-cultural or socio-political lines. This chapter argues that religious activism has been as conducive to the consolidation of democracy and the deepening of democratic practices in Spain as earlier forms of activism insofar as it has demanded a share of the public sphere, government involvement in safeguarding the public practice of Islam, and equal treatment of all religions represented in Spanish society.

From State Catholicism to Religious Pluralism

Spain has maintained a troubled relationship with secularism longer than most European nations. Historically, religious pluralism has been the *de facto* and *de jure* exception rather than the norm. In 1492, the Catholic Monarchs Ferdinand and Isabella expelled Spanish Jews and forcibly converted its Muslims after 800 years of settlement on the Iberian Peninsula. Between 1609 and 1614, Phillip III expelled the remaining Muslims that had converted to Catholicism, known as *Moriscos*. For most of its existence, Spain has been religiously and politically Catholic, with little separation of church and state.

Despite ferocious battles between liberals and traditionalists throughout the nineteenth century, Catholicism has remained the official religion of the country into the modern era. The otherwise progressive, liberal Constitution of 1812 declared that "The religion of the Spanish nation is, and ever shall be, the Catholic Apostolic Roman and only true faith; the

State shall, by wise and just laws, protect it and prevent the exercise of any other".[4] Religious pluralism and state neutrality reigned only during two brief republican interludes: the First Republic of 1873–1874 and the Second Republic of 1931–1939. Franco's Law of the Principles of the *Movimiento Nacional*, of 1958, resumed traditional religious orthodoxy: "The Spanish nation considers as a badge of honour observance of the Law of God according to the doctrine of the Holy Roman and Apostolic Catholic Church, the only true faith inseparable from the national conscience, and the inspiration for its legislation".[5]

As part of Franco's "National Catholicism", the state and its resources were placed at the service of the Catholic Church. In exchange, the Church offered Franco moral support, as well as indoctrination in schools and parishes in the complementary duty of obeying Franco's authoritarian regime. Franco cemented this relationship in 1953 by entering into a concordat with the Holy See. Among other things, the concordat mandated financial privileges for the Catholic Church, and it permitted Franco to appoint bishops.[6]

After a controversial debate between mostly traditionalist representatives from Spain and Italy and reformers from the United States as part of the Second Vatican Council (Vatican II), the Declaration on Religious Freedom "*Dignitatis Humanae*" was approved in 1965. It accepted religious freedom for the first time, rendering the concordat with Franco, signed just twelve years earlier, outmoded. Vatican II moved away from the principle of church freedom, "*libertas ecclesiae*", and embraced instead freedom of the individual, "*libertas personae*". Vatican II also concluded that concordats with individual states were not the best way to protect the Church's freedom; it called instead for the defense of the sacred rights of individuals, and it reminded states of their democratic duty to protect individual freedoms.[7] In response to Vatican II, Franco issued the 1967 Law on Exercising the Civil Right to Religious Freedom, which made it possible for Muslim organizations in Melilla and Madrid to legalize in 1968 and 1971, respectively.[8]

The 1978 Constitution simultaneously abolished the 1953 concordat and Catholicism's status as state religion. However, a year later the Spanish government signed four new Agreements of Cooperation with the Vatican that dealt with educational, cultural, financial, and military concerns.[9] The new democratic constitution guaranteed freedom of belief and religion, yet required the state to "maintain appropriate cooperation with the Catholic Church and other confessions".[10] Shortly thereafter, in 1980, Congress passed a new Law on Religious Freedom that permitted non-Catholic religious groups to register voluntarily with the Ministry of Justice in order to obtain legal status. The new democracy was now "neither typically secularist, belligerent, and hostile in many instances towards religion, nor . . . dogmatically denominational", argued one senator in 1980.[11]

The Law on Religious Freedom impelled the government to promote religious pluralism and to eliminate obstacles that prevented pluralism as a matter of individual religious rights and freedoms. The Law called for bilateral agreements between Spain and those religious denominations that sought legal recognition.[12] In 1980, this included Protestants, Jews, and Muslims, as well as Catholics, now a separate and unofficial religion, like all others, though the Law did not stipulate that religious groups were equal. It was not until twelve years later, in 1992, that Madrid would sign agreements to regulate public religious practices with Protestant, Jewish, and Muslim representatives.[13]

The 1980 Law would remain unchanged until in 2008, when the Socialist government tabled reforms to deepen commitments to religious neutrality and attempted to introduce the expression "state *laïcité*".[14] This was part of a larger and more ambitious agenda that Omar Encarnación has labeled "a second transition".[15] José Luis Rodríguez Zapatero's Socialist government broke the consensus among political actors achieved during the transition to democracy. It overturned the so-called "pact of silence" concerning the historical memory of crimes committed during the Spanish Civil War and under the Franco dictatorship. The Zapatero administration also passed legislation on abortion, female parity in politics, same-sex marriage, and attempted to tackle state neutrality on religious matters as well. Catholic officials denounced these moves as a form of French-style secularism. "The government cannot replace state secularism with *laïcité* that aims to reduce religion to the private sphere and denies it expression in public", said a politician of the Catalan Christian Democrat Party.[16] During Socialist Zapatero's two terms as prime minister, Catholics protested in the streets and launched nationwide campaigns. Three notable mobilizations included a campaign to oppose citizenship education in 2005, same-sex marriage in 2007, and legalized abortion in 2009. Catholics also managed to arrange two controversial visits to the country by Pope Benedict XVI.[17]

Muslims, however, supported the government's efforts to reform the 1980 Law on Religious Freedom. Muslim leaders called for "one-hundred percent state neutrality" in religious matters. "Considering the current state of affairs, the government's position to remain completely neutral in questions of faith and to work positively with those religions rooted in the country is understandable", argued Riay Tatary, one of the two secretary-generals of the Islamic Commission of Spain.[18]

During this period, Spanish society remained culturally Catholic and divided between theists and proponents of a secular state. Many devout Muslims agreed in principle with the Catholic theist stance yet disagreed that the state should prioritize Catholicism over other faiths. Because Spanish conservatives relied on traditional support from organized Catholics and the Catholic Church, the two Muslim national federations have traditionally aligned themselves with the PSOE on matters of religious pluralism. Catholic criticisms, compounded by the change of priorities brought about by the economic recession that hit Europe in 2008, forced the Socialist government to shelve reform of the 1980 Law on Religious

Freedom. The status quo on religious matters remains unchanged to this day, and the new conservative government, in power since 2011, is unlikely to modify the relationship of the state with the Catholic Church.

José Casanova reminds us that in countries like France, "religious traditions are now confronting the differentiated secular spheres, challenging them to face their own obscurantist, ideological, and inauthentic claims. In many of these confrontations, it is religion which, as often as not, appears to be on the side of human enlightenment".[19] In Spain, Catholics have been more of a threat to the precarious balance of theist and secularist interests than Muslims. Nonetheless, it is Muslims who are perceived as the greater, more insidious menace by mainstream society; they would certainly not be described by many Spaniards as "on the side of human enlightenment". This fact has more to do with inconsistencies on the part of the Spanish state in regards to religion and the place of religion in public life, as well as the widespread image of Muslims in Europe as threats to secular society.

The Construction of Spanish Islam

In Spain, as in other European countries, Muslim immigrants have embodied tremendous diversity from the start, even if non-Muslims have often seen them as a homogenous bloc. Ideology, ethnicity, geographic origin, gender, age, and socioeconomic standing split Spanish Muslims; they adhere to four broad schools of Sunni Islam as well as Shia and South Asian Ahmadiyya. They are Islamic revivalists and reformists; rural and urban; educated and illiterate; native converts, Africans, and Asians; white, black, and Semitic. To some, Islam is a private affair of the heart, and to others it is public and political. Some have legal status and others do not.

During the Spanish Civil War, Franco employed 70,000 North African mercenaries, known as "*regulares*", and constructed a mosque in Córdoba for them. While a number remained in Spain between 1936 and 1957 to serve as personal guards (*Guardia Mora*) to Franco, a large majority returned to North Africa.[20] While it is tempting, if only for the sake of irony, to begin the story of Islam's return to mainland Spain with Franco and his Muslim mercenaries, a more appropriate starting point was provided by the arrival, in 1946, of an Ahmadiyya preacher from Pakistan who chose Andalusia to carry on his proselytizing mission. The Ahmadis fled Pakistan after religious authorities began persecuting them as a heretical sect.[21] Outside of Pakistan, they struggled for recognition from other Muslims, including the Sunni Muslim Association of Spain, founded in 1971, which claimed they were not genuine Muslims.[22] The Ahmadis would go on to build Spain's third modern mosque in 1982, the Basharat Mosque in Pedro Abad, Córdoba.

While the Ahmadiyya community remained small for several decades, Sunni Muslims grew steadily in numbers. By 1977, the Muslim Association of Spain was active in Madrid, Zaragoza, and Valencia, and was a central hub for Muslims across Spain. It counted 1,000 practicing members and twenty-four native converts among its ranks.[23] Similar associations appeared throughout Spain in response to the greater influx of immigrants and the newly passed 1980 Law. Yet many of these associations remained unofficial, or were registered as cultural institutions because they did not know about the Ministry of Justice's list of religious organizations.

The first Sunni Muslims came from the Middle East as exchange students – many of whom would become influential professionals – or as economic migrants from Morocco. By the late 1980s, the students had thinned out. In Madrid, they dropped from 30,000 to 10,000. "Students from Arab countries can't come to Spain anymore", lamented a spokesperson of the Islamic Institute of Madrid: "Entrance exams are tougher, the cost of living is more expensive, and it is hard to secure a student visa. A few years ago all you had to do was enrol [in university]".[24]

These newcomers were joined by a small contingent of vocal native converts. As Lisa Abend has demonstrated, the numbers are difficult to estimate. By 2008, when the total number of Muslims in Spain was thought to be around 1 million individuals, the number of converts amongst this group was estimated at 20,000. While these numbers are uncertain, their origins can be traced to a Scottish convert, Ian Dallas (or Skaykh Abdalqadir As-Sufi al Murabit, as he was known after conversion), who started a movement in southern Spain in 1975 called the Morabitun, derived from the Almoravids, the first of the two Imazighen dynasties that ruled Al Andalus after the fall of the Umayyad Córdoba Caliphate. The Morabitun's Islam was both Sufi and Andalusian in its inspiration, features that would remain crucial for most converts. According to Abend, the Morabitun were "[s]elf-identified progressives – some would call them hippies; many at one time belonged to the Communist Party – [who] were drawn to the Morabitun critique of the West as exhausted and capitalism as corrupt".[25] Moreover, the choice of Islam provided an opportunity to oppose Franco's National Catholicism – in one stroke, converts could embrace the nation's reviled historical enemy, the Moor, and reject the dominant Catholic orthodoxy.

As internal dissidence divided the Morabitun, other institutions and leaders emerged. The most influential of these groups was Junta Islámica (The Islamic Council), based in Córdoba. The Islamic Council claimed that Spanish Islam, as the inheritor of the medieval Islam of Al-Andalus, was heterogeneous and heterodox. Among its many projects and campaigns, the Islamic Council published *Verde Islam*, the most important Islamic magazine in the country. The Islamic Council defined itself as

> a free, open, and pluralistic organization whose objectives were to find the best possible ways to integrate Islam into the lay space of Spanish society, to promote basic freedoms, human rights, inter-religious dialogue, gender equality, freedom of expression and belief, mutual respect, peaceful coexistence between humans, and to preserve the environment. The Islamic

Council supports a universal Islam that unites spiritual values with modernity and ... democracy.[26]

The sustained organization and lobbying efforts of converts, who have embraced the role of intermediary between non-Muslim ethnic Spaniards and Muslim immigrants, has upset traditionalists and nationalists who cling to old national narratives premised on the belief that the Islamic period in Spain represented a foreign occupation and that its historic achievements were 'un-Spanish'. They also upset the growing number of European intellectuals that question the concept and implementation of multicultural policies. Converts are "wolves disguised as sheep, Trojan horses for useful fools who believe in the myth of multiculturalism", wrote philosopher and feminist Rosa María Rodríguez Magda in *La España convertida al islam* [Spain converted to Islam].[27] Such rhetoric minimizes, even dehumanizes, converts and overlooks the contribution of many converts to the strengthening of religious freedom, the promotion of rights for women and homosexuals, and the denunciation of Islamic, not to mention Catholic, fundamentalism.

Many Spanish converts claim they are not "creating a new brand of the faith, but recovering a true one, one that held sway centuries ago in the same areas where convert communities are now based". Some embrace, while others reject, the notion of an Islam "made in Spain", but most claim that the religion they practice is European, both in its historical roots in Andalusia and its compatibility with European Enlightenment values. In this sense, their reformist interpretation of Islam in Europe, what some have called 'Euro-Islam', is closer to the views of Bassam Tibi than the writings of the most popular – though also the most controversial – advocate of Euro-Islam, Tariq Ramadan.[28]

Back in the Madrid of the 1980s, Spanish Muslims drew attention to themselves whenever international events, such as the Iranian Revolution of 1979, the war between Afghan *mujahedeen* and the Soviet military, the Hezbollah-backed bombing of the American Marine barracks in Beirut in 1983, and the bombing of Pan Am flight 103, allegedly by Palestinian and/or Libyan terrorists, made international headlines. In an echo of current sentiments voiced by Muslim immigrants today, a spokesperson of the Islamic Institute of Madrid argued defensively that "in Spain, we live according to the constitution and only ask that our customs be respected".[29]

With four small mosques, a cemetery administered by the Moroccan government in the small town of Griñón, outside Madrid, two private schools with Islamic instruction, and a handful of ethnic restaurants, Muslims were conspicuous in the capital. "Our biggest problems are a lack of cemeteries and schools", said the Islamic Institute.[30] As their numbers swelled, Muslims not only drew greater attention to themselves in the media, on the streets, and in public spaces, but their diversity as a community grew as well. Moroccan economic migrants established modest prayer sites with contributions from members and with imams who were uncertified but recognized by their congregations as knowledgeable in Islamic religious matters. Though the Moroccan authorities aided religious organizations and ran their own welfare associations, the *amicales*, prayer sites remained largely independent.[31]

As a result, funding for religious spaces and activities was a constant issue. "In Spain, some groups are highly influenced by their financial backers and cannot express themselves freely", explained one spokesman for the Shia community in Granada.[32] Saudi-backed, so-called "Oil Islam", funded the construction of large mosques in Málaga and Madrid and fought to win over small prayer sites throughout Spain, to which their funding agencies contributed free literature and imams' salaries. The Saudi European Council of Mosques, one such agency, supported the first prayer room in the Catalan city of Vic, which resulted in young residents "discovering a new religion that was different from the magic world that surrounded us in our first eight years of life", claimed the Vic writer Najat El Hachmi. Her first exposure to Saudi Arabian Wahhabi Islam occurred in Spain. It shook up the unorthodox, superstition-prone Islam that she had absorbed in rural, isolated Morocco. "Why did my own grandfather . . . who had brought me to the town mosque at midday on Fridays, not tell me I was forbidden to wear pants?" she wondered.[33]

Despite Saudi mediation, Islam in Spain was at first decentralized and non-hierarchical. This changed in the early 1990s when the PSOE, following the lead of French Minister of Interior Pierre Joxe, who had attempted to institutionalize the practice of Islam in France through the French Council of Thought on Islam, established an Agreement of Cooperation with Spanish Muslims.[34] The PSOE used the 500th anniversary of the Christian conquest of Granada and the expulsion of the Jews to mark a historic reversal in the religious policies of the preceding centuries. Spain would acknowledge Protestants, Jews, and Muslims as "deeply rooted" (*notorio arraigo*) and sign agreements with them, as it had done with the Catholic Church. As we saw in the previous chapter, the concept of rootedness had become a crucial tool in accessing citizenship, status, and religious rights for minorities and immigrants.

The Agreements were necessary to develop the 1980 Law on Religious Freedom and negotiations with Protestants and Jewish federations were advanced. Spain would be holding the 1992 Olympic Games in Barcelona and the Universal Exposition of Cultures in Seville and knew that the country's international image and democratic credentials would be enhanced with the official recognition of religious minorities. Even though the PSOE government was in a hurry, it refused to negotiate with a plethora of Muslim regional and splinter groups. Regional associations would have to assemble under a federal body and elect representatives as delegates to negotiate with the government. Madrid thereby brought an end to years of decentralized and horizontal Muslim organization; in its place, it imposed a hierarchy that it could better manage.

Muslim organizations were keen to gain state recognition and to enjoy the rights and privileges that this entailed. They worked to unite, with mixed results. In negotiations to establish the Federation of Islamic Religious Entities of Spain (FEERI) in 1989, Riay Tatary Bakry, a Syrian-born physician and the imam of Madrid's largest mosque, refused to join the federation and formed a splinter group called the Union of Islamic Communities in Spain (UCIDE). The government did not want to deal with two separate and feuding federations, so it forced them to come together under one banner, the Islamic Commission of Spain (CIE). The government then signed an Agreement of Cooperation with the CIE, which was then placed in charge of monitoring the implementation of the agreement through its two secretaries-general, one from each federation.[35]

Supporters of UCIDE and FEERI quarrelled over many issues. While UCIDE was perceived to be "traditionalist", led by Arab immigrants who had arrived as students and had become professionals, and aligned loosely with moderates of the Egyptian Muslim Brotherhood, FEERI was "moderate", led by Spanish converts, and supposedly unattached to foreign causes, though it drew funds from Saudi Arabia, Libya, Iran, and Morocco.[36] Mansur Escudero, a psychiatrist from Córdoba and a convert with links to left-wing Spanish politicians and Libya, and an uneasy relationship with Saudi Arabia, headed FEERI.[37] Escudero was also president of Córdoba's Islamic Council and the unanimous leader of Spanish converts.

Tatary and Escudero competed for leadership of the Muslim community in Spain. Tatary received funds from oil-rich Islamic countries to maintain his mosque in Madrid. The sheer variety of financial bakers ensured, he argued, the mosque's independence, even though it was in direct competition with a nearly complete, Saudi-financed grand mosque on the outskirts of Madrid. Tatary accused Escudero of increasing Moroccan and Saudi influence over Spanish Islam, while Escudero claimed that Tatary put personal ambition before the common good and was too orthodox for Spain. Jordi Moreras and Joan Lacomba question the division between "moderates" and "traditionalists", arguing instead that national origin and personal affinities, rather than theological background, better explain why organizations aligned with one or other federation.[38]

The influence of both groups varied over time. Of the twenty regional Islamic groups in Spain in 1991, most were affiliated with FEERI, but UCIDE soon caught up, enlisting more than half of the groups by the time the overall number rose to thirty-seven. After the Agreement of Cooperation, official Muslim groups increased steadily: fifty-one in 1994; seventy in 1996; 176 in 2001; and 616 in 2011. In twenty years, the number had multiplied by a factor of thirty, and of these, most went to UCIDE rather than FEERI.[39]

The Tatary-Escudero row had dire consequences for the community. As UCIDE and FEERI scrambled for endorsements from regional groups and refused to work together, Madrid used the feuding to postpone implementation of the Agreement of Cooperation.

"Worthless piece of paper"

The 1992 Agreement of Cooperation was a milestone. It recognized and accepted Islam in modern Spain for the first time and it would guide public practice of Islam in the country for years. The Agreement's preamble acknowledged that Islam played an "important role in the formation of Spanish identity" and reiterated that Islam was "deeply rooted" in the country. It granted imams special privileges – for example, exemption from then mandatory military service – and conferred legal protections on Islamic religious institutions and cemeteries as sacred spaces. It also recognized Islamic marriage as equal to Catholic and civil marriage. In the military, in prisons, in hospitals, in schools, and in other public institutions, the government agreed to accommodate Muslim religious practices and offered tax relief to groups registered with the Ministry of Justice. Finally, the agreement recognized religious festivals, the need for halal food production, and the need to preserve Spain's Islamic artistic and historic heritage.[40] The CIE was put in charge of monitoring religious practices, training and appointing imams, and overlooking Islamic education in the national, public education system.

On paper, the Agreement was generous – indeed it was one of Europe's most progressive. Yet it certainly paled in comparison to the privileges accorded to the Catholic Church. Indeed, it sharpened and institutionalized the division between Catholics and the various minority religions of Spain. Among points excluded from the Agreement was a provision for state funding of recognized Muslim institutions. Escudero blamed Tatary for the oversight, which in his view forced Spanish Muslims to rely on capital from abroad. As a resident of Madrid and a member of the Ministry of Justice's Advisory Commission on Religious Freedom, Tatary had more direct access to government but did not view foreign financing as an issue, as long as it came from a variety of sources rather than just one. Nonetheless, Escudero had a point: while in the short term the government avoided conflict and saved money, in the long term it fostered foreign involvement in Spain. Foreign involvement was indeed a reality. To cite one example from Escudero, Saudi funding of the grand mosque on the outskirts of Madrid essentially gave the Saudi ambassador direct foreign control over the facility – in effect, a veto on who could use the premises, one that favoured hard-line adherents to the faith.[41]

The Agreement of Cooperation between Catholics and the government included the provision of "adequate funding". Accordingly, the government helped finance the Church directly by allowing taxpayers to allocate a portion of income tax revenue directly to the Church, provided upkeep for its heritage sites, funded the salaries of public professors of religion, and subsidized religious schools; the Church was also offered exemptions from paying some taxes, such as property tax. Other religions could access a portion of this money but the imbalance was egregious. In 2005, the Catholic Church received 141 million euros in tax revenue, compared to 3 million euros for Jewish, Muslim, and Protestant groups combined. Moreover, while the government covered the salaries of 15,000 Catholic teachers, only 100 Protestant and 36 Islamic teachers were subsidized publicly. School funding reflected a similar imbalance: 1,860 Catholic schools versus four Protestant and two Jewish received public funding.[42]

Escudero called on Madrid to fund Islam to the same extent that it funded Catholicism. He also wanted citizens to have the option to contribute income tax to religious minority institutions in the same way that they could contribute to the Catholic Church. The Socialist government denied his requests, arguing that the income tax option was "a transitory measure that was a hangover from the Spanish state's former support of Catholicism and [as such] would soon disappear". Escudero was not opposed to the government funding of Catholicism; he merely wanted the same privileges for Muslims.[43]

FEERI was more critical than UCIDE of the Agreement of Cooperation. In a speech to the Mediterranean Intergroup of the Committee of the Regions of the European Parliament in July 1997, Escudero accused government measures of being unconstitutional. "In the Agreement of Cooperation, the Islamic faith is not permitted to express its institutional characteristics and particularities; the three non-Catholic agreements are almost the same, homogenous", he said. "The agreement only stresses subjects that come up in the Agreement of Cooperation for Catholics, such as marriage rites, places of worship, religious aid, education, and financing, without considering important aspects such as the media, culture, or public funding". In other words, the government had applied some of the provisions for the Catholic Church to Islam and other minority religions, without allowing for specificities or unique challenges.[44]

After five years of the Agreement, Spanish Muslims were disillusioned with the government's lack of will to implement it. They said the agreement was a "*papel mojado*", a worthless piece of paper. Escudero pointed to Ceuta and Melilla as examples of how government inaction endangered Muslim rights. At the time, Muslim children in Melilla were required to take a mandatory class in Catholicism, yet the Islamic Commission of Melilla was forbidden from offering similar instruction in Islam. School cafeterias, hospitals, prisons, and military barracks, meanwhile, failed to offer any halal options. Students were also forbidden from leaving school early to attend Friday prayers.[45]

Though these rights were enshrined in the Agreement of Cooperation, local governments and public authorities were reluctant to implement them, and Madrid was unenthusiastic about forcing the issue. The Muslim vote was still scant and a strong pro-Muslim stance could alienate the large, well-organized contingent of Catholics. This was particularly relevant between 1996 and 2004, when the PP was in government. "For many years the Conservatives failed to apply the agreement", claimed Ndeye Andújar, a convert. The PP government was more likely to support UCIDE because most converts and FEERI were closer to the PSOE, but it was even likelier to do nothing at all to guarantee the practice of Islam in Spain. Andújar claimed that the government "blockaded us [FEERI] and alleged that we [FEERI and UCIDE] did not get along during negotiations, that for example, both federations proposed separate curricula for a course in Islamic Religious Teaching. That is true, but the government has expressed little political will to apply the agreement also".[46] Supporters of the Islamic Council said that the PP favoured UCIDE because it was more complacent than FEERI. The Ministry of Justice, for instance, registered new Muslim groups with UCIDE, they claimed, without informing them that FEERI provided an alternative.[47] FEERI accused the PP of dividing Muslims to circumvent their legitimate demands. FEERI also problematically claimed to be more Spanish, democratic, and reasonable than UCIDE. Abdelm'min Aya, editor of *Verde Islam*, cautioned that

> The state's lack of interest in promoting a reasonable Islam like ours [converts'], will become clear when the state has to face Muslims who speak broken or no Spanish, have a radically different way of thinking, and are unwilling to deal with the government . . . The government needs us, so that Islam in the future does not get out of hand in this country.[48]

Jadicha Candela, another convert and member of the PSOE, expressed a similar foreboding:

> In the end the government preferred Muslims who did not ask for money, subsidies, or Islamic teachers in public schools, but rather turned to Saudi Arabia for mosques . . . Later, perhaps too late, the government will realize that in those mosques that were erected for free, a much more radical Islam will have arisen.[49]

The government of Spain, said Escudero, "needs to understand that Islam is part of Spanish culture. Either the government backs a home-grown reformist Muslim agenda or leaves it to foreign powers".[50]

The PP countered by saying that Islam in Spain had been divided long before the government became involved and that those divisions made it impossible for the government to implement the Agreement of Cooperation in a satisfactory manner.[51] By 2000, the rift between Tatary and Escudero had widened irredeemably; henceforth, the two leaders refused to speak to each other, and the government refused to discuss public funding with the CIE because of the split.

While blame for the bad blood among Muslim federations cannot be placed on the government, Muslim immigrants across the board expressed contempt for the government's general mismanagement of Islamic affairs. The government's "management has been chaotic and catastrophic", said Mohammed Chaib, founder of the immigrant association Ibn Battuta and Socialist member of the Catalan parliament from 2003 until 2011. "None of the points fleshed out in 1992 when the Islamic Commission of Spain was created have been fulfilled. Not religious teaching in schools, not freedom of religion – not one".[52] The Agreement of Cooperation itself, signed by a Socialist government, claimed Chaib, "is an attractive agreement that represents a brave step forward for the Muslim community in Spain". Yet later on, with the PP in power, Chaib would claim "there has been a lot of fighting between Muslims who want to build mosques and natives who don't want them built. The government has not defended freedom of religion in these conflicts".[53]

The government was not the only group to drag its feet in implementing the Agreement; UCIDE, FEERI, and the CIE, too, discouraged active involvement from emerging local Muslim groups. "The Islamic Commission has not been receptive to petitions from all groups of the Muslim community and has overlooked current realities", Chaib argued.[54] Chaib was referring to the fact that the Muslim community that signed the agreement in 1992 was markedly different from the much larger and more diverse Muslim community of the mid-2000s. Some of the Muslim communities that had been excluded were composed of newcomers from Morocco, Pakistan, or Sub-Saharan Africa, or had a regional power base. One such organization was the Islamic and Cultural Council of Catalonia, which Chaib founded in 2000. The council was founded as an interlocutor with the Catalan regional government and an attempt to break the heavy top-down management of the two federations and the CIE. The purpose of the group, explained Chaib, was to address "the chaotic situation in which the state managed Islam and the Islamic Commission's refusal to incorporate new immigrants from different Muslim countries".[55] Others, however, saw the group as less impartial. One Syrian-born imam claimed that Chaib's council focussed on the needs of Moroccan Muslims alone.[56]

As the number and variety of Muslim immigrants increased, so too did their influence on Muslim federations in the country. For example, in 2006, a group of orthodox Sunnis pushed the bulk of native Spanish converts out of the FEERI executive. Escudero resigned from the CIE and a heated debate on the role of native converts, who in the main belonged to no one federation, ensued. The media claimed that divisions were not "between fundamentalists and moderates, but [rather] between foreigners and Spaniards".[57] Yet in reality, things were more complicated. For instance, though the new president of FEERI was a native Spaniard, he was quite orthodox; by contrast, Moroccan-born Chaib was a moderate.

Converts' loss of power and influence was not just a question of numbers. To be sure, converts were outnumbered by immigrants, but they became marginal to the two national federations because immigrants resented the self-appointed role converts had been playing in negotiating with public authorities in the name of all Muslims. Many immigrants also disagreed with converts' claim that their progressive and unorthodox interpretation of Islam was the truly "Spanish" one, rooted in Al-Andalus and thus ideally suited to Spain's democratic rights and freedoms. The last stroke that divided converts and immigrant Muslims in Spain occurred in 2005, a year after the Madrid train bombing that killed 191 people, when Escudero, then leader of FEERI, proclaimed the first *fatwa* against Al Qaeda and terrorism in the name of Islam. Escudero's *fatwa* was perceived as a top-down proclamation from an increasingly unrepresentative and egocentric leader. It deepened the gap between progressive and traditionalist, converted and immigrant Muslims in Spain, and helped pushed converts out of FEERI.[58]

In order to preserve their influence, converts had been looking for a separate power base in the broader Spanish-speaking community, as well as the virtual world. Converts tried to find allies in Latin America, where Islam was eclectic and its adherents were native Spanish speakers. The international symposium "Islam across Continents" organized by converts not only aimed to create a network of Spanish-speaking Muslims, but also was an attempt at supporting converts in their fight over conflicting interpretations of Islam in Spain:

> We believe that the dynamic and self-reflexive character of Latin American Muslims proves wrong those that associate religion with immobility, cultural decline, and limits to fundamental rights ... We hope to show that the diffusion of Islam in the Spanish language can be done through dialogue, reflection, and a critical spirit. The reality of Latin American Muslims is refreshing.[59]

Thanks to their early online presence, Spanish converts found new allies and a new lease on life. A FEERI report claimed that in September 1998, the WebIslam site received 100,000 visitors and 7,000 emails after only eight months of operation. "FEERI generates 98 percent of information about Islam in Spanish", stated the report.[60] According to Escudero, the WebIslam portal, "plugged [converts] into the rapid growth of Islam in Spanish".[61]

Conflicts over Women's Rights

Foreign funding of mosques, access to government, and interpretations of scripture were some of the tensions that divided practicing Muslims in Spain. Another source of conflict was the role of women. Tensions were sparked, for example, by the publication of the controversial book *La mujer en el islam* ("Women in Islam"), by the Islamic scholar Mohamed Kamal Mustafa. Kamal Mustafa was imam of the mosque of Fuengirola, a seaside resort in southern Spain, director of an Islamic centre, and advisor on religious matters to FEERI. He was also Egyptian, had a poor command of Spanish, hardly any contact with non-Muslims, and little knowledge of Spain's value system. The controversy over *La mujer en el Islam* exemplifies the agency and active citizenship of Muslim women, the contribution of converts in driving conversations within the Muslim community on the rights of women, and the dangers of gendered Islamophobia.

Kamal Mustafa's book, printed in an edition of 1,668 copies, provided an analysis of Quranic verses, including verses from Sura 4:34, *An-Nisa* (The Women): "If you fear high-handedness from your wives, remind them [of the teaching of God], then ignore them when you go to bed, then hit them".[62] Kamal Mustafa, who claimed that he was "one of two men authorized to interpret the Qur'an in Spain", an assessment with which Spanish converts roundly disagreed, believed that the Qur'an permitted physical punishment of women who misbehaved, provided that the male had tried verbal admonishments, had abstained from sex with his spouse for a period, had undertaken beatings within strict guidelines, and did not mark the body. For example, "Only specific parts of the body, such as the feet and hands, may be struck", argued Kamal Mustafa. "Only a thin, light stick may be used, so the body is not scarred or bruised".[63]

In Egypt, as Eva Evers Rosander explains, "where the verses of the Koran are deeply respected and the gender ideology is related to and marked by a patriarchal and hierarchical interpretation of the Koran, Kamal Mustafa's explanations about wife beating would have had a different and more subtle resonance".[64] In Spain, however, Kamal Mustafa's book sparked heated debate within the Muslim community, forcing the author to claim publically that he was not "in favour of corporal punishment for women" and that "the regulation is there only as a preventative measure". He said Sura 4:34 needed to be put into historical context, but to condemn it was to condemn "all of the Qur'an". He continued: "Men and women enjoy the same rights and are subject to the same obligations under Islam, though the relationship between the two is not one of equality, nor superiority or inferiority, rather complementarity".[65]

The first people to criticize Kamal Mustafa were native female converts, who belonged to the Muslim feminist groups An-Nisa, led by lawyer Jadicha Candela, and Inshallah, led by writer Yaratullah Monturiol.[66] They called for bookstores across Spain to remove the book from their shelves because it sanctioned violence against women as a religious prerogative. Marian Cabezos, a FEERI representative in Catalonia, called Kamal Mustafa's views "intolerable". The three prominent women – Candela, Monturiol, and Cabezos – wrote an open letter to Kamal Mustafa and his publisher. "Our Prophet has protected us for fourteen centuries from the beatings that husbands have dealt to women systematically", they wrote. "The community's worst man is he who abuses his wife". Kamal Mustafa countered by saying that women were not permitted to interpret the Qur'an. The women's criticisms were thus "injurious, premeditated defamation that did not contribute anything new, only attacked".[67] FEERI's male leadership welcomed the attention and controversy because it shifted focus back onto the debate over "Spanish Islam", as distinct from foreign interpretations. Muslim feminists agreed that the trouble was not just Kamal Mustafa, but a fundamentalist, "misogynist interpretation of Islam" among the Muslim community in Spain.[68]

Following the lead of convert Muslim women associations, ninety women's groups, among them the Federation of Divorced and Separated Women, the Association of Assistance to Sexually Abused Women of Catalonia, and the Council of Women of Madrid brought civil action against Kamal for inciting gender violence. The Spanish branch of the powerful European Lobby of Women, representing an additional thirty groups, petitioned the Attorney General to charge Kamal Mustafa.[69]

Legally, the courts could do little because incitement of violence towards women was not a crime under Spanish law. Socially, however, women's groups and politicians applauded the feminist effort. Feminists called on a congressional committee on women's equality to push for legislation to curb domestic and sexual violence, as well as to empower the courts to prosecute incitement of violence towards women.[70]

Under hate laws, which were applied for the first time to gender violence, Kamal Mustafa was tried for inciting hatred and abuse of women and sentenced to a year and three months in prison. The judge also ordered the book to be removed from libraries and bookstores and destroyed. *La mujer en el islam* used "an obsolete tone of male chauvinism", explained the judge. "It does open harm to the constitution's principle of equality and encourages intolerable and criminally reproachable discriminatory behaviour for reasons of sex".

Kamal Mustafa spent a short period in prison before being freed on probation. During his probationary period, he participated in mandatory lessons on the Spanish constitution, and eventually he retracted his views on gender violence publically.[71] Kamal Mustafa's conviction "shows that male chauvinists who attempt to import, into our [Spain's] legal system, foreign systems that claim women are subordinate and inferior, will have to justify the arrogant views that they utter in the name of religious freedom", said Candela. If Islam was to exist and thrive in Spain, it would have to be practiced according to the constitution, which first and foremost would require upholding the rights of women.[72]

Kamal Mustafa's conviction was not solely the result of protests by Muslim converts, however. His book was launched at a time when, after decades of campaigning against domestic and sexual violence against women, feminist concerns had become mainstream and were forcing public authorities to act. In parliament, the scandal led to the unanimous approval of the 2004 Law on Protection against Gender Violence, and eventually to the 2007 Law on Equality between Men and Women. After 2006, the government launched annual nationwide campaigns to sensitize Spaniards to the issue of domestic violence.[73]

The Kamal Mustafa affair played a crucial role in granting Muslim women organizations led by converts an independent voice within the Muslim community, a national platform for their concerns, and strong allies within the larger feminist movement. But this came at a price. Even though convert Abdennur Prado considered the trial of Kamal Mustafa "a landmark in the process of the return of Islam to Al Andalus", the gap between Muslim organizations led by unorthodox converts and those led by immigrants widened, eventually limiting the influence and reach of converts' interpretations and vision of Spanish Islam.[74] It was just the beginning of more disagreements. Indeed, the only other moment to rival the inner tension of this period and to single out the most fundamentalist of the Muslim community was the Madrid commuter train attack of March 2004.

While the outspokenness of Muslim women in criticizing Kamal Mustafa conveyed the impression that gender relations and women's rights were as contested within the Muslim community as they had been (until very recently) in Spanish society at large, it also paradoxically reinforced Islamophobia. According to the 1997 Runnymede Trust Report "Islamophobia: A Challenge for Us All", one of the first attempts at understanding anti-Muslim discourse and behaviour in Europe, one type of Islamophobic discourse concerns the belief that "Muslim cultures mistreat women, but that other religions and cultures have outgrown patriarchy and sexism". Another characteristic of this discourse is the treatment of Islam as a "single monolithic bloc, static and unresponsive to new realities".[75] Despite converts' efforts to the contrary, the Kamal Mustafa affair promoted a media image that portrayed the most traditional and discriminatory consideration of women as a universal, essential, and unchangeable quality of Islam.[76]

Islamophobia also played a part in how fast and expeditiously public authorities and courts had acted in the Kamal Mustafa case. In normal circumstances, a sentence of less than two years in prison does not entail actual prison time if the individual has no police record, as was the case for Kamal Mustafa. Social and media pressure, however, meant that Kamal Mustafa would spend three weeks in prison before being forced to take lessons in constitutional rights, a penalty without precedent. The judge justified this prison time by saying that Kamal Mustafa constituted a "social danger" to society, with the Socialist deputy prime minister, María Teresa Fernández de la Vega, going so far as to say that Kamal Mustafa's release from jail was "absolutely stupid".[77]

The Kamal Mustafa controversy would not have played out as it did if Muslim women groups had not been organizing for years. Muslim women met at a national level for the first time in Barcelona in 1999. The agenda for the Barcelona conference included discussions on health, education, halal food, and the hijab. Participants, both converts and immigrants, debated the role of women in the community. They asked "to be heard" and encouraged Muslim women "to participate actively in mosques and other Islamic organizations".[78] The second conference, attended by hundreds of women representing every autonomous community of Spain and titled "Muslim Women in the 21st Century: For our Youth, the Light of the Future", was held a year later in Valencia. Muslim women were concerned about specific gender issues, such as wearing the hijab, but mostly they wanted to discuss their role as mothers and providers of religious education for their children. In so doing, they were claiming agency and autonomy, but within the constraints of accepted female roles as nurturers of family values and gatekeepers of tradition.

The experience of writers Laila Karrouch and Najat el Hachmi, who grew up in the Catalan town of Vic, exemplifies some of the concerns Muslim women had about their daughters growing up in Spain. Young Muslim students were often slighted, for example, for wearing hijabs or decorating their hands with henna on special religious occasions. As a child in Morocco, El Hachmi could not wait to beautify her hands. "I would run to wash the paste of the henna off, eager to find out how they now looked. I would admire them for a long time. The intensity of colour and the shades between folds of skin would fascinate me". Later, in Vic, she lost interest: "I stopped using henna during celebrations and waited for a long time before I asked my mother to put it on me again".[79] She described one particularly decisive encounter with an ethnic Catalan woman in the following terms:

> "What's on your hands?" the woman asked. She looked at me half surprised, half disgusted. "Go clean your hands, dear, they're filthy". I had hoped someone was going to congratulate me for the extra sharp lines my mother had drawn, to marvel, as my grandmother did, at the colour that she had achieved. But no, the excitement that henna had caused in me had become an odd sensation of ridicule, a shame I hadn't experienced before. Somewhere inside me, another delicate thread snapped.[80]

El Hachmi continued:

> From that moment on, I realized that there were two Najats in the world: one Moroccan, who followed annihilated customs, played at being bride with the handkerchiefs of her mother, dreamt of women belly dancing at parties – the woman of doors to the inside . . . the other Catalan, who was shown the doors to the outside. Neither of the two personalities spoke to each other. The pact of silence protected me from the feeling of shame I felt from comments like, "you shouldn't put that henna crap all over you, you are one of us now".[81]

Henna was not the only problem. Mannerisms and mores also changed. "The art of eating with your fingers without dirtying them, which my grand-mother had taught me with great patience . . . in one afternoon had become ridiculous", said El Hachmi.[82] She quickly self-censored all traces of her Maghrebian culture in public:

> I can't begin to describe all the things I left behind. Everything I thought was grotesque in the eyes of Catalans I reserved for my intimacy. I hid them like one might hide certain crimes. My clothes, once florid and happy, grew dark. I scrubbed my skin ferociously in an effort to whiten it, to go unnoticed. I was ashamed of the music my parents played. There was too much tambourine and the voice of singers was too sensuous. I feared, wrongly, that our neigh-

bours would criticize us for any North African feature that they could decipher in us.[83]

Chaib explained that immigrant youth often changed their names rather than insist on their original forms. Mustafa would become "Musti", and, more revealingly, Mohamed (Spanish for Muhammad) would become "Moha". "There were certain [native] individuals . . . who got a rise out of making fun of names: 'And you, why are you called Yasin and not Jacinto, which is easier to pronounce? Look how you like to complicate life for us'", reported Chaib. In order to protect his children, Chaib "told them to be proud of their names, that their identity and culture were no less Catalan than anyone else's".[84]

Muslim women, however, also attempted to gain a voice within the community that went beyond their gender and family concerns. The third conference, which focussed on the role of women in developing Spanish Islam in medieval and modern times, appropriately took place in Córdoba. After that Muslim women focussed on regional rather than national initiatives because they were easier to organize and attend.[85] Eventually, this activism paid off. In 2008, Amparo Sánchez Rosell, a convert, became the first woman elected to the prominent, mixed-gender Islamic Cultural Centre of Valencia.[86]

Some Muslims were eager to promote a more ambitious national and international agenda. In Catalonia in 2005, converts organized the first international conference on Islamic feminism that attracted men and women from Pakistan, Nigeria, Iran, Mali, and the United States. The organizer of the conference, the Islamic Council of Catalonia, aimed to "bring into focus Islamic feminism as an emerging reality all over the world".[87] The council argued that Islam

> is perfectly compatible with democracy, human rights, ecological welfare, and women's equality. We defend the right of Muslims to be governed by Islamic laws and denounce laws that are sexist and discriminate against women and sexual, racial, and religious minorities as deviations from the genuine Islam contained in the Holy Qur'an and typified by the Sunnah of Mohammad . . . We propose that Sharia law be reformed, democratized, and adapted to the new needs of Muslims in the 21st century.[88]

Zanan, a magazine founded by the Iranian journalist Shahla Sherkat in 1992 and closed down by the Iranian government in 2008, was one of the world's first Islamic feminist publications.[89] The magazine contended that gender inequality was not the result of Islam but misogynist interpretations of the Qur'an. It argued that women could interpret Islamic scripture and jurisprudence on their own, that mixed-gender prayers were possible under the Qur'an, and that women, as well as men, could lead prayers.[90] Indeed, *Zanan* argued, Islam was the only monotheistic religion to enshrine gender equality, at least in its founding texts. If relations between Muslim men and women were now unequal in Iran, it was due to the social and political order, not the divine order.[91]

According to Kent Blore, Islamic feminism "arose under the umbrella of postmodernism to counter Enlightenment universalisation of Western experience and ethnocentric condescension as epitomised by Western feminists". It sought to refute Western feminism's claim of universal application to the experience of Muslim women and "the orientalization of the experiences of Muslim women as a reassurance of Western moral superiority".[92] Yet Islamic feminism as practiced by converts to Islam in Spain has been less confrontational vis-à-vis Western feminism and more interested in building alliances within the feminist movement at large. It also faced different challenges than those Islamic feminists that operate under a theocratic regime in Muslim-majority countries. In Spain, even though women converts have argued that gender discrimination has no place in Islam, they have defended gender equality, not because of its sacred character, but rather because it is enshrined in the secular constitution. Imams like Kamal Mustafa could try to use a literal or traditional interpretation of the Qur'an all they wished; in the end, it was secular law, not scriptural interpretation, that reigned supreme.[93]

The Kamal Mustafa controversy was not the only conflict that targeted Muslim women specifically. While in other European countries such as France, the "headscarf affair" had begun in 1989, in Spain controversies over veiling only began to gather public attention after 2002.[94] On three occasions – in 2002, 2007, and 2010 – school authorities expelled Muslim students for refusing to remove their *hijabs*, which, they claimed, contravened rules calling for the removal of hats, motorcycle helmets, and general headgear indoors. The Spanish media contradictorily portrayed these young women as insubordinate to school regulations and submissive to the wills of their fathers.[95]

Veiling is a form of non-verbal communication whose meaning is far from clear. While many Europeans and North Americans associate the veil with submission and gender discrimination, many Muslim women see it as a religious duty, a choice, and not an indicator of adherence to literal or fundamentalist Islam. Moreover, Muslim women have argued that the veil shields them from unwanted attention from men and subverts Western-centric definitions of femininity. As Islamophobia has increased across Europe, so too has the adoption of the veil as a symbol of cultural pride and political resistance.[96] Regardless of intentions, wearing the veil is not easy or socially accepted in Spain. Participants in the first National Conference for Muslim Women discussed the overpowering social pressure exerted on women to remove their veils and conform to secular norms. In their memoirs of growing up in Spain, El Hachmi and Karrouch also emphasized the pressures their mothers faced to remove their veils in Spain after wearing them for decades in Morocco.[97]

The debate over veiling in Spain initially departed from other European countries, first because the education system in Spain does not endorse a strict secular public sphere. Catholicism is still taught in public schools at taxpayers' expense – though attendance is no longer mandatory – and privately-owned Catholic schools still receive public funding. Since schools have flexibility to determine their own regulations and guidelines, some forbid all head coverings, religious or secular, while others allow them. The rejection of veiled students in the classroom is not framed as a defense of secularism, as in France, but rather as a defiance of school regulations. In such instances, the Ministry of Education has prioritized the right of pupils to an education and has either forced schools to back down or transferred students to other institutions.[98] Often overlooked in the debate over school regulations is the violation of students' religious freedom. For example, the 1992 Agreement of Cooperation, negotiated without the contribution of any Muslim women, guarantees elective Islamic education but is silent on the matter of veiling in schools.

Secondly, the rights of Catholics have also benefited veiled Muslim women. In 1998, lawyer Iván Jiménez-Aybar successfully defended the right of Muslim women to be photographed for the National Identity Document in hijab. Jiménez-Aybar argued that Muslim women were entitled to the same privileges as nuns, who could be photographed in veil. Following his success in that case, Jiménez-Aybar is currently defending women's right to wear the hijab in Spanish schools.[99]

Thirdly, most Muslim feminists in Spain do not wear the veil, and the discussion has had less play than elsewhere in Europe as a result. Instead, Muslim agency in Spain has had more to do with women's ability to thwart the domination of male family members and to adapt Islam to a secular European context. Accordingly, Muslim women in Spain emphasize, not whether or not they should wear the veil, but rather their ability to choose. Sánchez Rosell, the president of the Islamic Cultural Centre of Valencia wears the hijab and traditional Moroccan *djellaba*; Mariam Isabel Romero Arias, general director of the Halal Institute, does not. Both are respected, prominent women in the community.

Lastly, even though immigration has become a politicized issue in Spain since 2000, the lack of powerful xenophobic and Islamophobic parties has enabled mainstream Spanish parties, unlike in some European countries, to keep headscarves off of the political agenda for quite some time. This did not change until 2010, when Spain joined the European wave of "hijabophobia" that resulted in the banning of full veiling in public places in France, Belgium, and Italy, with partial restrictions enacted in Germany and Denmark. As Ángeles Ramírez argues, the emergence of the Islamophobic party Platform for Catalonia (PxC) in the 2010 Catalan regional elections transformed the political discourse and started a race to ban full veiling in the region.[100] In Catalonia, several large cities, including Barcelona and Lleida, passed regulations to restrict full veiling in public places. The Catalan media portrayed veiled women as dupes of Salafist Islam, a Moroccan import that, if not pre-empted, would root itself in the land as it had in the Netherlands, Belgium, and the United Kingdom.

Municipal bans did not, however, withstand judicial scrutiny. When the Superior Court of Justice nullified them with the argument that a limitation of religious freedom could not be undertaken by local governments, the Catalan regional government announced it would pursue a ban in the regional parliament.[101]

While most Spanish Muslims opposed full veiling – which was, at any rate, rare in Spain – they viewed measures to restrict the practice as an attack on women's freedom of choice. The debate, they argued, was framed too narrowly and aggressively by both governments and the media. Many believed that new xenophobic parties, like the PxC, which had sixty-seven candidates elected in twenty towns in 2011, as well as mainstream parties who courted populist votes, motivated this debate, not real concern for the rights of women. "The debate empowers the populists and xenophobes; it produces rancour in society", claimed the secretary of the Union of Islamic Centres of Catalonia.[102]

Gendered Islamophobia, wrote Jasmine Zine, "operates socially, politically, and discursively to deny material advantages to Muslim women".[103] Indeed, while Muslims of all stripes have had to contend with deep prejudices in Spain, veiled Muslims have withstood the worst of anti-Islamic prejudice in the workplace, on the streets, in schools, and now with bans on veiling in many cities, in public venues, too.

The Public Practice of Islam in Spain

In France, *neutralité de la rue* ensures that religious expression does not occur in public spaces.[104] In Spain, where generations of Catholic practice has been intertwined into the fabric of secular society, this relationship is necessarily fuzzier. The argument that religious dress violates the principle of church-state separation and thus should be outlawed is not as frequently used in Spain, where Catholic rituals spill over into secular public realms. A tally of church-state overlap in Spain would place Catholicism well ahead of any other religion. Over half of national statutory holidays, including Epiphany, Maundy Thursday, Good Friday, the Assumption of Mary, All Saints' Day, the Immaculate Conception, and Christmas, are Catholic. For the autonomous communities, the proportion is even higher. In addition to national religious holidays, the government of Valencia recognizes Easter Monday, St. Vincent Ferrer's Day, St. John's Day, and St. Stephen's Day; to this list, the cities of Valencia and Barcelona add St. Vincent's Day and Our Lady of Mercy, respectively. Indeed, it is difficult to celebrate anything that does not ring of Catholicism in Spain, and if not Catholicism, then nationalism. Only in Ceuta and Melilla is a non-Catholic religious holiday recognized: the local governments there introduced Eid al-Adha, the Festival of Sacrifice, as a statutory holiday in 2010.

Both public financial support of Catholic activities and governmental representation at Catholic ceremonies go unchecked. In 1981, Córdoba's

Communist mayor reminded local Catholic officials that his post obliged him to acknowledge all the religions of residents, not just Catholicism. When the Bishop of Córdoba complained that the city had offered Muslims public facilities to create an Islamic museum and library, the mayor pointed to the exorbitant "cost to the city of processions during Holy Week, public worship of Corpus Christi, and other festivities, not to mention municipal chaplaincies at cemeteries". The mayor expressed frustration that many of his councillors were expected to chaperone Catholic dignitaries at public rituals, "which the mayor would never dream of attending for obvious reasons of respect and [ideological] integrity". Of course, ignoring Catholicism carries political consequences. In 2010, Prime Minister José Luis Rodríguez Zapatero was criticized for not attending the christening of the Sagrada Familia church in Barcelona during Pope Benedict XVI's visit to Spain.[105]

As "a discursive or agoric space in principle open to all citizens and all issues", the public realm does not belong to either the secular or the religious camp. Moreover, Casanova reminds us that "there is not a single public space; there are many competing and interrelated publics and a multiplicity of public spaces".[106] Muslims are carving out private spaces in centres of worship and even on the Internet, but mainstream Spanish society has hindered the practice of Islam in the public realm. According to Tariq Modood and Riva Kastoryano, this is a general trend across Europe:

> Those citizens whose moral, ethnic or religious communal identities are most adequately reflected in the political identity of the regime, those citizens whose private identity fits most comfortably with this political identity, will feel least the force of a rigidly enforced public/private distinction. They may only become aware of its coercive influence when they have to share the public domain with persons from other communities, persons who may also wish the identity of the political community to reflect something of their own community too.[107]

While Spanish society views Muslim calls for equal access to public space as irregular and provocative, it sees Catholic encroachment as somehow acceptable, customary, even banal. Muslim demands for the same access to public space as Catholics challenge the status quo and Spain's self-perception as secular; they also enforce religious pluralism where it is not wanted. Examples are plentiful. Perhaps one of the most striking is the Pakistani immigrants' celebration in Barcelona of the Day of Ashura, when Hussein ibn Ali, the grandson of Prophet Mohammad, was martyred at the Battle of Karbala in 680 CE. The Shia association Al Qaim thanked the city for permitting it to celebrate the day publicly. Yet many residents complained. "I don't understand a thing", claimed one resident. "Why do they have to block off roads for three whole hours for this procession?"[108]

Muslims organized as a group for the first time in the 1970s, their religion gained the status of "deeply rooted" in the 1990s, and they pushed to implement the Agreement of Cooperation and achieved a degree of success in the 2000s. In most areas – in education, in religious holiday recognition, in religious practices and customs, and in mosque construction – matters improved slowly, though ultimately not as much as most Muslims would like.

Education provides perhaps the best example of the difficulties Muslims have encountered in exercising the rights granted to them in the Agreement of Cooperation. In the post-Franco period, Madrid made Catholicism optional in public schools and a growing number of students chose not to study it. The Agreement of Cooperation extended the right to Islamic education in public schools to Muslims. In 1993, the CIE developed an appropriate Islamic curriculum for the public system, and in 1996 it signed an accord with the PSOE government to pay for the salaries of trained Islamic teachers. The move was controversial. School authorities and civil servants in the regional ministries of education were reluctant to hire teachers of Islam, while the national government did not enforce the move, effectively hindering the introduction of Islamic education in public schools. Escudero complained that schools failed to inform parents and students that they had a right to study Islam. He also claimed that the Office of Religious Affairs had contacted him and had expressed fear that Islamic instruction would lead to fundamentalism. The office said nothing about the radicalizing potential of Catholic instruction.[109] When the national government shifted from PSOE to PP, things did not improve. The PP government, however, explained that the accord, "except in Ceuta and Melilla, was not fulfilled because the two [Muslim] federations could not agree on the kind of [Islamic] teachers that they envisioned".[110]

In 2004, the PSOE, back in government, made the funding of Islamic education in public schools mandatory whenever ten or more students requested it. Islamic religious classes could be taken as electives and could replace classes in culture and society that dealt with religion. However, since education is a shared jurisdiction, the national law had to be adver-tised and implemented by regional governments, many of which enforced it reluctantly and unequally – particularly as it required most regions to pay the salaries of religious teachers. In some regions, educational author-ities attempted to manoeuvre around the state's laws on religious education, do away altogether with Islamic and Catholic instruction, and offer instead a joint secular course in the history of religion. Only in Ceuta, Melilla, and Andalusia, where the national Ministry of Education pays salaries directly, were teachers of Islam hired according to the law. By 2005, only thirty-six teachers of Islam were active in the public system across Spain.[111]

Arabic language instruction has not been as contentious as Islamic teaching, and the province of Madrid incorporated it as early as 1995. "Almost ten percent of students at my school are the children of immigrants, and half of those are Moroccans, so I stress the need to integrate ethnic minorities", claimed one school principal.[112] The principal was justifying

Arab language classes at her school and reaching out to minority students and their parents, whose culture she valued. She could have made a similar argument for religious instruction.

Though UCIDE and FEERI pushed hard for Islamic education, other Muslims felt it was an "unreasonable demand". "We as a society have more important questions to resolve than Islamic teaching in schools", said Chaib. If Islamic education was necessary at all, "it was of a second order" – priority had to be given to immigrant status and rights.[113] Indeed, Chaib questioned efforts to introduce religious education altogether:

> It's important to remember that schools are not the place to teach religion, any religion. The big problem I see for our society is that we can't tell Muslims that natives have the right to learn Catholicism at school while Muslims don't have the right to learn Islam. This constitutes visible discrimination.[114]

Chaib continued: "Religion is for the private sphere, in churches and mosques, but not schools, not as doctrine, only as a course in the history and culture of world religions". While most religious leaders disagreed with Chaib, many cultural Muslims and second-generation immigrants raised in secular surroundings supported his views.[115]

Included in the Agreement of Cooperation was the right to stop work early on Fridays for prayer, as well as during Ramadan, and to replace statutory holidays with major Islamic ones, provided employers could, in good faith, reschedule working hours. Yet if employers said that they could not accommodate the needs of Muslims, employees had no recourse. Increasing religious diversity in the workplace fell more in the hands of trade unions and secular immigrant groups than religious organizations.

This was the case in Almería, for example, where the Association of Moroccan Immigrant Workers in Spain (ATIME) worked with unions to ensure that the 12,000–15,000 migrant greenhouse workers were accommodated in their religious practices. In conjunction with the Workers' Commissions, ATIME fought to reduce hours during Ramadan. ATIME's aim, said the organization, was *convivencia*. "Some farmers understand Ramadan, but we want it written into our labour contract, and the Workers' Commissions intends to include this demand in the next round of collective bargaining", said the organization's vice-president.[116]

While the legal side of religious accommodation presented challenges, the larger battle was with mainstream social attitudes. "My [track] coach didn't like that I practiced Ramadan", explained Laila Karrouch. "She said that Ramadan would make me sick and that she didn't understand [why I wanted to practice it]. My classmates didn't understand either. Everyone asked me questions and I felt that, with the thousands of explanations I gave, I only confused people more".[117] Despite the lack of accommodation at the workplace and incomprehension by teachers and neighbours, celebrating Ramadan has slowly become a common feature in Spain and politicians of most parties attend festivities on the last day of Ramadan. In Catalonia, public television has even begun broadcasting the event.[118]

Perhaps the greatest success vis-à-vis the public practice of Islam in Spain has been related to Halal slaughtering practices. In 1986, the Islamic Council created the Halal Institute. Its executive director, Isabel Romero, a convert, patented a "Halal Certification Guarantee" and became an important intermediary between Spanish producers wishing to export to Muslim-majority countries and Muslims in the EU market.[119] Soon halal food was widely available and accepted. By 2005, more than 100 Spanish producers had begun a halal line of products and 15% of bovines slaughtered in the abattoirs of Barcelona were done so according to halal precepts. By 2010, this figure had risen to 50 percent.[120]

Part of the reason why Islamic education in schools and religious services in prisons and hospitals were so contentious was due to the tension among Muslims themselves over orthodox or reformist interpretations of Islam. The issue became charged after 11 September 2001 and the terrorist bombing of the Madrid commuter train system in March 2004. Secular organizations such as ATIME, worried about radical Islam, asked the governments of Spain and Morocco to monitor religious fundamentalism in Spain.[121] Regional governments had little idea of the vast array of splinter groups, warned Chaib, who wanted regional and national governments to become more involved in vetting religious officials. "It's not about control, as they sometimes say; it's about regulation, about meeting halfway . . . Everyone – government, society, and Muslims – would welcome a vetting initiative".[122]

Regulation, Chaib contended, would bring accountability as well as assistance in the integration of immigrants. "If religious leaders are irregular, how can we hope to have them contribute to integrating Muslims in Catalonia?" he asked. Because many imams were migrant workers who were elected to their posts by the community and had some experience in Spain, Chaib wanted to make them a visible bridge between Muslims and native society. "Imams are the first to want Catalans to see them and to recognize their role as normal, to see them as persons working to integrate Muslims in Catalonia". FEERI lobbied to establish a professional school for imam training similar to he European Institute of Human Sciences at Saint-Leger-de-Fougeret in France. We need such a school "to fill the hole of positions and circumvent those who could damage the community", argued FEERI.[123]

Muslim moderates, both immigrants and converts, worked hard to adapt Islam to Spanish society. They gained recognition for Muslims as "deeply rooted" and cooperated with public institutions. "[A]ll actual practices of secularism consist of institutional compromises and these can, should be, and are being extended to accommodate Muslims", argued Modood and Kastoryano.[124] As a neutral non-religious state that is obliged by its constitution to cooperate with major religions, Spain is equipped to manage its secular and religious spheres in a non-partisan manner. "Today the appropriate response to the new Muslim challenges is pluralistic institutional integration/assimilation, rather than an appeal to a radical public/private separation in the name of secularism", Modood and Katoryano have contended. While a minority of radical secularists look to French *laïcité* for inspiration, a majority of Spaniards have adopted a less provocative approach to religion, one which allows religion a presence in the public sphere. In adopting this stance, Muslim and non-Muslim Spaniards have been closer than many natives perhaps assumed.

4

Mosque Building, Catalan Nationalism, and Spain's Politics of Belonging, 1990–2010

In Spain, the presence of a mosque signifies not only the existence of a local Muslim community, but also the evolution of Islam itself from the private to the public realm. According to Jocelyn Cesari, once the social invisibility that had hitherto protected Islamic communities in Spain was removed, and Muslim prayer sites were made visible to the larger public, Islam went from being an object of indifference to one of contempt. Moreover, as Stefano Allievi points out, because "Mosques . . . constitute a form of symbolic ownership of the land . . . resistance to them becomes a very concrete and material sign of dominance and power over the territory. It is clear, therefore, that the conflict surrounding mosques is, above all, a genuine conflict of power".[1] Any discussion of the public practice of Islam in modern Spain, then, requires an analysis of the repeated attempts to build Islamic prayer sites in the country, and just as importantly, the anti-mosque backlashes they have often triggered.

In the broader European context, conflicts over the building of mosques have occurred in every country, but their intensity and outcome have depended on the degree to which local Muslims have acquired legitimacy in the public sphere, both at the local and national levels. This process has been highly uneven. According to Cesari, "in countries where immigration has a long history, such as France, Great Britain or Belgium, immediate resistance to the existence of a mosque is gradually losing its force".[2] The importance of electoral strategies and the consideration of the Muslim vote, as in the case of the Schaerbeek neighborhood of Brussels, for example, as well as the emergence of a new generation of educated Muslim leaders and of a Muslim middle class, help to explain the growing acceptance of Muslim visibility in these areas.[3]

Opposition to the building of a mosque by neighbourhood associations or local authorities, argues Cesari, should be understood as the first phase in a conversation over the use of public space and the balance between religious and secular interests. Simone Chambers concurs, arguing that voice rather than vote is the vehicle of empowerment in a mature democracy. Yet the primacy of voice over votes is predicated first and foremost on the assumption that debates in the public sphere are undertaken in an atmosphere of civility; that all parties appeal to logic rather than emotion; and that the use of persuasion is given precedence over the resort to force.[4]

Scholars have consistently shown, however, that in the dialogue over mosque building in Europe, Islamic voices have been either underrepresented or silenced altogether. In many such conflicts, Muslim communities have been forced to abandon their initial demands in an attempt to avoid anti-Muslim backlashes; often, they accept a far from ideal solution (usually a prayer site on the industrial outskirts of their given town). Indeed, the response of many Muslim communities in Europe can be summed up in the words of Hamza Piccardo, the representative of the Muslim community in the small northern Italian town of Lodi: "If the mosque is going to incite hatred, let us say not another word about it".[5] It is thus a paradox of this situation that the very same neighbourhood organizations that played such a crucial role in strengthening Spanish democracy during the post-Franco transition became, inadvertently and unwittingly, leading opponents of visible religious pluralism in the country.

In Spain, conflicts over mosques are still on the rise, with most of these taking place in the autonomous region of Catalonia. Between 1990 and 2008, ethnic Spaniards opposed proposals to build mosques and prayer rooms in sixty Spanish towns, forty of which (67 percent) were located in Catalonia. These conflicts have been triggered by Islamic communities' attempts to move from small prayer sites to newer, larger buildings, by the renovation of existing ones, or by attempts to construct purpose-built, grand mosques. As many scholars have pointed out, these conflicts are also related to the newly won visibility of, and the claim of permanence made by, various local Muslim communities in Spain, not to mention disparities between native and Muslim populations in terms of their access to public space, enjoyment of public resources, and protection by public authorities.[6]

Yet visibility and spatial and socio-economic inequality do not, in themselves, explain these conflicts, nor do they explain the widespread backing of the nativist position by Catalan politicians and intellectuals. Rather, the conflict over mosques in Catalonia needs to be understood in the context of the politics of belonging – in other words, "the political projects which construct particular modes of belonging and boundaries of belonging, in ways that usually promote the agent's own power within the group".[7] The assumption that mosques present a twofold challenge – to natives' demands for cultural assimilation and to the primacy of the Catalan nationalist project – is crucial to understanding why anti-mosque conflicts are more prevalent in Catalonia than elsewhere in Spain.

Democratic deepening entails a closing of the gap between formal legal rights in the civil and political arena – which Muslims obtained with the 1992 Agreement of Cooperation and the granting of residency or citizenship status – and the practical exercise of those rights in the real world.

Implicit in the outbreak of anti-mosque conflict is an attempt to pinpoint an acceptable level of cultural and religious pluralism in Spanish society, as well as the degree to which democratic practices have been embraced by civil society. Mosque building and anti-mosque activism can therefore help us to chart the circuitous process by which religious pluralism has become normalized in Spain in the post-Franco years.[8]

Mosque Building and Nativist Resistance in Spain

Spain's first modern mosque appeared in Córdoba during the Spanish Civil War, a gift for Franco's Muslim soldiers. This was followed, in 1981, with the erection of a mosque in Marbella, Málaga, in the town's most exclusive neighbourhood, though Muslims of all social classes and geographical origins were permitted to attend. In 1982, Ahmediyya Muslims in Pedro Abad, Córdoba, built a mosque as well.[9]

The country's most iconic mosque was built in Madrid, the nation's capital. Negotiations for its construction began as early as 1964, yet work on the structure did not commence in earnest until 1977, when the local government donated 1 hectare of land on the outskirts of the city – next to the M-30 highway – to the future king of Saudi Arabia, Fahd bin Abdul Aziz Al Saud. The Madrid mosque, popularly known as the M-30 mosque, was thus "an important project for both the Islamic community [as well as] Spanish relations with Arab countries", explained one representative of the Saudi government.[10] The mosque took another fifteen years to complete, due in part to disagreements over funding among Arab countries.[11]

By the time it was inaugurated in 1992, the Madrid mosque was the largest of its kind in Europe. King Juan Carlos I attended the ceremony and *El País* welcomed the opening as a further step "in the recuperation of tolerant traditions of past centuries".[12] While the M-30 mosque was under construction, smaller mosques appeared elsewhere. In the Madrid neighbourhood of Tetuán – named for the Moroccan city of Tetouan, after returning colonial soldiers were garrisoned in the neighbourhood in the 1860s – an old furniture factory was turned into a mosque whose funding, according to the mosque's imam, Riay Tatary, came from the "Muslims of the world" – mainly Qataris, Jordanians, Syrians, and Saudi Arabians. The Tetuán mosque provided a counterbalance to the M-30 project, which was seen by many as top-down and Saudi controlled.[13]

With the signing of the Agreement of Cooperation, religious bodies sprung up across Spain and Muslims gained notoriety. News of the publication of Salman Rushdie's *The Satanic Verses* and the *fatwa* that subsequently threatened his life reverberated throughout Europe. In France, Islamic head-dress in schools became an issue in the media. In Spain, mosques and prayer rooms became the object of attention not because of their particular theological line, though this would be a concern after the events of 11 September 2001, but because they shattered native assumptions that immigration was a temporary phenomenon, according to the sociologist Abdelmalek Sayad.[14] Natives thought that immigrants would soon return 'home', that they were labourers who filled shortages of undesirable work, rather than fellow citizens. (Accordingly, immigrants were initially excluded from the political and even social spheres, as we saw in previous chapters).

Mosques, by contrast, signified permanence, not transience. As natives challenged Muslims on their desire to remain in the country, Muslims pushed back and became, thereby, political agents rather than 'guests'. And as the spectre of Islamic terrorism came to loom ever larger over Western societies, mosques were thrown into the centre of this controversy. Spanish Muslims were understandably sensitive to this heightened anxiety; in Catalonia, for example, local Muslims and launched an 'open-door day' at local mosques to be held yearly at the end of Ramadan.[15]

Prayer rooms in Barcelona were originally defined by precariousness and caution. They were created in rental units that were not designed for large groups and lacked adequate safety features. Muslim immigrants were sensitive to the attitudes of natives and took care to conceal their places of worship. Unlike the activities of Spanish converts, who practiced Islam as publicly and didactically as they could, Muslim immigrants aimed to go unnoticed and thus avert any backlash from locals.[16]

In the politicized context of the 1990s, Muslim immigrants could not keep their prayer rooms and religious activities hidden. The first anti-mosque demonstration occurred in 1990 in the town of Vic. There, nativists who claimed that ethnic Spaniards should have more rights than newly arrived immigrants petitioned the city to close a prayer room because it was located in a street that was too narrow for high-volume traffic. The family that lived in the apartment above the prayer room also complained that it disturbed them.[17]

These same arguments – that Muslim prayer sites disrupt community harmony and override the interests of local Spaniards – would resurface repeatedly in coming years. Native protestors argued that mosques, especially on Fridays, crowded public spaces. Mosques often had trouble accommodating all of their congregants, with believers sometimes praying on sidewalks. Protestors claimed that public space was not meant to serve the needs of one particular religious community, but was rather the property of the citizenry as a whole. Moreover, in marginalized areas, protesters argued that publicly owned property or plots of land should be used for community centres, libraries, and sport and recreational facilities. In wealthier areas, protestors also claimed that mosques lowered property values.[18]

As the conflict over mosques evolved, so too did natives' arguments against them. From initial claims that took into account only natives' interests, protesters pointed to a host of technical arguments, such as inadequate sanitary and safety regulations, as well as fears of Islamic fundamentalism and terrorism – what Cesari calls the adoption of a metanarrative premised on considering Islam as a threat to Western values and security. Stefano Allievi divides arguments against mosques in Europe between "real" or "supposedly real" concerns about regulations, use of resources and public space, and "cultural" arguments, in other words, those that emphasize the "foreignness of Islam to 'our' culture; defence of women's rights; reciprocity; 'non integrability' and/or incompatibility of Islam with western/European/Christian values".[19]

The elaboration of similar cultural arguments in Holland, Germany, and Switzerland has revolved around architectural styles and the symbolism of minarets; in Italy, the weakness of Italian cultural identity and the need to protect it; and in Greece, the apparent 'foreign factor', which sees mosques as institutions working on behalf of Turkish state interests. In Catalonia, local discussions have centred on the visibility of immigrants in popular locations, as well as native-immigrant commingling, while at the regional level they have focused on the need to protect Catalan identity, culture, and language.[20]

Movements to oppose mosques tended to result in increased tension and social strife. Local authorities – sometimes reluctantly, as in the cases of Lodi in Italy or Premià de Mar in Catalonia, other times enthusiastically, as in the Catalan cities of Lleida and Reus – sided with natives and pressured Muslims to relocate to industrial parks or other unattractive locations on the outskirts of cities. Allievi has called this the peripheralization and marginalization of mosques to the suburbs or degraded areas.[21]

Mosques are not sites of worship alone, but places to gather and fraternize, too. The relegation of these institutions to city outskirts and other undesirable areas has therefore driven home to Muslims the message that they are outcasts from the wider community. "We are moved away from the people, as if we have leprosy", exclaimed Badalona's imam.[22] Riay Tatary appealed to legality: "They're supposed to apply the law equally, with the same barometer for everyone . . . Times are less than ideal here in Spain".[23]

The most widely studied backlashes transpired in two cities close to Barcelona, Premià de Mar and Badalona, in 2001–02 and 2005, respectively. The population of Premià was 4.4 percent Muslim, while in Badalona it was slightly higher. In Premià, natives mobilized shortly after 11 September 2001, and in Badalona, after the Madrid train attack, though neither mobilization made Islamic fundamentalism its central complaint. Indeed, native protestors showed little interest in or knowledge of the various Islamic sects. The movements were, rather, self-serving: they opposed mosques because they perceived them to be impositions by outsiders who did not belong. They held little regard for equality, fairness, or diversity.[24]

The most intense hostility took place in Premià de Mar because the Muslim community there owned a plot of land in the city centre and had received the required building permit from the city. It would have been the first purpose-built mosque in Catalonia. Native agitation put a halt to construction and the Muslim community was forced to relocate to a decommissioned school on the outskirts of town. "Regional governments need to intervene justly, but also realistically in religious conflicts", claimed Jordi Pujol, the nationalist Christian Democrat president of the Catalan government from 1980 to 2003 and the most influential Catalan politician of the post-Franco period. "The Muslims of Premià have the right to build a mosque in the centre of town, but the wellbeing of the population [sic] must also be considered. A balance would be to move the site elsewhere. The city needs to do that". Pujol went on to say that native actions stemmed from "intolerance" and that their demands were "unfair", but he did not hesitate to argue that the best way forward was for Muslims to relocate to a less conspicuous environment.[25]

In Catalonia, the series of conflicts over mosques triggered a government initiative to regulate places of worship. New regulations hoped to iron out inconsistencies in the treatment of religious minorities and to uphold health and safety measures. On paper the regulations promised to guarantee religious pluralism, yet in practice they helped local governments expedite the closing down of prayer rooms, claimed Abdennur Prado, a prominent Catalan convert.[26]

Native resistance to the building of new mosques – or even to the maintenance of existing prayer rooms – demonstrates how tenacious Muslims have had to be in their efforts to secure adequate prayer sites, as well as the general ineffectiveness of the Agreement of Cooperation. After decades of effort, Muslim immigrants have failed to attain suitable facilities and instead have had to accept anything they are offered: hundreds of unsafe, poorly located sites that are subject to constant regulatory scrutiny. In a genuine multicultural exchange, the burden of change should not lie with one side alone, argue Tariq Modood and Riva Kastoryano. Spanish nativists have, however, forced immigrants to shoulder this burden exclusively by refusing to embrace religious pluralism in a meaningful way.[27]

Barcelona and the Mosque that was Never Built

Plans for a grand mosque in Barcelona exemplify the difficulties faced by Muslims who have tried to exercise their religious rights in Catalonia. Following talks with the two national Islamic federations, the Spanish government agreed in 1992 to protect and recognize Muslim religious sites throughout the country. Shortly thereafter, grand mosques were inaugurated in Madrid and Valencia. However, in Barcelona, Spain's second-largest city and the city with the largest population of Muslims, the municipal and regional government obstructed similar efforts.[28] In Catalonia, more than elsewhere in Spain, mosques and devout Muslims were pushed to city outskirts, into industrial warehouses, storage sheds, and other inadequate venues.

In 1998, the Museum of Catalan History, in conjunction with the Government of Catalonia, organized an exhibition called "Islam and Catalonia", which showcased the Catalan-Islamic relationship from the medieval era to the present. Pujol figured prominently in the exhibition's catalogue. It was time for Catalonia to "settle accounts" with Islam, said Pujol. Catalans and Muslims had "fought each other, up and down the peninsula, for too long".[29]

The exhibition explained, among other things, that the Spanish crown had expelled the *Morisco* population between 1609 and 1614 because Christians believed they were "the same *moros* and dogs as before". A group of Middle Eastern ambassadors toured the exhibition. They paused at the final section dealing with "citizens of Catalonia", where new Muslim immigrants appeared. The section spoke of turning over a new leaf and putting old differences aside. Later, the ambassadors argued that Pujol should, in good faith, support Barcelona's Muslim community in their efforts to construct a grand mosque.[30] With the pending Universal Forum of Cultures, the largest event Barcelona had organized since the 1992 Olympic Games, the time was ripe, said the ambassadors, for such a move. (The same arguments were simultaneously being used in Greece, where local Muslims and their supporters justified the construction of the first grand mosque in Athens as a necessary preparation for the 2004 Olympic Games).[31]

Muslims from many denominations and origins believed that Barcelona was ready for a central, grand mosque, a place to unite the city's Muslim community. Of the 24 percent of Barcelona's religious infrastructure that was not Catholic in 2000, only 1 percent was Muslim (the remainder belonged to Protestant, Jehovah's Witness, or Buddhist organizations).[32] Sheikh Abdur-Rahman Al-Sudais, imam of the grand mosque in Mecca, visited Barcelona and offered his support. Though the Catalan government remained sceptical, it was now contemplating the idea.

During the summer of 1999, native residents of Tarrasa, 35 kilometres north of Barcelona, demonstrated and attacked Muslim immigrant homes. The riot was the first of its kind in Spain. The Catalan government was eager to distance itself from these events, if only because the Universal Forum of Cultures was approaching. Barcelona's deputy mayor, Xavier Casas, argued that an Islamic centre "would be good for Barcelona, given that the spirit of the Universal Forum is about dialogue between cultures".[33]

While politicians had initially supported Casas's comments, the idea of a grand mosque was abandoned once the media spotlight on nativist xenophobia began to fade. Regional Social Affairs Minister Antoni Comas warned Barcelonans that a grand mosque "could serve as cover for . . . fundamentalism". Muslims "have the right to have a mosque here [in Barcelona] because they have the right to practice their religion freely, but in their countries of origin do you think Catholic churches are permitted?" Comas was reacting to the sheikh's visit from Mecca and his particular fundamentalist interpretation of Islam, which indeed endorsed the Saudi Arabian government's ban on Christian churches. Comas's comments also echoed some politicians and media outlets in Italy, who have used the lack of reciprocal rights for Christians in Islamic-majority countries as a way to justify curtailing the rights of Muslims in Europe.[34]

Despite the admonishments of Pujol, Comas, and others, the construction of the grand mosque looked as if it might go through in the summer of 1999. Barcelona city hall had located a suitable, centrally located plot of land, but construction was delayed due to funding shortfalls and Muslim infighting. In response to the delay, Muslim activists redoubled their efforts. Syrian-born Mowafak Kanfash, founder of the well-known Arabic Book House of Barcelona, argued that a grand mosque "would be a great symbol of *convivencia*".[35] Kanfash and his embryonic Islamic Federation of Catalonia pledged to contribute 1 million dollars to its construction. The Saudi ambassador to Spain, Radi Shuaibi, pledged additional funds. Yet Saudi involvement raised eyebrows both among native Spaniards and other Muslim immigrants. The Islamic Cultural Council of Catalonia (CICC), a competing federation with Kanfash's Islamic Federation, included seventeen member mosques. The CICC was founded by Mohamed Chaib and supported by the Ibn Battuta Association, one of the most active cultural Islamic organizations in the city. It made a counterproposal in the hopes of avoiding Saudi involvement. The CICC wanted a grassroots mosque that was free from foreign control and that was built and paid for by Spanish Muslims, with input from the Catalan government.[36]

In the end, neither Saudi Arabia and Kanfash nor the CICC could agree on a funding structure.[37] While Chaib's CICC knew how to navigate local and regional government and could whip up opposition to the Saudis, it could not offer a financially viable alternative. To Chaib and his followers, no grand mosque for the time being was better than a Saudi-controlled one right away. A similar sentiment was shared in other parts of Spain.[38] In Granada, a Morabitun mosque with a view of the Alhambra would take over fifteen years to build, largely because of a nativist backlash but also because local Muslims refused to accept funding from Saudi Arabia and to suffer, in exchange, Saudi input. Instead, the Muslim community garnered finances from Libya, Morocco, and Malaysia.[39] The influence of Muslims in local politics – after all, Chaib was a member of the PSC and the PSC held Barcelona city hall – combined with the reluctance on the part of local authorities to encourage Saudi Islam, meant that the construction of a grand mosque in Barcelona would go unrealized.

Since 2005, the CICC has organized the annual Congress of Catalan Imams and Mosques to lobby local and regional governments to permit the construction of dignified prayer sites for Muslims. The Congress asked for "a dignified mosque to represent the fusion of Muslim and Catalan art", and "a good cultural centre in Barcelona, with room for Muslim women, where socio-cultural projects and religious activities could be organized".[40] Barcelona's existing prayer rooms were not large enough to accommodate all male worshipers, let alone Muslim women, who did not have a single prayer site of their own. The construction of a grand mosque, even if under Saudi control, would – paradoxically – offer Muslim women a public place to organize, socialize, and pray.

In response to Muslim disunity, Catalan politicians abandoned the idea of a grand mosque and offered instead to support small prayer rooms, which, they claimed, were more in tune with the multi-denominational character of Muslim immigrants in Catalonia. Yet even on this point, the Catalan government failed to deliver. In the summer of 2000, Pakistani Muslims, whose small prayer room in the El Raval neighbourhood could no longer accommodate their numbers, asked Barcelona city hall for help to find a new location. Pressured by nativist complaints, city hall turned their request down.

In each of the forty conflicts over proposed mosque and prayer room constructions in Catalonia between 1990 and 2008, natives were pitted against Muslim immigrants. A mosque, if not a grand mosque, was needed in Barcelona to send a message that Islam was welcome in Catalonia. Pierre Bourdieu has cautioned about the power of symbolic violence linked to identity and representation.[41] Symbolic violence does not necessarily take an exclusively active form, such as in the Festival of Moors and Christians; it can also be passive, for example, when a religious or ethnic minority's use of dignified and accepted symbols is denied. Had the opportunity not been missed in 1999, subsequent protests may have been avoided or more easily deactivated. As things stood, however, Catalan authorities did not find it problematic that Barcelona – together with Athens, Greece and Ljubljana, Slovenia – remained one of the few large European cities without a grand mosque.[42]

A Path towards Peace or "Ravalistan"?

Before the 1980s, El Raval was known as the "*barrio chino*": Chinatown, a red-light district replete with prostitutes, petty criminals, social misfits, and of course, immigrants (though very few of them were actually Chinese).[43] The first South Asian Muslims to arrive in Barcelona in the 1970s settled in this neighbourhood. Over the next two decades, Barcelona city hall committed to "revitalizing" El Raval. It promised improved housing and public utilities in preparation for the 1992 Olympic Games. When the games were over, the city opened up El Raval to the rest of Barcelona. It built a *rambla*, a pedestrian avenue with cafés, stores, and open spaces for concerts and other community events. This was inaugurated in September 2000, and it immediately transformed both the city and the neighbourhood. Tourists and residents flocked to El Raval to sample 'ethnic food' and to absorb the exotic atmosphere like never before.

To many Pakistani immigrants, the *rambla* of El Raval was also the *Udàs Rambla*, or "Rambla of Sadness", because it was on the thoroughfare's hard public benches that many waited for residency and work permits, for permission to reunite with family members, or generally lamented their difficult situations in Spain.[44] Revitalization brought not only the *rambla* to El Raval, but also museums, libraries, seniors' centres, community centres, and other public infrastructure. The Contemporary Art Museum of

Barcelona, MACBA, was built in El Raval in 1995; a cinematheque, complete with library, theatre, gallery, and archives, was under construction as of 2011.[45] Yet for immigrants, revitalization was a mixed blessing. The high-end museum and cinematheque increased foot traffic astronomically and set off a fierce wave of gentrification that has made it difficult for immigrants to find housing and venues for small businesses.[46]

Muhammad Iqbal left Pakistan in the early 1990s. Before settling in Barcelona, where his uncle lived, he worked in England and in other Spanish cities. Immediately upon arriving in Barcelona, Iqbal became active in the Pakistani immigrant community. He became fluent in both Spanish and Catalan and was well regarded in the Pakistani community. He has claimed that he is a Muslim first, a Pakistani second, and Spanish/Catalan third. Thanks to his fluency in Catalan, local nationalists have accepted him, even though he refuses to be pulled in to either side of the Catalan/Spanish dichotomy.[47]

Path towards Peace, an organization which works with city and regional authorities to promote religious understanding and tolerance, was founded in 1997, and in 2005, Iqbal was made its president. Despite pressure from adherents to the Deobandi school of Pakistani Sunni Islam, which defends a puritanical interpretation of Islam and promotes separation from native society, Path towards Peace encouraged dialogue between immigrants and native society. Iqbal fought for the right to build mosques in Spain and spoke out against Islamic terrorism, though he initially defended Pakistanis arrested in Barcelona, and later convicted of terrorism charges, in 2009.[48]

In 2000, after city authorities abandoned the idea of a grand mosque and pledged to support grassroots prayer rooms instead, Path towards Peace found itself at the centre of controversy. Its membership of religious adherents had swelled to 600 and its space could no longer accommodate these numbers during Friday prayers. The organization's leadership wanted to relocate, and to this end asked the city to help it find a larger venue in El Raval, where most of its members lived and worked.[49] City hall took four months to respond. It recommended that Path towards Peace find a venue outside of the downtown. Both Path towards Peace and FEERI rebuked city hall for its "negative attitude": "We're here legally and we pay our taxes. It pains us to hear the government say go away", complained community leaders. Path towards Peace reiterated that it did not wish to build a new mosque, and certainly not a grand mosque; it simply wanted help in securing a larger, more permanent facility and an interim location that it could use in the meantime for Friday prayers. City hall claimed that because El Raval was being revitalized and gentrified, it could not find a venue that was large enough to accommodate hundreds of Muslims. Later, back-tracking slightly, it offered a multiuse sports centre.[50]

Path towards Peace took the city up on its offer. Muslims, in much greater numbers than the organization had anticipated, flocked to the new complex. The crowd drew immediate suspicion from native residents, who complained that the city had prioritized public infrastructure for Muslims.

In the ensuing conflict, natives managed to convince the city to renege on its agreement with Path towards Peace. According to the downtown district manager, it was not the city's job to "find mosques or convert sports centres into places of worship . . . the city cannot, either, block streets every Friday for praying". After two months of Friday prayers in the complex, the district manager told Path towards Peace that "a facility for secular activities cannot be converted into a place of worship". Only on special occasions, on Eid al-Adha for instance, could it be used for this purpose.[51]

After being forced to return to their former location, Path towards Peace members noticed that local residents had stepped up complaints to the police about Muslims praying in the neighbourhood. The police threatened Path towards Peace with heavy fines if it did not find indoor space for prayer. It seemed the group could not win. In October 2000, FEERI and Path towards Peace called for a demonstration in front of Barcelona city hall and the seat of the Catalan regional government, located in the same square. The protest was called off at the last minute, however, because Muslims did not want to antagonize politicians and to create even more backlash. Conflicts over mosques have ended similarly in other European cities, with Muslims backtracking and compromising their rights in order to appease nativist reactions. By then a Catholic church in El Raval had offered the organization temporary space for Friday prayers. While it is not unusual in other parts of Europe for churches to help Muslims find sites of prayer, the Catholic Church in Spain has been reluctant to involve itself in this way. As a temporary solution, the offer pleased Muslims. They were anxious about provoking their neighbours further.[52]

In the end, the city did not find or offer alternative facilities. El Raval's revitalization proceeded in a spirit of complete disregard for one of the neighbourhood's most dynamic communities.[53] Moderate Muslims in organizations such as Path towards Peace were unable to find native allies in city hall. They also failed to muster support from Moroccan members of the Ibn Battuta Association or more strident Deobandi adherents of Pakistani origin, who saw them as competitors for Muslim allegiance. Barcelona, too, lost an opportunity: it alienated moderate Muslims who owned businesses, paid into the social-security system, and even drew tourists to the city. Hard-line Muslims, busy at work in the immigrant community, would not be so easy to disregard.[54]

Muslim Immigrants on Catalonia's Nationalist Fault Lines

Migrants who settle in societies already divided by language, ethnicity, and/or religion must develop specific strategies to adapt and survive.[55] Often, as vulnerable newcomers, they are pressured, even manipulated, into joining one side of a local conflict, though occasionally they manage to remain neutral. In Catalonia, tension between Spanish and Catalan speakers tends to drown out immigrant priorities and hinder the implementation of the religious rights of Muslims. Regional nationalists vie for political as much as cultural loyalty, and this process has managed to divide immigrants as well.

As we saw in Chapter 1, Franco's death brought a new constitution that granted unprecedented independence to Spain's autonomous communities. In Catalonia, nationalists wrestled for control of cultural affairs and attempted to "normalize" the Catalan language by introducing it into schools and government. Since the new constitution granted these communities jurisdiction over culture, labour relations, education, health, and policing, nationalists duly set about "Catalanizing" each of these sectors. Immigration, however, remained the prerogative of Madrid, something resented by Catalan nationalists. In 1992, Muslim immigrants won the right to religious and cultural expression throughout Spain. Yet in Catalonia, this would be less straightforward than in other regions of Spain. In practice, regional governments could restrict or ensure immigrant rights. In Catalonia, pledges to learn Catalan and identify with "Catalan values" took precedence over immigrants' rights to practice their own culture and religion openly.

Most scholars of nationalism agree that the origins and ethos of Catalan nationalism is mostly civic, as opposed to, say, Basque nationalism, which is predominantly ethnic.[56] Ethnic nationalism tends to draw boundaries more exclusively; for individuals to be accepted as a legitimate member of the national community, they are required to share certain attributes, such as ancestry, race, language, culture, religion, or birthplace. By contrast, civic conceptions of nationalism extend membership on a legal-rational basis, without making claims to cultural assimilation. All nationalist movements display elements from both of these two ideal types, but one usually predominates.

Differentiating civic and ethnic nationalism is not always feasible; indeed, many scholars find these categories problematic.[57] Nonetheless, a scholarly consensus maintains that Catalan nationalism is predominantly civic, if only because its ethnic markers, such as language and culture, are features that can be acquired. This was still an accurate assessment in the early 1990s, when "diversity" referred to linguistic and cultural differences between ethnic Catalans and internal migrants from other regions of Spain. For all their differences, these groups shared an adherence to social Catholicism, were equal citizens of Spain, and their cultures were more or less mutually intelligible. Under these conditions, Catalan nationalism remained overwhelmingly civic in nature.

Once international migration broadened the religious and ethnic diversity in Catalonia, however, Catalan nationalism came to be defined increasingly by its ethnic characteristics. In recent years, the debate has focused less on language – though that still weighs heavily – but rather on religion, skin colour, cultural assimilation, and political allegiance to the Catalan independence project. If race and religion are considered, then Catalan nationalism has certainly experienced an 'ethnic turn' since the arrival of international immigrants to the region. It is increasingly reliant upon language, whiteness, and Christianity to distinguish native Catalans from visible minorities.[58] The challenge, then, has been – and remains – to include visible minorities, particularly Muslims, in the imagined Catalan nation.[59] (This process is certainly not exclusive to Catalonia; one recent example can be seen in the Canadian Parti Quebecois's attempt at limiting the rights of religious minorities with the 2013 Charter of Quebec Values).[60]

The migrants that ethnic Catalans have decided to welcome into their nation have varied over the past half century. In the 1960s, Catalonia's population doubled with the arrival of migrants from other regions of Spain, in particular from Andalusia, almost all of whom were Spanish speaking, Christian, and ethnically Spanish. As Catalonia developed into a bilingual society, language emerged as a source of disagreement and a marker of difference. In the post-Franco quest to make Catalan the official language across the region, nationalists argued that Spanish, the dominant and historically more prestigious language, would overwhelm the use of Catalan if immediate action was not taken.[61]

In this conflict, Spanish-speaking internal migrants figured prominently. They were viewed by many Catalan nationalists as foot soldiers in a larger cultural conflict (whether these internal migrants viewed themselves in these terms is of course highly debatable). In an honest effort to integrate Spanish speakers, nationalists set about clarifying who, exactly, was to be considered Catalan. They hit on the gender-partial formula, "Every man who lives and works in Catalonia [is Catalan]", regardless of his language, culture, or birthplace.[62] It was at this point that myths of diversity, which saw Catalonia as "a land of passing" (*terra de pas*) or "welcoming land" (*terra d'acollida*), were developed to encourage ethnic Catalans to incorporate, and hopefully assimilate, their Spanish-speaking neighbours. This process did not go unchallenged, of course: for example, many self-styled "real Catalans" (*de soca-rel*) employed xenophobic epithets, such as mixed-race, or illegitimate (*xarnego*), to refer to Spanish-speaking migrants from other regions.[63]

In 1960s Catalonia, however, race and religion were non-issues. In the 1970s, the first Moroccan migrants arrived in Spain and by the 1990s they were conspicuous in demanding rights for themselves. While Catalan nationalists pushed for greater cultural control over the region, immigrants fought first and foremost for work and residency permits from Madrid, then for religious and cultural rights from autonomous communities like Catalonia. If during the Franco era, Catalan nationalists had defined themselves against Andalusian migrants, by the 1980s Muslim immigrants became the new counter-image, with Andalusians, who were Christian and much more familiar, joining the Catalan nation, so long as they identified primarily with Catalonia.[64]

Will Kymlicka is wary of assuming that regional nationalists and migrants can establish alliances in an attempt to counter the homogenizing effects of nation-states.[65] Minority nationalists claim though that a common alliance among disenfranchised groups to oppose Madrid's centralization of power and cultural dominance is not only possible, but actually desirable.[66] Evidence, however, undermines the reality of this alliance. In Catalonia, nationalists saw themselves as victims of state policy: if Catalonia was not defended, it would be annihilated, went the standard argument. In a replay of the 1960s, nationalists viewed immigrants who did not share this logic as suspicious, as impostors who did the dirty work of Spanish nationalists. For example, in 2000 Pujol roused native fears by stating that "Catalonia would be better off without immigrants". He was referring specifically to Latin Americans, who "have difficulty understanding the concept of Catalanness". Muslim immigrants, he argued, were better – "provided we leave religion aside" – because they did not bring with them the same linguistic baggage.[67] To nationalists like Pujol, immigrants were not companions in an effort to pluralize Spain; they were, rather, chess pieces in an old game that Catalonia had long played with Madrid.

The apparent championing of one group of immigrants over another was not genuine. For example, Marta Ferrussola, Pujol's wife, reflected Catalan Islamophobia by claiming that Moroccans who arrived in the 1980s represented "a different kind of avalanche than fifty years ago . . . Their culture and religion is distinctly different from ours and they demand that we respect them". To Ferrussola, religious accommodations – for instance, the ability to purchase halal food – were unacceptable. "It isn't enough to welcome them [Muslims], we're supposed to accommodate their food too! We need to be open as individuals, but . . . these impositions! Maybe mosques will replace Romanesque churches shortly as well". As with political discourse generally, Ferrussola struggled to find the acceptable terminology. Religious pluralism, in her view, was a euphemism for cultural imposition: "They can observe their religion, but we won't allow them to impose it on us!" she stated. She also warned: "If they impose their stuff on us, fine. All right. We'll move ahead with our language: we want them to speak Catalan". As her husband put it, Muslim migrants "not only have rights, they have responsibilities, which include respecting Catalan identity".[68]

In 2004, Pujol reiterated this stance by allowing for the integration of migrants provided that they did not mix ("*vigilar amb el mestissatge*") with native Catalans, since that would spell "the end for Catalonia".[69] In the political storm that followed, Catalan political parties scrambled to find a new meaning of identity, even if both left- and right-wing nationalists concurred with Pujol that Catalonia was at risk of disappearing due to the presence of migrants. The PSC and the United Left Party, however, rebuked Pujol, arguing instead for what they called "interculturalism". "Mixture is not the end", argued Pascual Maragall, the PSC president of the Catalan government. "If done right, it could be the beginning of everything".[70] The exchange showed that Catalan nationalism was multidimensional; within it, civic and ethnic tendencies coexisted and even vied for dominance.

While Pujol and Ferrussola echoed the common view that "old Catalans" should have more say in determining the way Catalan society operates, not all nationalists adhered to this line. Miquel Àngel Essomba, Director of UNESCO-Catalonia, Chair in Pedagogy at the Autonomous University of Barcelona, and a Barcelonan born to a Cameroonian father and Catalan mother, admitted that Catalan society struggled to adjust to diversity. Catalans "need to slightly change their established model. At times they open doors, but stress too forcefully established norms of behaviour", he argued. While to Pujol and Ferrussola, Catalonia was Catholic and Catalan speaking, to Essombra Catalonia also belonged to immigrants, people who "must be allowed to participate in developing the guidelines for *convivencia*".[71]

In response to migration, Catalan nationalists have imagined their nation differently over the past forty years. Their main response has been to re-value and reposition their conceptualization of language to suit their needs. In the 1970s and early 1980s, nationalists called for "Catalan: official language" (*llengua oficial*); however once Catalan achieved official status alongside Spanish, they upped their rhetoric and shifted to "Catalan: Catalonia's language" (*llengua pròpia*). The goal was to elevate Catalan above Spanish, rather than keep it on an equal level. Many nationalists wanted Spanish as removed as possible from Catalonia and there was widespread agreement for Catalan to be "the language of normal and preferential use in government and in the public media of Catalonia . . . [as well as] the education system". While everyone had "the right to use the two official languages" – nationalists could not eliminate Spanish as an official language as long as Catalonia remained politically part of Spain – "the citizens of Catalonia [had] the right and the duty to know the two languages".[72] The obligation to know Catalan was a step towards its normalization. It was no longer possible for Spanish speakers to live in Catalonia without at least a passive knowledge of Catalan.

As nationalist parties in the Catalan parliament busied themselves with legislating *llengua pròpia*, smaller cultural organizations lobbied to make Catalan the "common language" (*llengua comuna*), a deeper conception of linguistic dominance aimed at convincing immigrants that they should prioritize learning and using Catalan over Spanish and throw their allegiance with the nationalist project. Since 2007, the Platform for the Catalan Language (PCL) has organized activities for a day of celebration of Catalan culture, the Day of Sant Jordi, around the theme of *llengua comuna*.[73] The PCL wanted to show both immigrants and natives that they were linked through Catalan. Yet this position did not go unchallenged. Nobel Prize-winning novelist Mario Vargas Llosa and playwright and director Albert Boadella, among other influential intellectuals, considered Spanish, not Catalan, to be the common language of the region, and they made their positions known by issuing a pro-Spanish "Manifesto for the Common Language" in 2008.[74]

Matthew Tree, a long-term Barcelona resident born in Britain, compared the Spanish-Catalan rivalry to betting on a race. The moment migrants step inside Catalonia a bookie asks them for their bet.[75] As in Flanders, the Basque country, Quebec, and elsewhere, migrants presumably place this bet on the language of most utility and prestige, the one that will help them find employment, communicate on the street, and keep further mobility options open.[76] In Catalonia, that language has been Spanish, a reality that has provoked the ire of Catalan nationalists.

While immigrant children have had the opportunity to learn Catalan in school, their parents, despite many free government-funded courses, have not. First-generation immigrants were typically too busy with work, housing, education for their children, and community relations to take advantage of language courses for themselves. Nationalists have pushed to change this. They claim that for an immigrant to obtain status through *arraigo*, he or she should have to prove knowledge of Catalan.[77] Many immigrants perceive this policy to be unfair, since Catalan authorities were demanding cultural assimilation without having first guaranteed migrants' citizenship and religious rights. "Integration has nothing to do with the immigrant speaking Catalan", argued one Senegalese immigrant; "it's about having work, rights, and responsibilities".[78]

The Spectrum of Possibilities for Muslims in Catalonia

When Muslim immigrants first arrived in significant numbers in the 1970s, Spain was divided sharply along national and regional lines. Migrants to Catalonia had little choice but to cope with the conflict over cultural and linguistic identity. Though Catalan nationalists had long thought of themselves as a minority in Spain, they had given little reflection to the other minorities among them. In the quest to preserve their language and identity, many insisted on a version of cultural assimilation, with the Catalan language as a central pillar. Catalan was not yet the prestigious language of public institutions that it would eventually become; many ethnic Catalans believed that their language was inferior to Spanish, and switched to the latter when talking to a stranger or in public. From the nationalist point of view, bilingualism was a threat, a zero-sum game: the more people or immigrants chose Spanish, the less Catalan would become "normalized".

In order to explore the spectrum of possibilities for Muslim immigrants in the face of Catalan pressure to culturally assimilate, it is helpful to look at the linguistic choices, religious attachments, and political allegiances of five Muslim immigrants in Catalonia, chosen because they either wrote memoirs of their experiences growing up in the region, or are prominent community and religious activists. The more these immigrants accepted and internalized demands for cultural assimilation, the more nationalists granted them access to government and to the existing power structure. Those who refused to adopt Catalan nationalist values were pushed to the margins.

The writer Najat El Hachmi migrated to Vic in 1985 at the age of eight. Though she had strong memories of her childhood, she received most of her schooling in Spain, where she excelled in Catalan. She was still in high school when she received her first literary award for a short story in Catalan. El Hachmi said that she had to learn the language fast: "it was a vital necessity to learn. There were few Moroccans in Vic. Knowing Catalan opened doors to a new world; it held the keys to the inner world of the people of that land of fog".[79] Later, she would go on to publish *Jo també sóc catalana* ("I too am Catalan"), a memoir in which she pleaded with native society to adjust its rigid view of Catalan identity as necessarily white, Christian (or historically Christian), and middle class, in order to include people like her, who had been born in other countries but identified personally and culturally with the region.

El Hachmi's writing combines her strong critique of the narrowness of Catalan identity with an outspoken support for Catalan self-determination, as well as the "normalization" of the Catalan language. She supports the "ideal of a free nation under the Catalan flag of independence", the "spirit of resistance and recognition of symbols". Catalan nationalism, she writes, "made me feel one again, that where I was born and where my parents were born didn't matter".[80] In this regard, El Hachmi exemplifies not only the struggles that visible minorities face in Catalonia, but the rewards that are offered to them when they pledge allegiance to the nationalist cause. She has become a militant Catalanist and an atheist – a poster child held up by left-wing nationalists as proof that integration is possible. She is, in this regard, a sort of Catalan Ayaan Hirsi Ali, the Somali immigrant to Holland who gained a reputation in Europe as an outspoken female critic of Islamic misogyny and backwardness.[81] El Hachmi's novel *The Last Patriarch*, published in 2008, offers a similarly harsh criticism of patriarchy among Muslim immigrants in Europe, and it won her Catalonia's top literary prize, the Ramon Llull. She was the first immigrant to win this prestigious award.

El Hachmi is part of a left-wing nationalist school of thought that upholds immigrants from oppressed minorities as heroic – not unlike the Catalans vis-à-vis the Spanish. Catalan nationalists of this school have actively recruited Amazigh migrants to their cause. "Here in Catalonia, Moroccans of Berber descent differentiate themselves from Arabs and feel more Berber than Moroccan", explained Joan Soler Amigó, a member of the association Jameiat Essalam. "The situation of Berbers with respect to Arabs parallels that of Catalans with respect to Castilians", he added. In Catalonia, "the distance [from Morocco] reinforces Berber identity and clarifies the awareness of who Berbers are. Berbers become moved to express themselves . . . in front of Arab Moroccans. The two cultures become entangled in conflict".[82]

How much of this is true and how much is a projection of European-style nationalism, the recycling of language that the most militant nationalists want to hear, is difficult to say. Certainly, this mindset cannot be helpful to immigrants, especially Arab Moroccans, who in Soler Amigó's worldview are pitted against Imazighen Moroccans and are viewed in the same light as Castilian "invaders" in Catalonia.

Being rewarded and accepted by nationalist elites does not necessarily mean that El Hachmi has been acknowledged as part of the imagined nation on the street. As Chaib has pointed out, "Catalan could be a vehicle for *convivencia*" but only if ethnic Catalans made more of an effort to speak to immigrants in Catalan rather than Spanish.[83] Likewise, El Hachmi has complained that she is often addressed in Spanish rather than Catalan, since ethnic Catalans tend to switch instinctively to Spanish when addressing perceived outsiders. This happened to her, for example, when she approached the employee of a local shop: the man stopped speaking Catalan to another customer and switched into Spanish to speak to her. He was "annoyed . . . with rancour in his voice" that he had to switch.[84] Perhaps the employee, in good faith, was simply trying to be nice, and El Hachmi politely responded in Catalan. He still refused to speak to her in anything but Spanish. He could only see her as "a poor, ignorant immigrant girl, who didn't know a thing about reality in the country in which she lived", wrote Hachmi. Natives' refusal to speak to El Hachmi in Catalan made her "feel constantly . . . an outsider".[85]

She experienced a similar disappointment when she discovered that ethnic Catalans were only paying lip service to her when they said things like, "I like that, Najat, you've learned to speak Catalan . . . you're from here now, aren't you?" Native acceptance, she would learn over time, "was a heartbreaking mirage. All those people that accepted us didn't really accept us, not as we were. They only expressed their desire to homogenize us. They set their own minds at ease by thinking that they would make us, the foreigners, leave our pasts behind and convert us all to the Catalan cause".[86]

El Hachmi speculated that this refusal to speak Catalan to newcomers had something to do with the intimacy with which many Catalans treated their language. For many years, Catalan was reserved for the family, the household, a trusted inner circle to which visible minorities did not belong. In the decades after Franco, Catalans still hesitated to extend the use of their language into official, public spaces. This was also the explanation that nationalists gave. Nonetheless, evidence offered by Tree and other immigrants suggest that ethnic Catalans refuse to speak Catalan to visible minorities in an attempt to maintain their racial and socioeconomic privileges.[87]

Not all immigrants were troubled by natives' refusal to speak to them in Catalan. Indeed, most preferred to speak Spanish, even if it meant that the gulf between immigrants and natives remained wide as a result, as El Hachmi contended. The experience of growing up in the mostly Catalan-speaking Vic, in a period when immigrants were still relatively few – as opposed to growing up in Barcelona or its surrounding towns, where the social language is Spanish – explains why El Hachmi's experience is an exception rather than the rule. El Hachmi is an assimilated immigrant. She forwent attachments to Islam and internalized the values and concerns of her host society.

As John Crowley has suggested, immigrants like El Hachmi want to belong, which is a deeper sense of citizenship that goes beyond rights, duties, and official eligibility.[88] Of course, belonging is subjective; it is located somewhere between community identity, individual self-identification, and membership or acceptance in a wider group. El Hachmi identifies with Catalan culture, even supports Catalan independence from Spain, but natives do not as a rule accept her as Catalan, even if she is a citizen, speaks Catalan like a native, and was educated in Catalan schools. What comes across in *Jo també sóc catalana* is, more than anything else, a truncated sense of belonging.

Like El Hachmi, the writer and politician Chaib immigrated to Catalonia when he was a child. Yet unlike El Hachmi, Chaib experienced a twofold feeling of dislocation from the very beginning: "I found myself in a paradox: I was an immigrant twice over". He had first left for Spain with his family in 1966, when he was five years old, and a second time alone as a young man, after eight years in Morocco (Spanish authorities had unexpectedly prevented his family from returning to Spain after a family holiday). The move when he was a child, he said, was easy, but returning to Morocco when he was a teenager was difficult. By the time he could return to Catalonia, after marrying a Catalan woman, he had forgotten so much Catalan that the shock was severe once again. "The constant moving from one place to the next marked me, my personality, my way of being, the way I saw my two cultures – Muslim and Western – profoundly", he explains.[89]

Chaib, too, is a nationalist who has embraced Catalan culture. "Catalonia is everything . . . it is my land", he writes in his memoir.[90] Catalan "was for me the everyday language".[91] It was necessary to learn it "if you wanted to be equal", and Chaib attributed his success in politics to his language skills. In 2004, he became the first Muslim elected to the Catalan parliament. He ran for the PSC and championed a civic identity for Catalonia. The media compared him to José Montilla, a fellow PSC member and an Andalusian immigrant who became president of Catalonia. Knowing Catalan "helped me move smoothly between the different sectors of Catalan society . . . Catalan opened many doors".[92] Catalan, he claimed, should be "the vehicle of communication [in Catalonia], an open vehicle, problem free, not viewed as an imposition but a necessity".[93]

Unlike El Hachmi, Chaib is an observant Muslim, but one who believes religion should be a private matter. He lobbied the Catalan government to fund afterschool lessons in Arabic for immigrant children, yet he has not supported other Muslims' demand for Islamic instruction in schools. His understanding of religion is well suited to a secular context and has not been an impediment to his rise in Catalan politics, though he has kept a low profile during periods of religious controversy. (He quietly lobbied against Saudi efforts to build a grand mosque in Barcelona, stayed aloof of Muslims' attempts to find adequate prayer space in El Raval, and was even less visible during dozens of anti-mosque backlashes across Catalonia). Instead, Chaib used his CICC and Ibn Battuta Association to pressure slaughterhouses to produce halal meat and cemeteries to reserve space for Muslims. To Chaib, immigration in Catalonia is a two-way street. He compensates for his Moroccanness, he says, by being effusively Catalan, a strategy also adopted by El Hachmi.

Chaib reassured Catalans that immigration was not a danger. "Immigration does not have to be a problem as long as Catalonia maintains its language, culture, and identity", he wrote.[94] For Chaib, to be Spanish rather than Catalan in Catalonia was out of the question. He also worried that to natives, to be "Catalan and Muslim" was also, potentially, out of the question.[95] He reasoned: "it is possible to have split emotions and the symbolism of this is not negative . . . by combining two identities, Catalan culture is consolidated and strongly enriched by cultures from other places".[96] Chaib believed it worthwhile to "fight for people to be able to choose to be Catalan and Muslim at the same time. They are not incompatible", he insisted.[97]

Typically, nationalists saw no connection between how Catalan was repressed under Franco and how immigrants experienced language tensions in Catalonia. When natives told Muslim children that their Arabic or Amazigh names were strange, and that their cultures were inferior or languages dialectal, it was not unlike "when the Catalans [under Franco] were told to speak 'in Christian'", argued Chaib.[98] "Christian" harked back to the Spanish conquest, and Spanish nationalists used this as a synonym for Spanish and to ridicule Catalan, which they believed was a heathen language. Chaib felt that Moroccan immigrant culture in Catalonia required recognition in order to dignify those like himself who had multiple identifications and a complex background.[99]

The community activist Huma Jamshed was born in Karachi, Pakistan to a Punjabi Muslim family that settled in Pakistan after the partition of India in 1947. Jamshed migrated to Madrid along with her husband in 1997. She obtained a doctorate in chemistry from the Complutense University of Madrid, but has since found that, as an immigrant, her doctorate "has not been useful". She wanted to work as a scientist, but was turned down repeatedly by employers because of her appearance and name, she claimed.[100] Instead, she opened a successful travel agency in Barcelona with her husband. Jamshed became the president of the Cultural, Educational, and Social Association of Pakistani Women (ACESOP), an organization that advocates for the rights of Pakistani women in Barcelona. She also became the vice-president of the Barcelona Municipal Immigration Council.

Jamshed is a practicing Muslim but prays at home rather than in public venues. When she arrived in El Raval, no organization served the needs of Muslim women, so she set one up herself. She said that she did not feel Catalan, but that she loved Barcelona and considered it welcoming and diverse, despite overt nationalism and a lack of facilities for Muslims. The key to her success, she claimed, was her active participation in local politics:

"The city hall and Generalitat [Catalan government] find ways for immigrants to participate" she argued. "I have participated in so many activities that I think of Barcelona as my city and Catalonia as my country".[101]

Despite Jamshed's goodwill towards Barcelona, she resented the imposition of Catalan on newcomers. Requiring immigrants to learn Catalan when most natives refuse to speak it to them is hypocritical, she said: "No one speaks Catalan to immigrants . . . The authorities demand it because it is good for some jobs, but people don't use it with immigrants". Jamshed's experience looking for employment with a Spanish Ph.D., as well as the discrimination she experienced because of her ethnicity, made her doubt that "by speaking Catalan, immigrants will get those jobs in management where Catalan is needed". The question of language in Catalonia goes beyond knowledge, she said – it crosses over into identity, since here "they force you to *feel* Catalan". Jamshed feels more comfortable with Rachid Nini's understanding of identity: "I think the homeland is a portable concept. You find it inside of you".[102]

Jamshed's concern for the welfare of migrant women, interestingly enough, brought her closer to native society. "In Barcelona I have had to fight against my own compatriots, not against the government . . . [I fought] machismo and other things . . . In return, Catalans and Spaniards understand me perfectly well".[103] Since Jamshed has kept her religion private and has avoided strong identification with the nationalist cause, she has not received the same opportunities as El Hachmi or Chaib. However, as an educated, independent woman, a leader in her community, she stands out as an important figure in Catalan society.

The community activist Javed Ilyas was born in Pakistan to a minority Saraiki-speaking family. He studied political science in Pakistan before immigrating to Barcelona in 1991. He believed that it would be easier to obtain status, which he received in 1995, in Spain rather than in other European countries. Most Pakistanis in Barcelona are from the Punjab and Ilyas was not readily accepted by fellow Pakistanis; he had to remind them repeatedly that he, too, was from Pakistan. Ilyas spent many years working in the construction industry. Eventually he became the president of the Association of Pakistani Workers in Catalonia (APWC). APWC helped undocumented Pakistanis in Barcelona obtain status and was active during the church occupations of 2001. The association also mobilized to oppose the Iraq War in 2003. It hosts an annual celebration of Pakistan's Independence Day, and it has invited such renowned European-Pakistani intellectuals as Tariq Ali to speak in Barcelona. APWC, like other migrant organizations, serves as a bridge between immigrants and natives.

Like El Hachmi, Ilyas sympathized with the Catalan cause, since he himself is a member of a minority group. He said that he felt simultaneously Pakistani and Catalan, though he struggled to speak the language. He arrived when he was forty-one, too old, he believed, to learn Catalan, but he has encouraged his three children – all born in Pakistan but raised in Catalonia – to do so.[104] His sympathy for the Catalan cause has had a real impact on the organization he founded. APWC established a celebration for immigrant groups to honour Catalonia's national day and in the organization's offices, a large mosaic greets visitors with the motto: "In Catalonia, one speaks Catalan".[105]

Ilyas's Islam resembles Jamshed's. It is an internal, private expression of faith, rather than a public one. APWC is a secular institution. "At the mosque I pray, sure", Ilyas conceded, "but religion does not have a role to play in the political organization of the country. Where there is democracy, the country is secular".[106] Ilyas argued this point for years in El Raval's community magazine, *Massala* – published in Spanish, Catalan, Urdu, and Arabic – where he reflected on the Pakistani experience in Spain and debated different interpretations of morality, religion, and women's role in society.[107]

While El Hachmi, Chaib, and Ilyas accept Catalan nationalism as a viable strategy for integration, even if it means that they have to push away or ignore other identities, Jamshed and his compatriot Iqbal, spokesman for Path towards Peace, are more critical of pressures placed on them by Catalan society. Iqbal, more than the others, values his religion, and Jamshed identifies strongly with women and the universal cause of human rights. In a sense, the former individuals have gone the natives' route, while the latter have sought independent mechanisms of inclusion and preservation.

Osona: The Rise of the PxC and the Collapse of *Convivencia*

Located in central Catalonia, Osona is an immigrant-dense and largely Catalan-speaking county, with a population well in excess of 100,000 people. Its main industry is pork production and processing. Osona has been the theatre for the most innovative public policies to value and embrace cultural diversity, the most genuine of civil society's initiatives to build bridges between natives and Muslim immigrants, yet it has also witnessed an organized xenophobic and Islamophobic backlash to these efforts. In Osona, innovative policy planning and integrated community organizations, despite their best efforts, have failed to create long-lasting bridges among diverse communities largely because of natives' inability to work with Muslim immigrants as fellow citizens.

The NGO Jameiat Essalam was founded in Manlleu, Osona, in 1991. Manlleu was a major centre of textile and metal production until the 1980s, when it switched to food and chemical manufacturing. Drawn by the local industry, migrants have come to Manlleu since the 1940s. Initially, they came from the surrounding countryside as well as from southern Spain. Beginning in the 1980s, Moroccan immigrants also started to arrive. By 1981, nearly a quarter of the population was born outside of Spain. While in the last decade this share would drop to roughly one fifth, many native residents continue to believe that this region is a magnet for outside immigration.[108]

Migration to Osona came in waves, each of which led to overcrowding in the marginalized neighbourhoods of Vic and Manlleu. In the 1960s and seventies, overcrowding was resolved by a slew of construction projects; in the 1980s and nineties, no such projects were undertaken. The Barri de l'Erm ("barren ward") was built in the 1960s to house migrants. It quickly became known for the density of its population and its segregation from native Manlleu. "Since its very beginning, a series of invisible limits beyond which residents have often imagined 'another' city to lie have coloured l'Erm", wrote the historian Pere Casas and the architect Carles Crosas, a neighbourhood of poor Spanish-speaking people without roots in Manlleu.[109]

Two large housing projects capable of accommodating hundreds of migrant families dominate l'Erm. As was common during the Franco era, these projects were constructed with little regard for community needs, with large, plain, poorly designed buildings plunked down into growing industrial cities like Manlleu. They were perceived as "progressive" and "modern" because they were affordable and signalled growth and economic development. In 1970, 61 percent of apartment units in one project, Can Mateu, were inhabited by Andalusian families and 30 percent by ethnic Catalans. In another project, Can Gracia, 61 percent of units were inhabited by Andalusian families and 13 percent by ethnic Catalans. Most units were rentals and, because they were not considered permanent residences, they were not kept up. By 2002, with 62 percent of units in Can Mateu, and 79 percents of units in Can Gracia, now inhabited by Moroccan families – the highest density of Moroccans in the county – these buildings were in severe disrepair.[110]

While more and more Moroccans streamed into Manlleu, the city refused to increase its supply of affordable housing and focussed instead on high-end developments for wealthy natives.[111] Part of the explanation for this lay in the mindset of city hall: l'Erm was not so much a problem as a solution for city planners and politicians, whose ears were attuned to the needs of voting constituents, not immigrants. Many native residents preferred not to interact with immigrants at all, and pressured city hall to keep them away from the downtown and from new suburbs where they lived. On occasion, when the city responded to complaints of segregation in l'Erm by trying to build social housing in other parts of town, native neighbourhood associations were mobilized to prevent influxes of migrants into these districts.[112]

Founded in the Barri de l'Erm, Jameiat Essalam was one of the earliest immigrant organizations in Spain.[113] Its membership consisted of ethnic Catalans and Moroccans (mostly Imazighen), a reflection of its mandate to promote mutual understanding and peaceful coexistence between the two groups. The organization worked closely with the Miquel Martí i Pol Adult School (MMPAS), inspired by the writings and philosophy of the Brazilian educator Paulo Freire.[114] MMPAS was the first organization of its kind to offer language and settlement courses in Osona, beginning in 1989. Shortly thereafter, other schools, such as the Samba Kubally Adult School for African Migrants in the neighbouring province of Girona, began offering similar programming.

Adult schools were not perfect. They struggled to pay bills and were subject to frequent raids by police looking for undocumented migrants.[115] Natives also tended to dominate these institutions; it took a long time for these individuals to understand that they were not there to teach uncouth, uneducated migrants, but rather to work in partnership with them.

Until the existence of Jameiat Essalam, Moroccan immigrants "did not exist publicly or socially", claimed the NGO. Jameiat was their voice and face, and its impact on immigrants was felt immediately. Despite its success, the organization was plunged into a state of financial crisis in 1996. It no longer had the resources to deal with burgeoning legal, social, and cultural services. Its staff was comprised of unpaid volunteers and its supporters became demoralized and frustrated. At the same time, Madrid hardened immigration regulations. On the streets, immigrants met with a fresh round of chauvinism. "The 'moro' is rejected more than ever and racism is more vocal, more insolent . . . Jameiat Essalam has more detractors than before, even in government", wrote Soler Amigó.[116]

Inside the organization, too, conflicts erupted between newcomers and natives. Initially, migrant and native members of Jameiat Essalam were divided into two separate and unequal groups. While Moroccan migrants belonged to a wider assembly that discussed organizational strategy, natives belonged to an executive that acted on the assembly's behalf. When migrants complained that an assembly-based structure did not work for them, the executive dissolved itself, only to regroup in sub-committees and take charge of them. As much as natives claimed that they wanted immigrants to take on leadership roles, natives continued to act as spokespersons. In time, immigrants learned to be more assertive, asking for a more rigid hierarchy of decision-making, as in Morocco, rather than the loose, flattened structure that native activists preferred. Compromise appeared impossible and many immigrants left, claiming that the NGO was simply too "Catalan in its ways".[117]

Another source of tension was a lack of participation from Muslim women. While native activists insisted on involving more Muslim women, many Muslim men said that they did not want the sexes mixed. A group of l'Erm women who were independent from Jameiat Essalam organized Muslim women in a segregated fashion, but gender roles and women's rights continued to trigger further arguments among the group's members.[118]

Despite their good intentions, native activists did operate in a less than egalitarian way. Many were nationalists and held strict black-white views of "us" and "them", "immigrants" and "Catalans", "immigrant people and the people of the country [sic]". When the NGO teetered, in 1996, natives called it the immigrants' "coming of age", implying that immigrants had been naïve in their community activism.[119]

Jameiat Essalam could not resolve its internal differences, and it eventually decayed. In place of the volunteer services it offered, local government stepped in and provided some of the same services. New laws, including a regional Neighbourhoods Law [*Llei de barris*], were passed to deal with the historically uneven level of public investment in areas with high proportions of immigrants since the 1960s. These measures led to such renewal projects as "Let's Improve l'Erm, Let's Improve the City" in 2007. "Let's Improve l'Erm" mandated government to supply new services and to improve issues of social exclusion and segregation.[120] Though many of Jameiat Essalam's concerns were addressed, the government did not give the NGO a strong role to play, though it consulted its members whenever tensions flared in the community.[121]

The government's intervention achieved much more than Jameiat alone was capable of. A social centre, named after Federica Montseny, the anarchist Minister of Health during the Spanish Civil War, was built in the centre of l'Erm, beside Can Garcia. Rationalist in design, the centre included a cafeteria, concert hall, and meeting rooms for community groups. It aimed to draw residents from across Manlleu into l'Erm and thereby boost neighbourly goodwill. Natives loved the centre – they streamed in to use it – but immigrants did not. "Is [the centre] for Muslims, too?" asked a member of Jameiat Essalam, whose memory of the organization's exclusion from government planning was still strong years later.[122] While Manlleu's revitalization strategy for l'Erm lessened structural barriers and improved infrastructure, it also diminished immigrants' agency and meaningful involvement within NGOs like Jameiat Essalam.[123]

As Jameiat Essalam waned, the extreme-right Platform for Catalonia (PxC) waxed. The PxC was founded by the politician Josep Anglada i Rius in Vic in 2001. Vic, located in the Catalan interior, represents for many Catalans "Old Catalonia", an "authentic" Catalan place that is free from the increasing heterogeneity of Barcelona and other large cities. The PxC gained rapid success in Vic and spread from there to other surrounding towns. The party's mandate was to "better control immigration and improve security for citizens". It encourages segregation in housing, discourages religious pluralism, and refuses to accept Muslims as equals, in the same vein as the Austrian Freedom Party or the defunct Pim Fortuyn List in Holland.[124]

As with the leaders of some of these other hardline parties, Anglada has a checkered past. He belonged, for example, to two fascist groupuscules in the 1980s. Though he does not use the same Francoist language and tactics in the PxC, he does encourage a similar national pride and xenophobia. The PxC's constituency is native, Catholic, and middle class. The PxC does not prioritize the interests of Catalans over Spanish speakers. Through a consistently bilingual literature, it endorses the unity of the Spanish nation. It supersedes the entrenched dichotomy between Catalonia and Spain by stressing the "common enemy" – i.e., Muslim immigrants – and the need to unify under a regional identity compatible with a larger national one. PxC's slogan for the 2010 elections to the Catalan Parliament was "*primer, els de casa*" [those from home, first]. By simultaneously adopting an idiom that refers to "us", or "those from home", and avoiding identity battles – it is never specified whether this "us" refers to ethnic Catalans or ethnic Spanish – Anglada and his party have moved their discourse beyond the Catalan/Spanish dichotomy, adopting Islamophobia as a unifying feature.[125]

If in the 1990s, Osona was known for its innovative multicultural initiatives, media focus has since shifted to the PxC's provocative discourse. In the early 1990s, public and semi-public schools were forcibly integrated in Vic and Manlleu; when the number of immigrant students reached 15 percent, students were redistributed to other schools. The aim, said authorities, was to prevent educational segregation and stigmatization of immigrant children. If these numbers could be kept low, reasoned local authorities, native parents would not complain and white flight from local schools – occurring in Osona since the early 1990s – could be avoided.[126]

After fifteen years of the system known colloquially as the "Vic Model", the Catalan Ministry of Education flipped existing policy on its head and segregated new arrivals within the school system.[127] Rather than distribute migrants in mainstream integrated classrooms, as had previously been the case, the government restricted them to dedicated classrooms called *aules d'acollida* (welcome classrooms), issuing them a separate curriculum. The school system was responding to demands from native parents who could not afford to send their children to private schools that their children be sheltered from immigrants. The measure was enthusiastically backed by the PxC. "Each day, [The Catalan Ministry of] Education gets closer to the positions of the PxC", claimed Anglada. SOS Racismo denounced the new approach as discriminatory.[128]

In Osona and other parts of Catalonia where the PxC has gained ground, diversity has become a matter of containment, a separate reality relegated to another town, district, neighbourhood, or school. In Manlleu, the Barri de l'Erm is still that "other town", and in Vic a new peripheral, poor, and neglected area where many Muslims have relocated has been dubbed Vic II. Meanwhile, the "Real Vic" – affluent, central, and well-accommodated – continues to be populated by native Catalans who vote Catalan nationalist parties or PxC.[129]

Anglada believed that he would become Vic's mayor in the near future. In the November 2010 elections for the Catalan parliament, the PxC's first regional electoral appearance, the party received 75,321 votes, or 2.42 percent of the overall vote. In 2011, the party increased, by five, its presence in Catalan city halls.[130] Anglada has purposely adopted a strategy that is similar to that which allowed the French Front National to place second in the 2002 presidential elections: the securing of a local base as a platform for the transition to regional or even national politics.[131] So far, the mix of populist and Islamophobic discourse has not been as successful as in other European countries. Anglada's discourse, however, has made it more acceptable for mainstream parties to blame immigrants for crime and anti-social behaviour, and Muslims in particular for cleavages in social cohesion.[132] Had pioneer organizations such as Jameiat Essalam been able to consolidate and grow in Osona, they could have provided a bulwark against Anglada and his supporters. Their disappearance does not bode well for the social cohesion and political equality of Catalan Muslims.

Interculturalism

According to Jordi Pujol, "Catalonia need not have a complex. It has been more welcoming to immigrants than anywhere else in Spain".[133] Pujol was pointing to the fact that Catalonia was the first region in Spain to approve an Immigration Plan aimed at coordinating and streamlining how different levels of government dealt with migration. What he failed to mention was the fact that assimilationist demands were more strident in Catalonia; that hatred of Muslims and outsiders was prevalent in the region; and that Spain's first extreme-right xenophobic party, the PxC, had come from there. Catalan nationalists might be able to provide shining examples of visible minorities who had managed to integrate successfully, using them as proof of the welcoming nature of Catalan society, yet after three decades of immigration life for most migrants remained stark.

Essomba lamented the fact that nationalists simultaneously emphasized immigrants' need for acculturation while disregarding their own "*ombliguismo*" or naval gazing, a term coined by Juan Goytisolo. "I like cultural fusions, a mixture of styles", Essomba explained. "Building interculturalism is not about knowing the customs of others alone; it's about building new cultural products, creating new mixtures out of customs from different places".[134] He admitted that in Catalonia

> I guess I am part of an ethnocentric society which consumes essentially its own cultural products and rarely the products of other cultures . . . I have read few authors who are not from my [Catalan] culture. Indeed, I rarely open up to other worlds.[135]

While some Catalan politicians and academics advocate for "interculturalism", the rather sizeable nationalist contingent among them attempts to shield Catalan society from outside cultural influences. Use of the term interculturalism itself – rather than the despised multiculturalism of the Anglo-American world – reveals a lot about this mentality. Catalan scholars of migration believe that interculturalism suits the Catalan context better than multiculturalism because the latter creates ethnic enclaves and divides societies into cantons, they argue. In this misrepresented understanding of multiculturalism, governments are required to grant cultural communities distinct collective rights and the state, with a strong central government in the middle, is flattened into equal but rival subunits, in which "historical nationalities" become diluted. Multiculturalism is political pluralism, the

"Anglo-Saxon" way. Interculturalism, on the other hand, is the more familiar French model. It aims to develop a common civic culture based on the values of freedom, fraternity, and universal human rights, much in the mold of the European Enlightenment.[136]

In Catalonia and Quebec, as elsewhere in the world where the emphasis is on interculturalism, the "common civic culture" necessitates a degree of assimilation. In Catalonia, migrants are expected to learn Catalan and appreciate the received national culture before they can contribute to it. Only one sort of interculturalism, however, is welcomed; if cultural innovations bypass the Catalan language and culture, then they are actively opposed as contrary to the Catalan 'ethos'. Indeed, some Catalan nationalists still refuse to accept as Catalan certain intercultural artistic fusions, like the Catalan Rumba, a musical genre practiced by such world-renowned Catalan Roma musicians as the Gypsy Kings and Los Manolos.

Moreover, forty years after the arrival of the first Spanish-speaking internal migrants to Catalonia, fictional works in Spanish, written in and dealing with Catalonia, continue to struggle for acceptance in official Catalan culture, as illustrated by the Frankfurt Book Fair in 2007.[137] That year, Catalan served as the Fair's "cultural guest of honour" and the Ramon Llull Institute, a public institution financed by the government of Catalonia, was charged with "presenting the Catalan culture in all its diversity to the world". Of course, the Institute allowed only "writers in the Catalan language" to represent it.[138] While unknown writers from England, the Czech Republic, Benin, Valencia, the Balearic Islands, and elsewhere were invited to showcase their works in Catalan to the international publishing industry,[139] renowned residents of Catalonia who write in Spanish, including Juan Marsé, Eduardo Mendoza, Javier Cercas, Carlos Ruiz Zafón and others, were excluded.

As part of Catalan interculturalism, nationalists call on minorities to accept, value, and ultimately renew Catalan culture, while simultaneously encouraging natives to maintain a traditional outlook that perceives Catalan culture as under attack from Castilian and other "foreign" influences. Catalans "love to learn about their own traditions but struggle to learn about others", explains Mohamed Chair, a member of the Ibn Battuta Association. This is unfortunate because "if the environment in which the immigrant settles takes an interest in him, his level of integration and performance is higher".[140]

The reality of Catalan nationalism is premised not on equality but on privilege and the preservation of natives' culture and language, and no matter how much an immigrant assimilates through the gaining of citizenship, the learning of language and culture, or the embrace of nationalist values, he or she is still seen by many as an outsider, the *moro* or "*negret*" (little black). "At first people here pity you; later, when you are progressing, they distance themselves from you. You have to exert tremendous energy to convince them that you are equal or even better at some things than they are", claimed Chair.[141]

Pujol and Ferrussola's claim that Muslim demands for religious pluralism in Catalonia represented an imposition upon native society obeyed the ethnocentric logic of "Catalans first". "The historical continuity of a nation . . . [is something] immigrants can contribute to", but in the end is a matter for native society, not immigrants, argued Pujol.[142] In Catalonia, the nation is reserved for and by native Catalans, a view shared by the PxC, even though Pujol and many nationalists have distanced themselves from that party.

Recent debates over the burka and niqab in public venues in Catalonia have revealed the pervasiveness of PxC-like thinking. Over a span of two months, the four largest Catalan cities – Barcelona, Tarragona, Hospitalet, and Lleida – outlawed substantial religious headgear in public offices, schools, libraries, and hospitals. Except for the Catalan United Left Party (Iniciativa per Catalunya-Verds), all parties supported the ban. (Nationally, the PSOE opposed the ban, and because they were in power in Barcelona, debate was intense in that city). In smaller towns like Vendrell, where the PxC has been able to elect city councillors, local parties were more unanimous.[143] Unity among Catalan political parties, over other wide-ranging issues and policies, has rarely been as solid. This is one way in which Catalans are proving they are different: in the rest of Spain little political consensus exists for a similar ban, and the discourse of "Spaniards first" is only advocated by right-wing groupuscules.

Kymlicka reminds us that "symbolic gestures granting or denying recognition can have profound and continuing effects within a political culture in ways that directly affect the well being and self respect of citizens of minority cultures, as well as their enthusiasm to participate in the political life of the larger state".[144] If Catalan nationalists took seriously their own commitment to interculturalism, they would prioritize religious pluralism over cultural assimilation. Local authorities would then, perhaps, be able to support a purpose-built grand mosque in Barcelona that fused Romanesque with Moorish styles without undermining the pride they feel for Antoni Gaudi's Sagrada Familia.

5

Reclaiming Islamic Spain
From the Córdoba Mosque to the Festival of Moors and Christians, 1965–2010

In the post-Franco era, the discourse over collective memory and public commemoration has come to focus overwhelmingly on the legacy of the Spanish Civil War, in addition to the competing national narratives put forth by various peripheral nationalist movements, each with its own myth of origin and cannon of national heroes. Conflicts over the memory of the Civil War and Francoism have dominated Spanish society since the so-called "pact of silence", which had guided public discourse during the transition to democracy, was eroded in the late 1990s. The taboo that had once buried the multitude of crimes committed during the Civil War and under the Franco dictatorship – reinforced by the passing of the 1977 Amnesty Law, which forgave most political crimes committed under Francoism – was now literally exhumed, most famously in 2000, when journalist Emilio Silva recovered the unmarked grave in which the remains of his grandfather, killed in 1936, had rested for decades. Silva's example prompted thousands of other victims of political violence to ask the state for assistance in the recovery of their loved ones' remains from thousands of unmarked mass graves across the country. In the fervour that ensued – what Helen Graham has called "The Return of Republican Memory" – a plethora of NGOs went to work, transforming the way the Civil War and its victims are subsequently remembered. To be sure, the shockwaves set in motion by these debates have not yet subsided, and scandalous findings, such as the revelation of widespread child trafficking – the so-called *niños robados* (stolen children) – committed under Franco, continue to emerge.[1]

In an attempt to both reclaim and reinterpret Spain's Islamic past as an instrument of social inclusion and political legitimacy, Spanish Muslims, too, have helped to shine a light on aspects of Spanish history hitherto ignored. This process has involved both recovery and omission. On the one hand, Muslims have consciously distanced themselves from Franco's *Guardia Mora* (Moorish Guard) and the brutality of Muslim army units during the Spanish Civil War. On the other hand, they have helped to rewrite the myth of Al-Andalus by reclaiming the memory of Islamic Spain and advocating for the recognition of Córdoba's Mosque-Cathedral as an ecumenical site, a beacon of *convivencia* in the country. Moreover, Muslims in Spain have advanced their own legitimate claim to victimhood by recovering the memory of the *Moriscos*, Spanish Muslims forcibly converted to Christianity in the fifteenth century, only to feel the brunt of ethnic cleansing between 1609 and 1614. Finally, they have subverted the historical narrative underpinning the Festival of Moors and Christians as a celebration of the demise of Islamic Spain. These campaigns and controversies reflect the continuing struggle of Muslims in Spain for cultural rights and acceptance.

Islam in Spain's Memory Debates

Scholars agree that memory is a psychological process that takes place in the individual's mind regarding those events that the individual has directly experienced. Memory is, however, also socially framed and some scholars argue for the concept of "collective memory". According to the French sociologist Maurice Halbwachs, individual memories are structured by the groups to which the individual belongs – family, ethnicity, religion, and nation – and are socialized through symbolic or mnemonic cultural practices – rituals, commemorations, monuments, and museums – to create a social memory or a set of narratives concerning the past. These narratives are no longer based on the individual's experience, but on a shared understanding of a common past. Moreover, collective memory and the individual identities it sustains evolve in response to changing political and social circumstances that alter the framework through which individual experiences are understood and given meaning.[2]

The collective memory of Islam's status within European society is a highly contested one. This is natural to the extent that the Christian-Muslim relationship draws on centuries of contact, both martial and peaceful, mutually destructive and mutually beneficial. Spain, with its nearly eight-hundred year history of sustained contact between Muslims and Christians, remains at the centre of this debate. Historians have wrangled over the extent to which Islamic Spain, or Al-Andalus as it was called by contemporaries, embodied values of tolerance and pluralism and these arguments have spilled over into contemporary concerns about immigration. Was Islamic Spain a successful example of *convivencia* from which modern Europe could draw valuable lessons today, as scholars like María Rosa Menocal, a specialist in Iberian medieval literature, have argued? Menocal believes a genuine and exceptional spirit of tolerance prevailed in Islamic Spain. Proponents of this *convivencia* thesis emphasize the unique social structure that permitted certain *dhimmis*, or "protected people", to live in peace with their Muslim neighbours, even if it is true that Christians and Jews were accorded fewer rights than Muslims during the period.[3] Religious minorities were, Menocal argues, better off in Al-Andalus than Christian Europe. From a vast multi-religious exchange, multiculturalism flourished in Al-Andalus and eventually fuelled new scientific and philosophical developments during Europe's 'Dark Age'.[4]

Other historians downplay the tolerance of Al-Andalus by emphasizing the social and economic discrimination that allowed Muslim rulers to maintain power and to encourage the conversion of many Jews and *Mozarabs* (Christians living under Muslim rule) to Islam. According to these scholars, Jews, Muslims, and Christians clashed bitterly during this period, and little cultural and religious understanding occurred as a result. Bernard Lewis, an American historian of the Muslim world and an expert in the history of the Ottoman Empire, disagrees strongly that Jews and Muslims got along in Al-Andalus. He claims that *convivencia* is an ahistorical fiction.[5]

Thomas F. Glick, a historian of medieval Spain, believes that the problem with these opposing theses is that they pigeonhole the complex historical events they purport to understand. "Those historians who tend towards a conflictive view of the Spanish middle ages . . . play down the positive features of culture contact", he writes. At the same time, those who accept the idea of a peaceful *convivencia* equate acculturation – a cultural process – with assimilation – a social process – in the assumption that "the lessening of cultural distance must perforce result in the diminution of social distance". These scholars confuse "ethnic with social cleavages without realizing that these can be cross-cutting. From this fallacy follow a large number of generalizations concerning the cultural fusion of ethnic groups in Al-Andalus which political facts seem to contradict", argues Glick.[6]

Simon Doubleday explains that "claims of historical links between medieval and modern Spain are self-evidently politicized in public affairs" and they have been for most of the twentieth century.[7] The main academic proponents of the epic, primordial, *longue durée* thesis were the historians Marcelino Menéndez Pelayo (1856–1912) and Claudio Sánchez Albornoz (1893–1984). Menéndez Pelayo's definition of the Spanish nation was unequivocal: Spain's glory, according to Menéndez Pelayo, lay in its "Roman, apostolic, Catholic faith . . . the *substratum*, the essence, the greatest and most beautiful of the theologies, our philosophy, literature, and art".[8] Catholic Spain was the "evangelizer of half the world . . . the hammer on the heretics, light of Trent, sword of Rome, cradle of Saint Ignatius . . . [Catholicism] is our greatness and source of unity, we do not have another. The day we lose it, Spain will return to the cantonalism of the Arevaci and Vettones, of the Kings of the Taifas".[9] Menéndez Pelayo's firebrand Catholicism had gloriously beaten the Protestants and defended the Vatican. Its Inquisition had smothered heresy. If Spain were ever to lose sight of its divine mandate, it would be divided or conquered by an outside force. Likewise, Claudio Sánchez Albornoz saw the Muslim period as an embarrassing aberration in Spanish history. He argued that the Muslim conquest of 711 "ruptured Spain's unity and interrupted its natural process of evolution". According to Sánchez Albornoz, a continuous line that bypasses the Islamic period can be drawn between the Visigoth-Catholic heritage and modern Spain.[10]

Américo Castro challenged these ethnocentric notions of Spanish identity by turning his gaze once more on medieval Spain. Under the Franco regime, Castro argued that Spaniards only became a distinct ethnicity after the Islamic conquest of 711, when three distinct "casts" – Christians, Muslims, and Jews – emerged. He contended that coexistence shaped new cultural forms that defined the permanent essence of Spanish identity, a thesis that was almost unanimously attacked.[11] This historiographical tug-of-war did not disappear with the end of Francoism. For example, Juan Goytisolo and María Rosa Menocal have in recent years defended – albeit in a modified way – Castro's interpretation, while César Vidal, Serafín Fanjul, Rosa María Rodríguez Magda, and others have refortified the Menéndez Pelayo–Sánchez Albornoz thesis.[12]

The politicized history of Islamic Spain has not left Muslims in the country untouched. As a strategy to legitimize Islam and religious pluralism in the country, Spanish converts to Islam have vigorously reinterpreted Spanish history. The active WebIslam Internet portal, Córdoba's Islamic Council, and many other Spanish Islamic organizations have attempted to reclaim the legacy of medieval Al-Andalus, when Jews, Muslims, and Christians under Muslim rule allegedly lived in harmony. As Abdennur Coca put it in the Islamic magazine *Verde Islam*, "We, the Islamic citizens of Spain, do not vindicate Al-Andalus: we are Al-Andalus. As Spaniards, we vindicate the Spanishness of our project".[13] Native converts championed Américo Castro's vision of Spanish society, one that embraces and celebrates its three founding peoples – Jews, Muslims, and Christians. They have used *arraigo* to argue their case, claiming that their roots went back to Spain's Islamic past, which was a justification and defence for today's religious pluralism.

Writers like Coca were careful to select only those aspects of the past they wished to remember. Similarly, local and regional governments were careful to select the history that was convenient for them, lavishly celebrating the Christian conquest of Islamic Spain. In 2008, for example, the former territories of the Crown of Aragon commemorated the 800th anniversary of the birth of King James I, a conqueror of Muslims. The regional government of the Balearic Islands declared 2008 Year of James I and the governments of Aragon, Catalonia, and the Balearic Islands paid homage to James I at his place of burial, the Monastery of Poblet.[14] The regional government of Valencia organized and funded exhibitions and, together with Valencia city hall, put on an expensive parade to celebrate the 770th anniversary of the city's conquest by James I. The parade was an extravagant re-enactment by hundreds of actors of a 1428 parade organized by King Alfonso the Magnanimous to honour the 200th anniversary of James I's conquest.[15]

In the very same year, the Islamic Cultural Centre of Valencia (ICCV) celebrated the 1,000th anniversary of the creation of the Taifa Kingdom of Valencia and criticized city officials for honouring Valencia's Christian conquest exclusively. The city's "vision was skewed and partisan", claimed Amparo Sánchez Rosell, the group's president. It endorsed the Christian interpretation of history, glossing over the fact that the Taifa's roots were older and deeper than the Christian kingdom's.[16] The ICCV issued a manifesto entitled "Valencia was not born in 1238" in which it claimed that the Valencian people "are much older [than the Christian conquest], and in the formation of their personality they benefited greatly from different cultures, including significantly the Islamic culture". The ICCV offered to counterbalance the narrative of James I with an "epic of King Mubarrak", who declared Valencia independent from the Caliphate of Córdoba in 1009.[17]

While Valencian authorities celebrated James I, they completely overlooked the 400th anniversary of the ethnic cleansing of the *Moriscos* from Valencia a year later. The ICCV recovered this memory and countered official silence with an international symposium: "Islam Close to Home: The Valencian Moriscos".[18] The notion that the *Moriscos* were Valencians ("*moriscos valencians*") was novel.[19] The University of Valencia, as well as regional historical associations, did organize exhibitions of artefacts and historical symposiums, but in all instances chose wording that did not upset native sensitivities. The more neutral "expulsion" was used rather than "ethnic cleansing" or "forced transfer".[20] At a national level, little was done to mark the anniversary and commemorate the ethnic cleansing of *Moriscos*. In Madrid, the National Library of Spain organized an exhibition entitled "Remembering the Moriscos: The Writings and Stories of a Cultural Diaspora". While the term 'diaspora' suggested that the *Moriscos* were culturally Spanish, the exhibit would not go so far as to call them a 'Spanish diaspora' or 'Spanish *Moriscos*'. Sections of the exhibition were titled, for instance, "An Islam in Spanish", rather than 'A Spanish Islam'.[21]

Few of these academic activities actually included *Moriscos* or their North African descendants, though a small Valencian television crew did travel to Tunisia to trace the descendants of Valencian *Moriscos* and interview *Morisco* scholars. And the ICCV did go against the grain, once again, by making an effort to invite African academics to its symposium.[22]

One characteristic of a mature democracy is the issuing of government apologies for wrongs done in the past, either to other peoples or to its own minorities. The goal of these expressions of remorse for harm done to a given group is twofold: to accept collective responsibility for the commission of a shameful act and to strengthen national unity for the future. For example, the Japanese government apologized in 1993 and then again in 2007 for its country's use of so-called "comfort women" during World War II, and the Canadian government apologized in 2008 for the abuse of aboriginal children in residential schools.[23] While official apologies may at times consist merely of empty phrases, devoid of any real compensation or promise of further investigation, they have nevertheless been consistently welcomed by victimized populations or their descendants.

The government of Spain, however, has been reluctant to issue similar public apologies, even when the UN Human Rights Committee requested it to do so in the case of Rosalind Williams, a victim of racial profiling by Spanish police in the 1990s (discussed briefly in Chapter 2).[24] This is perhaps yet another legacy of the Spanish Civil War – the divisive memories it still triggers and the many unuttered apologies.[25] An official apology for the expulsion of Spanish Jews in 1492, the forced conversions of Muslims after the fall of Granada, and the ethnic cleansing of *Moriscos* between 1609 and 1614 would have gone a long way to signal to Muslim immigrants and converts that Spain welcomes them and that Spanish democracy is secure enough to recognize past wrongs and embrace a pluralistic future. A public apology would also have signaled to ethnic Spaniards that casual derogatory behavior towards religious and ethnic minorities is no longer acceptable, and that a pluralistic democracy must demand respect and dignity for all of its members.

To this end, migrant writers have reflected on the cultural dynamics of ethnic exclusion and have been at the forefront of denouncing the use of the word *Moro* ("Moor") to broadly refer to Arab and Muslim populations. The word *Moro* combines old imagery and new; it juxtaposes the medieval, belligerent, lascivious Moor, as well as Franco's reviled mercenary soldiers during the Spanish Civil War, with the poor, uneducated and undocumented Muslim immigrants of today.[26] The Algerian migrant Lyes Belkacemi explains that *Moro* is an irremediably belittling term and unacceptable in any context (even though in doing so he succumbs to the same stereotyping that he denounces): "Those are Europeans for you; they think we are all the same: Moors and that's it".[27] The efforts of migrants to overcome reductive labels have gone generally unacknowledged by ethnic Spaniards. As Mohamed Chaib explains,

> Simply to speak of "Moors" is scandalous. I have wound up red in the face many times because someone blabs away to me about the Moors. Many times it was friends. In every instance a justification of the word was offered, insisting it wasn't anything serious and that here in Catalonia it is a normal way of speaking and unimportant. But there is a racist and pejorative undertone in using this and similar words.[28]

Symbolic recognition of the worth, status, or existence of a group within a larger community is one of the cultural rights identified by Jacob Levy for which minorities within liberal democracies have long struggled.[29] This type of recognition may be as important to a group as many other, more substantive political rights. Perhaps the politicization of Islamic Spain is a strategy of inclusion that may backfire for Spanish Muslims, but if historical narratives will continue to be used to justify present realities, Spanish Muslims might as well enter the field and play with all the resources they can muster.

The Córdoba Mosque-Cathedral and the limits of *Convivencia*

In an attempt to reclaim their country's Islamic past and popularize important non-Christian historical figures, Muslims in Spain have struggled to overturn the self-referential nature of Spanish scholarship. In some regions of Spain, they have not been alone in these efforts. In Andalusia, for example, the government has endeavoured to reclaim the region's Islamic heritage as a source of regional pride as well as tourist revenue.[30] In 1993, the government there established the Andalusian Legacy Foundation to promote its Islamic past. The foundation organized the exhibitions "Ibn Khaldun, Between Al-Andalus and Egypt" and "Ibn Khaldun, Between Algeria and Al-Andalus", which attracted hundreds of thousands of visitors. The exhibitions were also brought to Egypt and Algeria, where the Spanish king and queen presided over their openings. The Ministry of Foreign Affairs used them to promote business and tourism from Muslim-majority countries to Spain.[31]

In 1999, Alfredo Sánchez Monteseirín, the PSOE mayor of Seville, explained at a conference on "Islam across Continents", organized by the Islamic Council, that

> We are not only remembering a splendid past, but a past which will be projected into the future. We are working to make Seville a node for the Orient and Occident, for Arab countries, Latin America, and Europe. We want Seville to be a nexus of union based on messages of peace and peaceful coexistence of citizens.[32]

Córdoba, too, endeavoured to repatriate a fuller picture of its past by celebrating such figures as Maimonides (Moses ben-Maimon), the medieval Jewish philosopher, and Averroes (Ibn Rushd), the Muslim polymath. Throughout his time in office (1979–1986), Julio Anguita, the Communist mayor of the city, worked with local converts to reclaim the legacy of Al-Andalus by promoting, for instance, the Roger Garaudy Foundation and Living Museum of Al-Andalus, located in the Islamic-era Calahorra Tower. In 1992, the city also offered the *Morabito*, a mosque built for Franco's Muslim troops during the Civil War, to the city's Muslim community. Currently, the *Morabito* serves as a place of worship and as a cemetery. In 2002, the Roger Garaudy Foundation was allowed to establish a library in the Palace of the Bailio, linked to the family of Gonzalo Fernández de Córdoba, "Great Captain" of the 1492 conquest of Granada. Spanish nationalists were outraged by the gesture.[33]

Rafael Merino, Córdoba's conservative mayor between 1995 and 1999, continued his predecessors's work. "Córdoba needs to recuperate its traditions of openness, sophistication, and tolerance", argued Merino. Together with the Islamic Council, he supported the Kurtuba Centre for Islamic Research and Cooperation.[34] In Merino's strategic plan to attract tourists and turn Córdoba into a gathering point for East and West, the involvement of local Muslims figured prominently. Collaboration was reciprocal and local authorities sanctioned the Halal Institute upon the request of local Muslims.[35]

The local government's newfound focus on Al-Andalus was, however, not universally endorsed. One lightening rod was the Cathedral-Mosque of Córdoba and the Catholic Church's resistance to embrace Islamic Spain. While local Muslims wished to transform the site of worship into an ecumenical space where Christians and Muslims could pray side by side, Catholic authorities dismissed the idea as insulting. The cathedral's history was long and venerated. It was originally a small temple of Christian Visigoth origin. Under Umayyad reign in Spain (711–1031 CE), it was expanded and made into a mosque, which it would remain for eight centuries. During the Christian conquest of Al-Andalus, Christians captured the mosque and consecrated it as a Catholic church. In the sixteenth century, Charles V destroyed and rebuilt portions of the building; he turned it into a large cathedral, but left much of its original Muslim character untouched (for example, he saved the famous "forest of columns" and the *mihrab,* a niche in the wall that indicates the direction of Mecca).

The proposition that Christians and Muslims could share the cathedral was both historical and practical. The remaining mosque section of the cathedral was separate from the Christian area and Muslims felt that their prayers there were compatible with the Christian services. Yet Catholics countered by saying that it was impossible to share the space, for under Catholic canon law non-Catholic rites were forbidden in Catholic cathedrals, except in extraordinary circumstances, which were not infrequent. One such event took place in 1974, a year before Franco's death, when Saddam Hussein, then vice-president of the Iraqi Revolutionary Command Council, was permitted to pray there. Also in 1974, Muslims were permitted to worship in the Córdoba mosque-cathedral alongside Christians during a three day conference on Christian-Muslim relations. In 1979, church authorities allowed local Muslims to celebrate Eid al-Adha in the mosque-cathedral. Muslim collective prayers also occurred there in 1982, 1985, and 1991. As late as 1995, the Bishop of Córdoba permitted Saudi Prince Abdul-Azzis al Saud and his entourage to pray in the cathedral.[36]

In 2004, at a meeting of the Pontifical Council for Inter-Religious Dialogue, Mansur Escudero, the most widely recognized leader of Spanish converts, called for the Córdoba Cathedral to be turned into "a multi-confessional space of worship, where the one and only God could be worshipped in all its forms". Escudero reassured his audience that Muslims "do not want ownership, exclusivity, or to change the name of the Córdoba Cathedral, we only want to be welcomed in to worship God". In Escudero's address to the Pope, he described the Cathedral of Córdoba as "a symbol of universality that the city wishes to reclaim as a positive identifying mark, as a symbol of free expression and pluralism, open to all forms of thought and worship, a place of meeting and peace".[37]

In a 2004 speech to the United Nations General Assembly, Prime Minister Rodríguez Zapatero proposed a Spanish-Turkish initiative called the Alliance of Civilizations, a sort of response to Samuel Huntington's controversial "Clash of Civilizations" thesis. Six months after the terrorist attacks on the Madrid commuter train system that killed 191 people,

Rodríguez Zapatero's initiative was aimed at combating terrorism non-militarily by deepening the political and cultural ties between the West and the Arab-Muslim world.[38] He emphasized the "need to build bridges of understanding between the different cultures of our planet", and advocated a "constructive dialogue between civilizations, peoples, cultures, and religions". The Alliance, he claimed, would help to overcome "misunderstandings between the Western and the Islamic worlds".[39]

In 2006, at a meeting between Zapatero and Spain's Muslim leaders aimed at preventing Muslim outrage over the publication of cartoons depicting Prophet Mohammed by Danish newspapers, Escudero reiterated his demand for Muslim prayer rights in the Córdoba Cathedral. Escudero argued that "the Cathedral-Mosque of Córdoba, and also the Hagia Sophia in Istanbul, could be converted into ecumenical temples in which Christians, Muslims, and believers of other religions could pray together to the same God and tighten spiritual and emotional bonds". Sharing the cathedral would be "a great opportunity to develop the Alliance of Civilizations . . . to promote inter-religious dialogue". Córdoban Socialists, the Socialist trade union UGT, and grassroots Catholic groups supported Escudero, but Zapatero ignored his plea, pointing out that the Cathedral was owned by the Catholic Church and it was up to the Church to decide how to use it.[40]

Similarly, the president of the Pontifical Council, Archbishop Michael Fitzgerald, argued that because the Cathedral of Córdoba "belongs to a specific community", ecumenical use of it was "problematic". "Peaceful coexistence between Christians and Muslims is difficult when one attempts to correct history or seek revenge. We must accept history and move forward", explained Fitzgerald. The Archbishop of Seville also rejected the proposal, claiming that "Many [Catholic] Córdobans would feel offended in their religious feelings". Sharing the space would "create problems for us, for them, and for the city . . . inter-religious dialogue does not mean sharing spaces, except in exceptional cases".[41]

In April 2010, the Cathedral of Córdoba drew international attention as a group of more than 100 Austrian Muslims toured its grounds and prayed there. When guards attempted to prevent them, an altercation broke out: two Muslims were arrested and two guards were injured. The Austrian Muslim Youth Association apologized for the incident, arguing that its members had believed they were in a mosque and were thus allowed to pray; the Córdoba Office of the Bishop disagreed, claiming that Austrian Muslims had, "in a pre-planned manner . . . provoked the episode of violence". Shortly thereafter, Bishop Demetrio Fernández argued in the national newspaper *ABC* that the term "Mosque of Córdoba" should be abandoned in favour of "Cathedral of Córdoba". "It is inappropriate", wrote the bishop, "to call the temple a mosque. It has not been a mosque for eight centuries and to call it a mosque now confuses visitors. Córdobans understand it as a cathedral". The United Nations Educational, Scientific and Cultural Organization (UNESCO) had already changed the official name of the monument from Mosque of Córdoba to Historic Centre of Córdoba in 1994, but the Córdoba city hall has been reluctant to part altogether with the famous name "Mosque of Córdoba".[42]

Following Escudero's death, in October 2010, no other articulate spokesperson has emerged to resume the fight over shared use of the Cathedral of Córdoba. Though strongly organized since the 1970s, the influence of converts over local politicians has diminished and Muslim immigrant leaders have chosen not to champion this symbolic fight. The Catholic Church has refused to participate in any revival of Al-Andalus or mythic *convivencia*, hindering Córdoba's efforts to draw tourists and to turn the city into a meaningful "Alliance of Civilizations". One reason is certainly a legitimate interest in protecting Catholic spaces of prayer. Yet an important factor in the Church's reluctance to cede exclusive control of the Córdoba Mosque-Cathedral has been the lucrative revenues generated by tourism to the site. In 2003, the Church earned an alleged 6 million euros from the sale of entrance tickets alone.[43] Moreover, it is unclear what, if anything, the Catholic Church would gain from sharing this symbolic temple with Spanish Muslims at the price of irritating its more fundamentalist members. While in other European countries, Christian organizations have collaborated with Muslim immigrants in securing sites of prayer and lobbying for religious rights, such collaboration has thus far been very scant amongst Spanish Catholics.[44]

The Festival of Moors and Christians

Every year for three to five days, hundreds of villages in Valencia, Catalonia, Andalusia, and Castile-La Mancha celebrate the Festival of Moors and Christians. Donning the medieval garb of Moors and Christians, ethnic Spaniards re-enact battles from the "Reconquest" of the medieval period. Divided into separate companies, each with its own dress code and name, both sides vie for control of a wooden castle. As per the script, the Christians always defeat the Moors, forcing them to convert to Christianity.

The Festival of Moors of Christians is for many towns the most important event of the year. Participants show off costumes that are often twelve months in the making. They hire marching bands to accompany them in the streets. Fireworks are set off to mark the opening and closing of festivities. Flags and other decorations are ubiquitous. The Festival not only marks the most important event in a town's calendar, but also structures the entire social life of the community. People gather at each company's headquarters for weekly suppers or dances and also use them to celebrate the baptism of their children or their wedding anniversaries. Towns pulsate at the rhythm of the Festival's celebrations throughout the year.

The spirit of the Festival is both religious and secular. Towns pay homage to local patron saints and hold processions and masses. Participants march through their towns in extravagant parades (*entradas*) and perform pieces of street theatre, such as calls to arms, in which are fired mock harquebuses filled with gunpowder. While the *entradas* and other parades throughout the Festival are carnivalesque and playful in nature, the theatre tends to be provocative, with verbal abuse hurled from side to side and humiliation a common theme. In most of the Festival's installments, it is generally not enough that Christian armies are victorious; Islam itself must be denigrated as well. In Alcoi, for example, participants are reminded that Islam is the "dirty rite of Muhammad" and a "wicked sect" based on "the perfidious Qur'an". Local Christians, therefore, must not allow the "Qur'an and sect of the Moor to triumph".[45] In Bocairent, the Moors are "the dogs of the Qur'an" and in Fontanars dels Alforins, an angel tells a Moorish captain that "the true religion, dear Moor, is Christianity. Islam is broken, vile, and vulgar superstition". [46]

Such degrading language is also expressed in the choice of company names, such as *pollosos*, the louse-ridden, [47] cannibals, or *penjamoros* ["Moor-Lynchers"]. Company names convey the message that Moors and Islam are objects of ridicule. Some names poke fun at Islam for not allowing Muslims to drink alcohol, for example *Alí Ben Bufat* (Ali is Very Drunk), *Muladins d'Alí Bufat* (Mullahs of the Drunkard Ali), *Alí Ben Begut* (Ali is Really Stoned), or *Mohamed-te-sed* (Muhammad Needs a Drink).[48]

Perhaps the most abhorrent feature of the Festival is the so-called "La Mahoma" ritual, which even some diehard supporters have criticized.[49] "Mahoma", in both Spanish and Catalan, is the traditional Catalan and Spanish derogatory name for Prophet Muhammad; La Mahoma is a four-metre tall, cartoon-like effigy of a man with a beard dressed in classical Moorish garb and wearing a large turban.

While the Christians fight for a specific patron saint or the Virgin Mary, parading their likeness around town, the Moors battle for La Mahoma and, temporarily victorious, place it atop the wooden castle. Defenders of this ritual argue that the effigy does not represent Prophet Muhammad. Yet in the town of Callosa d'en Sarrià, for example, the Moorish ambassador typically prays to La Mahoma before battle.[50] Once the Christians take control of the castle, they vandalize the effigy. In Beneixama, they used to blow up La Mahoma's head with firecrackers. In Bocairent, they threw the effigy from the castle, set it on fire, and buried it. In Alcoi, explained Joan Amades,

> Once the Christians retook the castle, they climbed up the tallest tower of town, threw away the Moors' flag, and lit a long wick attached to La Mahoma. La Mahoma caught fire immediately and since its head was full of fireworks, it exploded and the sound echoed a long distance. In the town square, people cheered joyously.[51]

Debate abounds as to why the effigy is referred to in the feminine as "*La Mahoma*", rather than the masculine "*El Mahoma*" or simply Mahoma. Max Harris claims that the feminine article places it on a parallel with La Virgen, the female virgin that is honoured in many towns, but this does not explain why the masculine article is not used for villages with male patron saints, such as the ubiquitous Saint George. Some have suggested that the feminine article comes from a figure in the Corpus Christi with a similar name, La Moma, but this is unconvincing since the two figures otherwise have nothing else in common. A more convincing explanation links the article to gender relations. By feminizing a figure that represents Muhammad, the Moors are emasculated and pacified. While the utmost veneration is paid to town virgins and patron saints, La Mahoma is made to look silly, a cartoon, and an object of laughter. The use of the feminine article when referring to the Prophet Muhammad is even more irreverent when considered in a Catholic context in which God and the prophets are exclusively male.[52]

According to Albert Alcaraz, La Mahoma is "singular and interesting"; no harm is done since La Mahoma is an "allegorical figure". Attendants at a national symposium on the Festival in 1974, however, realized that the effigy was rife with negative symbolism and advised "towns which . . . maintain the effigy . . . to meet and consider the difficulties such a symbol could entail for the outside world." Festival participants agreed to be cautious, but chose not to ban the ritual outright. The discussion at the symposium centred not on the inappropriate nature of the ritual, but rather on its potential to generate negative press.[53]

The climax of the Festival comes with a mass conversion. In the Ritual of Dispossession and Conversion, the Moorish captain accepts his conversion and, now a Christian, recovers his dignity. He denounces Islam in a long monologue and is publicly baptized. He then removes his turban and royal robe and disarms.[54] At the 1974 symposium, Salvador Vañó Silvestre reasoned that the "the conquest should not be imposed on the vanquished, rather the vanquished, stirred by the heavens, should be moved to convert".[55] Once the enemy has become Christian, conquerors' anxieties about the race, culture, religion, and allegiance of defeated Moors are placated.

The Festival is remarkable for its adherence to a traditional, self-aggrandizing nationalist narrative. Its participants insist on using the contentious term *reconquista* (or reconquest), rather than the more neutral *conquista* (or conquest). Reconquest, of course, implies that the Spanish Peninsula was stolen and then restored to its rightful (Christian) owners. The most didactic moments of the Festival are provided by a meeting of the opposing sides in a theatre piece known as "the Embassies", which takes place in front of the ceremonial wooden castle. The diplomats from each side recite well-known scripts – the oldest of which date back to the mid-nineteenth century – written by local, mostly anonymous, poets and writers.[56]

Even though a standard narrative based on the victory of Christians over the Moors is common to all manifestations of the Festival, the battle plays out in a slightly different way depending on the location. In Andalusia, for example, the Moors typically hold a sacred Christian relic – usually a town virgin – and Christians battle to recover it. In Valencia, towns re-enact the original conquest, or even a later Christian victory over Muslim resistance. In Alcoi, the location of the longest-running Festival and thus an example for many other villages, participants re-enact the suppression of a rebellion by the Muslim leader Al-Azraq in 1276.[57]

In all cases, however, it is the Christians that are depicted as virtuous, "native" saviours, while Muslims are evil, "foreign" invaders. The Christians are descendants of the Roman Iberians who escaped the Islamic invasion of the eighth century and regrouped in northern Spain. From this stronghold, they pushed the Moors southward for seven centuries until they managed to reclaim the entire Iberian Peninsula in 1492. In this narrative, "true Spain" is first and foremost Iberian, then Roman, then Visigoth, and finally Christian. The chain is then broken for centuries by barbarian hoards of Muslim invaders, only to be restored in 1492 when Christian freedom fighters, after centuries of reconquest, finally completed the liberation of the entire peninsula.

The Festival of Moors and Christians in many ways reproduces the Menéndez Pelayo–Sánchez Albornoz thesis. In Alcoi, the Moors are portrayed as "occupiers", the Christians represent the true nation, and the Prophet Muhammad is "the terror of all Spain". The Moorish guard calls out from the wooden castle, "Who's there?" to which the Christian ambassador answers, "Spain". The ambassador warns the Moors that the Christians will crush them and that the Visigoth victory at Covadonga in 722, led by the mythic instigator of the reconquest, Pelayo of Asturias, will repeat itself; the heroic El Cid will have his day again; and Kings García Iñigo and James I of Aragon will triumph.[58] In Bocairent, the ambassador explains, "Spain had a traitor, and if indeed Count Julián committed an outrageous offence, remember that in this walled town you will find a Guzmán again". Julián, Count of Ceuta, a legendary Visigoth governor in North Africa who helped the Umayyads conquer Spain, is pitted against Alonso "The Good" Pérez de Guzmán, Grandee of Spain and commander-in-chief of the Spanish navy, who successfully held the town of Tarifa against the Muslim Marinids in 1294. In La Vila Joiosa, the ambassador proclaims, "We are Spaniards, the noble blood of the sons of Pelayo, of the sons of Las Navas runs through our veins". The battle known alternatively as las Navas de Tolosa, or the Battle of Al-Uqab, as it was known to Spanish Muslims, opened Andalusia up to the armies of Castile in 1216. The battle was, in the eyes of Christian historians anyway, the definitive military blow to the Muslims.[59]

Interpreting the Festival of Moors and Christians

In Valencia, the region where its influence is most widespread, the Festival of Moors and Christians has changed significantly in the approximately 350 years since its inception. The earliest records of the Festival date back to 1668. In 1672, Enric Carbonell wrote that "a company of Christian Moors and Christian Catholics" had paraded through Alcoi "to honour and worship its Patron Saint, Saint George".[60] There were earlier records of dances and plays, in which townsfolk dressed up as Moors and Christians and held mock battles, generally to celebrate royal births, marriages, and visits, but Carbonell's description is the first to link Moors and Christians to a celebration of a patron saint, and hence a regular, yearly event.[61] Historians agree that the Festival is an amalgam of three traditional celebratory forms: military parading, theatre for royal celebrations, and festivals that pay tribute to patron saints and virgins. The street theatre of the Festival has also been connected to popular comedies concerning Moors and Christians from the seventeenth century.[62]

As for its chronology, the Festival seems to have arisen in the seventeenth century, only to disappear with the War of Spanish Succession (1701–1714). It re-emerged in 1740 in several villages within the economic and political orbit of the Valencian industrial city of Alcoi. Yet it was not until the 1860s, when Spanish colonialism surged in North Africa, that the Festival was codified and expanded. Under Franco, it was promoted as a means to reinforce Spanish Catholicism and national unity. After Franco's death, in November 1975, Spain's remaining colonies in North Africa were lost and Catholic observance plummeted, yet the Festival remained (it even underwent a colossal expansion in the 1960s and seventies, coinciding with the economic and tourist boom of that period).

In trying to explain the origins of the Festival of Moors and Christians, the majority of scholars have focused on cultural or ritual precedents. They have largely failed, however, to explore the connections between the Festival and the larger issue of collective memory. For example, the 1576 *Morisco* rebellion in the Alpujarras Mountains, which eventually led to the expulsion of the *Moriscos* from Spain between 1609 and 1614, is central to understanding the genesis of the Festival because it was in those regions with the largest numbers of *Moriscos* – and thus a history of forced baptism and fierce Muslim resistance – that the Festival first emerged. In Elx, the Festival incorporates a ritual called the "Baptism of the Moor", which purports to recreate the forced mass baptism of "*mudéjares*" (unconverted Muslims) during the 1519–1523 anti-feudal Revolt of the Brotherhoods.[63] In Alcoi, a company of *Moros viejos* (old or former Moors) refers directly to the forced conversion of Muslims in its imagery and symbolism. In Bocairent, the uniform of a Christian company called *Antigua española* (Old Spanish) is the same uniform Philip III's armed guards used when they physically removed the *Moriscos* in 1609. In the same town a company of *Moros viejos* relates to the 1611 mass baptism of Morisco toddlers, who Philip III forbade from leaving Spain with their parents and who were forcibly "adopted" by Christian families. This same company performs a ritual called the "Dispossession and Conversion of the Moor" before a statue of the town's patron saint.[64]

Festival supporters, as well as many Spanish scholars, downplay these references to Catholic domination and military conquest. In his 1966 study

Las danzas de Moros y Cristianos, Joan Amades, a renowned Spanish ethnologist and folklorist, wrote that the Festival "has at its core the notion of a fight, [but] it has nothing to do with religious struggle between Christianity and Mohammedism [sic]". Rather, argued Amades, the Festival "has its roots in agrarian ritual . . . One could argue that the great popularity of the Festival of Moors and Christians in the region of Valencia is not due to a lasting memory of the long presence of Muslims in the old kingdom, [but] rather that it pays tribute to the great importance and development of agriculture since time immemorial".[65] Yet the Festival appeared in the wake of a campaign of ethnic cleansing, a period when *Moriscos* were incapable of speaking up for themselves and when Christians, victors in the conflict between these two groups, were safe to interpret the past as they saw fit.

A 1974 national symposium on the Festival of Moors and Christians, which brought together representatives from dozens of participating villages, concluded that the Festival's *raison d'être* was indeed "to exalt religious and traditional values that recall the epic of the *Reconquista*".[66] Bocairent's archivist said in the meeting's opening address that the Festival "aims to dramatize the fight between Good and Bad, between truth and heresy".[67] The director of the National Library in Madrid perhaps put it best: "distilled in its purest form, the fight between Christian and Moor is fundamentally about the eternal struggle between Good and Evil".[68]

Despite some claims to the contrary, this interpretation of the Festival's meaning has been remarkably consistent. Thirty years after the first symposium, Albert Alcaraz Santonja, winner of the Bernat Capó Popular Culture Award in 2005 for his analysis of the Festival, claimed that "at its base, [the Festival of Moors and Christians] offers us a symbolic representation of the Muslim as it is found in ideological and religious arguments (the Moor as invader and infidel, who we must fight) . . . ". While Alcaraz claimed that "the current representation of the Muslim has little to do with the offensive and insulting image of the past, not to mention the antiquated nineteenth-century image produced by refined orientalism", he offered little evidence for this claim.[69]

Alcaraz suggested that Festival scripts that were used in the nineteenth century had changed drastically, and for the better, since the 1970s; as an example he cited the town of Alaquàs, which had introduced words like "concord", "peace", "justice", "respect", and "*convivencia*" as counterbalances to the old rhetoric. For example:

> Now that we have reached an agreement and peace is established between our nations, these doors to the castle, herein opened, will bring us justice, respect, and work. Today a new people is born. Our shared authority will be the law, *convivencia*, respect, and compliance with the law. Let our descendants be proud of our actions! Ahead, together, one people. Moors and Christians. Long live Alaquàs![70]

While this script certainly reads differently than older ones, it reproduces the same ontological divisions. Perhaps Alcaraz focused on Alaquàs because, despite his claim, Alaquàs is in fact an exception. The scripts of most towns persist in crudely replicating nineteenth-century ideas about national purity.

While the new scripts are in Catalan – unthinkable under Franco – they uphold the same essentializing rhetoric of the original Spanish ones. An edited 2008 script for the Treaty of Almizra between King James I and Prince Alfonso of Castile, for example, strongly echoed Menéndez Pelayo, even if it was written in Catalan. In the new version, "Saracen armies" posed a "threat" to Visigoth Spain, which consequently was forced to retreat to the north, regroup, and return in glorious "reconquest". This much-lauded script was published in book form by the University of Valencia Press with a forward by two former presidents of that institution.[71]

Outside of Spain, the scholarly consensus on the Festival is altogether different. Max Harris, an American anthropologist, has argued that the Festival represents a symbolic battle between the forces of religion and the forces secularism, not the forces of good and evil. "It is in the tension between these two juxtaposed and . . . intermingled fiestas [secular and religious], rather than in the officially celebrated conflict between Moors and Christians, that I understand the real significance of the *fiestas de moros y cristianos* to reside", wrote Harris.[72] Harris claimed that the real historical existence of the Moor had little to do with the Moor portrayed by the Festival, which was in reality a "secular Christian". The Festival was a dialogue among victors, and the Muslims were a convenient prop: a fight between religious Spaniards (represented by the Christian side) and secular Spaniards (represented by the Muslim side).

According to Harris, Festival participants "speak not in terms of victory, whether of Christians over Moors or of secular over religious . . . but of *convivencia* (living together with others)". Yet the apparent reconciliation that is dramatized at the end of the Festival involves the Moors foregoing their religion and joining Christian society. Harris believes that the "baptism of the Moorish king at the close of the fiestas . . . signals . . . the incorporation of the Moors and their heritage into Spanish Christian society". It is "the reincorporation of the *festeros* [participants] into the world that is not fiesta. 'It is . . . 'an act of forgiveness for everything done during the fiestas'".[73] In Harris's interpretation, "convivencia . . . embraces both the ancestral ethnic other and the suppressed 'sensual' other within oneself".[74] *Convivencia* is thus a reconciliation of Christians among themselves, an inward psychic rehabilitation. In making this argument, Harris has excised the Moors altogether and allowed Christians, on their own terms, to define them. While tension between religious and secular life certainly underpins the Festival, it is fanciful to claim that it is its only, or even dominant, theme. Like Spanish historians, Harris has glossed over very specific references to religious intolerance and forced conversion. He is thus able to tell us very little about how the Festival has influenced the worldviews of ethnic Spaniards.

Other non-Spanish scholars have managed to analyze the Festival without removing Moors from the picture.[75] Some have gone so far as to view the Festival's symbolism within the context of Muslim immigration in contemporary Spain. Daniela Flesler and Adrián Pérez Melgosa, following in the footsteps of David M. Guss, have argued that the Festival represents a "semiotic battlefield" in which participants play the roles of "host" and "guest". The celebration of the Christian victory is above all an assertion of ethnic Spaniards' right to control Spanish society – a tenuous claim, at best, since both groups have, at various points throughout Spanish history, made similar assertions. Flesler and Pérez Melgosa read the symbolic violence perpetrated against Moors as a veiled message to present-day Muslim immigrants; for example, their analysis of the Festival compares the re-enactment of a naval battle between Moors and Christians in La Vila Joiosa to recent encounters between Spanish coastal patrols in the Strait of Gibraltar and small boats and rafts (*pateras* and *cayucos*) transporting illegal migrants to mainland Spain.[76]

"Mooricization"

Why is it that Spaniards continue to celebrate a conquest that occurred eight centuries ago? Why has the Festival of Moors and Christians not withered away, as has happened with the commemoration of similarly controversial historical events in, say, present-day South Africa? Ann Kaplan argues that the very same mechanisms which affect the individual psyche can harm the social body and produce collective cultural trauma. Cultures, like individuals, "can be traumatized by events not cognitively processed and which intrude persistently", Kaplan writes. Following Kaplan, Flesler and Pérez Melgosa have argued that Spanish society, with its entrenched Catholic heritage, continues to commemorate the subjugation of Muslim Spain as a response to collective cultural and historic trauma.[77]

Though psychological trauma may occur at a societal level, constructivist explanations like those of Eric Hobsbawm and Terence Ranger, who contend that traditions are consciously invented, carefully selected, and conspicuously linked to power, seem more plausible. Moreover, they may help to explain the evolution of the Festival over time in ways that static reference to collective trauma cannot. The invention of tradition, argues Hobsbawm, is contingent upon "a set of practices...of a ritual or symbolic nature, which seek to inculcate certain values and norms of behaviour by repetition, which automatically implies continuity with the past".[78] The Festival's ability, since the late-nineteenth century, to adapt to and redefine the social and cultural milieu in which it takes place sheds more light on its longevity and success than does a theory of collective trauma.

According to Juan Goytisolo, "the Muslim enemy . . . became, over centuries, a sort of reviled figure who rallied the forces of Christianity and, due to his closeness and the push he exerted, Christians felt directly threatened".[79] However, after the Ottoman navy in the Mediterranean was defeated at the Battle of Lepanto in 1571, and the *Moriscos* were expelled from Spain shortly thereafter, the Islamic military threat abated. Muslims became a distant memory on the Iberian Peninsula, and the symbol of the Moor-as-invader, a useful device to tie together the Christian community around folklore and tradition, flourished. While the Muslim threat did not entirely disappear until the French invasion of Algeria in 1830 curtailed the last remnants of Muslim piracy in the western Mediterranean, piracy was, nevertheless, a lesser threat to Spaniards. Christians feared enslavement and loss of property, but not a wholesale occupation of Spanish territory, as had occurred in the eighth century.

During the period of the Festival's greatest expansion, from the mid-nineteenth century onward, Europeans dominated the Mediterranean. In Spanish coastal towns, the Festival was thus a reflection of Christians' moral and martial superiority. As the real Muslim threat waned, the "Moor" in the Festival was transformed and new enemies were transferred onto the template. As Vañó Silvestre explained at the national symposium in 1974, Christian companies "represent defenders of the faith and homeland, in any era, and the Moors are enemies of the faith and homeland, regardless of the time period".[80] At the turn of the nineteenth century, for example, as Napoleon's armies expanded across Europe, the French became the new Moors and companies of Spanish smugglers, students, and farmers – inspired by the resistance to the French occupation of the country – were incorporated into the Festival on the Christian side. Bocairent introduced a student company that paid tribute to Spanish youth who had fought Napoleonic troops, especially the legendary Student Artillery Regiment of the University of Valencia. Later, during the Carlist Wars, Liberals would play the Moors and traditionalist supporters of the pretender to the Spanish Crown formed new Christian companies: Biscayans, Catalans, Zouaves, and Navarrese. In 1860, a company of "Grenadiers" sported the uniform of the colonial army of the Spanish-Moroccan War of 1859–60 – itself viewed as yet another "war . . . against the Moors".[81]

On the Moorish side, a company of musketeers in Bocairent represented French Huguenots and Dutch Protestants, both rivals of Catholicism. A company known as "The Moroccans", dressed as anti-Spanish guerrilla fighters from 1859–60, was also added to the Moorish side.[82] Other companies, too, symbolized anti-colonial fighters, such as Kabylians, Riffians, and "Pacos", the name Spanish colonial troops gave to Imazighen snipers.[83] Others stood in for a host of generic enemies of imperial-age Europe: the Maasai, Sangali, Zimbabweans, "simbas" (Congolese rebels), Yemenis, Zairians, and Hindus. One of the newest Moorish companies, the "Mubaraks" (after the former Egyptian President Hosni Mubarak), represents contemporary authoritarian regimes in North Africa and the Middle East. This newer innovation updates old dichotomies: while Spain and Europe are currently democracies, the Moorish side is represented as their authoritarian antithesis.

The Festival has not only incorporated Spain's enemies; it has also acted as a forum for the expression of political ideology. In the nineteenth century, members of a Christian company of Biscayans in Bocairent declared their support for Prince Charles, pretender to the Spanish Crown during the First Carlist War (1832–39). The company then split into two factions; a company of Grenadiers allied with moderate Liberals, who were supporters of Isabel II, and a more traditionally minded company of Catalans, who were supporters of the anti-Isabel Carlists in the Second Carlist War (1846–49). The Catalan company later changed names and became the *Terç de Suavos*, or Papal Zouaves, in 1873, in tribute to fellow Spaniards who fought for Pope Pius IX in France and Italy in the 1860s and returned to fight the Spanish Republicans during the Third Carlist War (1872–76). The company used such traditional Carlist symbols as crosses and red berets. In other towns, rather than Papal Zouaves, people formed the company of Garibaldians to pay tribute to the Italian nationalist leader Giuseppe Garibaldi. Today these companies still parade with the Italian flag. To round off the spectrum of political concerns of the day, a Liberal company of contrabandists and an absolutist company of musketeers were also active in Bocairent.[84]

The politicization of the Festival decreased sometime between the Third Carlist War in 1873 and the Spanish-American War of 1898. Though the Americans were clearly Spain's new enemy, they were not "Mooricized" as others had been. Instead, contemporary political events were disassociated from the Festival and organizers refocused on the medieval past, a time when Spaniards were victors rather than a defeated colonial power. Organizers occupied themselves with the "true" historical narrative in an attempt to remove the anachronisms that apparently diminished the Festival's "seriousness". As part of this gradual "purification" and "medievalization", Biscayans, Catalans, and Navarrese were removed and new companies of Templars, crusaders, "Cids" (followers of the legendary Castilian mercenary, El Cid), Almogavers (Aragonese mercenaries), Mozarabs, Asturians, and mountaineers of Covadonga were introduced.[85]

While the Festival remained a symbolic theatre for defining didactically the enemies and heroes of the nation, contemporary politics moved to a different rhythm than the supposedly 'timeless' Festival. Crucial political events of the twentieth century, such as the Spanish Civil War, did not have a lasting impact in the Festival's features. The Second Republic (1931–39) introduced changes to costumes – for example, the monarchy's shield was eliminated from Alcoi's Cids – and rituals in an attempt to edit out the clergy's historical involvement. In Ontinyent, the clergy was banned from participating in Festival rituals and in the upheaval of the summer of 1936, the sacred Christ of the Agony, the town's patron saint, was immolated. During the Spanish Civil War, argues Goytisolo, "the spectre of Africa was used as a missile against the right and left, by colonialists, Marxists, fascists, and republicans".[86] When the war was over, the Festival rewound to before the Republican interlude.

Under Franco, the Festival maintained its epic nature, increased its religious (i.e., Catholic) content, and participants preferred to exalt historic Castilian leaders, reflected in such companies as the Cids, Guzmans, and Don Pelayos. In the democratic period, the Knights Templar and Knights of James I came to the fore, reflecting the resurgence of regional nationalism in the former territories of the Aragonese Crown. Since the 1970s, organizers have introduced local Christian heroes. The town of Manises, for example, introduced Artal de Luna, a nobleman to whom James I offered Manises as reward for his contribution to the Christian conquest.[87] Moorish companies have also changed. Names of great Muslim caliphates have now been included: Almoravids, Abbasids, Merinids, Umayyads, Almohads, and Nasrids. Legendary warriors, sultans, and caliphs such as Tarik, Al-Azraq, Suleiman, Al-Mansur Billah, and Abubaker have also been given companies. In Denia, Moorish company names have been rendered in Arabic: Alkamar (moon) and Saqaliba (eunuch).[88]

The Festival of Moors and Christians in Democratic Times

For ethnic Spaniards the Festival may represent an opportunity to have a good time, but in a country that at least on paper has mandated the separation of church and state, enshrined religious freedom and gender equality, and pledges protection against discrimination based on "birth, race, sex, religion, opinion, and other personal or social conditions or circumstances",[89] the Festival is problematic to say the least. Members of the Catholic Church, feminist organizations, and Islamic groups have questioned and challenged the Festival, but their success in initiating a genuine public conversation has been limited.

In 1965, the Second Vatican Council issued *Nostra Aetate*, a Declaration on the Relation of the Church with Non-Christian Religions. *Nostra Aetate* stated that the "Church regards with esteem also the Moslems . . . Since in the course of centuries not a few quarrels and hostilities have arisen between Christians and Moslems, this Sacred Synod urges all to forget the past and to work sincerely for mutual understanding".[90] Shortly after and influenced by changing views in the Vatican, some Catholics spoke out against the Festival's symbolic discrimination of Muslims in an attempt to change its tone.

In a few villages, organizers removed cruder Festival rituals, including La Mahoma in Alcoi, but did not challenge its core *modus operandi*: the Christian triumph over Islam. At the 1974 symposium, a group of Catholic priests proposed eliminating rituals that "could hurt religious sensibilities, even if [they were] not Christian". They called upon participants to avoid "acting dogmatically . . . [and] not reproduce the theatre of the festival as a behavioural model for everyday life. It is important not to impose [on others] forms of worship or thought", they argued.[91] They were attempting to address a consensus which said that to impose one's religious will on others was indeed fine. The majority of participants, however, voted against modifying the core content of the Festival.

Nostra Aetate's influence on the Festival was limited, and the spirit of reform did not return for two decades, when women's groups raised concerns of their own. Women's participation in the Festival has changed drastically since the 1970s. In 1974, eight of thirty-one participating villages discouraged the inclusion of women, and in one village, Ontinyent, women's participation was prohibited altogether. "The festival is for men", declared the 1974 symposium. Participation in it was reserved "for men, boys, and [young] girls", though women were "naturally supposed to honour male participants". In other words, they could watch the Festival and accompany their fathers, brothers, husbands, or children, but they were not supposed to actively participate. The expectation was that they should stay at home and prepare costumes, clean and put their homes on display, manage kitchen tasks, and entertain guests.[92]

The symposium explained that this gender division was natural. "The Festival of Moors and Christians is a celebration of the soldier and therefore essentially masculine", it pointed out. Femininity did not belong to "the gallantry, the male virtues that are put on display". It was not right, argued organizers, for women to "leave the home and walk about". Women should only do that when they are "extras, carollers, chorus girls, or majorettes". They most certainly should not participate in the mock gunpowder battles, because "the gunpowder and noise is not appropriate to their charms".[93]

Indeed, the quality of a Festival was measured by the extent of male-centredness; that is why "When women participate en masse, it is because the festival lacks quality [*solera*] and has been distorted". The symposium concluded that "it was fine for women to participate in the festival, but in their proper station, in accordance with traditional customs and the guidelines of town organizers". Moreover, "the participants of this symposium agree unanimously that women's participation in the festival should not do damage to their femininity".[94]

Despite this informal injunction, coupled with widespread fear that "the surrounding force of feminism invades everything", women did begin to participate en masse beginning in the 1980s.[95] Only in Alcoi did the Festival remain segregated. Young women could participate there, but only as dancers whose role it was to adorn their male captains. They dressed as odalisques and belly dancers, recalling the harem or *seraglio*, and were valued for their sexual allure. Alcoi did not ban women's participation as a matter of principal, but organizers made it effectively impossible for them to participate on equal terms with men. As of 2007, harassment remained so strong that the ratio of female to male participants was 1:1000, or 7 out of 7,000 total participants.[96]

To challenge gender segregation at the Alcoi Festival, a feminist association called Fonèvol, Friends of Alcoi's Festival of Moors and Christians, was founded in 2003. Fonèvol advocated for equal rights, organized public campaigns, denounced the Saint George Association, and lobbied the regional government of Valencia to cease funding and promotion of Alcoi's Festival.[97]

Though Fonèvol garnered sympathy outside of Alcoi, neither Alcoi's Saint George Association nor its city hall offered their support.[98] Local government, meanwhile, was more concerned with tourists than with women's grievances. Pressure, nevertheless, produced change, and in 2004 the Saint George Association approved new regulations for women's participation in the Festival. Yet these regulations continued to prohibit mixed parade groups, insisted women dress in traditional female costumes, and deprived women of the right to equal representation.[99] Even though women in Spain are allowed to serve in the armed forces, Civil Guard, and national and local police, they are still banned from carrying mock weapons at the Festival of Moors and Christians in Alcoi.

Fonèvol understood the Festival's symbolic value: it is "tightly related to society and has a great influence on the perpetuation of discrimination and democratization".[100] Fonèvol pointed out that, in limiting women's participation in the Festival, Alcoi's Saint George Association defied Article 14 of the Spanish Constitution concerning the equality of the sexes. According to Fonèvol,

> It is unacceptable to attempt to bring back now, into the festival, the mutilated model of citizenship that Franco designed for women, a model that submitted women to the authority of their fathers and husbands and prevented them from acting without male permission or mediation.[101]

A Fonèvol symposium on women's participation in the Festival concluded that "it seems easier today for a woman from Alcoi to become a member of the constitutional court than march in an *entrada*".[102] Yet as the same symposium put it, "traditions are like trees, rooted in the past but growing towards the future. Let us hope that that future is one of equality and democracy".[103]

One of Fonèvol's main concerns was that by excluding women, the Festival would become "merely an instrument of perpetuating inequality; the sense of community would disappear and the festival would lose its potential and ability to involve and recognize pluralism and diversity in the community. The cultural heritage would not be a shared one, rather it would be privatized for men alone".[104] Though Fonèvol's concern was for women, a similar argument could be made for Muslims. The group, however, did not make this connection, thereby limiting its criticism.

"We are not fanatics"

Spanish Muslims have had a conflicted relationship with the Festival. A minority have criticized the event's core philosophy: the celebration of conquest in the conqueror's land. Yet the majority have chosen to respond only when political and social events have forced them to, such as during the Danish cartoon controversy of 2005. While some feared a backlash from nativists in towns where Muslims comprised a small minority of the local population, others have boldly claimed that the Festival has "no place in a democratic Spain".[105]

During the 2002 Festival in Ontinyent, participants stomped over a giant rug decorated in Arabic calligraphy; this was, in fact, Quranic verses. Awat Khalil, the nominal president of the Medina Awara Mosque, and representative of nearly 400 practicing Muslims residents in the city, pointed out that this was "absolutely disrespectful of our religion and ourselves as followers of Islam".[106] The community did not pursue legal action because the Moorish captain that had used the rug, a female for the first time in the Festival's history, had stepped forward and apologized. (She said she was unaware of the origin and importance of the writing). The mayor of Ontinyent, Rafael Portero, formally apologized as well: "I hope this incident will not modify the peaceful way in which people born in other countries and natives have lived together for many years now, because we are all *onte-nienses* [residents in Ontinyent]".[107] The president of the Festival's organizing body claimed that, "[f]rom now on, we will work closely with the Muslim community", and signed a notarized agreement with Muslims to have all Arabic writing used in the Festival cleared first by a representative of the Islamic community.[108]

A few weeks later, twenty-eight mosques and Islamic centres in Valencia issued a statement of gratitude to the residents of Ontinyent. The statement thanked them for their sensitive and respectful reaction, but also called for enhanced cultural and religious understanding. More importantly, it congratulated Festival organizers on the participation of women. The suggestion was that the form of the Festival was not etched in stone; if women could find a place in it, perhaps Muslims could too, provided certain accommodations were made. It was also suggested that, for many local Muslims, "it is difficult to wrap one's head around the epic foundation of the festival. It could be refocused perfectly towards an enriching under-standing of many centuries of peaceful *convivencia*. War battles could be substituted by literary, philosophical, folkloristic, or gastronomic battles".[109]

Several hundred organizing committees, thousands of companies, and tens of thousands of Festival participants throughout Spain ignored the Muslim petition. Only in Bocairent did a historian and a philosopher write a series of articles and give talks on how to modify the Festival to suite a multicultural context.[110] Their impact was nominal.

In 2005, attention was focussed once again on the "La Mahoma" ritual after the controversy erupted – first in Denmark, and then around the world – over cartoons depicting Prophet Muhammad. Contrary to other coun-tries, Muslim responses to the cartoon controversy in Spain were peaceful. Zapatero met with Muslim leaders and published a statement together with Turkish President, Recep Tayyip Erdogan: "In a globalized world, in which the relationships and exchanges among different civilizations continue to multiply, and in which a local incident may have worldwide repercussions, it is vital that we cultivate the values of respect, tolerance, and peaceful coexistence". The pair claimed that while the publication of the Danish cartoons was legal, they "ought to be rejected from a moral and political standpoint".[111]

Yet these words of moderation were not embraced by Festival participants. In January 2006, the ritual execution of the "anonymous Moor" in Bocairent garnered unwelcome attention. While extensive media coverage and subsequent fear of international outcry made some participants consider banning the ritual, those who wanted to protect the status quo simply attacked journalists who had come to observe the event. Local authorities also tried to silence the media; "Nobody, not even the mayor, would tell me whether [the effigy] had been thrown from the castle", claimed a journalist from the national newspaper *El Mundo*. Participants had indeed seized La Mahoma, marched it up the castle, and thrown it down to the street below.[112]

Later, Bocairent's organizers debated what to do with La Mahoma in the long term. One tongue-in-cheek suggestion called for renaming the effigy, rather arbitrarily it must be said, "Little Thomas", while maintaining the same ritual. Organizers turned this suggestion down, and decided instead to ban the controversial practice – at least until things cooled off.[113]

Though Bocairent's La Mahoma was explosive, it received little national or international attention, and the reasons for its offensiveness were not assimilated by most of the Festival's participants. What was abundantly clear, however, was that organizers had to be careful, secretive, perhaps more politically correct. In Alcoi, whenever religious processions bore representations of St. George on horseback slaying Moors, organizers now made a point of placing flowers over the depictions of bloodied corpses. In the program of the 2006 Beneixama Festival, organizers simply changed the name "La Mahoma" to the more ambiguous "the effigy". They claimed that "La Mahoma" was "only a symbol of the Moorish side; we do not think of it as Muhammad".[114]

Some Muslim leaders welcomed these changes as they at least distanced the Festival from its original religious meaning. Yet not everyone agreed. Félix Herrero, president of FEERI and a convert to Islam, said the Festival had "no place in a democratic Spain" and should be suppressed "in the name of *convivencia*". In "a democratic Spain that recognizes all religious creeds, celebrations of conquest must disappear", said Herrero. He claimed the Festival was the equivalent of celebrating Franco's conquests, or the death and punishment the dictator had doled out to vanquished Republicans.[115]

Malik Ruiz, president of CIE and manager of the Granada Mosque Foundation, said that he did not object to the Festival itself, but certainly disagreed with the more provocative rituals, which "generated discord". Ruiz compared the Festival to the celebration of the conquest of Granada, which "not long ago was a source of tension and difficulty". He added that, for the Granada celebration, he would prefer that "rather than celebrate a conquest, a change of dynasty . . . be acted out". The president of the Islamic Council of Catalonia, Abdennur Prado, added his qualified agreement: "The Festival of Moors and Christians does not seem bad to us at all", he said; "In fact, it replays a shared history. Of course, it only seems right that offensive aspects of it be removed".[116]

In places where the Festival's influence was widespread, Muslim leaders were even more congenial than Ruiz and Prado. For example, the president of the Islamic Community of Alacant, Majed Kadem, argued that the Festival did "not represent an attack on Islam or the Prophet Muhammad . . . [rather] we see it as a *fiesta*". At the same time, Kadem called for the elimination of La Mahoma and asked that "there not be victors in the festival so that it is agreeable to everybody". Similarly, Imad Al Naddaf, president of the Islamic Council of the Valencian Region, claimed the Festival "was and always will be a *fiesta*." "Do not take the festival out of context", he warned; "It does not signify confrontation . . . or conflict". He reproved Muslims who wished to eliminate it. A spokesperson for the grand mosque of Valencia also deemphasized the gravity of the festival by using a common line of argument among ethnic Spaniards: "in many villages, people fight to be on the Moorish side". He argued that the Festival's battles were moments of joy, "with the two sides embracing each other in the end". As for La Mahoma: its modification was an "act of great responsibility" on the part of Festival organizers. In Crevillent, the local imam said the Festival "shows great respect for different cultures" and therefore did not offend his congregation.[117]

Amidst the confusion of the 2005 Danish cartoon controversy, Khader Ibeid, a Muslim Palestinian who had lived in Xàvia for thirty years and was known to residents as Jorge (or George), called for "common sense". Ibeid had been made president of Xàvia's Festival, a position that he was proud to occupy. He said that those who wanted the Festival suppressed were unrepresentative of the Muslim community in Spain. Criticisms of the Festival "are ridiculous . . . They [Herrero and his supporters] are free to express their views, but they must also be respectful of the customs and ways of life of the places where they now live".[118]

If in other towns the Festival was contentious, Ibeid went on, "in Xàvia it is an open celebration in which people from many nationalities participate: English, Belgian, German, and French". If in the past the Festival was a celebration of Christian conquest, "today it is nothing more than a *fiesta*, a *fiesta* that respects all religions". In addition to assuaging critics of the Festival, Ibeid was concerned with nativist backlash against what some might see as Muslims' qualified acceptance of Spanish society and culture. "Muslims are ordinary people", he made the point of saying. "We are not fanatics, we are peaceful people".[119] Ibeid's Eurocentric and assimilationist outlook can be contrasted to the harder, less compromising stance of Herrero, who had hoped to widen the scope of acceptable criticism and challenge the conventional view of the Festival as a mere party. In doing so, he aligned himself with the minority.

The scope of criticism available to Muslim leaders was limited due to the dominant stereotype of Muslims as "fanatics" or terrorists that the Madrid commuter train bombings and the Danish cartoon controversy, among other recent events, had helped to cement. Even if anti-Muslim outbursts were rare after the Madrid bombing, Muslim leaders and Festival organizers were certainly more careful about what they said in public.[120] Though many may have previously agreed with Herrero's claim that the Festival fit uneasily with democratic rights and values, they now kept quiet. And indeed, the closer they lived to traditional strongholds of the Festival, the quieter they kept.

Dynamics and Alternatives

Is the Festival of Moors and Christians merely a *fiesta*, as many of its partic-ipants, and even some Muslim leaders, assert? Does it promote understanding of Spain's Islamic past and empathy for its present-day Muslim inhabitants? Alacaraz remains steadfast in his view that the Festival does not promote harmful relations between Muslims and Christians since "some participants play the role of defenders of Islam". Moreover, he points out, "[e]veryday there is more interest in understanding the Islamic past of our country". Participants learn to identify with, not hate, Islam, he argues. Anthropologist Carmelo Lisón Tolosana claims that "at a very explicit level, the people opt for the Moors . . . much more than for the Christians". The Moors indeed have the more spectacular costumes, the most stirring music, and they often outnumber the Christians. According to anthropologist George M. Foster, "to be a Moor is considered more desirable than to be a Christian". At the 1974 symposium, some presenters pointed out that "The Moors are better dressed". Perhaps as a result, "more people want to be on the Moorish rather than the Christian side".[121]

Goytisolo claims that Spanish literature is Janus faced on this topic. When Moors were real military enemies, Spanish literature insulted and denigrated them; when they were defeated, it glorified and exalted them. "The image of the Other", he says, "unfolds in two; it undergoes a process of idealization, is festooned with positive adornments". In the sixteenth and seventeenth centuries, Christian rejection of *Moriscos* as "distinct compa-triots who were impossible to assimilate" occurred at the same time that "the enemy was exalted to mythic proportions on the literary plane". In other words, the Christian conquest and subsequent ethnic cleansing were prerequisites for the exaltation of the defeated Islamic enemy in a new kind of literature.[122]

Literary critic Ramón Menéndez Pidal has argued that once the Muslim military threat disappeared, ethnic Spaniards found themselves strangely attracted to "their exotic civilization, the luxurious oriental dress, the splendid ornamentation of buildings, the strange way of life, the manners of horse riding, of how to arm oneself, of fighting".[123] From a safe distance it was possible to recreate, reconstruct, and re-imagine the other. The victor's imagination, "prone to historical fantasy", became fuelled by a "longing for the extinct world which accentuated its favourable features". However, Maurophilia, admiration for the Moors and Moorish culture, "and respect for the vanquished and remote adversary do not insulate one . . . from the prejudices and clichés that grow out of a vain awareness and belief of moral superiority", argues Goytisolo.[124]

Both the Christians of the early modern period as well as the Festival participants of today have tended to represent their Moorish enemy with all the "ignorance of the triumphant imagination".[125] Yet in so doing they do not heighten their awareness of Islam, of the Moor, the *Mudéjar*, the *Morisco*, or the Muslim immigrant; rather they distance themselves from any real appreciation of them. They build up a romanticized representation around the real thing. As Goytisolo puts it,

> the identification with the figure of the subtle, remote, and exalted Moor increases . . . the distance between the painting and the original: admiration for the former contributed perhaps to excusing, in the eyes of the public, contempt for and rejection of the latter, the vulgar, corporeal Morisco, who was found daily on the street.[126]

Behind the idealized image of the Moor, continues Goytisolo, is a functional dynamic:

> Retreat into the past permits . . . [us] to avoid the intolerance of the present without suffering pangs of conscience: the fabrication of the Other in positive terms responds to the same social and psychic principles that prop up the phantoms and myths of the "barbarous" in [Spain's] complex and contradictory mental landscape.[127]

Festival participants may recreate the exotic, magnificent Moor, but they do not seem to want to live, work, or send their children to schools with the Muslim equivalents of today. A similar dynamic vis-à-vis the popular perception of Native Americans has been identified by the writer Thomas King. While many cultural products exalt and romanticize what King calls "Dead Indians", in other words "the stereotypes and clichés that North America has conjured up", those same products either ignore or denigrate "Live Indians". According to King, "[o]ne is a romantic reminder of a heroic but fictional past. The other is simply an unpleasant, contemporary surprise".[128]

It is unsurprising that at the height of Europe's global influence – not to mention the heights of Orientalism's influence over European art – Spain, cleansed of its erstwhile religious and cultural pluralism and obsessed with cultural homogeneity, purity of blood, and imperial grandeur, would embrace celebratory rituals of conversion and denigration. It is even less surprising that under Franco, local authorities, in their attachment to National Catholicism, maintained the core of the Festival. What is remarkable is the lack of critical scholarship and alternative views concerning the Festival during almost four decades of liberal democracy – a period which, as we have seen, also witnessed the Festival's exponential growth. Towns that have not traditionally celebrated it now do: between 1975 and 1980, twenty-two villages in Valencia began to celebrate the Festival, doubling the overall number of participating towns, and since then dozens more have joined this trend.[129]

The growth of the Festival in democratic times can be attributed to the preponderant role it plays in local economies, its transformation into an international tourist attraction, and its adoption by both pro-Catalan and pro-Valencian regional nationalists have allowed the Festival to become a marker of regional identity. The participatory, carnivalesque nature of the Festival, not to mention Spaniards' need to reinvent themselves after Franco, may also explains its success.

Indeed, the role of nationalism in the promotion of the Festival cannot be overestimated. In Valencia, where the rift between pro-Catalan and anti-Catalan nationalists runs deep, one of the famous slogans of the latter is "We'll be Moors before we are made Catalans" (*antes moros que catalans*) – the two most despised groups in their cultural lexicon.[130] Since the Festival was associated with the Catalan conquest, anti-Catalan nationalists were weary of it. Things began to change only once they re-branded Catalan monarchs as Christian ones.[131] For instance, anti-Catalan but pro-Valencian regionalists, such as Rita Barberà, the mayor of Valencia since 1991, have laid claim to James I, previously a symbol of pro-Catalan nationalism. Barberà seized on James I, not as the founding father of the Catalan language in Valencia, but as a valiant Christian soldier and king. This re-identification helped depoliticize James I's image, making it safe for anti-Catalan Valencians to participate in the Festival without fear of being stigmatized as pro-Catalan. The Catholic turn of anti-Catalan regionalists did not stop pro-Catalan nationalist from continuing their veneration of James I as the founding father of their imagined *Països Catalans* (or Catalan Countries).[132]

Whether conservative, pro- or anti-Catalan nationalist, or Marxist-Leninist, all have agreed on the need to celebrate the conquest of Valencia over Muslims as a matter of local pride, and the Festival has burgeoned as a result.[133] The arrival of large numbers of Muslim immigrants has refocused attention from differences between Castilians, Catalans, and Valencians, to differences between natives and recent non-Christian arrivals. In this sense, the Festival has rediscovered its roots.

Since its growth in the 1960s and seventies, the Festival, an international tourist attraction, has also become an important motor for local economies. A flourishing industry in costume rentals and design, marching bands, floats, props, and decorations survives and thrives entirely because of the

Festival. This is a strong motivator for a country that in recent years has seen unemployment rates twice that of the Eurozone average. Criticism of the Festival, especially in the international press, risks harming these regions' economic prosperity.

Nowhere has the Festival been promoted more to tourists than in Valencia. When Alcoi's companies were invited to the 2006 Columbus Day Parade in New York, the Saint George Association and the government of Valencia took this as an opportunity to shine a positive international light on the Festival. The Saint George Association allowed only Christian companies to participate, fearing that ethnic Spaniards dressed as Moors would offend American racial sensibilities following the events of 11 September 2001. In an op-ed piece, *The Financial Times* claimed that such "self-censorship" was shameless, a whitewash that attempted to garner international acceptance. The bishop emeritus of the Archdiocese of Valencia also called the Saint George Association's censorship "shameful" and "cowardly", but for entirely different reasons. In front of the world, the association had "mutilated" and "deprived the festival of its genuine historical meaning". "They shamed us in New York", claimed the bishop. "We need to defend what is ours, and the festival is the heritage of all *alcoyanos* [residents of Alcoi]".[134]

The PP Valencian government was also displeased with Alcoi's truncated representation. It called on the PSOE government in Madrid to file an application with UNESCO for recognition of the Festival as a Masterpiece of the Oral and Intangible Heritage of Humanity. The PP argued that Rodríguez Zapatero's Alliance of Civilizations "must never get in the way of . . . our best and most healthy traditions, including the Festival of Moors and Christians".[135] Further, the PP maintained that

> under no circumstances must we attend to the demands of those who wish to limit us. We are very proud of our festival, its traditions, and the spontaneity that we so intensely live, which in its splendour is so very important to our tourist sector.[136]

Muslim immigrants, by contrast, have tried to initiate a conversation about the epic nature, offensive rituals, and orientalist distortions of the Festival, though with little success. The public space for dissent and for constructive alternatives has been limited, but not entirely so. Part of the difficulty encountered by Muslims in Spain relates to the gradual nature by which democratic educational institutions and authorities revise and update national myths and narratives. In 1992, on the 500th anniversary of the Europeans' arrival in the Americas, King Juan Carlos I declared the conquest of Latin America a "great adventure of discovery, a double voyage . . . which connected Europe to America, the old world to the new".[137] The king said nothing about colonialism and the exploitation of indigenous peoples. The 1992 anniversary presented an opportunity for democratic Spain to revise the historical narrative clung to so violently under Franco, and before, during the colonial period. This was accomplished only in part. While this study concurs with Flesler and Pérez Melgosa's assessment that the 1992 Agreement of Cooperation between Spain and the CIE introduced the notion of "reconciliation" between Muslims and other Spaniards for the first time, this did not result in any substantial changes to the Festival of Moors and Christians. [138] Moreover, the history taught in schools and endorsed by public institutions has upheld the same time-honoured, positivist, self-aggrandizing national narrative. The language of textbooks has changed little, continuing to herald the Christian "reconquest" of Islamic Spain as the birth of the Spanish nation and celebrating the "conquest of the Americas" as a dawn of one of the world's greatest empires, as well as a "golden age" for Spanish literature and culture. [139]

Despite the persistence of epic narratives in both the Festival and popular culture at large, precedents for transforming the Festival into something more respectful and consistent with the values of liberal democracy do exist. In the 1990s, the Catalan cities of Móra d'Ebre and Lleida adopted nontraditional forms of celebration for their Festivals. When, in 1996, Lleida reintroduced the Festival after a lapse of almost a century, participants modified it by allowing the Moorish side to win biannually. This was not so much a rewriting of the history of Moors and Christians as it was a refocusing; the goal of organizers was to deemphasize the epic character and denouement of the war, a change that many, more traditional towns deplored. [140]

Móra d'Ebre went further. It named its Festival "Moorish Mora: Three Visions, One World", and recreated the three communities – Jewish, Muslim, and Christian – that had coexisted in the village during the fifteenth century. Rather than re-enact battles, participants recreated the different historic neighbourhoods of the town. The festival aimed to remind residents that at "the end of the fifteenth century, Móra d'Ebre had 34 Jewish, 51 Saracen, and 130 Christian families. The festival recreates a time in which Móra d'Ebre had a church, mosque, and synagogue, and Christian, Muslim, and Jewish cultures lived together in peace". [141]

Rachid Nini, a Moroccan journalist who published a diary of his experiences as an undocumented worker in Spain, pointed to the paradoxes presented by the Festival of Moors and Christians in a time of immigration. He witnessed the festival in the Valencian town of La Vila Joiosa:

> I think this way of communicating history to foreigners is interesting. The festival does not aim to teach the new generations about what really happened when the Arabs were expelled from Al-Andalus. The Inquisition. The killings. The collective expulsion. None of this would attract tourists. On the contrary. It would have altogether an inappropriate dramatic tone. It is for the best that the festival takes place in this way: a celebration of the expulsion of the Arabs. Of the Moors. There is no better way to delicately recount the travesty . . . the parading is incredible . . . For a second I felt vanity.

Suddenly, I felt that my presence there was more ridiculous than the imaginary competition on the beach. I was tired of hanging around the festival waiting to see if the police would come and I had to flee. I returned home before the festival was done, but I knew all too well how it ended.[142]

Spanish Muslims "spent centuries creating a grandeur that does not now merit the kind of naïve celebration that consists in little else than repeating to the young that the Moors were conquered", wrote Nini. The failure to think of Spain as pluralistic and diverse and the "ignorance of the triumphant imagination" could, in a modern, multicultural Europe, prove to be a handicap. Yet the conversation is now open. It will be up to Spaniards, both Muslim and non-Muslim, to determine the parameters of a fruitful multicultural dialogue or fall prey to uncompromising narratives premised upon a clash of civilizations.[143]

Conclusion

The struggle for civil rights in Spain was started by Muslims in the North African city of Melilla in 1985. Though at the time – and especially in Ceuta and Melilla – Muslims comprised a significant minority of the population, the first Immigration Act was ill-equipped to deal fairly with their demands for rights and citizenship. Nativists looked upon Muslims Melillans with suspicion, even though many had been born in Spanish territory, spoke Spanish, and were integrated into the culture. Muslim Melillans were seen as aliens, not fellow citizens, and lacked organizations and representatives in positions of authority to defend their interests.

The ensuing civil rights movement demanded Spanish citizenship for 20,000 undocumented residents, improvements to conditions in shanty neighbourhoods, and greater employment opportunities. This movement lasted for two years and for the first time, Muslims were visible on the streets, in the media, and in new organizations created to lobby local and national governments on their behalf. Above all, Spanish Muslims fought for recognition as Spaniards, not as outsiders, Moroccans, immigrants, etc. They argued that Spanish history was a complex affair and that "Spanish", like American or Canadian, meant more than being Catholic, white, or European. Moreover, Muslim Melillans claimed "cultural affinity" akin to Latin Americans, Portuguese, Filipinos, Andorrans, Equatorial Guineans, Sephardic Jews, and Gibraltarians – all of whom were granted special privileges under the 1985 Immigration Act. They argued that in modern Spain, it was now possible to "hyphenate" one's identity – a novel idea to many.

Perhaps the most significant outcome of the fight in Melilla – aside from citizenship for thousands of Muslim residents – was the concept of *arraigo* as a legal mechanism to move beyond the exclusionary nature of the 1985 Act. *Arraigo* ignored religion or ethnicity and focussed instead on 'rootedness' in Spanish territory or acculturation to Spanish customs. If one could claim to have been born in Melilla or had spent significant time in the country, one could thus qualify for status and citizenship (or at least be put on the citizenship track). *Arraigo* would remain the de facto qualifier for decades. Later on, undocumented migrants in mainland Spain would employ the concept to prove to the government that they belonged in Spain, that they had social and cultural ties commensurate with ethnic Spaniards.

On the mainland, Muslim immigrants who sought to free themselves from the paternalistic oversight of native NGOs and Moroccan authorities in Spain founded organizations such as ATIME and the Ibn Battuta Association. These bodies gave voice to immigrants and produced skilled leaders who could challenge the self-serving view of immigrants as helpless and speechless recipients of charity, incapable of defending their own interests. If, initially, many of these independent migrant organizations focussed on legal gains and political activism, they eventually grew into large service providers that devoted time to settlement and legal matters on their constituents' behalf.

Immigrant organizations, together with labour unions and other supporters, defended migrants' rights by waging a war on two fronts. On the one hand, they fought to establish regular channels through which to obtain official status. For example, in 1993, the Spanish government implemented a quota system on foreign workers: undocumented migrants could be legalized for employment if they met the conditions of the quota system. In 1999, the program's peak year, the quota system regularized 39,879 undocumented labourers. Advocates for immigration henceforth used this system and the language of *arraigo* to shape and maintain regular channels to obtain status.

On the other hand, immigrant groups and their supporters lobbied for extraordinary regularization programs when parliament attempted to modify the Immigration Act. They carefully monitored changes to immigration regulations. They fought for longer residency permits that were not contingent upon legal employment, for improvements to family reunification, and for more streamlined citizenship procedures. Between 1985 and 2005, six large-scale regularizations, and many smaller ones, took place. Nearly a million undocumented persons acquired status as a result of these programs.

Regularizations presented a window of opportunity for migrants to organize, expand their networks of allies, and influence policy-making. Among other campaigns, migrant activism pushed to incorporate the concept of "social integration" into the Immigration Act – a legal and social recognition that Spain had become a county of immigration – defended the extension of fundamental rights to non-status residents, and requested parliament incorporate racism as a crime into the legal code.

While migrant activism on the part of Muslims has achieved a degree of success in the struggle for citizenship, official status, and labour rights, their campaign for political rights has stalled. While other migrant communities – chief among them Latin Americans – have slowly obtained political rights in Spain, Muslim immigrants have not. The need for a democratic setting able to grant reciprocal political rights to Spaniards in the countries of origin of immigrants has left Muslims in a third-tier position amongst the country's immigrant communities: they neither enjoy privileged access to status and citizenship, nor do they have political rights in Spain.

In all of these struggles, Muslim women have played an important role, organizing and advancing their own agenda, as well as that of their larger community. The movement in Melilla transformed gender relations in the Muslim community. For the first time, women were active and visible in advocating their rights. Organizations such as the Committee of Muslim

Women, which organized rallies and protests for women, increased their desire for autonomy. Muslim women throughout Spain pushed for participation in mixed-gender organizations and created women's committees and independent groups. Within the secular ATIME, women formed the Al Amal caucus to fight for better conditions in domestic service and to counter the requirement that the legal status of married women depend on their marriages. The women of Al Amal also advocated for legal status that was independent of attachments to men and for appropriate reforms to family reunification requirements.

Women also created religious organizations, such as An-Nisa and Inshallah, which defended women's right to wear religious headgear and to be photographed for official identity documents in traditional dress. They lobbied for prayer spaces for women. They educated men about the rights of women under Islam and launched campaigns to oppose literalist interpretations of the Qur'an that contradicted Spanish constitutional law. Women converts played an important role in this process, too: in 2007, Amparo Sánchez Rosell became the first female president of the prominent Islamic Cultural Centre of Valencia; Isabel Romero has led the successful Halal Institute since its foundation in 1986; and Ndeye Andújar became editor of WebIslam, the main Islamic website in Spanish.

Socio-political activism on the part of immigrants peaked in 2000, and from its radical phase of church occupations and hunger strikes, it has adopted regular venues for influencing policy. Its visibility and determination have been transferred to the new religious activism that began to take shape in 1992 with the signing of the Agreement of Cooperation between the national government and CIE. The PSOE government treated the 500th anniversary of the Christian conquest of Muslim Granada as a symbol of the country's intention to turn a page over centuries of religious minority persecution and Spanish Muslims were eager to have Islam recognized on an official level, as an integral and historically rooted religion in Spain, as well as their right to practice it.

Practicing Muslims opposed French-style *laïcité* in Spain and instead supported state neutrality in matters of religion. Muslims reinforced the religious sphere and expanded religion's influence as a whole in the public realm, but their calls for equality and parity have also fortified the state's commitment to religious pluralism and neutrality. Unlike Catholics, Muslims have not demanded special consideration or privileges, but rather equal opportunity and state neutrality, a stance that has undermined the Catholic Church by questioning its de facto right to privileges. The Church has perceived Muslims as rivals and as competitors for limited religious public space, instead of as allies. Ecumenical struggles over the use of such religious space as the Mosque-Cathedral of Córdoba illustrate this tension.

Religious activism has been fuelled as well by the need to counter suspicion towards Muslims, which reached unprecedented levels after the attacks of 11 September 2001 and the March 2004 Madrid commuter train bombings. It has also been fuelled in part by nativist efforts to prevent new mosque constructions since 1990, as well as by dissatisfaction on the part of some Muslims with the 1992 Agreement of Cooperation. Although the Agreement pioneered state management of Islam in Europe, many Spanish Muslims have found that it was easily ignored by conservative national governments and regional governments of all political affiliations. Because the Agreement demanded unified representation, it also transformed Spanish Islam into a top-down hierarchy, which led to significant divisions within the community. Reform-minded native converts and more traditional Muslim immigrants formed two different federations. Internal rifts favoured those who were willing to compromise, rather than fully implement the Agreement. Activism persisted because politicians forestalled the Agreement, especially its provisions concerning education, the workplace, and prayer sites.

Muslims' right to dignified prayer sites has not been evenly challenged in Spain, with Catalonia becoming the region with the most sustained and intense anti-mosque backlashes. Almost 70 percent of anti-mosque protests in Spain have arisen there, and Barcelona has the dubious distinction of being the only major Spanish city without a grand mosque; elsewhere in Europe, only Athens and Ljubljana can make a similar claim. Muslims in Madrid are in many ways fortunate not just because they have more diversified and dignified sites of prayer, but also because they are not required to contend with two official languages and Catalan nationalists' widespread feelings of cultural injustice at the hands of a central, and to Catalans "foreign", power. In Catalonia, regional nationalists who battle "Castilian influence" demand that immigrants identify with one force or the other, not both, not a mix of each.

Catalan nationalists have encouraged Muslims to support the nationalist cause and to de-prioritize other religious or cultural commitments that are not perceived as traditionally Catalan. Early theorists of Catalan nationalism claimed that Catalan nationalism was mostly civic, premised as it was on political membership to the region. Its ethnic features, such as language or group loyalty, rather than inherited were qualities easy to acquire. This has changed with the arrival of visible minorities from non-Christian countries.

Spain's first new xenophobic party, the Platform for Catalonia, or PxC, has also used nationalism to forward its political agenda. The PxC advocates unity among Christian, ethnic Catalans, and ethnic Castilians by battling a new common enemy: Muslim immigrants. As parties like the PxC have grown in popularity, immigrant organizations such as Jameiat Essalam, which spent decades in the region of Osona mediating between natives and immigrants, have dwindled in influence. A new us-versus-them logic has become so powerful that mainstream parties in Catalonia, such as the PSC and PP, have begun to employ a similar xenophobic and anti-Muslim discourse.

Catalan authorities have implemented projects to avoid social fracture – for example, improvements in social housing and education – but they continue to reject multiculturalism as a kind of Bantustanism or

Balkanization, and opt instead for a French-style interculturalism that places Catalans' concern for language and cultural preservation at its core. The nationalist agenda to normalize the Catalan language and the sense of victimization that comes from being a small community contending with the second largest language in the world – in number of native speakers – has put the burden of cultural assimilation on immigrants to Catalonia.

A major project of Spanish Muslims has been to re-historicize the place of Islam in Spanish history. To this end, Muslims have organized lively academic debates and pushed for cities, such as Córdoba and Toledo, to revive the mythical *convivencia* between Christians, Muslims, and Jews of the past. Muslims have worked with museums and libraries to reanimate the past and have reclaimed Al-Andalus as their own. Their ecumenical position has subverted the strong Catholic favouritism in Spanish historiography, especially as it was practiced by public institutions in such celebrations as the Christian conquest of Valencia and Majorca, or the birth of James I in Aragon. In Valencia, Muslims commemorated instead the 1,000[th] anniversary of the Muslim Taifa Kingdom of Valencia, as well as the 400th anniversary of the expulsion of the *Moriscos*.

Some non-Muslims have collaborated with Muslims in this project of historical revision. During Vatican II, Catholic community groups took measures to avoid portraying Muslims as natural enemies and criticized the Church hierarchy's support of the Festival of Moors and Christians. Women's groups, who criticized the Festival's exclusion of women, particularly in the city of Alcoi, argued the Festival had to be made consistent with constitutional rights and democratic values of inclusion, such as equality for women.

The centuries-old Festival of Moors of Christians has drawn attention from Muslims due to its unflattering depiction of outsiders, its epic overtones, and its rigidly parochial worldview. The Festival goes to the heart of the crudest nativist arguments about immigration: that the true Spain is Catholic, that those that are not born into the country's good society or have the right genes are imposters who must be vanquished. According to the Festival's narrative, Spain was first Iberian, then Roman, then Visigoth, then hijacked by Muslim outsiders, before being restored to its Christian roots.

In response to their critics, Festival organizers have defended the event's traditionalism and refused to make changes, though they have toned down more offensive rituals for fear of international scorn, particularly after the Danish cartoon controversy of 2005. So far, the Festival has changed little due to its economic role and social function, even though it defies both Spain's commitment to the UN Alliance of Civilizations, an initiative meant to engender mutual respect and understanding between the West and the Islamic World, as well as the country's own recent embrace of cultural and religious pluralism. The conversation is nevertheless open and Muslim voices will increasingly be in a position to better defend their cultural rights and symbolic place in Spanish society.

Altogether, the civic engagement of Muslim immigrants has not only helped fellow immigrants obtain rights and become active Spanish citizens; more generally, it has made Spain a more dynamic, democratic society. Muslim immigrants, religious and secular, male and female, radical and moderate, have laid the foundation for a new *convivencia* in Spain. And while some battles, such as those waged by nativists in Melilla, are safely in the past, many struggles are just beginning. The emerging language of equality and mutual respect will do much to cement the sense of belonging of Muslims in Spain and strengthen Spaniard's commitment to democratic values. Our understanding of democratization in post-Francoist Spain must, therefore, recognize the contributions of Muslims, native and immigrants, in consolidating democratic institutions, enfranchising and protecting the political and social rights of minorities, deepening democratic attitudes amongst Spaniards, and integrating cultural rights into the country's democratic framework.

Notes

Introduction

1   The Imazighen (singular: Amazigh) are an indigenous people found across North Africa, west of the Nile River. They are also known as Berbers but opt, in self-reference, for the former designation.

2   Karrouch, *De Nador a Vic.*

3   Laila Karrouch, interview with author, Vic, March 12, 2008.

4   Spanish Constitution, Preamble.

5   Ibid., article 13.1.

6   Ibid., article 2 and 4.

7   For critical assessments of nationalism in the democratic period, see Balfour and Quiroga, *The Reinvention* and Mar-Molinero and Smith, *Nationalism.*

8   In Southern Europe, governments tied regularizations to reforms of immigration laws. In Spain, national regularizations took place in 1985, 1991, 1996, 2000, 2001, 2003, and 2004. In Italy, regularizations occurred during parliamentary approvals of the Martelli Law in 1990, the Turco-Napolitano Law in 1998, and the Bossi-Fini Law in 2002. In Portugal, regularizations and reforms occurred in 1992, 1996, and 2001.

9   UN Department of Economic and Social Affairs, *World Population Policies 2005*, 414 [Spain], 214 [France], and 222 [Germany].

10 INE, http://www.ine.es/prensa/np648.pdf.

11 Ibid.

12 UCIDE, *Estudio* and López García, "La evolución," 213–221.

13 Beckman, "Democratization," 162.

14 Dahl, *Polyarchy*, 4, 129. See also Young, *Inclusion*, and Wolbrecht and Hero, *The Politics.*

15 A "nativist" favours the interests of established citizens over those of immigrants or perceived immigrants. For historical examples of the use of the concept, see Higham, *Strangers* and Lucassen, *The Immigrant Threat.*

16 Kymlicka and Norman, "Return of the Citizen," 353.

17 Radcliff, *Making Democratic Citizens*, 12.

18 Ibid., 11.

19 Geoff Eley, *Forging Democracy.* My focus is on immigrant movements, something Eley does not cover.

20 Galston, *Liberal Purposes*, 227

21 Kymlicka and Norman, *Citizenship in Diverse Societies* 10,

22 Cazorla-Sánchez, *Fear and Progress*, 95–172 and Radcliff, *Making Democratic Citizens.*

23 For the transition, see Carr and Fusi, *España*, Castellano, *Por Dios*, Cebrián, *La España*, and Preston, *El triunfo*.

24 For a detailed description of the difference between consolidation and deepening of democracy, see Schedler, "What is Democratic Consolidation," 91–107 and Fung and Wright, *Deepening Democracy*.

25 Pérez-Díaz, *The Return of Civil Society*, 3–4. Pérez-Díaz differentiates between transition (ending in 1978), consolidation (ending some time during the first Socialist government from 1982 to 1986), and institution-alization (a process with a long way to go).

26 Heller, "Democratic Deepening," 125.

27 Ibid., 124.

28 Gellner, *Muslim Society*; Huntington, *The Clash of Civilizations*; Halliday, *Islam*; Goddard, "Islam and Democracy," 3–10, and Esposito and Burgat, *Modernizing Islam*.

29 Fallaci, *The Rage*; Ye'or, *Eurabia*; Bawer, *While Europe Slept*. Some popular counter examples also exist. See Buruma, *Murder in Amsterdam* or Saunders, *The Myth of the Muslim Tide*.

30 See Bruckner, *Misère*.

31 See Hirsi Ali, *The Caged Virgin*.

32 See Tibi, *Political Islam*; Roy, *Secularism*; and Kepel and Milner, *Allah in the West*.

33 See Garton Ash, *Free World*; Modood and Kastoryano, "Secularism," 162–178; and Cesari and McLoughlin, eds., *European Muslims*.

34 AlSayyad and Castells, eds., *Muslim Europe* and Nielsen, "The Question of Euro-Islam," 34–48.

35 A "native" or "ethnic Spaniard" in this book is a person who is indigenous to Spain, who is culturally Catholic, and whose mother tongue is Spanish, Catalan, Basque, or Gallego.

36 Perry, "Memory and Mutilation," 80–81. Martín Corrales, "Maurofobia/Islamofobia."

1 The Fight for Citizenship and Inclusion in a Borderland City: Melilla, 1985–1988

1 Spanish Constitution, 5th Transitory Disposition, and Law 2/1995, on the Statute of Autonomy of Melilla.

2 Despite the importance of the struggle for civil rights in Melilla, and to a lesser extent in Ceuta, only a handful of scholars have studied Muslim activism there. Even those scholars, such as Peter Gold and Ana I. Planet, who analyze the events of 1985–87 in Melilla, focus on the triangular rela-tionship between Morocco, Spain, and the enclaves, rather than on the contributions of Muslim activists to democratizing Spain. They, however, correctly conclude that Muslim mobilization ultimately reinforced Spain's geopolitical position in North Africa. Gold, *Europe or Africa?*, 91–119 and Planet, *Melilla and Ceuta*, 85–106.

3 INE, historical census data. 1970 census, Volume II, Provincial Data, http://www.ine.es/inebaseweb/pdfDispacher.do?td=144968.

4   M.N., "Un puerto muy franco," *El Periódico*, August 23, 2010, 15. See Cazorla-Sánchez, *Franco*, 23–24.

5   Ferrer Gallardo, "Theorizing," 1–24.

6   Castan Pinos, "Identity Challenges," 67–68.

7   Hopkin, *Party Formation*.

8   INE, http://www.ine.es. For more on the 1986 census, see Planet, *Melilla and Ceuta*, 30–37. Rocío García, "Chapas de perro," *El País*, June 10, 1985.

9   Government delegates (*delegados del gobierno*) are representatives of the national government in autonomous regions and cities. They supervise areas under the jurisdiction of the national government and coordinate efforts with regional administrations.

10 Luis Rincón, "Melilla no es tierra de todos, es tierra de unos," *Melilla Hoy*, May 2, 1985, 8–9.

11 Kaplan, "Territorial," 31–49 and Kaplan, "Conflict," 100–107.

12 The idea of multiple identities, particularly simultaneous regional and national identities, has become more prevalent in Spain. See for instance Moral, *Identidad* and García Ferrando et al., *La conciencia*.

13 Spanish Constitution, art. 13.1.

14 Sagarra Trias, *La Legislación*, 121–128.

15 See "Ruiz-Giménez apoya una reforma profunda de la ley de extranjería," *El País*, February 13, 1986. Editorial, "Los extranjeros, la Constitución y el Ministerio del Interior," *El País*, October 19, 1985. The role of the Office of the Ombudsman, created in 1981, is to protect and defend the fundamental rights and freedoms of citizens. The Ombudsman cited as possibly unconstitutional the articles that granted freedoms of assembly and association only to legal residents; that permitted the government to deport status-less immigrants without judicial oversight; and that stated that appeals could not impede the deportation process. In 1987 the Constitutional Court sided with the Ombudsman's appeal.

16 Article 26 (deportation), Article 4 (constitutional rights), Article 5 (suffrage rights), Article 7 (freedom of assembly), Article 8 (freedom of association), Preface, and Article 23 (preferential treatment). Law 7/1985.

17 Ricardo Crespo, "Algunas interrogantes sobre la Ley de Extranjería," *Melilla Hoy*, November 22, 1985, 6.

18 Aomar Mohamedi Duddu, "La Ley de Extranjería en Melilla o la legalización de la esclavitud," *Melilla Hoy*, December 11, 1985, 6.

19 Editorial, "Moros y cristianos," *El País*, December 17, 1985.

20 Malkki, "National Geographic," 31, 27. For historical arboreal interpretations of migration, see Handlin, *The Uprooted* and Bodnar, *The Transplanted*.

21 This book uses Spanish transliterations of Arabic names as they appear in Spanish sources, except for Duddu, whose name appeared either as Duddu, Dudú, or Duddú.

22 Alex Grijelmo, "Entrevista a Abdelkáder Mohamed Alí," *El País*, November 7, 1988. For a fictionalized attempt to understand Duddu, see Crespo, *Entre moros y cristianos*. For historical accounts of ethnic entre-

preneurs, see Harney, "Montreal's," 57–84 and Zhou, "Revisiting," 1040–1074.

23 To distinguish the two main ethnic groups in Melilla, this chapter uses "European descendant" or "ethnic European" and "African descendant" or "Muslim Melillan."

24 Adem Çaylak proved that although Islamist groups in Turkey in the 1980s tended to replicate the patterns of state authoritarianism in their organizational structures, they nevertheless performed a democratic function by encouraging alternative perspectives and providing a public milieu for discussion. Çaylak, "Autocratic or Democratic?" 115–151.

25 Ricardo Crespo, "Terra Omnium," *Melilla Hoy*, May 1, 1985, 3. Prior to Terra Omnium, Duddu and his supporters operated under the umbrella of the Muslim Association. Bureaucratic difficulties and infighting forced the group to branch out on its own.

26 Carlos Yárnoz, "Cierre de comercios del colectivo musulmán de Melilla," *El País*, December 8, 1985.

27 Differences in how Muslims in Melilla and Ceuta mobilized can be explained by the fact that Ceuta is geographically closer to mainland Spain and its leaders approached Madrid differently. The outlooks of the government delegates in both cities also varied. While Muslim Ceutans spoke highly of their delegate, Manuel Peláez López, for his neutrality and defence of Muslims, Muslim Melillans disparaged Antonio Moreno for his partisan support of nativists. Mimuntz Mohamed, a Melillan activist, speculated that differences between the cities were due to a greater ethnic bond amongst Melilla's predominantly Amazigh Muslims, as compared to the largely Arab Ceutans. Mimuntz Mohamed, interview with author, Melilla, August 24, 2010.

28 Editorial, "Racismo español," *El País*, May 26, 1985. Carlos Yárnoz, "El incierto futuro de Ceuta y Melilla," *El País*, February 17, 1985. C.Y., "Un militante del PSOE dice que fue expulsado por criticar el racismo en Melilla," *El País*, September 2, 1985.

29 Enrique Chueca, "Dudú evita pronunciarse sobre la españolidad de Melilla," *El País*, November 15, 1986.

30 Abdelkader Mohamed Alí, interview with author, Melilla, August 23, 2010. Bauman, *Identity*. For an anthropological study of how Muslim women in Ceuta negotiate their multiple identities, see Rosander, *Women in a Borderland*.

31 Modood, "Anti Essentialism, Multiculturalism," 186 and Jacobson, "Perceptions of Britishness."

32 "Protesta musulmana 'a la argentina'," *Melilla Hoy*, January 26, 1986, 5 and Avelino Gutiérrez, "300 mujeres musulmanas se manifiestan en Melilla contra la ley de Extranjería," *El País*, January 26, 1985.

33 Editorial, "Situación límite," *Melilla Hoy*, January 29, 1986, 1, 6, 7 and Avelino Gutierrez, "La policía reprime en Melilla con porras y botes de humo una manifestación pacífica de mujeres musulmanas," *El País*, January 29, 1986.

34 Gutierrez, "La policía reprime" and Editorial, "Situación límite," 1

35 Isabel de Torre, "¿Dónde estabas, Aomar?" *Melilla Hoy*, February 2, 1986, 3 and "Nosotras también pensamos," *Melilla Hoy*, February, 4, 1986, 6. Mimuntz Mohamed.

36 Karmentxu Marín, "Musulmanas en Melilla: Dejadas de la mano de Alá: La falta de documentación y el ambiente familiar dificultan la incorporación de las mujeres islámicas a la sociedad," *El País*, March 30, 1986. Abderramán Benyahya, interview with author, Melilla, August 24, 2010.

37 Most Muslim women who worked outside of the home did so as domestic servants or cleaners. Marín, "Musulmanas en Melilla."

38 Ibid.

39 Ibid.

40 The original Spanish reads: "*Ser morita y ser mujer ya es muy difícil. Ser morita ante los españoles y ser mujer ante los moritos musulmanes [es incluso más difícil.]*"

41 Marín, "Musulmanas en Melilla."

42 "Protesta musulmana 'a la argentina'"; "La Asamblea del colectivo musulmán terminó con aviso de bomba," *Melilla Hoy*, December 29, 1985, 1; Karima Tufali; "Continúa la huelga de hambre en la mezquita de Garbía Cabrelles," *Melilla Hoy*, January 24, 1986, 1; and Abdelkader Mohamed Alí.

43 "Comunicado de APROME," *Melilla Hoy*, January 14, 1986, 5.

44 Zine, "Unveiled Sentiments," 239, 240. See also Hamdan, "The Issue."

45 Cited in Fernando Orgambides, "Hassan II afirma que la situación de Ceuta y Melilla es anacrónica," *El País*, March 8, 1986. Saddiki, "Ceuta and Melilla Fences," 8.

46 Juan Goytisolo, "De la OTAN a la ley de extranjería," *El País*, March 6, 1986 and Carlos Yárnoz, "El incierto futuro de Ceuta y Melilla," *El País*, February 17, 1985.

47 A "nativist" favours the interests of established citizens over those of immigrants or perceived immigrants.

48 Cited in Carlos Yárnoz, "El incierto futuro."

49 Aomar Mohamedi Duddu, "Legalizar Melilla," *El País*, May 11, 1985

50 Joaquín Aranda Gallego, "La economía de Ceuta y Melilla," 278–287.

51 Duddu, "Legalizar Melilla."

52 Ricardo Crespo, "Discriminación," *El País*, December 8, 1985.

53 Noé Villaverde, "Ceuta y Melilla," *El País*, June 1, 1985.

54 Editorial, "Racismo español." The number of Muslim Melillans with Spanish citizenship was low due to an expensive and convoluted citizenship application process. Lawyers charged Muslims the equivalent to three months' salary for an unskilled worker to process their claims, and requested a report of good conduct from the government delegate. From 1975 to 1982, Spain granted citizenship to 2,000 Muslim Melillans; after 1982, less than 20 applications were processed per year. By 1985, more than 700 applications awaited processing. García, "Chapas de perro" and Carlos Yárnoz, "El Gobierno."

55 Editorial, "Racismo español."

56   Martín Sagrera, "Antipatriotas y suicidas," *El Correo Gallego*, December 10, 1985, reprinted in *Melilla Hoy*, January 2, 1986, 3.
57   Editorial, "La vergüenza de Melilla," *El País*, January 29, 1986 and Editorial, "Racismo español."
58   Doorenspleet, "Deviant democracies," 200.
59   Galston, *Liberal Purposes*, 221–4.
60   Duddu, "Legalizar Melilla."
61   "El Gobierno garantiza a Hassan II que no habrá expulsiones masivas," *El País*, December 7, 1985.
62   Fernando Orgambides, "Los nacionalistas marroquies, decididos a 'liberar' Ceuta y Melilla," *El País*, December 10, 1985; Fernando Orgambides, "Nacionalistas marroquíes convocan una concentración cerca de Melilla," *El País*, February 7, 1986; and Emma Roig, "Interior afirma que los musulmanes arraigados en Ceuta y Melilla tendrán la nacionalidad española," *El País*, February 8, 1986; Fernando Orgambides, "El Istiqlal advierte a los musulmanes de Ceuta y Melilla de los riesgos de ser españoles," *El País*, February 14, 1986.
63   Seddon, "Winter of Discontent," 7–16.
64   "El Gobierno asegura que facilitará la plena integración de los musulmanes de Ceuta y Melilla," *El País*, November 30, 1985.
65   Ibid.
66   "La vergüenza de Melilla."
67   "Esta noche, protesta del colectivo musulmán por la Ley de Extranjería," *Melilla Hoy*, October 30, 1985, 1; and Carlos Yárnoz, "Extranjeros en su tierra," *El País*, November 29, 1985. "Foreigners in our own land" is still an expression used by Muslim Melillans; Mohamed Alí; Karima Tufali, interview with author, Melilla, August 23, 2010.
68   Avelino Gutiérrez, "El delegado del Gobierno en Melilla amenaza a quienes asistan a la asamblea musulmana," *El País*, November 9, 1985; "Las peticiones del campo de fútbol del Tesorillo y del salón de actos del Instituto Leopoldo Queipo, han sido denegadas," *Melilla Hoy*, October 30, 1985, 1; and Abdelkader Mohamed Alí.
69   Avelino Gutiérrez, "Incidentes en Melilla ante la manifestación musulmana contra la ley de extranjería," *El País*, November 21, 1985; "La manifestación contra la Ley de Extranjería obedece a una mala información," *Melilla Hoy*, November 16, 1985, 1.
70   "Posturas radicalizadas sobre la Ley de Extranjería y la manifestación de hoy," *Melilla Hoy*, November 23, 1985, 7.
71   "Convocatoria a la manifestación," *Melilla Hoy*, November 23, 1985, 7. Capitalization in the original.
72   Editorial, "¿Empieza una nueva era en Melilla?" *Melilla Hoy*, November 24, 1985, 3 and Enrique Chueca, "Miles de musulmanes se manifiestan en Melilla contra la ley de extranjería," *El País*, November 24, 1985.
73   Avelino Gutiérrez, "Los partidos políticos de Melilla convocan una manifestación a favor de la ley de extranjería," *El País*, November 27, 1985.
74   "Aumenta la solidaridad hacia la manifestación del 6 de diciembre," *Melilla Hoy*, November 28, 1985, 1. The statement was by Manuel Soler.

Cited in Carlos Yárnoz, "10.000 banderas españolas para la marcha a favor de la ley de Extranjería," *El País*, November 30, 1985.

75 Carlos Yárnoz, "La manifestación en favor de la ley de extranjería se convirtió en un acto de reafirmación de la españolidad de Melilla," *El País*, December 7, 1985.

76 Ibid.

77 Carlos Yárnoz, "Banderas españolas engalanan Melilla ante la manifestación en favor de la ley de extranjería," *El País*, December 6, 1985. European Parliament Member Records, accessed September 10, 2010, http://www.europarl.europa.eu/members/archive/term4/view.do?langua ge=EN&id=2279.

78 "Comunicado de la Asociación Musulmana, COPM, Terra Omium y Unión Provincial de Comisiones Obreras de Melilla," *Melilla Hoy*, December 5, 1985, 12.

79 Avelino Gutiérrez, "Los musulmanes de Melilla rechazan las propuestas presentadas por Interior," *El País*, December 15, 1985; "Las Asociaciones de Vecinos colaborarán en la manifestación del día seis," *Melilla Hoy*, November 29, 1985, 1; "Aomar Mohamedi expulsado por el alcalde," *Melilla Hoy*, December 11, 1985, 1; and Mohamed Alí.

80 "Ayer comenzó la protesta blanca," *Melilla Hoy*, January 18, 1986, 7; "El colectivo muslmán declara días de ayuno hasta el sábado 25," *Melilla Hoy*, January 23, 1986, 7; Emma Roig, "El Gobierno retrasa la entrada en vigor de la ley de extranjería hasta el próximo 1 de marzo," *El País*, January 28, 1986.

81 "El Gobierno garantiza a Hassan II que no habrá expulsiones masivas," *El País*, December 7, 1985.

82 Emma Roig, "Comienza el diálogo en Interior sobre la situación en Ceuta y Melilla," *El País*, February 10, 1986. The Agreement stipulated that Muslim organizations were to create a census of undocumented Muslim residents in Ceuta and Melilla; that the Immigration Act was not applicable to Ceuta and Melilla residents who could show "*arraigo*," a concept to be defined with input from Muslims; and that the Ministry of Justice was to expedite citizenship applications for Melillans. "Las bases del pacto," *El País*, February 11, 1986, Emma Roig, "Interior llega a un acuerdo con los lideres de los musulmanes de Ceuta y Melilla sobre la ley de extranjería," *El País*, February 11, 1986; Editorial, "Un principio de acuerdo para Ceuta y Melilla," El País, February 11, 1986.

83 Avelino Gutiérrez, "5.000 musulmanes de Melilla han presentado los documentos para solicitar ser españoles," *El País*, April 2, 1986.

84 Carlos Gómez, "Los partidos políticos de Melilla protestan por el acuerdo entre Interior y los musulmanes," *El País*, February 12, 1986.

85 J.G., "Los nacionalistas desconvocan la protesta contra Barrionuevo," *El País*, April 2, 1986.

86 Emma Roig, "El Gobierno aprobará una dotación de 15.000 millones para Ceuta y Melilla," *El País*, March 21, 1986; "Iniciadas las obras para reforzar la frontera de Melilla con Marruecos," *El País*, May 16, 1986; and Emma

Roig, "El Gobierno amplía por tercera vez el plazo para que los extranjeros regulen su situación en España," *El País*, February 22, 1986.

87   Carlos Yárnoz, "El Consejo del Poder Judicial abre una investigación sobre la discriminación de los musulmanes melillenses," *El País*, El Viajero, June 14, 1986 and "Investigación judicial sobre posible discriminación a los musulmanes de Melilla," *El País*, June 14, 1986.

88   Emma Roig, "El líder musulmán melillense acusa al Gobierno de no cumplir sus compromisos," *El País*, June 5, 1986 and Avelino Guitérrez, "El alcalde de Melilla prefiere dimitir antes que readmitir a Dudú en el Ayuntamiento," January 2, 1987.

89   Carlos Yárnoz, "Dirigentes musulmanes de Melilla apoyan la creación de una administracion paralela en la ciudad," *El País*, November 10, 1986.

90   Muslim Melillans campaigned in three languages: Spanish, Arabic, and Cherja. Carlos Yárnoz, "Campaña con mensajes electorales en árabe," *El País*, June 20, 1986; Editorial, "¿Arde Melilla?" *El País*, June 19, 1986.

91   "Jóvenes musulmanes de Melilla reparten claveles blancos como gesto de amistad," *El País*, July 1, 1986; Editorial, "Convivencia en Melilla," *El País*, August 23, 1986; and Editorial, "La demagogia y el avestruz," *El País*, November 11, 1986.

92   Carlos Yárnoz, "Representantes políticos de Melilla pedirán hoy al Gobierno que releve a su delegado y aplique la ley de extranjería," *El País*, August 22, 1986; and "Los musulmanes de Melilla rompen las negociaciones con el Gobierno," *El País*, November 7, 1986.

93   Avelino Gutiérrez and Enrique Chueca, "Los musulmanes de Melilla convocan una huelga general de cuatro días y una manifestación para el día 22," *El País*, November 12, 1986.

94   "Barrionuevo: 'No hay más salida para Melilla que la integración de los musulmanes'," *El País*, November 13, 1986. The government delegate claimed that 2,500 people had participated, while organizers claimed a number ten times larger. Enrique Chueca, "Miles de musulmanes se manifiestan en Melilla sin incidentes," *El País*, November 23, 1986.

95   Yárnoz, "El Consejo del Poder Judicial."

96   A rift had opened in late 1986 among Muslims who supported Spain and Muslims who supported Morocco. Pro-Morocco leaders in Melilla demanded the withdrawal of all 7,000 citizenship applications. Pro-Spanish Muslims, such as Ahmed Moh, wanted to continue participating in the Joint Commission until a new agreement could be reached. Carlos Yárnoz, "Decisiones sorprendentes con consecuencias imprevistas," *El País*, February 2, 1987.

97   "Barrionuevo: 'No hay mas salida para Melilla que la integración de losmusulmanes'," *El País*, November 13, 1986.

98   Fernando Orgambides, "El viaje a Rabat, inicio del 'cambio de rumbo'," *El País*, November 12, 1986; "El Gobierno asegura que hay avances en la integración," *El País*, November 10, 1986; and Editorial, "La demagogia y el avestruz."

99   Fernando Orgambides, "Crece la preocupación en Rabat por los acontecimientos en Melilla," *El País*, November 17, 1986.

100 Enrique Chueca, "Miles de musulmanes."

101 Avelino Gutiérrez, "Aomar Dudú viaja nuevamente a Marruecos, 'para meditar'," *El País*, December 12, 1986; "Dudú realiza una nueva visita a Rabat," January 7, 1987; "Interior negocia con los musulmanes y Dudú afirma que Melilla es marroquí," *El País*, January 14, 1987; and Avelino Gutiérrez, "Políticos de Melilla piden que se prive a Dudú de la nacionalidad española," January 15, 1987.

102 Duddu, "La Ley de Extranjería," 6 and Luis Rincón, "Interview with Aomar Mohamedi Duddú. Melilla no es tierra de todos, es tierra de unos," *Melilla Hoy*, May 2, 1986, 8–9. See also Habermas, *The Postnational Constellation*.

103 Abdelkader Mohamed Alí and Mimuntz Mohamed.

104 Avelino Gutiérrez, "Dudú se 'autoexilia' en la localidad marroquí de Nador," *El País*, January 31, 1987; Fernando Orgambides, "'He encontrado en Marruecos la seguridad que no tenía en Melilla', afirma Dudú," *El País*, February 1, 1987; and "Céspedes afirma contar con el apoyo del Gobierno," *El País*, February 2, 1987.

105 "Cinco heridos graves en Melilla en enfrentamientos entre miembros de las dos comunidades," February 2, 1987; Editorial, "Un nuevo aviso viene de Melilla," *El País*, February 2, 1987; Abdelkader Mohamed Alí; and Mimuntz Mohamed.

106 Fernando Orgambides, "Dudú afirma que Céspedes lleva a cabo una 'política de terror'," *El País*, February 4, 1987 and Alex Grijelmo, "El juez procesa a Dudú por incitar a la subversion," *El País*, February 5, 1987.

107 According to the police version of events, Hammu and other demonstrators had attacked a young nativist, Miguel Sánchez Luque, with a knife as he returned home, which made his father shoot at the assailants with a rifle. Hassan Hammed and Hassan Alí, two witnesses to the event, said Sánchez Luque's father shot at demonstrators first and they only attacked Sánchez Luque with a knife in self-defence. The police arrested both the father and son. Alex Grijelmo, "La muerte de un musulmán herido el sábado pasado reaviva la tensión en Melilla," *El País*, February 7, 1987.

108 In May 1981, ETA tried to assassinate a Spanish general, Joaquín de Valenzuela. A few days later, three tortured, charred, and bullet-ridden bodies turned up outside Almería. The Spanish Civil Guard claimed that a shootout with an ETA commando had occurred, though it was later revealed that the deaths were the results of reckless actions by Lieutenant Colonel Carlos Castillo Quero and eleven of his subordinates. The victims were innocent civilians. Though Darío Fernandez, the lawyer for the victims' families, received death threats and went into hiding for a time, he managed to get Castillo Quero and three guards sentenced for their crimes. Santiago Aroca, "Carlos Castillo Quero: Condenado por el 'caso Almería'," *El Mundo*, April 5, 1994; Alex Grijelmo, "Una ciudad dominada por los rumores," *El País*, February 8, 1987; and Lola Galán, "Nadie puede ser un agente en su tierra," declara el líder musulmán," *El País*, February 19, 1987.

109 Alex Grijelmo, "Tambores para un delito," *El País*, February 6, 1987.

110 Alex Grijelmo, "Los dirigentes musulmanes presos califican de 'ofensivo' el haber sido procesados por el delito de sedición," *El País*, February 10, 1987.

111 Grijelmo, "Los dirigentes musulmanes presos" and Alex Grijelmo, "Nosotros abrazamos la Constitución," declaran los nueve musulmanes presos," *El País*, February 12, 1987.

112 "Instrucciones sobre autorización de residencia y trabajo en las ciudades de Ceuta y Melilla," Directive, July 2, 1986; "Normas sobre tramitación y resolución de solicitudes de permisos de trabajo a extranjeros," Communication, 12/87, March 6, 1987; Antonio Gala, Juan Goytisolo, Manuel Vázquez Montalbán et al., "Por la distensión en Melilla y Ceuta," *El País*, February 13, 1987.

113 See, for example, Abdallah et al., *J'y suis, j'y reste!*

114 In total, 14,000 Muslims were nationalized, which still left 4,000 undocumented. José Antonio Carrizosa, "Dudú es un cadáver político y la comunidad musulmana permanece dividida," *El País*, November 27, 1988.

115 Przeworski, "Conquered or Granted?" 291–321.

116 The Coalition for Melilla was the third most voted party in 1995 and the second in 1999. Toñi Ramos, "Un musulmán gobernará la ciudad autónoma de Melilla con apoyo socialista y del GIL," *El País*, July 4, 1999.

117 The new leadership of Terra Omnium was presided over by Abderramán Mohamed who believed that "Duddu's betrayal has damaged the Muslim community in Melilla. For us Duddu is a political cadaver who will never have anything more to say here." José Antonio Carrizosa, "Los árabes de Melilla critican a Dudú en el tercer aniversario de las primeras movilizaciones," *El País*, November 19, 1988.

118 Grijelmo, "Entrevista a Abdelkáder Mohamed."

119 Fernando Orgambides, "Dudú rindió fidelidad a Hassan II en Rabat," *El País*, March 5, 1987; Ignacio Cembrero, "¿Puede un gobernador marroquí concurrir a las elecciones en Melilla?" *El País*, May 15, 2011; and Grijelmo, "Entrevista a Abdelkáder Mohamed Alí."

120 Goytisolo, "De la OTAN."

2 The Struggle for Voice, Rights, and Status in Mainland Spain, 1989–2005

1 On regional nationalist protest, see Núñez Seixas, "The Reawakening," and Llera, Mata, and Irvin, "ETA," 106–134.

2 On the decline of protest in the post-Franco era, see Hipsher, "Democratization," 273–287. On the mobilization of women, see Threlfall, "The Women's Movement," 44–73 and Radcliff, "Imagining Female Citizenship," 498–523. On the rise of the environmental movement in the 1990s, see Jiménez, "The Environmental," 359–378. On the anti-globalization movement of the 2000s, see Karamichas, "Key Issues," 273–294. On the lesbian, gay, transsexual, and bisexual movement, see Calvo, "Sacrifices," 295–314.

3 King and Rodríguez-Melguizo, "Recent Immigration," 75 and Castles and Miller, *The Age of Migration*.

4   Spain is not the only European country that has experienced an immigrant-led civil rights movement. For a survey, see Laubenthal, "The Emergence," 101–133.

5   Tarrow, *Power in Movement.*

6   Begoña Aguirre, "El comité regional del Año contra el Racismo excluye a los inmigrantes," *El País,* June 4, 1997.

7   "La Iglesia católica critica la situación en la que viven los inmigrantes en España," *El País,* November 6, 1989; Bernabé López García et al., "De los inmigrantes ilegales," *El País,* March 5, 1991; Bernabé López García and Carlos Celaya, "La metáfora del extranjero," *El País,* July 11, 1995; Goytisolo and Naïr, *El peaje.*

8   "Interview with Abdelhamid Beyuki: Los sentimientos xenófobos son difíciles de frenar una vez activados," *Consumer Eroski,* February 1, 2001, accessed December 10, 2009, http://revista.consumer.es/web/es/20010201/entrevista/28167.php. Chaib, *Enlloc,* 116.

9   Begoña Aguirre, "Beyuki Abdelhamid se ha convertido en el líder de los inmigrantes marroquíes," *El País,* February 15, 1991. On the 1984 bread riots, see Seddon, "Winter," 7–16.

10 Nini, *Diario,* 28.

11 I.C., "El ministro de Exteriores de Marruecos pedirá el fin de las expulsiones de inmigrantes," *El País,* July 2, 1990.

12 See, for instance, Testas, "Maghreb-EU," 64–80 and Zniber, "Maroc," 46–47. On Spain, see Mancho, *Emigración.*

13 Ana Camacho, "5.000 marroquíes duermen a la intemperie en las afueras de Madrid para eludir a la policía," *El País,* May 27, 1990.

14 Ibid.

15 "ATIME: Quienes somos," accessed December 10, 2009, http://www.atime.es/quien.html.

16 Chaib, *Enlloc,* 116. For more on Moroccan activism in Catalonia, see Moreras, *Actors.*

17 "ATIME: Quienes somos" and "Interview with Abdelhamid Beyuki."

18 One of the reasons that AEME was pushed off the political map was because the attorney general used against AEME an article from the Immigration Act on human trafficking that was meant for mafia groups, rather than immigrant organizations who helped undocumented workers.

19 Begoña Aguirre, "La asociación de inmigrantes denuncia 'corrupción' en el consulado marroquí," *El País,* April 15, 1991.

20 Begoña Aguirre, "Inmigrantes marroquíes denuncian el retraso de sus permisos de trabajo," *El País,* September 3, 1991 and Lorenzo Romero and Joanquín Prieto, "Contrabando de inmigrantes," *El País,* September 22, 1991.

21 Maite Rico, "Ciudadanos marroquíes, contra la corrupción de su embajada en Madrid," *El País,* Septembre 23, 1991.

22 Lorenzo Romero and Joaquín Prieto, "Marruecos sustituye a los responsables del consulado denunciado por corrupción," *El País,* October 12, 1991. Francesc Peirón, "La presión diplomática obliga al juez a tomar

declaración por escrito al cónsul marroquí," *La Vanguardia*, November 28, 1991, 38.

23 Maite Rico, "Más de 4.000 inmigrantes marroquíes piden su legalización," *El País*, March 2, 1991.

24 Belkacemi, *Amazic*, 119, 103.

25 Nini, *Diario*, 197.

26 Ibid., 180; Hage, *Cockroach* and Belkacemi, *Amazic*, 84. See also Santa Ana, "Like an Animal," 191–224.

27 Nini, *Diario*, 41. For a fictionalized account of Spain's migrant criminal underworld, see Ben Jelloun, *Leaving Tangier*.

28 Nini, *Diario*, 51.

29 Belkacemi, *Amazic*, 47 and Nini, *Diario*, 63.

30 Nini, *Diario*, 207.

31 Chaib, *Ètica*, 10, 25, 115.

32 L.S.M., "El Gobierno ratifica la exigencia de visado a marroquíes y tunecinos," *El País*, April 13, 1991. López García et al., "De los inmigrantes ilegales."

33 Izquierdo Escribano, "La inmigración," 18–38. Francisco Mercado, "Los inmigrantes ilegales en España oscilan entre 72.000 y 124.000 según un estudio," *El País*, March 18, 1991.

34 "Cristianisme i Justicia sugiere que España pida perdón por la colonización de América," *El País*, January 3, 1989.

35 Royal Decree 155, on the Regulations of Law 7/1985 and "Aprobado el Plan para la Integración Social de los inmigrantes," *El País*, December 3, 1994.

36 Maite Rico, "Los socialistas piden la legalización de todo inmigrante que esté 'arraigado'," *El País*, April 9, 1991.

37 Maite Rico, "El Congreso aprueba la legalización de los inmigrantes que demuestren 'su arraigo'," *El País*, April 10, 1991.

38 Maite Rico, "Un proceso bien acogido," *El País*, June 13, 1991.

39 Rico, "El Gobierno facilitará" and José Carlos Rodríguez Soto, "Africanos, ¿los perdedores de siempre?" *El País*, September 12, 1991.

40 Izquierdo Escribano, "La inmigración,"18–38.

41 Ana Camacho, "Las emigrantes magrebíes crean una comisión para reivindicar sus derechos," *El País*, May 20, 1991.

42 Ibid and Begoña Aguirre, "Encierro de 30 empleadas de hogar marroquíes contra la explotación laboral," *El País*, January 19, 1992. The power of immigration to shake up gender roles was not unique to Spain. For the American context, see Hondagneu-Sotelo, *Gender*, and Aitchison, *Geographies*, and Predelli, "Interpreting."

43 Aguirre, "Encierro."

44 Ibid. and Arancha García de Sola, "El fin de la clandestinidad," *El País*, December 8, 1991.

45 Luis Fernando Durán, "Los trabajadores marroquíes piden una ley que les proteja en el mercado laboral," *El País*, December 14, 1992.

46 Begoña Aguirre, "Inmigrantes marroquíes denuncian el retraso de sus permisos de trabajo," *El País*, September 3, 1991.

47 Victorino R. de Azúa, "Inmigrantes marroquíes critican la Ley de Extranjería y piden 'derechos para todos'," *El País*, December 9, 1991 and "Concentración de inmigrantes en Madrid contra la ley de extranjería," *El País*, December 16, 1991.

48 "Interior asegura que sólo quedarán sin legalizar los delincuentes," *El País*, December 9, 1991; Victorino Ruiz de Azúa, "Interior anuncia la expulsión 'con todas las garantías' de los inmigrantes ilegales," *El País*, December 12, 1991.

49 Durán, "Los trabajadores marroquíes piden."

50 Jesús Duva, "Inmigrantes marroquíes piden una ley que tipifique el racismo," November 24, 1991. On Lucrecia Pérez's assassination, see Calvo Buezas, *El crimen*. See also Law 4/1995.

51 Begoña Aguirre, "34 marroquíes, en huelga del hambre al aumentar las expulsiones por la guerra," *El País*, February 8, 1991; and "Grupos 'ultras' amenazan por carta a una asociación de trabajadores marroquíes," *El País*, June 21, 1992.

52 Nini, *Diario*, 87, 153.

53 "*Controles policiales selectivos en función de la raza*" and "*controles policiales con sesgo racista*," literally, "selective police controls on the basis of race" and "police controls with racial bias." European Parliament, *Boletines terminológicos y normativos* 51, accessed September 25, 2010, http://www.europarl.europa.eu/transl_es/plataforma/pagina/celter/bol51 .htm. *Profilage racial* is well established in French and *racial profiling* is widely accepted in Italian.

54 Nini, *Diario*, 64.

55 Joseba Elola, "Identifíquese, es usted negra," *El País*, August 30, 2009; Anaís Berdié and Rebeca Carranco, "Detenido el único negro de la fila," *El País*, February 17, 2009. For Rosalind William's case, see http://www.opensocietyfoundations.org/litigation/williams-v-spain and http://www. opensocietyfoundations.org/sites/default/files/decision-en_20090812.pdf.

56 Candel, *Els altres Catalans*, 292–298.

57 Ana Torregrosa, "Un millar de inmigrantes protesta en Almería para reclamar unas condiciones dignas de vida," *El País*, April 12, 1999. For more on housing segregation in El Ejido, see Martínez Veiga, *El Ejido*. Nini, *Diario*, 31.

58 Ana Torregrosa, "Un centenar de trabajadores extranjeros se manifiesta por las calles de Vícar," *El País*, Sept. 27, 1999 and EUMC "Muslims in the European Union."

59 El Hachmi, *Jo també sóc catalana*, 78.

60 Chaib, *Enlloc*, 100.

61 Begoña Aguirre, "Los abogados de inmigrantes se quejan de la escasez de tiempo para defenderlos," *El País*, May 30, 1991.

62 Chaib, *Enlloc*, 112.

63 See the Red Acoge website, http://www.redacoge.org/ and http://www.murcia-acoge.com; "Grupos 'ultras' amenazan por carta."

64 For detailed information on the migrant quota system, see Plewa and Miller, "Postwar," 73–74.

65 Milagros Pérez Oliva, "Las organizaciones de inmigrantes califican de burla y trampa la regularización de este año," *El País*, September 18, 1995.

66 Ibid. See also López García et al., "La política," 257–8 and CEIMIGRA, "El contingente."

67 "Aprobado el Plan para la Integración Social de los inmigrantes," *El País*, December 3, 1994 and *Plan para la integración*.

68 "La marginación la fomenta el Gobierno," *El País*, January 8, 1995 and Ana Camacho, "España deja de ser un país de tránsito para los inmigrantes y se convierte en un destino estable," *El País*, January 8, 1995.

69 Royal Decree 490/1995.

70 Editorial, "Inmigrantes legales," *El País*, April 29, 1996.

71 While the Workers' Commissions argued that a job contract was unnecessary for the regularization, the UGT sided with the government and said that it was necessary. See González Enríquez et al., *Los sindicatos ante la inmigración*, 92.

72 Editorial, "Inmigrantes legales."

73 Begoña Aguirre, "El tortuoso camino hasta llegar a los 'papeles'," *El País*, November 17, 1996.

74 Begoña Aguirre, "El comité regional."

75 Ernesto Núñez, "Las asociaciones civiles piden crear un ministerio de migraciones," *El País*, August 20, 1998.

76 A.H.R., "Organizaciones católicas reclaman la regularización de 50.000 'ilegales'," *El País*, January 14, 1999; "¿Regularizaría a todos los inmigrantes 'sin papeles'?" *El País*, June 5, 1999.

77 Article 3, Law 4/2000. See also Miguel González, "Los extranjeros que residan legalmente en España no serán iguales en derechos a los españoles," *El País*, June 16, 2000 and Editorial, "Más que una reforma," *El País*, June 18, 2000.

78 In November 2000, when the Centro de Investigaciones Sociológicas asked a sample of Spaniards what they believed were Spain's top three problems, "immigration" ranked eight out of thirty. A year later it had moved to sixth place; by November 2002 it was fourth; by 2005 it was second; and by 2006 it was tied for first with "unemployment." Source: Barómetros del CIS. http://www.cis.es, accessed December 22, 2009.

79 See Eliseo Aja, "Inmigración: ¿reformar la ley o impulsar el consenso?" *El País*, June 29, 2000.

80 "Las asociaciones sociales inician hoy protestas en defensa de la ley," *El País*, November 25, 1999; Jorge A. Rodríguez, "Sindicatos y ONG convocan protestas contra la 'burla a la democracia' de las enmiendas del PP, *El País*, December 10, 1999; and Jorge A. Rodríguez, "Las organizaciones sociales dejan el consejo consultivo del Gobierno sobre la inmigración," *El País*, December 11, 1999.

81 "Las asociaciones sociales inician hoy protestas en defensa de la ley," *El País*, November 25, 1999 and Rodríguez, "Sindicatos y ONG."

82 Articles 7, 8, 9, 11, and 29.3, Act 4/2000.

83 Editorial, "Es de ley," *El País*, November 12, 1999.

84 Jorge A. Rodríguez, "De la precariedad a la integración social," *El País*, November 12, 1999 and Carlos E. Cué, "La integración, principio básico," *El País*, December 23, 1999.

85 Editorial, "Un éxito de la democracia, una grave derrota del Ejecutivo," *El País*, December 23, 1999.

86 Following the January 2000 riots in El Ejido, Moroccan migrants rallied to fight labour exploitation, housing segregation, and poor living conditions generally. They signed a series of agreements with regional authorities and agri-business associations, however their situation changed little and most chose to relocate to other areas of Spain. SOS Racismo, *El Ejido*; Checa, ed. *El Ejido*; Martínez Veiga, *Organización*. For the agro-business perspective, see Azurmendi, *Estampas*.

87 "500 personas piden en Valencia que se regularice la situación de los inmigrantes," *El País*, February 18, 2000.

88 *Balance 2001* (Madrid: Delegación del Gobierno para la Extranjería y la Inmigración, 2002): 30 and Estrada and Serraller, "Un proceso de regularización."

89 Editorial, "Gobierno e inmigración," *El País*, May 28, 2000 and Miguel Pajares, "Ley de Extranjería y política de inmigración," *El País*, June 16, 2000.

90 Eliseo Aja, "Inmigración: ¿reformar la ley o impulsar el consenso?" *El País*, June 29, 2000.

91 The European Council meeting in Tampere, Finland approved the creation of a common asylum and immigration policy for the EU. The meeting called for fair treatment of third-country nationals and tougher legislation for the illegal trafficking of migrants. See "Tampere European Council 15 and 16 October 1999. Presidency Conclusions," accessed April 24, 2010, http://www.europarl.europa.eu/summits/tam_en.htm. "SOS Racismo denuncia al PP por 'reproducir los tópicos racistas'," *El País*, November 22, 1999.

92 Instituto Nacional de Estadística, *Encuesta nacional de inmigrantes 2007: Una monografía* (Madrid: INE, 2007): 145. Javier Pradera, "Siervos sin derechos," *El País*, December 20, 2000 and Tomás Bárbulo, "La llegada a Canarias de inmigrantes en pateras se cuadruplica en sólo dos años," *El País*, January 28, 2003. "'El Gobierno nunca ha tenido voluntad política de sacar esta ley,' afirman los inmigrantes marroquíes," *El País*, December 9, 1999.

93 Begoña Aguirre, "Las ONG sostienen que la nueva ley supone la 'muerte civil' de los extranjeros 'sin papeles'," *El País*, November 20, 2000 and M. González and J.A. Rodríguez, "Toda la oposición rechaza el recorte de los derechos de los inmigrantes," *El País*, October 6, 2000.

94 T.C., "Más de 500 entidades piden otra política inmigratoria al Gobierno," *El País*, August 2, 2000.

95 T.C., "El 19% de inmigrantes no regularizados en el país reside en Almería," *El País*, October 25, 2000.

96 Ana Torregrosa, "Fracasa la reunión entre los inmigrantes encerrados en Almería y el Gobierno," *El País*, September 27, 2000.

97 A.T. and T.C., "Los recursos de inmigrantes de Almería excluidos de la regularización desbordan el turno de oficio," *El País*, October 20, 2000.

98 Lluís Visa, "Los inmigrantes que vivían en la plaza de Catalunya, considerados refugiados," *El País*, July 27, 2000; T.C., "Acuerdo para estudiar una salida para los inmigrantes de la plaza de Catalunya," *El País*, November 11, 2000; and Jorge A. Rodríguez, "El Gobierno legalizará a parte de los 57.000 inmigrantes a quienes denegó la regularización," *El País*, November 7, 2000.

99 Tomás Bárbulo, "La regularización del Gobierno discrimina a los inmigrantes por su lugar de residencia," *El País*, December 23, 2000.

100 "Más de 300 grupos sociales ven insuficiente la 'repesca' de 57.000 inmigrantes," *El País*, November 8, 2000.

101 Tomás Bárbulo, "La oposición denuncia la regularización de inmigrantes por 'discriminatoria y chapucera'," *El País*, December 27, 2000.

102 Estrada and Serraller, "Un proceso de regularización."

103 Pablo Ordaz, "Los ecuatorianos muertos trabajaban para un empresario condenado por explotación," *El País*, January 5, 2001.

104 Raúl Jiménez, "La marcha por la vida," 2001, accessed April 25, 2010, http://www.eurosur.org/ruminahui/marcha.htm.

105 Óscar Muñoz and Susana Quadrado, "Los inmigrantes rechazan una oferta del Govern y siguen su encierro en Barcelona," *La Vanguardia*, January 25, 2001, 28.

106 Papers per Tothom was short for the Platform to Support Immigrants in Resistance. For a list of protests across Spain in January-March 2001, see "3 meses de encierros de sin papeles," *Mugak* 14 (2001), accessed April 20, 2010, http://revista.mugak.eu/articulos/show/126.

107 Óscar Muñoz, "Más de trescientos 'sin papeles' inician una huelga de hambre en Barcelona," *La Vanguardia*, January 22, 2001, 31. See also Sellés i Vidal, *Moviment obrer*.

108 Derocher, *L'asile religieux*; Coutin, *The Culture of Protest*; and Suárez Navaz, *La lucha*.

109 Luis Benvenuty, "El Ayuntamiento de Santa Coloma rechaza la ley y garantiza derechos a los inmigrantes," *La Vanguardia*, January 31, 2001, 27.

110 Isabel Ramos Rioja, "La Iglesia da apoyo a los 'sin papeles'," *La Vanguardia*, January 27, 2001, 25. See also Aierbe, "La irrupción."

111 Isabel Ramos Rioja, "La Iglesia da apoyo a los 'sin papeles'," *La Vanguardia*, January 27, 2001, 25.

112 For instance, the Catalan government "received a delegation of undocumented migrants . . . but rejected dealing with numerous community representatives and having so many translations." "Entrevista a Norma Falconi."

113 Cited in Isabel Ramos Rioja, "Entrevista a Miren Santiago: Nosotros no decidíamos nada," *La Vanguardia*, February 10, 2001, 31.

114 "Entrevista a Norma Falconi." An undocumented Pakistani, Khalid

Salimi, was also, at times, a spokesman for the occupation at Santa Maria del Pi.

115 "Mujeres inmigradas: Encierro de Barcelona," *Mugak* 14 (2001), accessed April 27, 2010, http://revista.mugak.eu/articulos/show/127.

116 Ibid.

117 "Entrevista a Norma Falconi."

118 Isabel Ramos Rioja, "El Gobierno acepta que sindicatos y ONG participen en la revisión de la regularización," *La Vanguardia*, January 31, 2001, 26 and Isabel Ramos Rioja, "Los inmigrantes encerrados abren la vía a conversaciones directas con el Gobierno," *La Vanguardia*, February 8, 2001, 30; and "Entrevista a Norma Falconi."

119 "Entrevista a Norma Falconi."

120 Isabel Ramos Rioja, "El Gobierno acepta tramitar los expedientes de todos los inmigrantes en 60 días," February 10, 2001, 31.

121 M.N., "La 'pequeña Islamabad' catalana," *El País*, March 2, 2001. The area has, however, also been given the derogatory name of "Ravalistan." Moreras, "¿Ravalistán?" 119–132.

122 B.A., "Dos marchas a pie contra la Ley de Extranjería salen de Pinto y Alcalá," *El País*, March 15, 2001; Ana Torregrosa, "Un grupo de 39 inmigrantes deja el encierro en la Universidad de Almería," *El País*, March 11, 2001; Fernando Arnaiz, "Huelga de hambre en Lepe y manifestación en Zaragoza," *El País*, March 5, 2001; Jaime Prats, "Cientos de personas reclaman en las calles de Valencia y Alicante que se regularice a los inmigrantes," *El País*, March 1, 2001; Editorial, "Clamor inmigrante," *El País*, February 12, 2001; Estrada and Serraller, "Un proceso de regularización"; and "Rajoy anuncia la extensión a toda España de la regularización por arraigo," *El País*, June 6, 2001. Law 8/2000.

123 Ramos Rioja, "Los inmigrantes abandonan."

124 Judt, *Postwar*, 350.

125 On denizens, permanent residents without political rights, see Hammar, *Democracy* and Ong, *Flexible Citizenship*.

126 "Rajoy anuncia" and "Arraigar," *Diccionario de la Real Academia Española*, accessed January 14, 2011, http://buscon.rae.es/draeI/.

127 Malkki, "National Geographic," 28. Editorial, "El irregular existe," *El País*, June 6, 2001.

128 Castles and Miller, *The Age of Migration*, 245–276. Mazkiaran, "Recorrido."

129 Patricia Castán and Jordi Morera, "Final d'una acció reivindicativa," *El Periódico*, June 7, 2004, 30; and "Organitzacions d'immigrants i altres grups de suport no consideren els tancaments una sortida adient per a la problemàtica," *Vilaweb*, June 8, 2004.

130 Gómez-Quintero, "Inmigración," 25, 45 and Veredas Muñoz, "Las asociaciones," 207–225.

131 Warren, *Democracy*, 61.

132 See also Aja and Díez Bueso, "La participación."

3 Religious Pluralism, Secularism, and Women's Rights, 1968–2010

1   Casanova, "Secularization," 17.
2   Ibid., 12–13.
3   Planet, "Melilla y Ceuta."
4   "The Political Constitution of the Spanish Monarchy."
5   "Law of the Principles of the Movimiento Nacional," May 17, 1958, accessed February 18, 2011, http://bib.cervantesvirtual.com/servlet/SirveObras/02449421981244052976613/index.htm.
6   For a comprehensive history of the involvement of the Catholic Church in Spain, see Callaghan, *The Catholic Church in Spain.* "The Spanish Concordat between the Holy See and Spanish State," August 27, 1953, accessed February 20, 2011, http://www.vatican.va/roman_curia/secretariat_state/archivio/documents/rc_seg-st_19530827_concordato-spagna_sp.html.
7   "Declaration on Religious Freedom *Dignitatis Humanae.*" Raguer, *Réquiem.*
8   See Law 44/1967, on Exercising the Civil Right to Religious Freedom. Blanco, "La primera," 119–186; Tusell, "El impacto," 377–90; and Polo, "La significación," 255–282.
9   Instruments of Ratification of the Agreement between the Spanish State and Holy See on Legal Matters, Economic Matters, Education and Cultural Matters, Religious Service for the Military and the Military Service of Priests and Clergy, Signed in Vatican City on January 3, 1979.
10 Spanish Constitution, Art. 16.
11 "Senate Session Minutes," June 10, 1980, cited in Escudero, "El Islam," 9.
12 Article 7, Law 7/1980, on Religious Freedom, July 5, 1980.
13 Law 26/1992; Law 24/1992, and Law 25/1992.
14 The draft bill eliminated, among other things, Catholic state burials and religious symbols such as crucifixes in public spaces. Ignacio Cembrero and Mónica Ceberio Belaza, "Ni crucifijos ni funerales católicos," *El País,* June 13, 2010.
15 Encarnación, *Spanish Politics,* 150–164.
16 "Preocupación ante la reforma de la ley de Libertad Religiosa en España," *LibertadReligiosa.net,* May 15, 2008, accessed September 10, 2009, and Jorge Otero, "Zapatero: 'La Ley de Libertad Religiosa es conveniente, no urgente'," *Público,* November 11, 2010.
17 The Church hierarchy and fundamentalist Catholic movements led massive demonstrations and campaigns. Rosa Jiménez Cano, "Ataques a las políticas del Gobierno en el 'acto por la Familia Cristiana'," *El País,* December 30, 2007; Juan G. Bedoya, "Revuelta en la Iglesia contra los obispos por el aborto y la libertad," *El País,* April 14, 2009; and Pedro Simón, "La 'marcha por la vida' recorre Madrid en contra del aborto," *El Mundo,* March 29, 2009. On the Pope's visit in 2006, see "Benedicto XVI culmina su visita a Valencia con una misa multitudinaria," *El Mundo,* July 10, 2006.
18 Islamic News Agency, "En España no se ha producido aun la transición religiosa, Mansur Escudero dimite como presidente de la FEERI,"

WebIslam, October 1, 2000 and L.D., "Los líderes musulmanes ya reclaman al Gobierno que equipare su religión con la Iglesia católica," *LibertadDigital.es*, May 8, 2008, accessed September 10, 2009.

19   Casanova, "Secularism," 14–15.

20   See Sánchez Ruano, *Islam*.

21   See Khan, "Persecution," 217–244.

22   Jesús de las Heras, "La Asociación Musulmana, en defensa de la fidelidad al Islam," *El País*, February 24, 1977.

23   Ibid.

24   "La otra cara del Islam," *El País*, November 20, 1989.

25   Abend, "Spain's New Muslims," 135.

26   Islamic Council, "Quienes somos," accessed January 20, 2010, http://www.juntaislamica.org/presentacion.

27   Rodríguez Magda, *La España*, 161. See also her more recent book, Rodríguez Magda, *Inexistente Al Andalus*, which received the Jovellanos Essay International Prize in 2008. See also Rahola, *La República*. For responses from converts, see Abdennur Prado, "Sobre 'La España convertida al islam'," *WebIslam*, June 26, 2006 and Prado, *El Islam en democracia*.

28   See Tibi, *Political Islam*; Ramadan, *To be a European Muslim*; Ramadan, *Western Muslims*, and Ramadan, *What I Believe*. Ramadan advocates for a moratorium on stoning rather than its abolition. Spanish converts criticised him for this view. Abdennur Prado, "Llamamiento a Tariq Ramadán: a propósito de una moratoria," *WebIslam*, April 2, 2005.

29   "La otra cara del Islam."

30   Ibid.

31   Francesc Valls, "Musulmanes en el laberinto español," *El País*, February 23, 1991.

32   Ibid.

33   Ibid. and El Hachmi, *Jo també sóc Catalana*, 107.

34   Riva Kastoryano, "Race," 66–88.

35   Francesc Valls, "Los musulmanes se coordinan para tener pactos similares a los de la Iglesia con el Estado," *El País*, April 16, 1989; Alex Rodríguez, "El Estado reconoce derechos religiosos a otras confesiones sin equiparalas a la católica," *El País*, March 3, 1992; and Francisco Valls, "Las mil y una federaciones," *El País*, February 23, 1991.

36   Luís Gómez, "Los musulmanes radicales desplazan a los moderados en la comunidad islámica de España," *El País*, September 21, 2001.

37   González, "A fondo con Mansur," 29–39.

38   Lacomba, "La inmigración," 53 and Moreras, "Muslims," 133.

39   Moreras, "Muslims," 134; Registry of Minority Faiths, Ministry of Justice, accessed January 15, 2011, http://dgraj.mju.es/EntidadesReligiosas/NCindex.htm.

40   Law 26/1992; Preamble, Art. 2.2 [sacred spaces], Art. 4.1 [military services], Art. 7.1 [marriage], Art. 8 [military], Art. 9 [prisons and hospitals], Art. 10 [education,], Art. 11 [tax exemptions], Art. 12 [sacred days], Art. 13 [heritage], and Art. 14 [halal].

41   Tomás Bárbulo, "Los Hermanos Musulmanes y Arabia Saudí financian las

mezquitas más importantes," *El País*, October 1, 2000 and Agencia Islámica de Noticias, "La Comisión Islámica de España envía una propuesta formal al Gobierno para desarrollar el Acuerdo de Cooperación en materia económica," *WebIslam*, October 24, 1999.

42   Cadena Ser, last accessed March 20, 2011, http://www.cadenaser. com/static/especiales/documentos/aportaciones_Iglesia.html. For the Catholic Church's justification of their public funding, see Giménez Barriocanal, *La financiación*.

43   Escudero, "El Islam," 13.

44   Escudero, "El Islam," 11. For Tatary's view, see Tatary, "Libertad religiosa," 165–172 and Tatary, *25 años de libertad*.

45   Escudero, "El Islam," 11–12.

46   Ndeye Andújar Chevrollier, "El islam y los musulmanes en Europa," June 26, 2006, 17, accessed November 13, 2010, http://ndeyeandujar. files.wordpress.com/2008/02/el-islam-y-los-musulmanes-en-europa.pdf.

47   Chaib, *Ètica*, 43.

48   Gómez, "Los musulmanes radicales."

49   Ibid.

50   Cited in Javier Valenzuela, "España, en el ojo del huracán," *El País*, January 27, 2002.

51   Gómez, "Los musulmanes radicales."

52   Chaib, *Ètica*, 42.

53   Ibid., 37, 42.

54   Ibid., 39, 43.

55   Ibid., 44.

56   Joaquina Utrera, "Los musulmanes de Cataluña crean un consejo islámico para negociar sus reivindicaciones con la administración," *El País*, May 10, 2000.

57   Tomás Bárbulo, "Los Hermanos Musulmanes y Arabia Saudí financian las mezquitas más importantes," *El País*, October 1, 2000 and "Miembros de la Federación Española de Entidades Religiosas Islámicas (FEERI) planean su escisión tras la llegada a la dirección del Imam de la M-30," *WebIslam*, January 31, 2006.

58   CIE, "La Comisión Islámica de España emite una fatua condenando el terrorismo y al grupo Al Qaida," *WebIslam*, March 11, 2005. Agustí Iglesias i Sala, "La fatua de la Comisión Islámica de España contra el terrorismo: un documento que va más allá del dictamen religioso," *WebIslam*, November 2, 2007.

59   Islamic News Agency, "Islam en las dos orillas," November 1, 2002.

60   Islamic News Agency, "Informe de Gestión a la Asamblea de la Federación Española de Entidades Religiosas Islámicas (FEERI)," *WebIslam*, October 2, 1998.

61   Islamic News Agency, "Islam en las dos orillas,"

62   Abdel Haleem, trans., *The Qur'an*, 4:34, 54. There are many other translations of this controversial passage. For the most prominent translation that refutes the idea of beating, see Bahtiar, *The Sublime Quran* and sublimequran.org.

63   Javier Arroyo, "Dejadlas solas en el lecho, pegadles," *El País*, July 16, 2000
      and Joaquina Utrera, "El imam de Fuengirola explica formas de pegar a las
      mujeres," *El País*, July 16, 2000. The sole remaining copy of Kamal's book
      can be found at the Biblioteca Nacional in Madrid. Kamal Mustafa, *La
      mujer y el islam.*

64   Rosander, "Religion," 153.

65   Arroyo, "Dejadlas solas en el lecho."

66   Monturiol Virgili, *Dones a l'Islam.*

67   Utrera, "El imam de Fuengirola" and Arroyo, "Dejadlas solas en el lecho."

68   Arroyo, "Dejadlas solas en el lecho."

69   Leonor García, "Las asociaciones de mujeres denuncian al imam de
      Fuengirola," *El País*, July 22, 2000.

70   Utrera, "El imam de Fuengirola."

71   "Condenado a 15 meses de cárcel el imán que incitó a la violencia contra
      las mujeres en un libro," *El Mundo*, January 15, 2004 and Santiago Tarín,
      "Un catedrático de Derecho enseñará la Constitución al imam de
      Fuengirola," *La Vanguardia,* September 28, 2005.

72   Jadicha Candela, "Derecho a la igualdad frente al fanatismo misógino,"
      Madrid, January 14, 2004, accessed March 23, 2011, http://www.an-
      nisa.es/ensayos/igualdadfanatismomisogeno.htm.

73   Law 1/2004, on Comprehensive Protection against Gender Violence and
      Law 3/2007, on the Equality of Men and Women. For the national
      campaigns against gender violence, see the website of the Ministry of
      Health, Social Services, and Equality, http://www.msssi.gob.es/
      campannas/campanas06/home.htm.

74   Rosander, "Religion," 161.

75   The Runnymede Trust, "Islamophobia," 7 and 5.

76   See, for instance, the press coverage of Kamal Mustafa's case at Web Islam,
      http://www.webislam.com/tag/kamal/.

77   Rosander, "Religion," 154, 158.

78   Conference proceedings accessed March 12, 2011, http://www.webcciv.
      org/Actividades/Congresos/mujeres_musulmanas_1.html.

79   El Hachmi, *Jo també sóc catalana,* 66, 67.

80   Ibid., 66.

81   Ibid., 67.

82   Ibid., 68.

83   Ibid., 68–69.

84   Chaib, *Enlloc,* 130, 131. Nini explained that "I wound up with a new name
      . . . Miguel called me Richard [instead of Rashid] because it was easier for
      him to remember, and it stuck. My friend also got a new name. He was
      Raúl, not Rafel . . . Rafel said that with time we would get used to our new
      names." Nini, *Diario,* 133. In El Hachmi's *The Last Patriarch*, one character
      changes his name from Mimoun to Manel and another from Ahmed to
      Jaume. El Hachmi, *L'últim patriarca,* 157.

85   CCIC, "Manifiesto del segundo Encuentro de Mujeres Musulmanas," 35.

86   For a detailed study of the ICCV, see Lacomba, *El Islam.*

87   Another national conference was organized in Madrid in 2010 with the

title "Muslim Women Beyond the Stereotypes." For the speakers and concluding statements of the four international conferences on Islamic feminism organized thus far, see "Congreso Internacional de Feminismo Islámico," accessed March 23, 2011, http://feminismeislamic.org/es.

88 "Consell Islàmic de Catalunya," accessed March 23, 2011, http://feminismeislamic.org/es/home.

89 Eftekhari, "*Zanan*," 15–22. Some scholars criticize Islamic feminism as the "only homegrown, locally produced, and hence culturally suitable project for changing the lot of women in Iran and indeed in Muslim-majority countries." Moghissi, "Islamic Feminism Revisited," 76–84.

90 Spanish converts backed the American Progressive Muslim Union's support of mixed-gender Friday prayers led by Amina Wadud Muhsin, an anti-racist activist and professor at Virginia Commonwealth University in 2005. Abdennur Prado, "About the Friday Prayer led by Amina Wadud," accessed September 25, 2010, http://abdennurprado.wordpress.com/2005/03/10/about-the-friday-prayer-led-by-amina-wadud. See also Wadud Muhsin, *Qur'an and Women*.

91 Badran, *Feminism in Islam*.

92 Blore, "A Space," 5 and 7.

93 See the CCIC, "Manifiesto del segundo Encuentro de Mujeres Musulmanas de Catalunya," 23.

94 See Scott, *The Politics of the Veil*.

95 A.A.L. "La Comunidad de Madrid ordena al colegio admitir 'sin condiciones' a la niña marroquí," *ABC*, February 17, 2002, 38; "La niña del pañuelo islámico de Gerona vuelve a la escuela con normalidad," *ABC*, October 2, 2007; and Pilar Álvarez and M. Guerra, "El Consejo Escolar del colegio de Pozuelo decide mantener el reglamento que prohíbe el uso del velo islámico," *El País*, April 20, 2010. Ángeles Ramírez points to media coverage highlighting similarities in the supposed nomadism and foreignness of Muslim families and Roma minorities. Ramírez, *La trampa del velo*, 111–124.

96 See Haddad, "The Post-9/11," 253–267.

97 See El Hachmi, *Jo també sóc catalana*, 153–55 and Karrouch, *De Nador a Vic*, 47, 59.

98 Mijares and Ramírez, "Mujeres," 121–135 and Alicia Rodríguez de Paz, "España descarta una norma específica sobre el uso del velo en la escuela," *La Vanguardia*, April 21, 2010.

99 Pilar Álvarez and Ignacio Cembrero, "Interview with Ivan Jiménez-Aybar: Najwa no es ni quiere ser la Juana de Arco del Islam," *El País*, May 1, 2010.

100 Ramírez, *La trampa del velo*, 111–139.

101 Jesús García, "Contra el 'burka' (que da votos)," *El País*, June 2, 2010. Pere Ríos, "La Generalitat prohibirá por ley el uso del 'burka' en los espacios públicos," *El País*, July 4, 2013.

102 García, "Contra el 'burka'." Ministry of Interior, 2001 local elections official results, http://elecciones.mir.es/resultados2011/99MU/DMU99999TO_L1.htm, accessed June 20, 2011.

103 Zine, "Unveiled Sentiments," 240.

104 The French used the expression "*neutralité de la rue*," meaning secularism of the public sphere in, for instance, the Commission de reflexion sur l'application du principe de laïcité dans la Republique and the Conseil d'État. See also Moreras, "Musulmanes."

105 Sebastián Cuevas, "El obispo de Córdoba ataca al alcalde, del PCE, por ceder dos edificios a la comunidad islámica," *El País*, March 7, 1981 and "Bono afirma que 'a Zapatero se le puede pedir que gobierne, pero no que rece'," *El Mundo*, November 8, 2011.

106 Casanova, "Secularization," 14.

107 Modood and Kastoryano, "Secularism," 170.

108 Antonio Baquero, "Passió xiïta a Barcelona," *El Periódico*, February 10, 2006, 42.

109 Escudero, "El Islam," 13.

110 Gómez, "Los musulmanes radicales."

111 Catalonia and the Basque region contemplated a single course on the history of religion. Escudero, "El Islam," 12 and Cadena Ser.

112 Begoña Aguirre, "200 hijos de inmigrantes marroquíes reciben clases de árabe en la escuela," *El País*, May 1, 1995. For a comprehensive analysis of Moroccan children in Spanish schools, see Mijares Molina, *Aprendiendo*.

113 Chaib, *Ètica*, 67.

114 Ibid., 66.

115 Ibid., 66. See Moreno Álvarez, "El Islam."

116 M.J. López Días, "Ayuno bajo plástico," *El País*, December 22, 1998. See López Duro et al., *La diversitat*.

117 Karrouch, *De Nador a Vic*, 56.

118 Spanish public television broadcasts mass on Sunday mornings and on holy days, but it is rare that similar coverage is offered to other religions or denominations. "Les comunitats islámica i cristiana de Barcelona celebren juntes el final del Ramadà i el principi del Nadal," *Vilaweb*, December 19, 2000.

119 Halal Institute website, accessed February 22, 2011, http://www.instituto-halal.com.

120 Antonio Baquero, "Mercabarna mira la Meca," *El Periódico*, November 19, 2005, 3 and Ferran Cosculluela, "Els escorxadors burlen l'obligació d'atordir el bestiar abans de degollar-lo," *El Periódico*, October 29, 2010.

121 Elsa Granda, "La mayor asociación de marroquíes propone un control estricto de mezquitas e imanes," *El País*, August 26, 2004 and Ramírez and Mijares, "Gestión," 77–104.

122 Chaib, *Ètica*, 40.

123 Ibid., 40, 47. J.L. G., "Las entidades islámicas formarán a los imanes para evitar discursos radicales," *Levante*, April 13, 2007 and Husson, *Training*. See also Lacomba, "La inmigración," 155–193 and Moreras, "Els imams."

124 Modood and Kastoryano, "Secularism," 173.

4 Mosque Building, Catalan Nationalism, and Spain's Politics of Belonging, 1990–2010

1 Cesari, "Mosque," 1015–1024 and Allievi, *Conflict*, 38.
2 Cesari, "Mosque," 1018.
3 Manço and Kanmaz, "From Conflict," 1105–1123 and McLoughlin, "Mosques," 1045–1066.
4 Kymlicka and Norman, *Citizenship in Diverse Societies*, 9. Chambers, 'A Critical Theory,' 90–112.
5 Cited in Saint-Blancat and Schmidt di Friedberg, "Why are Mosques a Problem?" 1093. On the silencing of Islamic voices during mosque controversies, see Triandafyllidou and Gropas, "Constructing Difference," 957–977; Triandafyllidou, "Religious Diversity," 117–142.
6 Moreras, "Una mesquita al barri," 52. See also Astor, "Mezquita no!" 4.
7 "Interview with Professor Nira Yuval Davis," 129.
8 Carens and Williams, "Muslim Minorities," 157–86.
9 Ahmadiyya Community of Spain, accessed January 13, 2010, http://www.islamahmadiyya.es/ahmadia/espana.html. As in Córdoba city, the mayor of Pedro Abad was a Communist.
10 Pedro Montoliu, "La construcción de un gran Centro Cultural Islámico junto a la M-30 comienza el lunes," *El País*, March 21, 1987.
11 "Los países islámicos invertirán setencientos millones en la construcción de una mezquita en Madrid," *El País*, February 1, 1980.
12 Editorial, "Paso tolerante," *El País*, September 22, 1992 and "El Rey inaugural la catedral de Alá," *El País*, September 22, 1992.
13 Emma Roig, "Desde Madrid se ve La Meca," *El País*, April 7, 1988.
14 Sayad, *L'immigration*.
15 Chaib, *Ètica*, 11.
16 Moreras, *Musulmanes en Barcelona* and Moreras, "Pluralidad."
17 Moreras, "Una mesquita al barri," 7.
18 Astor, "Mezquita No! In the cases of Madrid and Valencia, grand mosques did not alter the demographics or the economic standing of the neighbourhoods in which they were located. Allievi has similarly found that claims that mosques lower property value are unsubstantiated. Allievi, *Conflict*, 61.
19 Cesari, "Mosque," 1019; Allievi, *Conflicts*, 60.
20 Landman and Wessels, "The Visibility," 1125–1140; Jonker, "The Mevlana," 1067–1081. Triandafyllidou and Gropas, "Constructing Difference," 957–977 and Triandafyllidou, "Religious Diversity," 117–142. See also Zapata-Barrero and de Witte, "Muslims in Spain," 181–198.
21 Allievi, *Conflict*, 42.
22 Ricard González, "Una mezquita en Badalona," *La Insignia*, May 12, 2006, accessed April 5, 2010, http://www.webislam.com/?idn=5755.
23 Cristina Andreu, "Los representatntes de las mezquitas de Cataluña reclaman una ley 'igual para todos'," *El País*, February 14, 2000.
24 Zapata-Barrero and de Witte, "Muslims in Spain," 181–198. For the role of the media on the Premià de Mar controversy, see Moreras, "Una mesquite al barri," 101–110.

25 "Pujol pide a los inmigrantes que respeten la identidad catalana," *El País*, March 20, 2003.

26 Prado, *El Islam en democracia.* The relevant regulation was inscribed in Law 16/2009, on Centres of Worship. On using these regulations to close prayer rooms, see Abdennur Prado, "Contra la llei de centres de culte de la Generalitat," July 16, 2009, accessed September 10, 2010, http://abdennurprado.wordpress.com/2009/07/16/contra-la-llei-de-centres-de-culte-de-la-generalitat.

27 Modood and Kastoryano, "Secularism," 172.

28 Moreras, *Musulmanes en Barcelona.*

29 Jacinto Antón, "Una exposición revisa la relación histórica de Cataluña con el islam," *El País*, November 26, 1998.

30 Jacinto Antón, "Países islámicos piden ayuda a Pujol para edificar una mezquita en Barcelona," *El País*, December 19, 1998.

31 David Martínez, "El islam busca un hueco en la cultura catalana," *El País*, January 4, 1999. Triandafyllidou and Gropas, "Constructing Difference," 964.

32 Marta Costa-Pau, "Casi una cuarta parte de los equipamientos religiosos de Barcelona son no católicos," *El País*, May 22, 2000.

33 Clara Tarrero, "Barcelona busca solar para la casa de Alá," *El País*, August 9, 1999.

34 "Comas teme que la futura mezquita de Barcelona sea un foco integrista," *El País*, August 7, 1999. For discourses in Italy, see Triandafyllidou, "Religious Diversity."

35 Tarrero, "Barcelona busca solar para la casa de Alá."

36 "El Consejo Islámico busca apoyo para abrir una mezquita en Barcelona," *El País*, June 5, 2000.

37 J.U. and M.P., "Barcelona se queda sin gran mezquita," *El País*, May 7, 2001.

38 Muslim in-fighting, rather than resistance from local authorities or neighbours, is not uncommon as the primary obstacle for Mosque construction in some contexts. Cesari, "Mosques in French Cities," 1025–1043.

39 Joaquima Utrera, "División en la comunidad islámica de Barcelona por la oferta saudí para construir una mezquita," *El País*, March 5, 2000 and Coleman, "The Persistence."

40 Consejo Islámico Cultural de Catalunya, "Manifiesto del cuarto Congreso," and Consejo Islámico Cultural de Catalunya, "Manifiesto del segundo Encuentro."

41 Bourdieu, "L'identité," 63–72.

42 The Hellenic Centre for Culture and Civilization in Athens is not an official place of worship. Triandafyllidou and Gropas. "Constructing Difference," 964; Tamsin Smith, "Mosque bid stirs feelings in Slovenia," *BBC News*, April 2, 2004.

43 McDonogh, "The Geography of Evil," 174–184.

44 "Interview with Javed Ilyas Qureshi: de la Rambla del Raval en diem Udàs Rambla, la 'Rambla de la Tristesa'," *Vilaweb*, accessed August 30, 2010, http://www.comunitats.info/paquistan/cat/entrevista.html.

45 "El Pla de Barris, un nou impuls pel Raval deu anys després de l'obertura

de la Rambla," accessed August 30, 2010, http://www. fomentciutatvella. net/noticies_fitxa.php?idNoticia=79.

46   Higher prices in El Raval, together with smaller apartments and lack of services for families, encouraged Pakistani migrants to relocate to the towns of Badalona and Hospitalet. Similar transfers from downtown to suburban areas occurred in other parts of Europe. For Britain, see Werbner, *The Migration Process*.

47   Muhammad Iqbal, interview with author, Barcelona, September 5, 2008.

48   "Els paquistanesos del Raval, contra l'estigmatització del barri," *Vilaweb*, February 23, 2009 and Muhammad Iqbal.

49   Moreras, "¿Ravalistán?" 119–132.

50   Joaquim Utrera, "Las mezquitas de Ciutat Vella carecen de capacidad para acoger a los fieles," *El País*, October 17, 2000.

51   Ibid.

52   Saint-Blancat and Schmidt di Friedberg, "Why are Mosques a Problem?," 1094–95; Allievi, *Conflict*, 75–76; Joaquim Utrera, "Los musulmanes del Raval rezarán en un local de una parroquia católica," *El País*, October 27, 2000; and Joaquim Utrera, "Mezquita provisional para cuatro semanas en el Raval," *El País*, November 4, 2000.

53   Tolsanas Pagès, "Las calles," 33–56; Solé Aubia and Roca, "Pakistaníes," 97–118; and Shah, "La emigración," 89–96.

54   Moreras, "¿Ravalistán?" 119–132.

55   See Guelke, *Democracy* and Gilligan and Ball, "Introduction," 153–170.

56   For versions of this argument, see Conversi, *The Basques*; Conversi, "Language or Race?" 50–70; Guibernau, *Catalan Nationalism*; and Shafir, *Immigrants and Nationalists*. For dissenting views, see Hargreaves, *Freedom for Catalonia?*, 16–38.

57   For a critical look at civic nationalism, see Shulman, "Challenging," 554–586; Yack, "The Myth," 193–211; and Xenos, "Civic Nationalism," 213–231.

58   Though whiteness is certainly a contested descriptor, it is one of the many social constructions used to distinguish native society in Spain from visible immigrant minorities. For more on the invention of whiteness, see Roediger, *Towards* and Arnesen, "Whiteness," 3–32.

59   For more on the invention of the nation, see Anderson, *Imagined Communities*.

60   Bill 60/2013, Quebec National Parliament.

61   Woolard, *Double Talk*.

62   The motto is attributed to both Pujol and PSUC. The civic conception of identity dates back to the period 1946–62, when nationalists aimed to preserve a shred of regional autonomy under Franco's strictures. Silveira Abrão, "Nacionalismo," 148–209. See also Jordi Pujol, "Immigració."

63   Hughes, *Barcelona*, 30

64   For an eye-witness account of the transformations in internal migrants' sense of belonging in Catalonia since the 1960s, see Candel, *Els altres Catalans* and Candel and Cuenca, *Els altres catalans del segle XXI*.

65   Kymlicka, *Politics in the Vernacular*, 275–89.

66   Muñoz, "Minority Nationalism."
67   "Pujol cuestiona las demandas de los musulmanes y enoja a las ONG y a los sindicatos," *El País*, October 31, 2000.
68   Antoni Puigverd, "Ferrusola expresa su preocupación por el 'alud de la inmigración'," *El País*, February 21, 2001 and "Pujol pide a los inmigrantes que respeten la identidad catalana," *El País*, March 20, 2003.
69   "Pujol alerta que el 'mestissatge' suposarà 'el final' de Catalunya," *El Periódico*, August 24, 2004, 14.
70   "Sols ERC recolza la crítica de Pujol al mestissatge," *El Periódico*, August 25, 2004, 13 and M. Baldomà and O. Merino, "Maragall defensa la bondat del mestissatge davant la crítica de Pujol," *El Periódico*, August 26, 2004, 13. For more on Catalan national identity and immigration, see Kleiner-Liebau, *Migration.*
71   Jamshed and Essomba, *Diàlegs*, 30.
72   Article 1 and 2, Law 6/2006, on the Reform of the Statute of Autonomy of Catalonia. In 2010, Spain's Constitutional Court deemed an article that granted the Catalan language preferential status in regional government to be unconstitutional. Court Sentence No. 8045/2006, Constitutional Court, accessed August 16, 2010, http://estatico.lavanguardia.es/lavanguardia/docs/20100709/SENTENCIA.pdf.
73   See "El català, llengua comuna: Takatalaniyt, Tutlayt Ax Islmann," accessed August 16, 2010, http://www.plataforma-llengua.cat/media/assets/1680/ manifest_amazic_def.pdf.
74   See "Manifiesto por la lengua común," accessed August 16, 2010, http://estaticos.elmundo.es/documentos/2008/06/22/manifiesto.pdf.
75   Tree, *Aniversari*, 20.
76   For analysis on immigration and bilingualism, see Juarros-Daussà and Lanz, "Rethinking," 1–21; Gore, "The Catalan Language," 91–102; and Lipski, "Double Talk," 117–119.
77   The Spanish ombudsperson raised concerns about Catalonia's interpretation of the law, arguing that the Catalan government could not, under the Spanish constitution, discriminate against Spanish speakers and prioritize the Catalan language in services for immigrants and access to status. "La Defensora del Poble recorre que Catalunya primi el català en l'acollida d'immigrants," *El Periódico*, August 17, 2010.
78   Interview with Sheriff Jarju, "Vaig venir caminant," *Vilaweb*, accessed August 24, 2010, http://www.comunitats.info/subsahara/cat/entrevista.html.
79   El Hachmi, *Jo també sóc catalana*, 38.
80   Ibid., 75–77 and 47.
81   In 2004, Ayaan Hirsi Ali was put under permanent police surveillance after controversial filmmaker Theo van Gogh, with whom she had worked, was assassinated by a Dutch-Moroccan Muslim in Amsterdam. See Hirsi Ali, *The Caged Virgin*; Hirsi Ali, *Infidel*; and Hirsi Ali, *Nomad.* See also Buruma, *Murder in Amsterdam.*
82   El Hachmi, *Jo també sóc catalana*, 20, 23, 24, 27, 52, 54. Soler Amigó, *Jameiat Essalam*, 17. See also "Interview with Mohamadi Bouziane: un

immigrant ha de ser una persona exemplar," *Vilaweb*, accessed August 30, 2010, http://www.comunitats.info/amazic/cat/entrevista.html.

83 Chaib, *Ètica*, 35. For additional examples of language discrimination in Europe, see Linke, "There," 149–173.

84 El Hachmi, *Jo també sóc catalana*, 49, 50.

85 Ibid., 50.

86 Ibid., 89–90.

87 Tree, *Aniversari*, 32.

88 Crowley, "The Politics of Belonging," 22. See also Tzanelli and Yar, "Paradoxes of Belonging," 473–478.

89 Chaib, *Enlloc*, 81, 41–42, 7.

90 Ibid., 107.

91 Ibid., 103;

92 Ibid., 103–4, 105 and Chaib, *Ètica*, 34, 35.

93 Karrouch, *De Nador a Vic*, 151. Also, see Jamshed and Essomba, *Diàlegs* and Chaib, *Ètica*, 35–36.

94 Chaib, *Ètica*, 36.

95 Ibid., 35.

96 Ibid., 78.

97 Ibid., 61 and Moreras, "¿Un islam en Cataluña o un islam catalán?," 335–351.

98 Chaib, *Enlloc*, 131.

99 El Hachmi was ridiculed for both being Muslim and for not "speaking Christian [sic]." El Hachmi, *Jo també sóc catalana*, 76.

100 Huma Jamshed, interview with author, Barcelona, September 9, 2008 and Jamshed and Essomba, *Diàlegs*, 15.

101 Huma Jamshed and Jamshed and Essomba, *Diàlegs*, 36.

102 Nini, *Diario*, 65. Huma Jamshed and Jamshed and Essomba, *Diàlegs*, 49.

103 Jamshed and Essomba, *Diàlegs*, 44 and Helena López, "Dona sense fronteres," *El Periódico*, October 31, 2010.

104 Javed Ilyas, interview with author, Barcelona, September 10, 2008.

105 Silvia Barroso, "Em dic Javed i sóc catalanista," *Avui*, November 8, 2009 and "Col·lectius d'immigrants residents a Catalunya donen suport a les consultes," *Vilaweb*, December 13, 2009.

106 "Interview with Javed Ilyas Qureshi."

107 See, for instance, Ilyas, "Pakistán," and Ilyas, "Comunitat pakistanesa."

108 Casas and Crosas, *Nouvinguts*, 92.

109 Ibid., *Nouvinguts*, 93. One of the major differences that fuelled the stigmatization of l'Erm as a separate entity and not part of Manlleu was the fact that most residents of downtown spoke Catalan and supported F.C. Barcelona, while l'Erm residents spoke Spanish and supported Real Madrid. "Fem Barri," 5.

110 Casas and Crosas, *Nouvinguts*, 67, 70, 80. An equivalent cleavage between residents of downtown Manlleu (mostly Catalan speaking) and residents in l'Erm (mostly Spanish speaking), occurred in l'Erm between old residents (Spanish speakers) and new residents (Tamazigh speakers). "Fem Barri," 5.

111 Casas and Crosas, *Nouvinguts,* 79.

112 Pere Prat, interview with author, Manlleu, July 24, 2008.

113 The Barri de l'Erm, despite its stigma and small geographical size, has been impressively community oriented and active. Other important organizations to emerge were a Flamenco society, a neighbourhood association, and the MMPAS. Cáritas and the Workers' Commissions maintained offices in the neighbourhood.

114 Miquel Casanova, interview with author, Manlleu, July 23, 2008.

115 Soler Amigó, *Jameiat Essalam,* 19–22.

116 Ibid., 66.

117 Ibid., 25–29.

118 Hassan Akioud, interview with author, Manlleu, July 24, 2008.

119 Soler Amigó, *Jameiat Essalam,* 65, 69.

120 The "Let's Improve L'Erm Project" grew out of the older "Plan of Reception and Welcoming for Manlleu," and "Project of Comprehensive Intervention for the Neighbourhood of l'Erm, Manlleu," once funding from the regional government became available for vulnerable neighbourhoods.

121 Most key demands of Jameiat Essalam and other NGOs were incorporated into "Fem Barri: Programa per la millora de la convivencia i la cooperació."

122 Hassan Akioud, Ibid.; Fabio López, interview with author, Manlleu, July 24, 2008; and Llorenç Espinal, interview with author, Manlleu, July 24, 2008. During a visit to the city in July 2008, the author observed that only ethnic Spaniards were using the facility.

123 "Projecte d'Intervenció Integral del Barri de l'Erm de Manlleu;" "Projecte d'Intervenció Integral del Barri de l'Erm: Pla de convivencia;" Ana Marta Roca, Manlleu city hall, interview with author, Manlleu, July 23, 2008; and Betlem Parés, interview with author, Manlleu, July 23, 2008.

124 For more on PxC ideology, see "Informe sobre Plataforma per Catalunya," August 22, 2010, accessed September 20, 2010, http://www.pxcatalunya.com/web/historiacast.htm. See also Anglada, *Sin mordaza* and Erra and Serra, *Tota la veritat.* For a comparison of far-right European parties in modern times, see Betz and Meret, "Revisiting Lepanto" and Meret, "The Danish People's Party."

125 Josep Anglada, interview with author, Vic, July 22, 2008. See also the pioneering research of Casals, *La Plataforma* and Casals, *Ultracatalunya.*

126 Pascual Saüc and Riera, *Identitat.*

127 Carbonell Sebarroja, *Magribins* and Vila, *Llengua.*

128 Josep Anglada and "Ple municipal," *Osona.com,* March 3, 2008, accessed July 29, 2010, http://www.osona.com/noticia/6587/ple/municipal/vic/construira/piscina/coberta/publica/sud/ciutat. See also SOS Racismo, "Comunicat de SOS Racisme davant la proposta de la Generalitat de crear centres educatius especials per als immigrants que arriben amb el curs ja començat," accessed July 29, 2010, http://www.fapac.cat/system/files/Comunicat%20Sos%20Racisme%20Centres%20Acollida%20Inicial%20%282008%29.pdf.

129 The same phenomenon has occurred in the Catalan cities of Badalona, Mataró, and Santa Coloma. Astor, "Mesquita No!" 27.

130 Miquel Noguer, "El partido xenófobo de Anglada quintuplica su resultado en Cataluña," *El País*, May 24, 2011.

131 Simmons, *The French.*

132 Toni Sust, "CiU ignorarà la reobertura de la causa contra Albiol per xenophobia," *El Periódico*, May 25, 2011.

133 Pujol, "Immigració."

134 Goytisolo, "Pájaro." Jamshed and Essomba, *Diàlegs*, 60.

135 Jamshed and Essomba, *Diàlegs*, 59.

136 Ros et al., *Interculturalitat*; Garreta Bochaca and Llevot Calvet, *El espejismo*. For a theoretical analysis and policy applications of interculturalism, see Zapata Barrero "The Three Strands." For a discussion on liberal societies and multiculturalism, See Parekh, *Rethinking Multiculturalism.*

137 Stewart King, "Catalan Literature," 253–264.

138 "Frankfurt 2007 Objectives," accessed December 24, 2009, http://www.frankfurt2007.cat/eng/fira/objectius.shtml?seccio=fira. For a list of invitees, see "Autors," http://www.frankfurt2007.cat/eng/cultura/cultura_catalana_autors.shtml?seccio=cultura&subseccio=autors.

139 The Beninese author Agnès Agboton, Slovenian author Simona Škrabec, British author Mathew Tree, and Czech author Monika Zgustova – all of whom write in Catalan – were invited to attend the Frankfurt Fair.

140 Guillem Martínez, "Entrevista with Mohamed Chair. 'Al catalán le gusta que asimiles sus tradiciones, pero le cuesta aprender otras'," *El País*, April 30, 2000.

141 Ibid.

142 "Pujol pide a los inmigrantes que respeten la identidad catalana," *El País*, March 20, 2003.

143 Juan Ruiz Sierra, "El PSOE insta els alcaldes socialistes a no impulsar més vetos al burca," *El Periódico*, June 23, 2010, 25 and Juanjo Robledo, "España se blinda contra la burka," *BBC World*, June 23, 2010. Ramírez, *La trampa del velo*, 124–139.

144 Kymlicka and Norman, "Citizenship," 29.

5 Reclaiming Islamic Spain: From the Córdoba Mosque to the Festival of Moors and Christians, 1965–2010

1 Graham, "The Spanish," 313–328.

2 Halbwachs, *The Collective Memory.*

3 The Qur'an mandates that *dhimmis*, or the Peoples of the Book (Muslims, Jews, and Christians), must be protected from interference in religious practices.

4 Menocal argues that from the standpoint of Al-Andalus, there was no Dark Age. Translations by Andalusi scholars of Plato, Aristotle, and other important thinkers, Menocal argues, laid the groundwork for the European Renaissance. Menocal, *The Ornament*. See also Mann, Glick, and Dodds, *Convivencia.*

5 Lewis, *The Jews* and Lewis, *Islam.*

6   Glick, *Islamic*, 165.

7   Doubleday, "Introduction," 16.

8   Menéndez Pelayo, "El brindis," 152.

9   Menéndez Pelayo, "Epílogo," 146.

10   Sánchez Albornoz, *El Islam*, 32. See also Sánchez Albornoz, *Ensayos*.

11   Doubleday, "Introduction," 16. Castro, *España* and Castro, *Sobre el nombre*. See also Subirats, ed., *Américo Castro*.

12   See Goytisolo, "El Ayer," 51–58; Goytisolo, *Crónicas*; Ugarte, "Juan Goytisolo," 353–364; Menocal, *The Ornament*; Vidal, *España*; Fanjul, *Al-Andalus*; and Rodríguez Magda, *La España*.

13   Coca, "Federalía," 52. See also Ruíz Romero, "El resurgir," 61–68.

14   Esther Celma, "Camps planta els presidents socialistes de la Corona d'Aragó," *El Periódico*, March 31, 2008, 19.

15   *9 d'Octubre de 2008: Recreació de la cavalcade de 1428 organitzada per Alfons el Magnànim en memòria del rei Jaume I*, Generalitat Valenciana, 2008, accessed January 10, 2009, http://www.anyjaumeprimer.com/castellano/programa.php.

16   Cited in José Parrilla, "El reino de Taifa frente a Jaume I," *Levante*, October 18, 2008.

17   Ibid. For more on language and cultural conflicts in Valencia, see Guia, *La llengua negociada*.

18   ICCV, accessed September 20, 2010, http://www.webcciv.org/Actividades/Congresos/moriscos.html.

19   See Mira, *Vida i final*.

20   Many local historical associations remembered the anniversary. The Institute of Municipal Studies of Bajo Vinalopó, for instance, organized the exhibition, "The Moriscos of Southern Valencia: Remembrance of a Forgotten People," http://www.iecbv.com/catala/conferencies-moriscos.pdf. The largest exhibition was organized by the University of Valencia, "Between Land and Faith: Muslims in the Christian Kingdom of Valencia (1238–1609)." Benítez et al., *Entre Terra i Fe*.

21   "Remembering the Moriscos: The Writings and Stories of a Cultural Diaspora," accessed March 10, 2011, http://www.bne.es/es/Micrositios/Exposiciones/MemoriaMoriscos.

22   "De terra endins, de mar enllà," *Dossiers*, Canal 9, September 22, 2009 and "El Islam cercano: Los moriscos valencianos," accessed November 20, 2011, http://www.webcciv.org/Actividades/Congresos/moriscos_ponentes.html.

23   Tom Zeller Jr, "The Politics of Apology for Japan's 'Comfort Women'," *The New York Times*, March 5, 2007 and government of Canada, "Prime Minister Harper offers full apology on behalf of Canadians for the Indian Residential Schools system," June 11, 2008, http://pm.gc.ca/eng/media.asp?id=2149.

24   Joseba Elola, "Identifíquese, es usted negra," *El País*, August 30, 2009.

25   When in October 2013, the Vatican beatified 522 Civil War Catholic martyrs, Pope Francis lost an opportunity to ask for forgiveness for the

Catholic Church's involvement in Franco's *coup d'état* and subsequent dictatorship. Natalia Junquera, "Las víctimas exigen al Papa que la Iglesia pida perdón por apoyar a Franco," *El País*, October 11, 2013.

26   For more on the link between the historic Moor and today's immigrant, see Martín Muñoz, "Percepciones," 97–104; Martín Corrales, *La imagen*; and Zapata-Barrero and van Dijk eds., *Discursos*.

27   Belkacemi, *Amazic*, 14. *Moro* was an equivalent in the 1950s–1970s to the word *xarnego* (mixed-race, illegitimate), which ethnic Catalans applied to Spanish-speaking immigrants. While the use of *xarnego* tends to be frowned upon today, *Moro* remains common currency. Guillem Martínez, "Lo peor que te pueden decir no es 'charnego', es 'moro'," *El País*, May 1, 1998.

28   Chaib, *Enlloc*, 128.

29   Levy, "Classifying Cultural Rights."

30   See, for instance, Cortés Peña, "Nacionalismo,"137–152 and Moreno Navarro, "Etnicidad," 13–38.

31   "Legado Andalusí," http://www.legadoandalusi.es/. For the Ibn Khaldun exhibition, see "Ibn Jaldún: Entre Al-Ándalus y Egipto," http://www.ibnjaldun.com/index.php?id=104&tx_ttnews[tt_news]=113 &cHash=e76f995f27. The Foundation also organized exhibitions on the Almoravids, Almohads, and the Umayyads and hosted tours on the Caliphate of Córdoba and the Nasrid dynasty.

32   Cited in Agencia Islámica de Noticias, "Islam en las dos orillas."

33   "Biblioteca Viva de Al-Ándalus," http://www.bibliotecavivadeal-andalus.org/. For more on the Spanish nationalist reaction, see Pedro Insa Rodríguez, "Variaciones sobre Al-Ándalus," *El Catoplebas* 9 (November 2002), http://www.nodulo.org/ec/2002/n009p15.htm. Ildefonso Olmedo, "El sueño de rezar en la mezquita," *El Mundo-Crónica* 445, April 25, 2004.

34   "Proyecto Kurtuba," 84–88.

35   "Halal Institute," http://www.institutohalal.com.

36   J. Morán, "Cristianos y musulmanes, juntos pero no revueltos," *Suplementos de La Opinión A Coruña*, April 18, 2010; Manuel Planelles, "El doble rasero de la Iglesia: Saddam Hussein y varios príncipes saudíes sí pudieron rezar en la Mezquita de Córdoba," *El País*, January 9, 2007; Félix Bayón, "Los musulmanes celebraron la Fiesta del Cordero," *El País*, November 2, 1979; and Olmedo, "El sueño de rezar en la mezquita."

37   Mansur Escudero, "Mezquita-Catedral de Córdoba: Un espacio para el encuentro," *WebIslam*, March 2, 2006.

38   Rodríguez Zapatero, "Speech of the Spanish Prime Minister (2004)," 26.

39   Rodríguez Zapatero, "Speech of the Spanish Prime Minister (2005)," 43.

40   I. Barajas, "Cómo convertir la catedral de Córdoba en mezquita," *La Razón*, February 19, 2006; "Por un futuro ecuménico de la Mezquita-Catedral," *WebIslam*, March 4, 2006; and "Córdoba – La Junta Islámica dice que el rezo musulmán en la Mezquita que defiende Moussa ayuda al diálogo interreligioso," *WebIslam*, October 10, 2007. For information on Zapatero's Alliance of Civilizations, see "Alliance of Civilizations," http://www. unaoc.org.

41 Cited in Barajas, "Cómo convertir la catedral de Córdoba en mezquita"; Manuel Planelles, "El obispo de Córdoba rechaza el rezo musulmán en la mezquita," *El País*, December 28, 2006; and P.C. Córdoba, "¿Rezar a Alá en la Mezquita de Córdoba?" *ABC*, November 11, 2009.

42 Giles Tremlett, "Two arrested after fight in Córdoba's former mosque," *The Guardian*, April 1, 2010; Rachel Donadio, "Name Debate Echoes an Old Clash of Faiths," *New York Times*, November 4, 2010; and Demetrio Fernández, "Tribuna Libre," *ABC*, October 10, 2010. For the relevant UNESCO documents, see "Historic Centre of Córdoba," http://whc.unesco.org/en/list/313/documents.

43 J. Prieto, "El Ayuntamiento pretende fomentar el turismo religioso y en familia," *ABC*, January 31, 2009. Olmedo, "El sueño de rezar en la mezquita."

44 Allievi, *Conflict*.

45 Alcaraz, *Moros i Cristians*, 104 and Amades, *Las danzas*, 32–50.

46 Alcaraz, *Moros i Cristians*, 104–105.

47 This is not a uniquely Spanish stereotype. Urbanized Muslims sometimes described Bedouins as *imámlin*, lousy. Jamal, *Lluny*, 64.

48 Alcaraz, *Moros i Cristians*, 87, 92, 98. Other racialized company names include the Papua Blacks, the Senegalese Blacks, the Egyptian Blacks, the Zulu Blacks, the Maasai, Sangali, Yemenis, Zairians, Hindus, Mubaraks, and Saudis.

49 La Mahoma is performed in Biar, Bocairent, Beneixama, Banyeres, Castalla, and Villena, all in the region of Valencia. The ritual was performed in the past but has been discontinued in Alcoi, Callosa d'en Sarrià, Onil, Petrer, and Elda.

50 Salvá Ballester, *Bosqueig*,140.

51 Amades, *Las danzas*, 51.

52 Harris, "Muhammad," 52 and Amades, *Las danzas*, 49.

53 Alcaraz, *Moros i Cristians*, 76 and "Conclusiones," *I Congreso Nacional*, 854.

54 The ritual takes place in several villages of Valencia. In Bocairent, records date it as far back as 1890. Vañó Silvestre, "Historia," 675.

55 Vañó Silvestre, "La religión," 124.

56 See, for instance, Cervino y Ferrero, *Embajadas*.

57 For a typical hagiographical account, see Momblanch González, *Al Azraq*. See also Burns, "The Crusade," 80–106.

58 Amades, *Las danzas*, 32–39, 40–50, and 54–60.

59 Alcaraz, *Moros i Cristians*, 102. See also Goytisolo, *Reivindicación*.

60 Enric Carbonell, *Célebre Centuria*, cited in Berenguer Barceló, "Fundamento religioso," 148.

61 Records of rituals involving Moors and Christians in Lleida go back to 1150. Mansanet Ribes, "La Fiesta," 357.

62 See Asociación de San Jorge de Alcoy, *Nostra Festa*; Bernabeu Rico, *Significados sociales*; and Carrasco Urgoiti, *El moro*. Seventeenth-century comedies of Moors and Christians include Lope de Vega's *El cerco de Santa*

Fe or Calderón de la Barca's *Origen, pérdida y restauración de la Virgen del Sagrario.*

63   See Garcia Càrcel, *La revolta.*
64   Vañó Silvestre, "La religión," 119.
65   Amades, *Las danzas,* 115.
66   "Conclusiones," *I Congreso Nacional,* 853.
67   Vañó Silvestre, "La religión," 112.
68   Soler García, "Crónica del Congreso," 55.
69   Alcaraz, *Moros i Cristians,* 7, 9.
70   Ibid., 9.
71   Domènech Llorens, *El tractat,* 36–37.
72   Harris, "Muhammad," 47.
73   Ibid., 48.
74   Ibid.
75   Driessen, "Mock Battles," 105–115 and Baumann, *The 'Moors.*
76   Flesler and Pérez Melgosa, "Battles of Identity," 153, 157 and Flesler, *The Return,* 97–131. See also Zapata-Barrero and de Witte, "Muslims in Spain," 181–198.
77   For South Africa, see Thompson, *The Political.* Kaplan, "Trauma," 308. Flesler and Pérez Melgosa, "Battles of Identity," 152. For more on collective trauma and historical memory in Spain, see Flesler, "Contemporary" and Doubleday, "Introduction."
78   Hobsbawm, "Introduction," 1.
79   Goytisolo, *Crónicas,* 9.
80   Vañó Silvestre, "Historia," 649–650.
81   Ibid., 663–4 and 657.
82   Ibid., 670, 667.
83   "*Paco*" was onomatopoeia for sniper shots.
84   Vañó Silvestre, "Historia," 649–662 and Alcaraz, *Moros i Cristians,* 83.
85   Vañó Silvestre, "Historia," 624, 650 and Alcaraz, *Moros i Cristians,* 84–88.
86   Goytisolo, *Crónicas,* 11.
87   For a long list of villages that have begun to celebrate the festival in the last three decades, see Alcaraz, *Moros i Cristians,* 90–91.
88   Ibid., 92–98. These names refer to Tariq ibn Ziyad, the Umayyad general who launched the Islamic conquest of the Iberian Peninsula in 711; Al-Azraq, a Mudéjar nobleman who refused to submit to Christian authority in Alcoi in 1275; the Ottoman sultan Suleiman I; Yaqub al-Mansur, the third Amir of the Almohad period; and the first Islamic Caliph, Abu Bakr.
89   *Spanish Constitution,* Articles 14 and 16 [on religious pluralism].
90   Pope Paul VI, *Declaration.*
91   Bonet Camarasa, Pardo Garcia et al., "La religión," 161.
92   Mansanet Ribes, "La Mujer," 269 and 266. Rojas Navarro, "Presente," 213 and 226 and Chico Amat, "La mujer," 246.
93   Mansanet Ribes, "La Mujer,"265. Rojas Navarro, "Presente," 226. Chico Amat, "La mujer," 246.
94   Chico Amat, "La mujer," 247. "Conclusiones," *I Congreso Nacional,* 855.
95   Mansanet Ribes, "La Mujer," 268–9.

96 Fonèvol, "Els fets."

97 M. González and R. Navarro, "La sanción privaría a los 'Moros' de Alcoy de 180.000 euros y su proyección internacional," *El Mundo,* April 12, 2008.

98 The provincial ombudsman claimed that Alcoi city hall was hostile to the rights of women in October 2004 and February 2005. Josep Miquel Martínez, "La valentia de Trames," *Barcella* 24, February 2005, accessed April 2, 2009, http://barcella.banyeres.com/carpeta_anteriors/anteriors. html.

99 Saint George Association, "Ordenanza de la Fiesta," Art. 13, 51, 57, 59, and 70, accessed April 2, 2009, http://associaciosantjordi.sollutia.com/ news/noticia.asp?DocumentID=273.

100 Fonèvol, "Conclusions," *Primera Jornada sobre la dona en la Festa,* Alcoi, March 27, 2004, accessed April 2, 2009, http://www.fonevol.net/Qüestions concretades i visió global.pdf.

101 Ibid.

102 Fonèvol, "Conclusions," *Tercera Jornada sobre la Dona en la Festa,* Alcoi, March 8, 2008, accessed April 2, 2009, http://www.fonevol.net/conclusions 3a jornada.htm.

103 Fonèvol, "Conclusions," *Primera Jornada.*

104 Fonèvol, "Conclusions," *Segona Jornada sobre la Dona en la Festa,* Alcoi, March 11, 2006, accessed April 2, 2009, http://www.fonevol.net/conclusions 2a jornada.htm.

105 Malik Ruiz and Félix Herrero respectively, cited in "El presidente de las entidades islámicas exige la suspensión de la fiesta de moros y cristianos," *Levante,* October 5, 2006 and "Una federació islàmica exigeix la fi de les festes de moros i cristians," *El Periódico,* October 6, 2006.

106 Anna Pinter, "El desfile de festeras sobre una alfombra con versos del Corán ofende a los musulmanes de Ontinyent," *Levante,* August 28, 2002.

107 Ibid.

108 Anna Pinter, "Los musulmanes revisarán los textos del 'bando moro' en Ontinyent," *Levante,* August 31, 2002.

109 F.B., "Los musulmanes sugieren cambiar 'el fondo épico' de los Moros y Cristianos," *Levante,* 3 September, 2002.

110 Verdú Navarro and Calabuig Gómez, "Els moros i cristians." See "Moros i cristians. Convivència i conflictes," *Trames: Revista d'estudis de Bocairent* 2 (2004).

111 Recep Tayyip Erdogan and José Luis Rodríguez Zapatero, "A Call for Respect and Calm," *International Herald Tribune,* February 5, 2006.

112 Amparo García, "¿Los Moros y Cristianos, amenazados?" *El Mundo-Revista Crónica,* February 12, 2006. Adelaida Ferre Tortosa, interview with author, Beneixama, June 25, 2006.

113 F.D.C., "Ni se quema La Mahoma, ni se pisa el Corán," *Las provincias,* February 4, 2007. Xavi Pascual, interview with author, Bocairent, June 26, 2006.

114 Many other villages censored images of Santiago "*Matamoros,*" the patron saint of Spain, slaughtering Muslims. Lucía Gadea, "Pueblos valencianos suprimen de las fiestas actos ofensivos a Mahoma," *El País,* October 2,

2006. Maria Ángeles Rivas, interview with author, Beneixama, June 27, 2006. Juan Ruiz Sierra, "La crema de Mahoma desapareix per por en les festes valencianes," *El Periódico*, October 1, 2006.

115 Cited in "Una federació islàmica" and "El presidente de las entidades."

116 Ibid. For the ritual celebrations of the conquest of Granada, see Rogozen-Soltar, "Al-Andalus," 863–886.

117 "El presidente de las entidades." "El Consejo Islámico reitera su apoyo a los Moros y Cristianos," *Levante*, October 22, 2006. Carlos Aimeur, "Donde todos quieren ser moros," *Magazine El Mundo*, November 19, 2006.

118 Ibid. and A.P.F., "Khader Ibeid: 'Los musulmanes no somos fanáticos'," *Levante*, October 20, 2006.

119 A.P.F., "Khader Ibeid."

120 Jordan, Mañas, and Horsburgh. "Strengths," 17–39.

121 Alcaraz, *Moros i Cristians*, 9. Lisón Tolosana, *Invitación*, 152 and Foster, *Culture*, 224. Peidró Pastor, "Coloquio," 197–98.

122 Goytisolo, *Crónicas*, 11, 12.

123 Cited in Goytisolo, *Crónicas*, 12.

124 Goytisolo, *Crónicas*, 12, 19. See also Martín Corrales, "Maurofobia," 39–51.

125 Southern, *Western*, 2.

126 Goytisolo, Crónicas, 13.

127 Ibid.

128 King, *The Inconvenient Indian*, 53, 66.

129 Alcaraz, *Moros i Cristians*, 129–200.

130 For anti-Catalan regionalism, see Viadel, *No mos* and Flor, *Noves*.

131 In 1986, the anti-Catalanist cultural organization Lo Rat Penat pressured the mayor of Valencia to forbid representations of Moors and Christians in the yearly celebration of James I's conquest of Valencia. Navarro Pastor, "Lo Rat Penat," 325. For an anti-Catalan perspective, see Recio, *La batalla*.

132 In 1997, a pro-Catalan association created a network of James I community centres, and during Valencia's annual celebration of its Christian conquest, pro-Catalan nationalists gather in front of a large monument of James I. See, for instance, http://fundaciocasal.blogspot.ca/.

133 The Socialist Party for National Liberation, on the far left end of the political spectrum, organizes a yearly rally in the city where James I launched his conquest of Valencia.

134 J.E.M., "El *Financial Times* destaca la 'autocensura' en la fiesta de moros y cristianos," *Levante*, October 17, 2006; Aimeur, "Donde todos quieren ser moros"; Mario Candela, "Las 'filaes' alcoyanas recorren la Quinta Avenida sin el bando moro," *Levante*, October 9, 2006; and "Sanus ve una 'vergüenza' que no desfilaran los moros en Nueva York," *Levante*, October 28, 2006.

135 "El PP quiere que los Moros y Cristianos sean Patrimonio de la Humanidad," *Levante*, October 14, 2006.

136 Ibid.

137 "Palabras de Su Majestad el Rey."

138 Flesler and Pérez Melgosa, "Battles of Identity."

139 Mijares, *Aprendiendo*; Caramés and Garriga, "La imagen," 55–60. See also Boyd, *Historia Patria*.

140 See "Festa de Moros i Cristians. Lleida," accessed April 2, 2009, http://www.miclleida.org/.

141 "Mora Morisca: Tres visions, un sol món," http://personal.telefonica. terra.es/web/launespress/morisca/index.html.

142 Nini, *Diario*, 37–3.

143 Ibid., 98 and Goytisolo, *Crónicas*, 9.

Bibliography

Primary Sources

Legal and Government Documents

The Political Constitution of the Spanish Monarchy. Promulgated in Cádiz, the nineteenth day of March, 1812. Accessed February 10, 2011. http://www.cervantesvirtual.com/obra-visor/the-political-constitution-of-the-spanish-monarchy-promulgated-in-cadiz-the-nineteenth-day-of-march-0/html/.

Law 44/1967, on Exercising the Civil Right to Religious Freedom, June 28, 1967, *Boletín Oficial del Estado (BOE)* 156, July 1, 1967, 9191–9194.

Spanish Constitution, December 27, 1978. Accessed March 23, 2011. http://www.senado.es/constitu_i/indices/consti_ing.pdf.

Instrument of Ratification of the Agreement between the Spanish State and Holy See on Legal Matters, Signed in Vatican City on January 3, 1979, *BOE* 300, December 15, 1979, 28781–28782.

Instrument of Ratification of the Agreement between the Spanish State and Holy See on Economics Matters, Signed in Vatican City on January 3, 1979, *BOE* 300, December 15, 1979, 28782–28783.

Instrument of Ratification of the Agreement between the Spanish State and Holy See on Education and Cultural Matters, Signed in Vatican City on January 3, 1979, *BOE* 300, December 15, 1979, 28784–28785.

Instrument of Ratification of the Agreement between the Spanish State and Holy See on the Religious Services for the Military and the Military Service of Priests and Clergy, Signed in Vatican City on January 3, 1979, *BOE* 300, December 15, 1979, 28785–28787.

Law 4/1979, on the Statute of Autonomy of Catalonia, December 18, 1979, *BOE* 306, December 22, 1979, 29363–29370.

Law 7/1980, on Religious Freedom, July 5, 1980, *BOE* 177, July 24, 1980, 16804–16905.

Law 7/1985, on Rights and Freedoms of Foreigners in Spain, July 1, 1985, *BOE* 158, July 3, 1985, 20824–20829.

Law 24/1992, on Approval of a Cooperation Agreement between the State and Federation of Evangelical Religious Organizations of Spain, November 10, 1992, *BOE* 272, November 12, 1992, 38209–38211.

Law 25/1992, on Approval of a Cooperation Agreement between the State and the Federation of Israelite Communities of Spain, November 10, 1992, *BOE* 272, November 12, 1992, 38211–38214.

Law 26/1992, on Approval of a Cooperative Agreement between the State and the Islamic Commission of Spain, November 10, 1992, *BOE* 272, November 12, 1992, 38214–38217.

Plan para la integración social de los inmigrantes. Madrid: Ministerio de Trabajo y Asuntos Sociales, 1995.

Law 2/1995, on the Statute of Autonomy of Melilla, March 13, 1995, *BOE* 62, November 14, 1995.

Law 4/1995, on Modifying the Criminal Code to Include the Crime of Vindication of Genocide, May 11, 1995, *BOE* 113, May 12, 1995, 13800–13801.

Royal Decree 490/1995, on the Creation of a Forum for the Social Integration of Immigrants, April 7, 1995, *BOE* 87, April 12, 1995, 10976–10978.

Royal Decree 155, on the Regulation of Law 7/1985, February 2, 1996, *BOE* 47, February 23, 1996, 6949–6977.

Law 4/2000, on the Rights and Freedoms of Foreigners in Spain and their Social Integration, January 11, 2000, *BOE* 10, January 12, 2000, 1139–1150.

Law 8/2000, on the Reform of Act 4/2000, on the Rights and Freedoms of Foreigners in Spain and their Social Integration, December 22, 2000, *BOE* 307, December 23, 2000, 45508–45522.

Court Sentence No. 03104, Criminal Court No. 3, Barcelona, January 12, 2004, regarding Mohamed Kamal Mustafa, iman of Fuengirola.

Law 1/2004, on Comprehensive Protection against Gender Violence, December 28, 2004, *BOE* 313, December 29, 2004, 42166–42197.

Court Sentence No. 8045/2006, Constitutional Court, Madrid, June 28, 2010.

Law 6/2006, on the Reform of the Statute of Autonomy of Catalonia, July 19, 2005, *Diari Oficial de la Generalitat de Catalunya* 4680, July 20, 2006, 31875–31904.

Law 3/2007, on the Equality of Men and Women, March 22, 2007, *BOE* 71, March 23, 2007, 12611–12645.

Law 52/2007, on Recognizing and Extending Rights and Establishing Compensatory Measures to those persecuted or victims of violence during the Civil War and Dictatorship, December 26, 2007, *BOE* 310, December 27, 2007, 53410 a 53416.

Provincial Court Sentence No. 319/06, Alicante, September 7, 2006, regarding the Saint George Association and the Navarra Company.

Law 16/2009, on Centres of Worship, July 22, 2009, *Diari Oficial de la Generalitat de Catalunya* 5432, July 30, 2009, 60449–60456.

Bill 60/2013, Quebec National Assembly, Charter affirming the values of State secularism and religious neutrality and of equality between women and men, and providing a framework for accommodation requests, http://www.nosvaleurs.gouv.qc.ca/medias/pdf/Charter.pdf.

Unpublished Municipal Documents

"Fem Barri: Programa per la convivència i la cooperació," l'Erm, Manlleu, December 2003.

"Pla de Gestió de la Diversitat de Manlleu," Manlleu City Hall, April 29, 2003.

"Pla de recepció i acollida de Manlleu (PRAM)," Manlleu City Hall, 2005.

"Projecte d'Intervenció Integral del Barri de l'Erm: Pla de convivencia," Manlleu City Hall, May 2006.

"Projecte d'Intervenció Integral del Barri de l'Erm de Manlleu," Manlleu City Hall, December 2007.

Newspaper Collections

ABC, 1968–2011.
El Mundo del Siglo XXI, 1989–2011.
El País, 1976–2011.
El Periódico de Cataluña, 1978–2011.
La Vanguardia, 1985–2011.
Levante-El Mercantil Valenciano, 1985–2011.
Melilla Hoy, 1985–1988.

Community Periodicals

Barcella: Pobles de la Mariola, 1994–2010.
L'Erm: Butlletí de l'Associació de Veins del Barri de l'Erm, 1997–2008.
Massala, 2001–2005.
Plataforma per Catalunya: Informatiu, 2001–2010.
Trames: Revista d'estudis de Bocairent, 2003–2006.
Verde Islam, 1995–2003.
WebIslam.com, 1997–2010.

Archives

Archive of ATIME, Madrid.
Archive of UCIDE, Madrid.
Archive of FEERI, Madrid.
Archive of ICCV, Valencia.
Archive of the Association Ibn Battuta, Barcelona.
Archive of Jameiat Essalam, Manlleu.
Archive of MMPA, Manlleu.
Archive of ACESOP, Barcelona.
Archive of APWC, Barcelona.
Archive of the Asociación San Jorge, Alcoi.
Archive of Fonèvol, Alcoi.
Barcelona Municipal Archive.
Manlleu Municipal Archive.
Melilla Historical Archive.
Melilla Central Archive.
Melilla Government Delegation Archive.
Ministry of Interior Archive.
Ministry of Justice Archive.

Interviews

Akioud, Hassan. Jameiat Essalam. Manlleu, 23/07/ 2008.
Anglada, Josep. Plataforma per Catalunya. Vic, 22/07/2008.
Azouzi, Mohamed. Islamic Cultural Centre of Manlleu. Manlleu, 24/07/2008.
Benyahya, Abderramán. Muslim activist. Melilla, 24/08/2010.

Casanova, Miquel. Professor of MMPAS. Manlleu, 23/07/2008.

Costa, Empar. Municipal archivist. Manlleu, 23/07/2008.

Espinal, Llorenç. Casal Cívic Federica Montseny. Manlleu, 24/07/2008.

Ferre Tortosa, Adelaida. Festival participant. Beneixama, 25/06/2006.

Hamshed, Juma. ACESOP. Barcelona, 09/09/2008.

Ilyas Qureshi, Javed. AWPC. Barcelona, 10/09/2008.

Iqbal, Muhammad. Path towards Peace. Barcelona, 05/09/2008 and 10/09/2008.

Karrouch, Laila. Nurse and writer. Vic, 12/03/2008 and Valencia, 06/10/2009.

López, Fabio. Associació de Gent Gran. Manlleu, 24/07/2008.

Mohamed Alí, Abkelkader. Terra Omnium. Melilla, 23/08/2010.

Mohamed, Mimunt. Muslim activist. Melilla, 24/08/2010.

Nahima. Resident of l'Erm. Manlleu, 23/08/2008.

Parés, Betlem. Institut de Desenvolupament de l'Erm. Manlleu, 23/07/2008.

Pascual, Xavi. Bocairent's Marrocs. Bocairent, 26/06/2006.

Prat, Pere. Mayor of Manlleu. Manlleu, 24/07/2008.

Riera, Miquelina. Principal, Antoni Pous Secondary School. Manlleu, 23/07/2008.

Rivas, Maria Ángeles. Beneixama's city councillor. Beneixama, 27/06/2006.

Roca, Ana Marta. Manlleu City Hall. Manlleu, 23/07/2008.

Rubia, Toni. L'Erm youth worker, Manlleu, 24/07/2008.

Saliba, Ghassan. CITE Catalunya. Barcelona, 05/09/2008.

Sánchez Gueldos, Miquel. Workers' Commissions at l'Erm. Manlleu, 23/07/2008.

Tufali, Karima. Muslim activist. Melilla, 23/08/2010.

Vila, Jordi. Catholic priest, Saint Paul Church, l'Erm, Manlleu. Manlleu, 23/07/2008.

Published Sources

Primary Sources

I Congreso Nacional de Fiestas de Moros y Cristianos (Villena, 1974) Vol. I & *II* Alicante: Editorial Confederación Española de Cajas de Ahorros, 1976.

"Entrevista a Norma Falconi: Los inmigrantes sin papeles organizados han de tener su propia identidad, su propio protagonismo." *Mugak* 14 (2001). Accessed April 26, 2010. http://revista.mugak.eu/articulos/show/124.

"Proyecto Kurtuba: Entrevista con el Alcalde de Córdoba." *Verde Islam* 2 (1995): 84–88.

Anglada, Josep. *Sin mordaza y sin velos.* Barcelona: Rambla Media Ediciones, S.L., 2010.

Asociación de San Jorge de Alcoy, *Nostra Festa: Alcoy.* Alicante: Gráficas Ciudad, 1982.

Belkacemi, Lyes and Francesc Miralles. *Amazic: L'odissea d'un algerià a Barcelona.* Barcelona: Llibres de l'Índex, 2005.

Berenguer Barceló, Julio. "Fundamento religioso de los Moros y Cristianos de Alcoy." In *I Congreso Nacional de Fiestas de Moros y Cristianos (Villena, 1974) Vol. I*, 145–155. Alicante: Editorial Confederación Española de Cajas de Ahorros, 1976.

Bonet Camarasa, Rafael and Ginés Pardo García. "La religión y la fiesta." In *I*

Congreso Nacional de Fiestas de Moros y Cristianos (Villena, 1974) Vol. I, 156–170. Alicante: Editorial Confederación Española de Cajas de Ahorros, 1976).

Candel, Francisco. *Els altres Catalans.* Barcelona: Edicions 62, 1967.

Candel, Francisco and Josep Maria Cuenca. *Els altres catalans del segle XXI.* Barcelona: Planeta, 2001.

Cervino y Ferrero, Joaquín José. *Embajadas del moro y del cristiano: Para las fiestas que se celebran en la villa de Onteniente al Santísimo Cristo de la Agonía.* Valencia: Librerías Paris-Valencia, 1996.

Chaib, Mohammed. *Enlloc com a Catalunya: Una vida guanyada dia a dia.* Barcelona: Empúries, 2005.

———. *Ètica per una convivència.* Barcelona: La Esfera de los Libros, 2005.

Chico Amat, Juan N. "La mujer en la Fiesta." In *I Congreso Nacional de Fiestas de Moros y Cristianos (Villena, 1974) Vol. I*, 240–262. Alicante: Editorial Confederación Española de Cajas de Ahorros, 1976.

Coca, Abdennur. "Federalía." *Verde Islam* 6 (1997): 49–53.

Colectivo IOÉ. "Relatos desde la entraña de los hogares: Voces de inmigrantes en el servicio doméstico." In *Historias de vida e inmigración,* María Jesús Criado et al., Ofrim suplementos 8 (2001): 37–60.

Consejo Islámico Cultural de Catalunya. "Manifiesto del Cuarto Congreso de Imanes y Mezquitas de Catalunya." *La Factoría* 38 (2009).

———. "Manifiesto del segundo Encuentro de Mujeres Musulmanas de Catalunya." *La Factoría* 35–36 (2008).

Crespo, Ricardo. *Entre moros y cristianos.* Granada: Editorial Andalucía, 1985.

Domènech Llorens, Salvador. *El tractat d'Almisrà,* edited by Maria Conca and Josep Guia. Valencia: University of Valencia, 2008.

El Gheryb, Mohamed and Pascual Moreno Torregrosa. *Dormir al raso.* Madrid: Ediciones VOSA, 1994.

El Hachmi, Najàt. *Jo també sóc catalana.* Barcelona: Columna, 2004.

———. *L'últim patriarca.* Barcelona: Planeta, 2008.

Escudero, Mansur Abdussalam. "El Islam y el incumplimiento de las libertades consitucionales." *Verde Islam* 7 (1997): 8–15.

González, Ali. "A fondo con Mansur." *Verde Islam* 12 (1999): 29–39.

Hage, Rawi. *Cockroach.* Toronto: Anansi, 2008.

Hirsi Ali, Ayaan. *Infidel.* New York: Free Press, 2007.

———. *Nomad: From Islam to America: A Personal Journey through the Clash of Civilizations.* New York: Free Press, 2010.

———. *The Caged Virgin: An Emancipation Proclamation for Women and Islam.* New York: Free Press, 2006.

Ilyas, Javed. "14 de agosto: Día de la independencia de Pakistán." *Massala* 10 (2002): 12.

———. "Comunitat pakistanesa i treball a Barcelona." *Massala* 11 (2002/03): 12

———. "Esclavos de la modernidad." *Massala* 4 (2001): 10–13.

———. "El Primer Ministre del Punjab visita Barcelona." *Massala* 23 (2005): 14.

———. "Qué significa civilización y cultura." *Massala* 5 (2001): 12–13.

Jamal, Salah. *Lluny de l'horitzó perfumat.* Barcelona: La Magrana, 2005.

Jamshed, Huma, Miquel Àngel Essomba and Xavier Febrés. *Diàlegs a Barcelona.* Barcelona: La Magrana, 2009.

Juan Carlos I, "Palabras de Su Majestad el Rey a los participantes en la V Conferencia Iberoamericana de Comisiones del V Centenario del Descubrimiento." San Juan, Puerto Rico, May 26, 1987. Accessed February 5, 2009. http://www.casareal.es/noticias/news/2333-ides-idweb.html.

Kamal Mustafa, Mohammed. *La mujer y el Islam.* Fuengirola: Centro Cultural Islámico Sohail, 1999.

Karrouch, Laila. *De Nador a Vic.* Barcelona: Columna, 2004.

Joan Lacomba. *Las voces del Islam: Veinte entrevistas con inmigrantes musulmanes.* Valencia: Tirant Lo Blanch, 2006.

Mansanet Ribes, José Luis. "La Fiesta de Moros y Cristianos como institución y su ordenación." In *I Congreso Nacional de Fiestas de Moros y Cristianos (Villena, 1974) Vol. I,* 350–372. Alicante: Editorial Confederación Española de Cajas de Ahorros, 1976.

——. "La Mujer y la Fiesta." In *I Congreso Nacional de Fiestas de Moros y Cristianos (Villena, 1974) Vol. I,* 263–280. Alicante: Editorial Confederación Española de Cajas de Ahorros, 1976.

Monturiol Virgili, Yaratullah. *Dones a l'Islam: Autodeterminació.* Barcelona: Edicions El Trabucaire, 2008.

Nini, Rachid. *Diario de un ilegal,* trans. G. Fernández Parrilla and M. Embarek López. Guadarrama: Ediciones del Oriente y del Mediterráneo, 2002.

Peidró Pastor, Jorge. "Coloquio." In *I Congreso Nacional de Fiestas de Moros y Cristianos (Villena, 1974) Vol. I,* 195–210. Alicante: Editorial Confederación Española de Cajas de Ahorros, 1976.

Pope Paul VI. *Declaration on the Relation of the Church to non-Christian Religions, Nostra Aetate.* October 28, 1965. Accessed March 20, 2009. http://www.vatican.va/archive/hist_councils/ii_vatican_council/documents/vat-ii_decl_19651028_nostra-aetate_en.html.

——. *Pastoral Constitution on the Church in the Modern World. Gaudium et Spes.* December 7, 1965. Accessed March 20, 2009. http://www.vatican.va/archive/hist_councils/ii_vatican_council/documents/vat-ii_cons_19651207_gaudium-et-spes_en.html.

Prado, Abdennur. *El Islam en democracia.* Córdoba: Junta Islámica, 2006.

Pujol, Jordi. "Immigració: Gent i País" [paper presented at the Institut d'Estudis Catalans, Barcelona, November 10, 2004]. Accessed August 16, 2010. http://www.jordipujol.cat/files/articles/immigracio.gent.pais.pdf.

Roca, Maria Àngels, Àngels Roger, and Carmen Arranz. *Marroquins a Barcelona: Vint-i-dos relats.* Barcelona: Editorial Laertes, 1983.

Rodríguez Zapatero, José Luis. "Speech of the Spanish Prime Minister." 59th Period of Sessions of the United Nations General Assembly, New York, September 21, 2004. In *Alliance of Civilizations.* Madrid: Ministerio de Asuntos Exteriores y Cooperación, November 2005. Accessed April 20, 2009. http://www.unaoc.org/repository/statement_foreign_ministry_english.pdf

——. "Speech of the Spanish Prime Minister." Summit of the League of Arab States, March 22, 2005. In *Alliance of Civilizations.* Madrid: Ministerio de Asuntos Exteriores y Cooperación, November 2005. Accessed April 20, 2009. http://www.unaoc.org/repository/statement_foreign_ministry_english.pdf.

Rojas Navarro, Alfredo. "Presente y futuro de la fiesta." *I Congreso Nacional de*

Fiestas de Moros y Cristianos (Villena, 1974) Vol. I, 210–234. Alicante: Editorial Confederación Española de Cajas de Ahorros, 1976.

Ruíz Romero, Manuel. "El resurgir de Al-Ándalus según Blas Infante." *Verde Islam* 14 (2000): 61–68.

Soler García, José María. "Crónica del Congreso." *I Congreso Nacional de Fiestas de Moros y Cristianos (Villena, 1974) Vol. I*, 29–60. Alicante: Editorial Confederación Española de Cajas de Ahorros, 1976.

Tatary, Riay. "Libertad religiosa y acuerdo de cooperación entre el Estado español y la Comisión Islámica de España." In *Comunidades Islámicas en Europa*, edited by Montserrat Abumalham, 165–172. Madrid: Trotta, 1995.

———. *25 años de libertad*. Madrid: Asociación Musulmana en España y Unión de Comunidades Islámicas de España, 2007.

Textos de embajadas: Monforte del Cid (Alicante). Monforte del Cid: City Hall of Monforte del Cid, 1999.

Tree, Matthew. *Aniversari: Quatre reflexions sense cap mena d'importància després d'haver viscut exactament vint anys entre els catalans*. Barcelona: Columna, 2005.

Vañó Silvestre, Salvador. "Historia de la Fiesta de Moros y Cristianos en Bocairente." In *I Congreso Nacional de Fiestas de Moros y Cristianos (Villena, 1974) Vol. II*, 648–682. Alicante: Editorial Confederación Española de Cajas de Ahorros, 1976.

———. "La religión y la fiesta de Moros y Cristianos." In *I Congreso Nacional de Fiestas de Moros y Cristianos (Villena, 1974) Vol. I*, 115–144. Alicante: Editorial Confederación Española de Cajas de Ahorros, 1976.

Verdú Navarro, Vicent and Pablo Calabuig Gómez, "Els moros i cristians com a festa intercultural." Xerrada a la fresca, August 19, 2003 [unpublished paper].

Secondary Sources

"Interview with Professor Nira Yuval Davis: After Gender and Nation." *Studies in Ethnicity and Nationalism* 9, 1 (2009): 128–138.

Abdallah, Mogniss Hamed, ed. *J'y suis, j'y reste! Les luttes de l'immigration en France depuis les années soixante*. Paris: Editions Reflex, 2000.

Abdel Haleem, M.A.S., trans. *The Qur'an*. New York: Oxford University Press, 2005.

Abend, Lisa. "Spain's New Muslims." In *In the Light of Medieval Spain: Islam, the West, and the Relevance of the Past*, edited by Simon R. Doubleday and David Coleman, 133–156. New York: Palgrave Macmillan, 2008.

Aierbe, Peio. "La irrupción de los sin papeles." *Mugak* 14 (2001). Accessed April 26, 2010. http://revista.mugak.eu/articulos/show/123.

Aitchison, Cara, Peter Hopkins, and Mei-po Kwan, eds. *Geographies of Muslim Identities: Diaspora, Gender and Belonging*. Aldershot, England: Ashgate, 2007.

Aja, Eliseo and Joaquín Arango, eds. *Veinte años de inmigración en España: Perspectivas jurídica y sociológica (1985–2004)*. Barcelona: CIDOB Edicions, 2006.

Aja, Eliseo and Laura Díez Bueso. "La participación política de los inmigrantes."

La Factoría 10 (1999–2000). Accessed January 23, 2011. http://www.lafactoriaweb.com/articulos/aja10.htm.

Alcaraz Santonja, Albert. *Moros i Cristians: Una festa*. Picanya: Edicions del Bullent, 2006.

Allievi, Stefano. *Conflict over Mosques in Europe: Policy Issues and Trends*. London: NEF and Alliance Publishing Trust, 2009.

AlSayyad, Nezar and Manuel Castells, eds. *Muslim Europe or Euro-Islam: Politics, Culture, and Citizenship in the Age of Globalization*. Lanham, Md.: Lexington Books, 2002.

Álvarez Junco, José and Adrian Shubert. *Spanish History since 1808*. London: Arnold; New York: Oxford University Press, 2000.

Amades, Joan. *Las danzas de moros y cristianos*. Valencia: Institució Alfons el Magnànim, 1966.

Anderson, Benedict R. *Imagined Communities: Reflections on the Origin and Spread of Nationalism*. London: Verso, 1983.

Arnesen, Eric. "Whiteness and the Historians' Imagination." *International Labor and Working-Class History* 60 (2001): 3–32.

Aranda Gallego, Joaquín. "La economía de Ceuta y Melilla: Desaceleración en un entorno expansive." *Papeles de economía española* 64 (1995): 278–287.

Astor, Avi. "Mezquita No! The Origins of Mosque Opposition in Spain." *GRITIM Working Paper Series* 3 (2009): 1–42.

Azurmendi, Mikel. *Estampas de El Ejido: Un reportaje sobre la integración del inmigrante*. Madrid: Taurus, 2001.

Badran, Margot. *Feminism in Islam: Secular and Religious Convergences*. Oxford: Oneworld, 2009.

Bahtiar, Laleh. *The Sublime Quran*. Chicago: Kazi Publications, 2009.

Balfour, Sebastian and Alejandro Quiroga. *The Reinvention of Spain: Nation and Identity since Democracy*. Oxford; New York: Oxford University Press, 2007.

Barth, Fredrik, ed. *Ethnic Groups and Boundaries: The Social Organization of Culture Difference*. Boston: Little Brown, 1969.

Baumann, Roland. *The 'Moors and Christians' of Valor: Folklore and Conflict in the Alpujarra (Andalusia)*. Ann Arbor: University of Michigan, 1995.

Bauman, Zygmunt. *Identity: Conversations with Benedetto Vecchi*. Cambridge, UK; Malden, MA: Polity Press, 2004.

Bawer, Bruce. *Surrender: Appeasing Islam, Sacrificing Freedom*. New York: Doubleday, 2009.

——. *While Europe Slept: How Radical Islam is Destroying the West from Within*. New York: Doubleday, 2006.

Beckman, Ludvig. "Democratization and Inclusion." In *Routledge Handbook of Democratization*, edited by Jeffrey Haynes, 161–174. New York: Routledge, 2012.

Ben Jelloun, Tahar. *Leaving Tangier*. London: Arcadia Books, 2009.

Benítez, Rafael, ed. *Entre terra i fe: Els musulmans al regne cristià de València (1238–1609)*. Valencia: University of Valencia Press, 2009.

Bernabeu Rico, José Luis. *Significados sociales de las fiestas de moros y cristianos*. Alicante: Universidad Nacional de Educación a Distancia, 1981.

Betz, Hans-Georg and Susi Meret. "Revisiting Lepanto: The Political

Mobilization Against Islam in Contemporary Western Europe." *Patterns of Prejudice* 43, ¾ (2009): 313–334.

Blanco, María. "La primera ley española de libertad religiosa." *Anuario de derecho eclesiástico del Estado* 14 (1998): 119–186.

Blore, Kent. "A Space for Feminism in Islamic Law? A Theoretical Exploration of Islamic Feminism." *eLaw Journal: Murdoch University Electronic Journal of Law* 17, 2 (2010): 1–12.

Bodnar, John. *The Transplanted: A History of Immigrants in Urban America.* Bloomington: Indiana University Press, 1985.

Bourdieu, Pierre. "L'identité et la représentation. Eléments pour une réflexion critique de l'ideé de region." *Actes de la Recherche en Sciences Sociales* 35 (1980): 63–72.

Boyd, Carolyn P. *Historia Patria: Politics, History, and National Identity in Spain, 1875–1975.* Princeton, NY: Princeton University Press, 1997.

Bruckner, Pascal. *Misère de la prospérité: la religion marchande et ses ennemis.* Paris: Grasset, 2002.

Burns, Robert I. "The Crusade against Al-Azraq: A Thirteenth-Century Mudejar Revolt in International Perspective." *The American Historical Review* 93, 1 (1988): 80–106.

Buruma, Ian. *Murder in Amsterdam: The Death of Theo van Gogh and the Limits of Tolerance.* New York: Penguin Books, 2005.

Calavita, Kitty. *Immigrants at the Margins: Law, Race, and Exclusion in Southern Europe.* Cambridge, UK; New York: Cambridge University Press, 2005.

Callahan, William J. *The Catholic Church in Spain, 1875–1998.* Washington, D.C.: Catholic University of America Press, 2000.

Calvo Buezas, Tomás. *El crimen racista de Aravaca.* Madrid: Jóvenes contra la Intolerancia, 1993.

Calvo, Kerman. "Sacrifices that Pay: Polity Membership, Political Opportunities and the Recognition of Same-Sex Marriage in Spain." *South European Society and Politics* 12, 3 (2007): 295–314.

Caramés, Lito and Valentí Garriga. "La imagen del otro: El Islam en los libros de texto." *Etnopolis* 5 (1996): 55–60.

Carbonell Sebarroja, Jaume. *Magribins a les aules: El model de Vic a debat.* Vic: Eumo, 2002.

Carens, Joseph H., and Melissa S. Williams. "Islam, Immigration and Group Recognition." *Citizenship Studies* 2, 3 (1998): 475–500.

——. "Muslim Minorities in Liberal Democracies: The Politics of Misrecognition." In *The Challenge of Diversity: Integration and Pluralism in Societies of Immigration,* edited by R. Bauböck, A. Heller, A. and A. R. Zolberg, 157–86. Aldershot: Avebury, 1996.

Carr, Raymond and Juan Pablo Fusi. *España de la dictadura a la democracia.* Barcelona: Planeta, 1979.

Carrasco Urgoiti, María Soledad. "Christians and Moors in Spain: History, Religion, Theatre." *Cultures* 3, 1 (1976): 87–116.

——. *El moro retador y el moro amigo (Estudios sobre fiestas y comedias de moros y cristianos).* Granada: University of Granada, 1996.

Casals, Xavier. *La Plataforma per Catalunya: La eclosión de un nacional-popu-*

lismo catalán (2003–2009), Working Papers 274. Barcelona: Institut de Ciències Polítiques i Socials, 2009.

——. *Ultracatalunya: L'extrema dreta a Catalunya: De l'emergència del búnker al rebuig de les mesquites (1966–2006).* Barcelona: L'Esfera dels Llibres, 2007.

Casanova, José. "Secularization Revisited: A Reply to Talal Asad." In *Powers of the Secular Modern: Talal Asad and his Interlocutors,* edited by David Scott and Charles Hirschkind, 12–30. Stanford, Calif.: Stanford University Press, 2006.

Casas Trabal, Pere and Carles Crosas Armengol. *Nouvinguts a la ciutat: La construcció urbana de Manlleu, 1900–2005.* Manlleu: Museu industrial del Ter/Eumo Editorial, 2007.

Castan Pinos, Jaume. "Identity Challenges affecting the Spanish Enclaves of Ceuta and Melilla." 2008 European Conference of the Association of Borderlands Studies. 65–80

Castellano, Pablo. *Por Dios, por la patria y el rey: Una visión crítica de la transición española.* Madrid: Temas de Hoy, 2001.

Castles, Stephen and Mark J. Miller. *The Age of Migration: International Population Movements in the Modern World.* New York: Guilford Press, 1993.

Castro, Américo. *España en su historia: Cristianos, moros y judíos.* Barcelona: Crítica, 2001.

——. *Sobre el nombre y el quién de los españoles.* Madrid: Taurus, 2000.

Cazorla-Sánchez, Antonio. *Fear and Progress: Ordinary Lives in Franco's Spain, 1939–1975.* Chichester, UK; Malden, MA: Wiley-Blackwell, 2010.

——. *Franco: The Biography of the Myth.* London: Routledge, 2014.

Cebrián, José Luís. *La España que bosteza: Apuntes para una historia crítica de la transición.* Madrid: Taurus, 1980.

CEIMIGRA. "El contingente laboral de trabajadores extranjeros no comunitarios." *Miradas sobre la Inmigración* 22. Valencia: Bancaja. Accessed September 20, 2010. http://www.ceimigra.net.

Cesari, Jocelyne. "Mosque Conflicts in European Cities: Introduction." *Journal of Ethnic and Migration Studies* 31, 6 (2005): 1015–1024.

——. "Mosques in French Cities: Towards the End of a Conflict?" *Journal of Ethnic and Migration Studies* 31, 6 (2005): 1025–1043.

Cesari, Jocelyne and Seán McLoughlin, eds. *European Muslims and the Secular State.* Aldershot, Hants, England; Burlington, VT, USA: Ashgate Pub. Co., 2005.

Chambers, Simone. "Critical Theory and Civil Society." In *Alternative Conceptions of Civil Society,* edited by W. Kymlicka and S. Chambers. 90–112. Princeton: Princeton University Press) 1998.

Checa, Francisco, ed. *El Ejido: La ciudad-cortijo: Claves socioeconómicas del conflicto étnico.* Barcelona: Icaria, 2001.

Choudhury, Tufyal et al. *Perceptions of Discrimination and Islamophobia: Voices from Members of Muslim Communities in the European Union.* Vienna: EMCR, 2006.

Colectivo IOÉ. *Discursos de los españoles sobre los extranjeros: Paradojas de la alteridad.* Madrid: Talasa, 1995.

Coleman, David. "The Persistence of the Past in the Albaicín: Granada's New

Mosque and the Question of Historical Relevance." In *In the Light of Medieval Spain: Islam, the West, and the Relevance of the Past,* edited by Simon R. Doubleday and David Coleman,157–188. New York: Palgrave Macmillan, 2008.

Conversi, Daniele. *The Basques, the Catalans, and Spain: Alternative Routes to Nationalist Mobilisation.* London: Hurst, 1997.

———. "Language or Race? The Choice of Core Values in the Development of Catalan and Basque nationalisms." *Ethnic and Racial Studies* 13, 1 (1990): 50–70.

Cortés Peña, Antonio Luis. "Nacionalismo/regionalismo andaluz, ¿una invención de laboratorio?" *Historia social* 40 (2001): 137–152.

Coutin, Susan Bibler. *The Culture of Protest: Religious Activism and the U.S. Sanctuary Movement.* Boulder: Westview Press, 1993.

Crowley, John. "The Political Participation of Ethnic Minorities." *International Political Science Review / Revue internationale de science politique* 22, 1 (2001): 99–121.

———. "The Politics of Belonging: Some Theoretical Consideration." In *The Politics of Belonging: Migrants and Minorities in Contemporary Europe,* edited by Andrew Geddes and Adrian Favell, 15–41. Aldershot: Ashgate, 1999.

Çaylak, Adem. "Autocratic or Democratic? A Critical Approach to Civil Society Movements in Turkey." *Journal of Economic and Social Research* 10, 1 (2008): 115–151.

Dahl, Robert. *Polyarchy: Participation and Opposition.* New Haven, CT: Yale University Press, 1971.

Derocher, Lorraine, ed. *L'asile religieux: entre desobeissance civile et obligation legale.* Sherbrooke, Que.: Editions Revue de droit de l'Universite de Sherbrooke, 2009.

Doorenspleet, Renske and Petr Kopecky. "Against the Odds: Deviant Cases of Democratization." *Democratization* 15, 4 (2008): 697–714

Doubleday, Simon R. "Introduction: 'Criminal Non-Intervention': Hispanism, Medievalism, and the Pursuit of Neutrality." In *In the Light of Medieval Spain: Islam, the West, and the Relevance of the Past,* edited by Simon R. Doubleday and David Coleman, 1–32. New York: Palgrave Macmillan, 2008.

Driessen, Henk. "Mock Battles between Moors and Christians: Playing the Confrontation of Crescent with Cross in Spain's South." *Ethnologia Europaea* 15, 2 (1985): 105–115.

Edles, Laura Desfor. "A Culturalist Approach to Ethnic Nationalist Movements: Symbolization and Basque and Catalan Nationalism in Spain." *Social Science History* 23, 3 (1999): 311–355.

———. *Symbol and Ritual in the New Spain: The Transition to Democracy after Franco.* Cambridge; New York: Cambridge University Press, 1998.

Eftekhari, Roza. "*Zanan*: Trials and Successes of a Feminist Magazine in Iran." In *Middle Eastern Women on the Move: Openings for and the Constraints on Women's Political Participation in the Middle East,* Haleh Esfandiari et al., 15–22. Washington, DC: Woodrow Wilson International Center for Scholars, 2003.

Eley, Geoff. *Forgin Democracy: The History of the Left in Europe, 1850–2000.* Oxford: Oxford University Press, 2002.

Encarnación, Omar G. *Spanish Politics: Democracy after Dictatorship.* Cambridge, UK; Malden, MA: Polity, 2008.

Erra, Miquel and Joan Serra. *Tota la veritat sobre Plataforma per Catalunya (PxC): L'ultradretà Josep Anglada al descobert.* Barcelona: Ara Llibres, 2008.

Esposito, John L. and François Burgat. *Modernizing Islam: Religion in the Public Sphere in the Middle East and Europe.* New Brunswick, New Jersey: Rutgers University Press, 2003.

European Monitoring Centre on Racism and Xenophobia, *Muslims in the European Union: Discrimination and Islamophobia.* Vienna: EMCR, 2006.

Fallaci, Oriana. *The Rage and the Pride.* New York: Rizzoli, 2001.

Fanjul, Serafín. *Al-Andalus contra España: La forja de un mito.* Madrid: Siglo Veintiuno de España, 2002.

Ferrer Gallardo, F. "Theorizing the Spanish-Moroccan Border Reconfiguration: Framing a Process of Geopolitical, Functional and Symbolic Rebordering." *CIBR/WP06,* 2006.

Flesler, Daniela. *The Return of the Moor: Spanish Responses to Contemporary Moroccan Immigration.* West Lafayette, IN: Purdue University Press, 2008.

——. "Contemporary Moroccan Immigration and Its Ghosts." In *In the Light of Medieval Spain: Islam, the West, and the Relevance of the Past,* edited by Simon R. Doubleday and David Coleman, 115–132. New York: Palgrave Macmillan, 2008.

Flesler, Daniela and Adrián Pérez Melgosa. "Battles of Identity, or Playing 'Guest' and 'Host': The Festivals of Moors and Christians in the Context of Moroccan Immigration in Spain." *Journal of Spanish Cultural Studies,* 4, 2 (2003): 151–168.

Flor, Vicent. *Noves glòries a Espanya: Anticatalanisme i identitat valenciana.* Catarroja: Editorial Afers, 2011.

Foster, George M. *Culture and Conquest: America's Spanish Heritage.* Chicago: Quadrangle Books, 1960.

Fung, Archon and Erik Olin Wright et al. *Deepening Democracy: Institutional Innovations in Empowered Participatory Governance.* London; New York: Verso, 2003.

Galston, William A. *Liberal Purposes: Goods, Virtues, and Diversity in the Liberal State.* Cambridge; New York: Cambridge University Press, 1991.

Garcia Càrcel, Ricard. *La revolta de les Germanies.* Valencia: Institució Alfons el Magnànim, 1981.

García Ferrando, Manuel, Eduardo López-Aranguren, and Miguel Beltrán Villalva. *La conciencia nacional y regional en la España de las autonomías,* Madrid: CIS, 1994.

Garreta Bochaca, Jordi and Núria Llevot Calvet. *El espejismo intercultural: La escuela de Cataluña ante la diversidad cultural.* Madrid: Ministerio de Educación, Cultura y Deporte, 2003.

Garton Ash, Timothy. *Free World: America, Europe, and the Surprising Future of the West.* New York: Vintage Books, 2005.

Gellner, Ernst. Muslim Society. Cambridge; New York: Cambridge University Press, 1981.

Gilligan, Chris and Susan Ball. "Introduction: Migration and Divided Societies." *Ethnopolitics: Formerly Global Review of Ethnopolitics* 10, 2 (2011): 153–170.

Giménez Barriocanal, Fernando. *La financiación de la Iglesia Católica en España.* Madrid: Conferencia Episcopal Española-Edice Editorial, 2007.

Glick, Thomas F. *Islamic and Christian Spain in the Early Middle Ages.* Princeton, NJ: Princeton University Press, 1979.

Goddard, Hugh. "Islam and Democracy." *Political Quarterly* 73, 1 (2002): 3–10

Gold, Peter. *Europe or Africa? A Contemporary Study of the Spanish North African Enclaves of Ceuta and Melilla.* Liverpool: Liverpool University Press, 2000.

Gómez-Quintero, Juan David. "Inmigración y ciudadanía: Legitimación social de la desigualdad." *Acciones e Investigaciones Sociales* 25, 2 (2008): 25–45.

González Enríquez, Carmen, ed. *Los sindicatos ante la inmigración.* Madrid: Ministerio de Trabajo e Inmigración, 2008.

——. "Undocumented Migration: Counting the Uncountable. Data and Trends across Europe. Country Report: Spain." http://irregular-migration.net//typo3_upload/groups/31/4.Background_Information/4.4.Country_Reports/Spain_CountryReport_Clandestino_Nov09_2.pdf

Gore, Sarah. "The Catalan Language and Immigrants from Outside the European Union." *International Journal of Iberian Studies* 15, 2 (2002): 91–102.

Goytisolo, Juan. *Crónicas sarracinas.* La Coruña: Ruedo Ibérico, 1982.

——. "El Ayer, hoy y mañana de la España de Américo Castro." In *Contra las sagradas formas,* 51–58. Barcelona: Círculo de Lectores and Galaxia Gutenberg, 2007.

——. "Pájaro que ensucia su propio nido." In *Tradición y disidencia,* 13–32. Monterrey: Instituto Tecnológico y de Estudios Superioreos de Monterrey; Madrid: Fondo de Cultura Económica, 2003.

——. *Tradición y disidencia.* Monterrey: Instituto Tecnológico y de Estudios Superioreos de Monterrey; Madrid: Fondo de Cultura Económica, 2003.

——. *Reivindicación del Conde Don Julián.* México: J.M Ortiz, 1970.

Goytisolo, Juan and Sami Naïr. *El peaje de la vida: Integración o rechazo de la emigración en España.* Madrid: Aguilar, 2000.

Graham, Helen. "The Spanish Civil War, 1936–2003: The Return of Republican Memory." *Science & Society* 68, 3 (2004): 313–328.

Guelke, Adrian. *Democracy and Ethnic Conflict: Advancing Peace in Deeply Divided Societies.* Hampshire, Eng.: Palgrave Macmillan, 2004.

Guia, Aitana. "De lenguas y horizontes: Europa vista por sus escritores inmigrantes de cultura islámica." *Extravío. Revista electrónica de literatura comparada* 5 (2010).

——. "Molts mons, una sola llengua: La narrativa en català escrita per immigrants." *Quaderns de Filologia. Estudis literaris* 12 (2007): 229–248.

——. *La llengua negociada: El manteniment del conflicte polític sobre la llengua.* Valencia: 3 i 4, 2001.

Guibernau, Montserrat. *Catalan Nationalism: Francoism, Transition, and Democracy.* London; New York: Routledge, 2004.

Habermas, Jürgen. *The Postnational Constellation: Political Essays,* Cambridge, UK: Polity Press, 2001.

Haddad, Yvonne Yazbeck. "The Post-9/11 Hijab as Icon." *Sociology of Religion* 68, 3 (2007): 253–267.

Halbwachs, Maurice. *The Collective Memory.* New York: Harper & Row, 1980.

Halliday, Fred. *Islam and the Myth of Confrontation: Religion and Politics in the Middle East.* London: I. B. Tauris, 1996.

Hamdan, Amani. "The Issue of Hijab in France: Reflections and Analysis." *Muslim World Journal of Human Rights* 4, 2, article 4 (2007).

Hammar, Tomas. *Democracy and the Nation State: Aliens, Denizens and Citizens in a World of International Migration.* Aldershot, Hants, Eng.: Brookfield, Vt.: Avebury; Gower Pub. Co., 1990.

Handlin, Oscar. *The Uprooted: The Epic Story of the Great Migrations that Made the American People.* Boston: Little, Brown, 1951.

Harney, Robert F. "Montreal's King of Italian Labour: A Case Study of Padronism." *Labour / Le Travail* 4 (1979): 57–84.

Harris, Max. "Muhammad and the Virgin: Folk Dramatizations of Battles between Moors and Christians in Modern Spain." *The Drama Review* 38, 1 (1994): 45–61.

Hargreaves, John. *Freedom for Catalonia? Catalan Nationalism and the Barcelona Olympic Games.* Cambridge; New York: Cambridge University Press, 2000.

Haynes, Jeffrey. "Introduction." In *Routledge Handbook of Democratization,* edited by Jeffrey Haynes, 1–10. New York: Routledge, 2012.

Heller, Patrick. "Democratic Deepening in India and South Africa." *Journal of Asian and African studies* 44 (2009): 125.

Higham, John. *Strangers in the Land: Patterns of American Nativism, 1860–1925.* New Brunswick, NJ: Rutgers University Press, 1955.

Hipsher, Patricia L. "Democratization and the Decline of Urban Social Movements in Spain and Chile." *Comparative Politics* 28, 3 (1996): 273–287.

Hobsbawm, Eric. "Introduction: Inventing Traditions." In *The Invention of Tradition,* edited by Eric Hobsbawm and Terence Ranger, 1–14. Cambridge: Cambridge University Press, 1983.

Hobsbawm, Eric and Terence Ranger, eds. *The Invention of Tradition.* Cambridge: Cambridge University Press, 1983.

Hondagneu-Sotelo, Pierrette. "Overcoming Patriarchal Constraints: The Reconstruction of Gender Relations among Mexican Immigrant Women and Men." *Gender and Society* 6, 3 (1992): 393–416.

———. *Gender and U.S. Immigration: Contemporary Trends.* Berkeley: University of California Press, 2003.

Huntington, Samuel P. *The Clash of Civilizations and the Remaking of World Order.* New York: Simon and Schuster, 1997.

Husson, Jean-François. *Training Imams in Europe: The Current Status.* Brussels: King Baudouin Foundation, 2007.

Hopkin, Jonathan, *Party Formation and Democratic Transition in Spain: The*

Creation and Collapse of the Union of the Democratic Centre, New York: St. Martin's Press, 1999

Hughes, Robert. *Barcelona*. New York: Knopf: Random House, 1992.

Interculturalitat, educació i llengües: Seminari de treball, Barcelona, Girona, Lleida i Tarragona, May 5–6, 2000. Barcelona: CC.OO., 2002.

Izquierdo Escribano, Antonio. *La inmigración en España: 1980–1990*. Madrid: Ministerio de Trabajo y Seguridad Social, 1992.

———. "La inmigración ilegal en España: Análisis de la operación extraordinaria de regularización 1985–86." *Economía y sociología del trabajo* 11 (1990): 18–38.

———. *La inmigración inesperada: La población extranjera en España, 1991–1995*. Madrid: Editorial Trotta, 1996.

Jacobson, Jessica. "Perceptions of Britishness." *Nations and Nationalism* 3/2 (1997): 181–200.

Jiménez, Manuel. "The Environmental Movement in Spain: A Growing Force of Contention." *South European Society and Politics* 12, 3 (2007): 359–378.

Jonker, Gerdien. "The Mevlana Mosque in Berlin-Kreuzberg: An Unsolved Conflict." *Journal of Ethnic and Migration Studies* 31, 6 (2005): 1067–1081.

Jordan, Javier, Fernando M. Mañas, and Nicola Horsburgh. "Strengths and Weaknesses of Grassroot Jihadist Networks: The Madrid Bombings." *Studies in Conflict and Terrorism* 31, 1 (2008): 17–39.

Juarros-Daussà, Eva and Tilman Lanz. "Rethinking Balanced Bilingualism: The Impact of Globalization in Catalonia." *Language Problems and Language Planning* 33:1 (2009), 1–21.

Judt, Tony. *Postwar: A History of Europe since 1945*. New York: Penguin Books, 2005.

Kamen, Henry. *Imagining Spain: Historical Myth and National Identity*. New Haven, Conn.; London: Yale University Press, 2008.

Kaplan, Ann E. "Trauma, Aging and Melodrama (With Reference to Tracey Moffatt's *Night Cries*)." In *Feminist Locations: Global and Local, Theory and Practice*, edited by Marianne DeKoven, 304–328. New Brunswick, NJ: Rutgers University Press, 2001.

Kaplan, David. "Territorial Identities and Geographical Scale." In *Nested Identities*, edited by H. Guntram and D. Kaplan, 31–49. New York: Rowman & Littlefield, 1999.

Kaplan, David. "Conflict and Compromise among Borderland Identities in Northern Italy." *Tijdschrift voor Economische en Sociale Geografie* 95, 1 (2000): 100–107.

Karamichas, John. "Key Issues in the Study of New and Alternative Social Movements in Spain: The Left, Identity and Globalizing Processes." *South European Society and Politics* 12, 3 (2007): 273–294.

Kastoryano, Riva. "Race and Ethnicity in France." In *Social Inequalities in Comparative Perspective*, edited by Fiona Devine and Mary Waters, 66–88. Malden, Mass.: Blackwell Pub., 2004

Kepel, Gilles, and Susan Milner. *Allah in the West: Islamic Movements in America and Europe*. Stanford, Calif: Stanford University Press, 1997.

Khan, Amjad Mahmood. "Persecution of the Ahmadiyya Community in

Pakistan: An Analysis under International Law and International Relations." *Harvard Human Rights Journal* 16 (2003): 217–244.

King, Rusell and Isabel Rodríguez-Melguizo. "Recent Immigration to Spain: The case of Moroccans in Catalonia." In *Into the Margins: Migration and Exclusion in Southern Europe*, edited by Floya Anthias and Gabriella Lazaridis, 55–82. Aldershot, UK: Ashgate, 1999.

King, Stewart. "Catalan Literature(s) in Postcolonial Context." *Romance Studies* 24, 3 (2006): 253–264.

King, Thomas. *The Inconvenient Indian: A Curious Account of Native People in North America*. Toronto, ON: Doubleday Canada, 2012.

Kleiner-Liebau, Désirée. *Migration and the Construction of National Identity in Spain*. Madrid; Frankfurt am Main: Iberoamericana; Vervuert, 2009.

Kymlicka, Will. *Politics in the Vernacular: Nationalism, Multiculturalism, and Citizenship*. Oxford: Oxford University Press, 2000.

Kymlicka, Will and Wayne Norman. "Return of the Citizen: A Survey of Recent Work on Citizenship Theory," *Ethics* 104 (1994): 353.

———. "Citizenship in Culturally Diverse Societies: Issues, Contexts, Concepts." In *Citizenship in Diverse Societies*, edited by Will Kymlicka and Wayne Norman, 1–45. Oxford: Oxford University Press 2000.

Kymlicka, Will and Wayne Norman, eds. *Citizenship in Diverse Societies*. Oxford: Oxford University Press 2000.

Lacomba Vázquez, Joan. *El Islam inmigrado: Transformaciones y adaptaciones de las prácticas culturales y religiosas*. Madrid: Ministerio de Educación, Cultura y Deporte, 2001.

———. "La inmigración musulmana en España: Inserción y dinámicas comunitarias en el espacio local." *Migraciones* 18 (2005): 47–76.

———. "La inmigración musulmana y el Islam institucionalizado: La figura de los 'imames' inmigrados." *Migraciones* 7 (2000): 155–193.

Landman, Nico and Wendy Wessels. "The Visibility of Mosques in Dutch Towns." *Journal of Ethnic and Migration Studies* 31, 6 (2005): 1125–1140.

Laubenthal, Barbara. "The Emergence of Pro-Regularization Movements in Western Europe." *International Migration* 45, 3 (2007): 101–133.

Levy, Jacob T. "Classifying Cultural Rights." In *Ethnicity and Group Rights: NOMOS XXXIX*, edited by W. Kymlicka and I. Shapiro. New York: New York University press, 1997.

Lewis, Bernard. *Islam and the West*. New York: Oxford University Press, 1993.

———. *The Jews of Islam*. Princeton, NJ: Princeton University Press, 1984.

Linke, Uli. "There is a Land where Everything is Pure: Linguistic Nationalism and Identity Politics in Germany." In *Race, Nature, and the Politics of Difference*, edited by D.S. Moore, J. Kosek, and A. Pandian, 149–173. Durham, NC: Duke University Press, 2003.

Lippert, Randy K. *Sanctuary, Sovereignty, Sacrifice: Canadian Sanctuary Incidents, Power and Law*. Vancouver: UBC Press, 2005.

Lipski, John M. "Double Talk: Bilingualism and the Politics of Ethnicity in Catalonia." *Journal of Linguistic Anthropology* 1, 1 (1991): 117–119.

Lisón Tolosana, Carmelo. *Invitación a la antropología cultural de España*. Madrid: Akal Bolsillo, 1980.

Llera, Francisco J., Jose M. Mata, and Cynthia L. Irvin. "ETA: From Secret Army to Social Movement – The Post-Franco Schism of the Basque Nationalist Movement." *Terrorism and Political Violence* 5, 3 (1993): 106–134.

López Duro, Paco, ed. *La diversitat cultural en l'àmbit laboral: Arguments i opinions al voltant de la immigració al País Valencià.* Valencia: CC.OO.-Valencia, 2008.

López García, Bernabé, ed. *Inmigración magrebí en España: El retorno de los moriscos.* Madrid: Editorial Mapfre, 1993.

———. "La evolución de la inmigración marroquí en España, 1991–2003." In *Atlas de la Inmigración Marroquí en España 2004*, edited by Bernabé López García and Mohamed Berriane, 213–220. Madrid: UAM, 2004.

López García, Bernabé, Ángeles Ramírez, and Ana I. Planet, "La política de contingentes en 1993 y 1994." In *Atlas de la Inmigración Marroquí en España 2004*, edited by Bernabé López García and Mohamed Berriane, 257–8. Madrid: UAM, 2004.

Lucassen, Leo. *The Immigrant Threat: The Integration of Old and New Migrants in Western Europe since 1850.* Urbana: University of Illinois Press, 2005.

Malkki, Liisa. "National Geographic: The Rooting of Peoples and the Territorialization of National Identity among Scholars and Refugees." *Cultural Anthropology* 7, 1 (1992): 22–44.

Mancho, Santiago. *Emigración y desarrollo español.* Madrid: Instituto Español de Emigración, Ministerio de Trabajo, 1978.

Manço, Ural and Meryem Kanmaz. "From Conflict to Co-operation Between Muslims and Local Authorities in a Brussels Borough: Schaerbeek." *Journal of Ethnic and Migration Studies* 31, 6 (2005): 1105–1123.

Mann, Vivan, Thomas F. Glick, and Jerrilynn D. Dodds, eds. *Convivencia: Jews, Muslims, and Christians in Medieval Spain.* New York: G. Braziller in association with the Jewish Museum, 1992.

Mar-Molinero, Clare and Angel Smith, eds. *Nationalism and the Nation in the Iberian Peninsula: Competing and Conflicting Identities.* Oxford, Eng.; Washington, DC: Berg, 1996.

Martín Corrales, Eloy. *La imagen del magrebí en España: Una perspectiva histórica, siglos XVI–XX.* Barcelona: Bellaterra, 2002.

———. "Maurofobia/islamofobia, maurofilia/islamofilia en la España del siglo XXI." *Revista CIDOB d'Afers Internacionals* 66–67 (2004): 39–51.

Martín Muñoz, Gema. "Percepciones de la inmigración magrebí en España." *Tropelias: Revista de teoría de la literatura y literatura comparada* 11 (2000): 97–104.

Martínez Veiga, Ubaldo. *El Ejido: Discriminación, exclusión social y racismo.* Madrid: La Catarata, 2001.

———. *Pobreza, segregación y exclusión espacial: La vivienda de los inmigrantes extranjeros en España.* Barcelona: Icaria, 1999.

Mazkiaran, Mikel. "Recorrido por las leyes de extranjería en España." *Mugak* 29 (2004). Accessed January 10, 2011. http://revista. mugak.eu/ articulos/ show/315.

McDonogh, Gary W. "The Geography of Evil: Barcelona's Barrio Chino." *Anthropological Quarterly* 60, 4 (1987): 174–184.

McLoughlin, Seán. "Mosques and the Public Space: Conflict and Cooperation in Bradford." *Journal of Ethnic and Migration Studies* 31, 6 (2005): 1045–1066.

Menéndez Pelayo, Marcelino. "Epílogo a *Historia de los heterodoxos españoles.*" In *Textos sobre España*, ed. Florentino Pérez Embid, 141–148. Madrid: Ediciones Rialp, 1955.

———. "El brindis del Retiro." In *Textos sobre España*, ed. Florentino Pérez Embid, 149–153. Madrid: Ediciones Rialp, 1955.

Menocal, Maria Rosa. *The Ornament of the World: How Muslims, Jews, and Christians Created a Culture of Tolerance in Medieval Spain.* Boston: Little, Brown, 2002.

Meret, Susi. "The Danish People's Party, the Italian Northern League and the Austrian Freedom Party in a Comparative Perspective: Party Ideology and Electoral Support." Ph.D. Series 25, University of Aalborg, 2010.

Mijares Molina, Laura. *Aprendiendo a ser marroquíes: Inmigración, diversidad lingüística y escuela.* Madrid: Ediciones del Oriente y el Mediterráneo, 2006.

Mijares Molina, Laura and Ángeles Ramírez. "Mujeres, pañuelo e islamofobia en España: Un estado de la cuestión." *Anales de historia contemporánea* 24 (2008): 121–135.

Ministerio de Trabajo y Asuntos Sociales, *Anuario de Migraciones 2002.* Madrid: MTAS, 2002. Accessed March 11, 2011. http://www.mtas.es/migraciones/anumigra/contenido/AnuMigra02Compl eto.pdf.

Mira, Joan Francesc. *Vida i final dels moriscos valencians.* Alzira: Bromera, 2009.

Modood, Tariq. "Anti Essentialism, Multiculturalism, and the 'Recognition' Of Religious Groups." In *Citizenship in Diverse Societies*, edited by Will Kymlicka and Wayne Norman, 175–197. Oxford: Oxford University Press 2000.

Modood, Tariq and Riva Kastoryano. "Secularism and the Accommodation of Muslims in Europe." In *Multiculturalism, Muslims and Citizenship: A European Approach*, edited by Tariq Modood, Anna Triandafyllidou, and Ricard Zapata-Barrero, 162–178. Toronto and New York: Routledge, 2006.

Moghissi, Haideh. "Islamic Feminism Revisited." *Comparative Studies of South Asia, Africa and the Middle East* 31, 1 (2011): 76–84

———. *Muslim Diaspora: Gender, Culture, and Identity.* New York: Routledge, 2006.

Moghissi, Haideh and Halleh Ghorashi, eds. *Muslim Diaspora in the West: Negotiating Gender, Home and Belonging.* Farnham, Surrey; Burlington, VT: Ashgate Pub., 2010.

Momblanch González, Francisco de P. *Al Azraq: Capitán de moros.* Alicante: Caja de Ahorros de Alicante y Murcia, 1977.

Moral, Félix. *Identidad regional y nacionalismo en el Estado de las Autonomías*, Madrid: CIS, 1998.

Moreno Álvarez, Luis Fermín. "El Islam positivo: La religión de los jóvenes musulmanes en España." *Migraciones* 10 (2001): 249–294.

Moreno Navarro, Isidoro. "Etnicidad, conciencia de etnicidad y movimientos nacionalistas: Aproximación al caso andaluz." *Revista de estudios andaluces* 5 (1985): 13–38.

Moreras, Jordi. *Actors i representacions: L'associacionisme d'origen marroquí a Catalunya*. Barcelona: Generalitat de Catalunya, Departament d'Acció Social i Ciutadania, Secretaria per a la Immigració, 2009.

———. "Muslims in Spain: Between the Historical Heritage and the Minority Construction." *The Muslim World* 92 (Spring 2002): 129–142.

———. *Musulmanes en Barcelona: Espacios y dinámicas comunitarias*. Barcelona: CIDOB Edicions, 1999.

———. "Musulmanes en Europa occidental." *La Factoría* 9 (1999). Accessed December 10, 1999. http://www.lafactoriaweb.com/articulos/moreras9.htm.

———. "Pluralidad, reconocimiento y cotidianidad: La integración del islam en Europa." *Mugak* 15 (2001). Accessed September 20, 2010. http://revista.mugak.eu/articulos/show/136.

———. "¿Ravalistán? Islam y configuración comunitaria entre los paquistaníes en Barcelona." *Revista CIDOB d'Afers Internacionals* 68 (2005): 119–132.

———. *Una mesquita al barri: Conflicte, espai públic i inserció urbana dels oratoris musulmans a Catalunya*. Barcelona: unpublish report, 2009. Accessed September 20, 2009. http://www.migracat.cat/document/270c6e54dbe97b1.pdf.

———. "¿Un islam en Cataluña o un islam catalán?" In *El islam plural*, edited by Maria Àngels Roque Alonso, 335–351. Barcelona: Icaria Editorial, 2003.

Muñoz, Jordi. "Minority Nationalism and Attitudes towards Immigration: Catalonia and Basque Country." In *Nationalism: Theories Formations and Future*, edited by A. Bhattachrya. Hyderabad: ICFAI University Press, 2009.

National Institute of Statistics. *Encuesta nacional de inmigrantes 2007: Una monografía*. Madrid: INE, 2007.

Navarro Pastor, Vicent Xavier. "Lo Rat Penat en la primera época autòmica (1980–1990)." In *Historia de Lo Rat Penat*, edited by Federico Martínez Roda, 320–345. Valencia: Lo Rat Penat, 2000.

Nielsen. Jørgen S. *Muslims in Western Europe*. Edinburgh: Edinburgh University Press, 2004.

———. "The Question of Euro-Islam: Restriction or Opportunity?" In *Islam in Europe: Diversity, Identity and Influence*, edited by Aziz Al-Azmeh and Effie Fokas, 34–48. New York: Cambridge University Press, 2007.

———. *Towards a European Islam*. New York: St. Martin's Press, 1999.

Núñez Seixas, Xosé Manoel. *Los nacionalismos en la España contemporánea (siglos XIX y XX)*. Barcelona: Hipòtesi, 1999.

———. "The Reawakening of Peripheral Nationalisms and the State of the Autonomous Communities." In *Spanish History since 1808*, edited by Adrian Shubert and José Álvarez Junco, 315–330. London: Edward Arnold, 2000.

Ong, Aihwa. *Flexible Citizenship: The Cultural Logics of Transnationality*. Durham, NC: Duke University Press, 1999.

Parekh, Bhikhu. *Rethinking Multiculturalism: Cultural Diversity and Political Theory*. Cambridge, Mass.: Harvard University Press, 2000.

Pascual Saüc, Jordi and Carles Riera. *Identitat cultural i socialització dels fills d'immigrats magrebins a la comarca d'Osona.* Barcelona: CIREM, 1991.

Pérez Embid, Florentino. "Estudio preliminar." In *Textos sobre España*, edited by Florentino Pérez Embid, 11–138. Madrid: Ediciones Rialp, 1955.

Pérez-Díaz, Víctor. *The Return of Civil Society: The Emergence of Democratic Spain.* Cambridge, Mass.: Harvard University Press, 1993.

Perry, Mary Elizabeth. "Memory and Mutilation: The Case of the Moriscos." In *In the Light of Medieval Spain: Islam, the West, and the Relevance of the Past*, edited by Simon R. Doubleday and David Coleman, 67–90. New York: Palgrave Macmillan, 2008.

Planet, Ana I. "Melilla y Ceuta, dos ciudades de frontera en el Mediterráneo occidental." *Mugak* 11 (2000). Accessed November 20, 2010. http://revista.mugak.eu/articulos/show/54.

——. *Melilla and Ceuta: Espacios-frontera hispano-marroquíes.* Melilla: Ciudades Autónomas de Melilla y ceuta/UNED, 1998.

Plewa, Piotr and Mark J. Miller. "Postwar and Post-Cold War Generations of European Temporary Foreign Worker Policies: Implications from Spain." *Migraciones Internacionales* 3, 2 (2005): 58–83.

Polo, José R. "La significación histórica en España del Concilio Vaticano II y el derecho de libertad religiosa." *Revista de la Facultad de Derecho de la Universidad Complutense* 89 (1997–98): 255–282.

Predelli, Line Nyhagen. "Interpreting Gender in Islam: A Case Study of Immigrant Muslim Women in Oslo, Norway." *Gender and Society* 18, 4 (2004): 473–493.

Preston, Paul. *El triunfo de la democracia en España: 1969–1982.* Barcelona: Plaza y Janés, 1986.

Przeworski, Adam. "Conquered or Granted? A History of Suffrage Extensions." *British Journal of Political Science* 39, 2 (2008): 291–321.

Radcliff, Pamela Beth. "Imagining Female Citizenship in the 'New Spain': Gendering the Democratic Transition." *Gender and History* 13, 3 (2001): 498–523.

——. *Making Democratic Citizens: Civil Society and the Popular Origins of the Transition, 1960–1978.* Houndmills, UK: Macmillan Publishers Limited, 2011.

Raguer, Hilari. *Réquiem por la cristiandad. El Concilio Vaticano II y su impacto en España.* Ediciones Peninsula, Barcelona, 2006.

Rahola, Pilar. *La República Islámica de España.* Barcelona: Editorial RBA, 2011.

Ramadan, Tariq. *To be a European Muslim: A Study of Islamic Sources in the European Context.* Leicester, UK: Islamic Foundation, 2005.

——. *Western Muslims and the Future of Islam.* New York: Oxford University Press, 2004.

——. *What I Believe.* New York: Oxford University Press, 2010.

Ramírez, Ángeles. *Migraciones, género e Islam: Mujeres marroquíes en España.* Madrid: Agencia Española de Cooperación Internacional, 1998.

——. *La trampa del velo: El debate sobre el uso del pañuelo musulmán.* Madrid: Catarata, 2011.

Ramírez, Ángeles and Laura Mijares. "Gestión del Islam y de la inmigración en Europa: Tres Estudios del caso." *Revista Migraciones* 18 (2005): 77–104.

Recio, Carles. *La batalla de Valencia.* València: Asociación Cultural Confluencia Valenciana, 1999.

Rodríguez Magda, Rosa María. *La España convertida al islam.* Barcelona: Áltera, 2006.

——. *Inexistente Al Andalus: De cómo los intelectuales reinventan el Islam.* Oviedo: Nobel, 2008.

Roediger, David R. *Towards the Abolition of Whiteness: Essays on Race, Politics, and Working Class History.* London, New York: Verso, 1994.

Rogozen-Soltar, Mikaela. "Al-Andalus in Andalusia: Negotiating Moorish History and Regional Identity in Southern Spain." *Anthropological Quarterly* 80, 3 (2007): 863–886.

Ros, Adela, ed. *Interculturalitat: Bases antropològiques, socials i polítiques.* Barcelona: Pòrtic Editorial, 2003.

Rosander, Eva Evers. *Women in a Borderland: Managing Muslim Identity Where Morocco Meets Spain.* Stockholm, Sweden: Department of Anthropology, Stockholm University, 1991.

——. "Religion, Secularism, and Politics in Contemporary Spain: The Case of the Imam of Fuengirola." In *Religion, Politics, and Globalization: Anthropological Approaches,* edited by Galina Lindquist and Don Handelman, 145–168. New York: Berghahn Books, 2011.

Rothenberg, Paula S., ed. *White Privilege: Essential Readings on the Other Side of Racism.* New York: Worth Publishers, 2005.

Roy, Olivier. *Secularism Confronts Islam.* New York: Columbia University Press, 2007.

Runnymede Trust. Commission on British Muslims and Islamophobia. "Islamophobia: A Challenge for Us All." The Runnymede Trust, 1997.

Sagarra Trias, Eduard. *La Legislación sobre extranjería e inmigración: una lectura.* Barcelona: Publicacions de la UB, 2002.

Saddiki, Said. "Ceuta and Melilla Fences: A Multidimensional Border?" CPSA Conference, 2010. http://www.cpsa-acsp.ca/papers-2010/Saddiki.pdf. Accessed April 17, 2013.

Said, Edward W. *Orientalism.* London; New York: Penguin Books, 1978.

Saint-Blancat, Chantal and Ottavia Schmidt di Friedberg. "Why are Mosques a Problem? Local Politics and Fear of Islam in Northern Italy." *Journal of Ethnic and Migration Studies* 31, 6 (2005): 1083–1104.

Salvá Ballester, Adolf. *Bosqueig històric i bibliogràfic de les festes de moros i cristians.* Alicante: Instituto de Estudios Alicantinos, 1958.

Sánchez Albornoz, Claudio. *Ensayos sobre historia de España.* Madrid: Siglo XXI, 1973.

——. *El Islam de España y el Occidente.* Madrid: Espasa Calpe, 1974.

Sánchez Ruano, Francisco. *Islam y guerra civil española: Moros con Franco y con la República.* Madrid: La Esfera de los Libros, 2004.

Santa Ana, Otto. "'Like an Animal I was Treated': Anti-Immigrant Metaphor in US Public Discourse." *Discourse Society* 10, 2 (1999): 191–224.

Santamarina Campos, Beatriz. "Moros y cristianos: De la batalla festiva a la discursiva." *Gaceta de Antropología* 24, 1 (2008). Article 16. Accessed March 22, 2010. http://hdl.handle.net/10481/6996.

Saunders, Doug. *The Myth of the Muslim Tide: Do Immigrants Threaten the West?* Toronto: Knopf Canada, 2012.

Sayad, Abdelmalek. *L'immigration ou les paradoxes de l'altérité: L'illusion du provisoire.* Paris: Éditions Raisons d'agir, 2006.

Schedler, Andreas. "What is Democratic Consolidation." *Journal of Democracy* 9, 2 (1998): 91–107

Scott, Joan Wallach. *The Politics of the Veil.* Princeton, NJ: Princeton University Press, 2007.

Seddon, David. "Winter of Discontent: Economic Crisis in Tunisia and Morocco." *MERIP Reports* 127 (1984): 7–16.

Sellés Vidal, Elionor. *Moviment obrer, canvi polític, social i cultural. Comissions Obreres a Catalunya (1964–1978).* PhD Thesis. Universitat de Barcelona, 2005.

Shafir, Gershon. *Immigrants and Nationalists: Ethnic Conflict and Accommodation in Catalonia, the Basque Country, Latvia, and Estonia.* Albany: State University of New York, 1995.

Shah, Nasra M. "La emigración laboral pakistaní: nuevos destinos en Europa." *Revista CIDOB d'Afers Internacionals* 68 (2005): 89–96.

Shubert, Adrian. *A Social History of Modern Spain.* London: Routledge, 1992.

Shulman, Stephen. "Challenging the Civic/Ethnic and West/East Dichotomies in the Study of Nationalism." *Comparative Political Studies* 35, 5 (2002): 554–586.

Silveira Abrão, Janete. "Nacionalismo cultural y político: La doble cara de un proyecto único: Cataluña." Ph.D. diss., Universidad de Barcelona, 2006.

Simmons, Harvey G. *The French National Front: the Extremist Challenge to Democracy.* Boulder, Colo.: Westview Press, 1996.

Smith, Anthony D. "The Ethnic Sources of Nationalism." In *Ethnic Conflict and International Security,* edited by Michael E. Brown, 27–42. Princeton, NJ: Princeton University Press, 1993.

Solé Aubia, Montserrat and Josep Roca. "Pakistaníes en España: Un estudio basado en el colectivo de la ciudad de Barcelona." *Revista CIDOB d'Afers Internacionals* 68 (2005): 97–118.

Soler Amigó, Joan. *Jameiat Essalam: Associació d'Osona per la Pau.* Barcelona: Fundació de Serveis de Cultura Popular, 1999.

SOS Racismo, *El Ejido: Racismo y explotación laboral: Balance un año después.* Barcelona: Icaria, 2001.

Southern, R. W. *Western Views of Islam in the Middle Ages.* Cambridge, Mass.: Harvard University Press, 1962.

Suárez Navaz, Liliana. *Rebordering the Mediterranean: Boundaries and Citizenship in Southern Europe.* Oxford and New York: Berghahn Books, 2004.

Suárez Navaz, Liliana, Raquel Macià Pareja, and Ángela Moreno García, eds. *La lucha de los sin papeles y la extensión de la ciudadanía: Perspectivas críticas desde Europa y Estados Unidos.* Madrid: Traficantes de Sueños, 2007.

Subirats, Eduardo, ed. *Américo Castro y la revisión de la memoria: El Islam en España.* Madrid: Libertarias, 2003.

Tarrow, Sidney. *Power in Movement.* New York: Cambridge University Press, 1994.

Testas, Abdelaziz. "Maghreb-EU Migration: Interdependence, Remittances, the Labour Market and Implications for Economic Development." *Mediterranean Politics* 6, 3 (2001): 64–80.

Threlfall, Monica. "The Women's Movement in Spain." *New Left Review* 151 (1985): 44–73.

Thompson, Leonard. *The Political Mythology of Apartheid.* New Haven: Yale University Press, 1985.

Tibi, Bassam. *Political Islam, World Politics and Europe: Democratic Peace and Euro-Islam Versus Global Jihad.* London; New York: Routledge, 2008.

Tolsanas Pagès, Mònica. "Las calles de Barcelona, las casas de Paquistán: Transnacionalismo y generación posmigratoria." *Revista CIDOB d'Afers Internacionals* 78 (2007): 33–56.

Triandafyllidou, Anna. *Immigrants and National Identity in Europe.* London; New York: Routledge, 2001.

——, ed. *Irregular Migration in Europe: Myths and Realities.* Farnham, England; Burlington, VT: Ashgate Pub, 2010.

——. "Religious Diversity and Multiculturalism in Southern Europe: The Italian 'Mosque Debate'." In *Multiculturalism, Muslims and Citizenship: A European Approach*, edited by Tariq Modood, Anna Triandafyllidou, and Ricard Zapata-Barrero, 117–142. London: Routledge, 2006.

Triandafyllidou, Anna and Ruby Gropas, "Constructing Difference: The Mosque Debates in Greece." *Journal of Ethnic and Migration Studies* 35, 6 (2009): 957–977.

Tusell, Javier. "El impacto del Concilio Vaticano II en la política y en la sociedad española." In *El Posconcilio en España*, edited by Juan María Laboa, 377–90. Madrid, Ediciones Encuentro, 1988.

Tzanelli, Rodanthi and Majid Yar, "Paradoxes of Belonging: Migration, Exclusion and Transnational Rights in the Mediterranean." *Development* 52 (2009): 473–478.

UCIDE. *Estudio demográfico de la población musulmana: Explotación estadística del censo de ciudadanos musulmanes en España referido a fecha de 31/12/2010.* Madrid: UCIDE. 2010. Accessed May 2, 2011. http://oban.multiplexor.es/estademograf.pdf.

Ugarte, Michael. "Juan Goytisolo: Unruly Disciple of Americo Castro." *Journal of Spanish Studies: Twentieth Century* 7, 3 (1979): 353–364.

United Nations, Department of Economic and Social Affairs, *World Population Policies 2005.* United Nations Publication: 2006.

Varela, Amara. "Residency Documents for All! Notes to Understand the Movement of Migrants in Barcelona." *Refuge* 26, 2 (2009): 121–132.

Veredas Muñoz, Sonia. "Las asociaciones de inmigrantes en España: Práctica clientelar y cooptación política." *Revista Internacional de Sociología* 36 (2003): 207–225.

Viadel, Francesc. *No mos fareu catalans: Història inacabada del blaverisme.* Valencia: Universitat de València, 2009.

Vidal, César. *España frente al Islam: De Mahoma a Ben Laden.* Madrid: Esfera de los libros, 2005.

Vila, Ignasi. *Llengua, escola i immigració: Un debat obert.* Barcelona: Graó, 2006.

Wadud Muhsin, Amina. *Qur'an and Women: Rereading the Sacred Text from a Woman's Perspective.* Oxford: Oxford University Press, 1999.

Warren, Mark E. *Democracy and Association.* Princeton NJ: Princeton University Press, 2001.

Werbner, Pnina. *The Migration Process: Capital, Gifts and Offerings among British Pakistanis.* New York: Berg, 1990.

Wolbrecht, Christina and Rodney E. Hero, eds. *The Politics of Democratic Inclusion.* Philadelphia, PA: Temple University Press, 2005.

Woolard, Kathryn A. *Double Talk: Bilingualism and the Politics of Ethnicity in Catalonia.* Stanford, Calif.: Stanford University Press, 1989.

Xenos, Nicholas. "Civic Nationalism: Oxymoron?" *Critical Review* 10, 2 (Spring 1996): 213–231.

Yack, Bernard. "The Myth of the Civic Nation." *Critical Review* 10, 2 (1996): 193–211.

Ye'or, Bat. *Eurabia: The Euro-Arab Axis.* Madison, NJ: Fairleigh Dickinson University Press, 2005.

Young, Iris Marion. *Inclusion and Democracy.* Oxford: Oxford University Press, 2000.

Yurdakul, Gökçe. *From Guest Workers into Muslims: The Transformation of Turkish Immigrant Associations in Germany.* Newcastle, UK: Cambridge Scholars Publishing, 2009.

Zapata-Barrero, Ricard. "The Muslim Community and Spanish Tradition: Maurofobia as a Fact, and Impartiality as a Desideratum." In *Multiculturalism, Muslims and Citizenship: A European Approach,* edited by Tariq Modood, Anna Triandafyllidou, and Ricard Zapata-Barrero, 143–161. Toronto and New York: Routledge, 2006.

——. "The Three Strands of Intercultural Policies: a Comprehensive View." GRITIM Working Paper No. 17, 2013.

Zapata-Barrero, Ricard and Nynke de Witte. "Muslims in Spain: Blurring Past and Present Moors." In *Muslims in 21st Century Europe: Structural and Cultural Perspectives,* edited by Anna Triandafyllidou, 181–198. Milton Park, Abingdon, Oxon; New York, NY: Routledge, 2010.

Zhou, Min. "Revisiting Ethnic Entrepreneurship: Convergencies, Controversies, and Conceptual Advancements." *International Migration Review* 38, 3 (2004): 1040–1074.

Zine, Jasmin. "Unveiled Sentiments: Gendered Islamophobia and Experiences of Veiling among Muslim Girls in a Canadian Islamic School." *Equity and Excellence in Education* 39, 3 (2006): 239–252.

Zniber, Khalil. "Maroc: des exilés qui rapportent." *Jeune Afrique* 34 (1993): 46–47.

Index

ACESOP (*Associació Cultural Educativa i Social Operativa de Dones Pakistaneses*), 120
  see also Jamshed, Huma
AEME (*Asociación de Emigrantes Marroquíes en España*), 45–6, 52–3, 56, 72, 177–18n
Agreement of Cooperation, 7, 75–6, 81–6, 94, 97–8, 102–3, 106, 159, 163–4
agriculture, 43, 47, 54–7, 65, 144
Ahmadiyya, 78
Al Amal, 51–2, 59, 163
  see also Mellagi, Aicha
Al-Andalus, 79, 86, 130–3, 136–7, 139, 159, 165, 195–4n
Alcoi, 140, 142–3, 148–9, 150–1, 153, 158, 165, 198–49n, 199–88n, 199–98n
Alianza Popular, 12
  see also Partido Popular
Alliance of Civilizations, 137–9, 158, 165, 197–40n
Allievi, Stefano, 101, 105, 189–18n
Almería Acoge, 56
Almería, 3, 55, 60, 64, 69, 98
Almería Case, 36, 175–108n
Amazigh, 1, 18, 29, 39, 55, 67, 117, 120
Andalusia, 3, 10, 11, 39, 54, 63–4, 78–80, 97, 113, 119, 123, 136, 139, 141–2
Anglada, Josep, 125–7, 194–124n
Anguita, Julio, 136
APWC (*Associació de Treballadors Pakistanesos de Catalunya*), 121–2
arraigo, 15, 31, 39, 48–9, 58, 61–2, 69–71, 81, 116, 133, 161–2, 173–82n
assimilation, 8, 100, 102, 112–13, 116, 118, 127–9, 132, 153–5, 165
Athens, 107, 109, 164, 190–42n
ATIME (*Asociación de Trabajadores Inmigrantes Marroquíes en España*), 42–6, 51–2, 55–7, 61, 63, 65, 69, 72, 98–9, 161, 163
  see also Beyuki, Abdelhamid

Autonomous Communities, 2, 10, 90, 95, 112
Aznar, José María, 58, 62–3
  see also Partido Popular

Barberá, Rita, 157
  see also Partido Popular
Barri de l'Erm, 54, 123–6, 193–109n, 193–110n
Barrionuevo, José, 27, 31
Basque Country, 1, 44, 112, 116
Bassets, Julio, 30
Belkacemi, Lies, 46–7, 135,
belonging, 101–2, 119, 166, 191–64n
Beyuki, Abdelhamid, 42–3, 53, 57, 59–61
bilingualism, 113, 116, 125
Bocairent, 140, 142–4, 147–8, 152–3, 198–49n, 198–54n
borderlands, 10, 12–14, 25, 39–40
Britain, 18, 22, 61, 101, 115, 191–46n

Candel, Francisco, 54, 191–64n
Candela, Jadicha, 85, 88–9
Castro, Américo, 133
Catalan language, 112, 115–17, 128, 157, 165, 192–72n
Catalan nationalism, 101, 112, 114, 117, 122, 128, 164
Catalonia, 1–3, 6, 54–5, 66, 71, 86, 88–9, 92, 94–5, 99, 102, 104–9, 111–22, 125–29, 133, 135, 139, 154, 164–5
  see also Pujol, Jordi
Catholic Church, 41–2, 74–78, 81, 83–4, 107, 111, 137–9, 149, 163, 183–6n, 185–42n, 196–25n
CCIC (*Consell Cultural Islàmic de Catalunya*), 108, 120
  see also Chaib, Mohamed
Cesari, Jocelyn, 101, 104, 190–38n
Ceuta, 2, 4–5, 10–11, 14–15, 17, 22–3, 26–9, 31, 33, 37, 40, 44, 64, 84, 95, 97, 142, 161, 170–27n

CGT (*Confederación General del Trabajo*), 66–7
Chaib, Mohamed, 42, 44, 47, 55–6, 85–6, 92, 98–9, 108, 118–22, 135
church occupations, 64, 66–9, 80, 121, 163
CIE (*Comisión Islámica de España*), 7, 75, 82–3, 85–6, 97, 163
citizenship, 3–9, 10, 14–18, 20, 23–7, 29–35, 37–8, 41, 44, 47, 70, 72, 77, 81, 87, 102, 116, 119, 128, 151, 161–2
civil rights, 4, 10, 18, 23, 37, 161
civil society, 4, 8, 16, 25, 38, 72, 103, 122
colonialism, 2, 3, 10, 12, 14–15, 19, 22, 24–5, 35, 40, 103, 143, 147–8, 158–9
commemoration, 130–1, 146
companies, 139, 147–9, 152, 158
see also Festival of Moors and Christians
conquest, 10–11, 81, 120, 132–4, 136–7, 139, 141–3, 145–6, 149, 151, 153–5, 157–9, 163, 165
consolidation of democracy, 7, 9, 17–18, 25, 75, 168–24*n*
constitutional patriotism, 28, 34, 39
converts to Christianity, 9, 14, 75, 131, 139, 141
converts to Islam, 3, 5, 9, 78–80, 82, 84–90, 92–93, 99, 104, 106, 133, 135–7, 139, 153, 163–4, 184–27*n*, 187–90*n*
convivencia, 16, 47, 62, 98, 108, 115, 118, 122, 131–2, 135, 139, 144–5, 152–3, 165–6
Córdoba Mosque, 130, 135, 137–9, 163
Córdoba, 78–9, 82, 92, 95–6, 103, 130, 133–9, 163, 165
Crespo, Ricardo, 14, 16, 23
cultural rights, 8–9, 113, 131, 135, 165–6

Danish cartoon controversy, 138, 152–5, 165
deepening of democracy, 7, 9, 75, 102, 166, 168–24*n*
democratization, 3–8, 17–18, 25, 151, 166
Denmark, 94, 152
diversity, 2, 9, 25, 78, 80, 98, 105, 112–13, 115, 122, 126, 128, 151
Duddu, Aomar Mohamedi, 15–19, 21, 23–4, 26–7, 29–39, 44

Ecuadorians, 3, 48, 65, 67
education, 6, 16, 27–9, 38, 45, 57, 59, 61–2, 76–7, 83–4, 90, 93–4, 97–9, 112, 115–16, 120, 126, 138, 158, 164
EEC (European Economic Community), 3, 11, 13, 22, 27
El Ejido, 39, 54, 56, 62, 64, 180–86*n*
El Hachmi, Najat, 55, 81, 91,93, 117–22
El País editorials, 17, 24, 27, 58
El Raval, 54, 66, 69, 109–11, 119–20, 122, 182–121*n*
Erdogan, Recep Tayyip, 152
Escudero, Mansur, 82–7, 97, 137–9
see also Junta Islámica
ETA (Basque Country and Freedom), 1, 41
Euro-Islam, 8, 80
exclusion, 4–6, 12, 14, 25, 37, 41–2, 125, 135, 161, 165

Falconi, Norma, 67–8, 70
family reunification, 51–2, 61, 68, 162–3
fanaticism, 23, 151, 154–5
Fanjul, Serafín, 133
FEERI (*Federación Española de Entidades Religiosas Islámicas*), 82, 84–8, 98–9, 110–11, 153
Festival of Moors and Christians, 6, 109, 130–1, 139, 142–4, 146, 149–51, 154–5, 158–9, 165
see also Fonèvol; La Mahoma; Saint George Association
Fonèvol, 150–1
France, 2, 3, 37, 61, 74, 78, 81, 93–5, 99, 101, 103, 148
Franco Bahamonde, Francisco, 1, 2, 5–7, 9, 11, 13, 17, 22–3, 25, 30, 41, 64, 66, 70, 74, 76–79, 97, 102–3, 106, 112–13, 118, 120, 123, 125, 130, 133, 135–7, 143, 145, 149, 151, 153, 157–8
Frankfurt Book Fair, 128

Gendered Islamophobia, 21, 87, 95
Germany, 3, 94, 105
Gibraltar, 11, 14, 22, 48, 53, 63–4, 146, 161
González, Felipe, 10, 33, 58
government delegate, 12, 27, 31, 33, 35, 64, 67, 169–9*n*
Goytisolo, Juan, 22, 39, 42, 127, 133, 146, 148, 155–6

Granada, 81, 108, 135–6, 153–4, 163
Greece, 105, 107, 109

halal food, 83–4, 90, 99, 114, 120
Halal Institute, 94, 99, 136, 163
  see also Romero Arias, Mariam Isabel
Hassan II, 22–3, 26, 33, 38, 44, 46
headscarf affair, 93
  see also veiling
Hernández, Gonzalo, 22, 29, 32
Hirsi Ali, Ayaan, 117, 192–81*n*
historical narratives, 6, 7, 9, 11, 23, 63,
    80, 104, 130–1, 134–5, 141–2, 148,
    158–60, 165
HOAC (*Hermandad Obrera de Acción
    Católica*), 56, 66
Hobsbawm, Eric, 146
human rights, 2, 16, 29–30, 33, 38, 42, 44,
    52, 54, 56, 59, 61, 63, 70, 79, 92, 122,
    128, 134
hunger strikes, 17, 21, 30, 40, 53, 56, 64,
    66–7, 69, 163

Ibn Battuta Association, 42, 44, 56, 71–2,
    85, 108, 111, 120, 128, 161
Ibn Khaldun, 136
Ibn Rushd (Averroes), 38, 136
ICCV (Centro Cultural Islámico de
    Valencia), 133–4
identification, 12–13, 23, 35–7, 39, 46, 52,
    119–21, 156–7
  see also identity
identity, 9, 12–14, 18, 23, 35, 39, 44, 54,
    67, 83, 92, 94, 96, 105, 109, 114,
    116–17, 119–21, 125–6, 133, 157,
    161, 163
  see also identification
Ilyas, Javed, 121–2
  see also APWC
Imam of Fuengirola, 87
  see also Kamal Mustafa, Mohamed
imams, 80–3, 86–7, 93, 99, 103, 105,
    107–8, 154
Imazighen, 10, 33, 79, 118, 123, 147
  see also Amazigh
Immigration Act of 1985, 1, 3, 4, 13–17,
    22, 26–31, 33, 37, 44, 49, 52, 58, 59,
    60–2, 71–2, 161
Immigration Act of December 2000, 63,
    66, 68–9, 71–2
Immigration Act of January 2000, 59–65,
    162

integration, 23–5, 31, 46, 49, 57–61, 63,
    70, 99, 100, 114, 116–17, 122, 128,
    162
interculturalism, 114, 127–9, 165
internal migrants, 112–13, 128, 191–64*n*
  see also Candel, Francisco
Iqbal, Muhammad, 110, 122
  see also Path Towards Peace
Islam, 3, 8, 9, 78, 80, 81
  and democracy, 8
  and women's rights, 20–1, 87–95
  grand mosques, 82–3, 102, 106–10,
    119, 129, 154, 164
  institutionalization of, 75, 82–7
  practice of, 2, 5, 7, 16, 39, 75, 81, 83, 85,
    95–101
  Shia, 78, 81, 96
  Sunni, 78–9, 86, 110
  see also Agreement of Cooperation;
    CCIC; CIE; converts to Islam;
    FEERI; ICCV; Islamic Spain; *Junta
    Islámica;* mosques; UCIDE
Islamic feminism, 92–3, 150, 187–87*n*,
    187–89*n*
Islamic Spain, 9, 79–80, 130–1, 133, 135,
    137, 159
Islamophobia, 21, 90, 93, 95, 114, 126
  see also gendered Islamophobia
Istiqlal, 26–7
Italy, 12, 76, 94, 105, 107, 148

Jameiat Essalam, 117, 122–5, 127, 164
James I, 133–4, 142, 145, 149, 157, 165,
    201–131*n*
Jamshed, Huma, 120–22
  see also ACESOP
Judt, Tony, 70
Junta Islámica (Islamic Council), 79, 82,
    85, 92, 99, 133, 136, 154

Kamal Mustafa, Mohamed, 87–90, 93
  see also Imam of Fuengirola
Karrouch, Ahmed, 1–3
Karrouch, Laila, 1, 91, 93, 98
King Juan Carlos I, 1, 17, 29, 103, 158
Kymlicka, Will, 6, 113, 129

La Mahoma, 140–1, 149, 152–4, 198–49*n*
La mujer en el Islam, 87, 89
La Vila Joiosa, 142, 146, 159
Lleida, 56, 64, 94, 105, 129, 159
Lodi, 102, 105

López García, Bernabé, 42
Lorca, 65–6

Madrid, 3, 11, 36, 42–6, 50–3, 56, 59–60,
    66, 69, 71, 76, 78–83, 87, 89–90, 97,
    99, 103, 105–6, 120, 134, 137,144,
    155, 163–4
Málaga, 10–12, 29, 69, 81, 103
Manlleu, 54, 122–3, 125–6, 193–109*n*,
    193–110*n*
Melilla City Hall, 11, 15, 17, 29–30,
    32–33
Melilla, 2, 4–5, 7, 10–40, 44, 49, 52, 75–6,
    84, 95, 97, 161–2, 166
    see also Duddu, Aomar Mohamedi;
    nativism; OCMP; Terra Omnium
Mellagi, Aicha, 51
    see also Al Amal
memory, 11, 25, 77, 125, 130–1, 134,
    143–4, 147
Menéndez Pelayo, Marcelino, 132–3,
    142, 145, 155
migrant activism, 40, 45, 52, 56, 70–1,
    162
migrant associations, 42, 72, 85
migrant workers, 3, 43, 49, 56, 58–9, 67,
    70, 98–9
MMPAS (*Escola d'Adults Miquel Martí i
    Pol*), 123, 194–113*n*
Model Vic, 126
Mohamed Alí, Abdelkader, 16, 18, 30, 32,
    35–9
Mooricization, 146, 148
Mora d'Ebre, 159
Morabitun, 79, 108
Moreno, Antonio, 28–9, 33, 170–27*n*
Moriscos, 9, 14, 25, 75, 107, 131, 134–5,
    143–4, 147, 155–6, 165
Moro (Moor), 20–1, 23, 39, 53, 79
    see also Festival of Moors and
    Christians
Moroccans, 3, 23, 26–9, 31, 39, 41, 43, 46,
    48, 51, 53, 55, 65, 97, 114, 117–18,
    123, 147, 161
Morocco, 3, 11–22, 14, 22, 23, 26–8, 31,
    33–39, 43–4, 46, 50–1, 62, 79,
    81–2, 86, 91, 93, 99, 108, 117,
    119, 124
Moses ben-Maimon (Maimonides), 136
mosques
    conflicts over, 6, 86, 101–11, 119–20,
    163–4

in Catalonia, 101–2, 104–11, 114, 122,
    129, 159
in Melilla, 17, 20, 28, 32, 36
in other European countries, 102
in other Spanish regions, 78, 80–85, 90,
    97–8, 103, 130, 135–9, 152–4, 163
    see also Córdoba Mosque; imam of
    Fuengirola; Lodi; prayer sites
Multiculturalism, 80, 106, 126–7, 131,
    152, 160, 164
Murcia Acoge, 56
Murcia, 3, 56, 65, 69
Muslim Association (Melilla), 16, 38
Muslim women, 18–21, 26–8, 87–95,
    108, 120, 124, 162–3, 170–30*n*,
    170–37*n*, 187–87*n*

nationalism, 2, 6, 13, 95, 101, 112, 114,
    117, 120, 122, 128, 149, 157, 164
    see also Catalan nationalism
nativism, 4, 22–39, 49, 102–4, 106–9, 111,
    152, 154, 161, 163, 165–6, 167–15*n*,
    171–47*n*
NATO, 3, 22, 48
neighbourhood associations, 66, 101,
    123, 194–113*n*
Netherlands, 94
Nini, Rachid, 43, 46–7, 53, 55, 93, 121,
    159–60

OCMP (*Comité Organizador del Pueblo
    Musulmán*), 16–8, 28–32, 34
Ombudsman, 14–15, 169–15*n*
Osona, 122–3, 126–7, 164

Pakistan, 3, 78, 86, 92, 110, 120–1
Pakistanis, 66–7, 72, 96, 109–11, 120–2
Papers per Tothom, 66–7, 72, 181–106*n*
    see also Falconi, Norma
papers, 20, 42, 46–7, 51–2, 55, 65–7, 72
Path Towards Peace, 109–11, 122
PCL (*Plataforma per la Llengua*), 115
peripheralization, 105, 126
political rights, 16, 60, 72, 75, 135, 162
politics of belonging, 101–2
PP (*Partido Popular*), 58–63, 65–6,
    68–71, 84–6, 97, 158, 164
    see also Alianza Popular; Aznar, José
    María; Barberá, Rita
prayer sites, 80–1, 101–2, 104, 106, 108,
    164
    see also mosques

Premià de Mar, 105
prisons, 21, 36–7, 49, 83–4, 89, 90, 99
PSC (*Partit dels Socialistes de Catalunya*), 66, 71, 108, 114, 119, 164
PSOE (*Partido Socialista Obrero Español*), 12, 15, 17–9, 22, 24, 27, 29, 30, 32, 37, 45, 49, 58, 69, 71, 77, 81, 84–5, 97, 129, 136, 158, 163
    see also Barrionuevo, José; González, Felipe; Moreno, Andrés; Rodríguez Zapatero, José Luis
Pujol, Jordi, 106–8, 114–15, 127, 129
    see also Catalan nationalism
PxC (*Plataforma per Catalunya*), 94–5, 122, 125–7, 129, 164, 194–124*n*
    see also Anglada, Josep

Québec, 113, 116, 128

racial profiling, 52–4, 134, 178–53*n*
racism, 24–5, 42, 52–3, 55, 59, 61, 124, 162
Ramadan, Tariq, 80
Ravalistan, 109, 182–121*n*
regional nationalism, 2, 13, 149
    see also Catalan nationalism
regularizations, 42, 45–53, 56–8, 60, 62, 64–6, 69–71, 162
religious pluralism, 2, 5, 9, 74–7, 96, 102–3, 106, 114, 125, 129, 133, 163, 165
residency permit, 13–4, 30, 37, 52, 57, 60, 72, 113, 162
rituals, 6, 79, 95–6, 131, 138, 140–1, 143–4, 146, 148–9, 152–3, 157–8, 165
    see also Festival of Moors and Christians
    see also La Mahoma
Rodríguez Magda, Rosa María, 80, 133
Rodríguez Zapatero, José Luis, 77, 96, 137–8, 152, 158
Romero Arias, Mariam Isabel, 94, 99, 163
    see also Halal Institute
Rushdie, Salman, 103

Saint George Association, 150–1, 158
    see also Alcoi; Festival of Moors and Christians
Salafism, 94
Sánchez Albornoz, Claudio, 132–3, 142

Sánchez Rosell, Amparo, 92, 94, 133, 163
    see also ICCV
Santa Maria del Pi, 66–7
Saudi Arabia, 81–3, 85, 103, 107–8, 119, 137
secularism, 8, 16, 74–8, 93–101, 111, 119, 122, 139, 145
segregation, 12, 18, 20–1, 35, 39, 51–2, 54, 60, 123–6, 150, 180–86*n*
social capital, 39
SOS Racismo, 42, 53, 61, 65–6, 126
Spain
    "pact of silence", 77, 130
    democracy, 4, 69, 102, 135
    Guardia Mora, 130, 142
    regulares, 78
    see also Franco Bahamonde, Francisco; Immigration Act of 1985; Immigration Act of December 2000; Immigration Act of January 2000; PP; PSOE; Spanish Civil War; Spanish Constitution of 1978; Transition to democracy; UGT; Workers' Commissions
Spanish Civil War, 77–8, 103, 125, 130, 135–6, 148
Spanish Constitution of 1978, 1, 2, 5–6, 10, 12–13, 25, 29–31, 35, 37, 71, 74, 76, 80, 89–90, 93, 99, 112, 151, 163, 165
Spanish intellectuals, 9, 17, 42, 49, 56, 62, 80, 102, 115
    see also Goytisolo, Juan
Statistics Card, 12, 15

Tamazight, 29, 67
Tatary, Riay, 77, 83–3, 85, 103, 105
Terra Omnium, 16, 18–19, 30, 32, 35–8
terrorism, 28, 36, 41, 60, 71, 80, 87, 99, 104, 110, 137–8, 142, 155
tourism, 57, 109, 111, 136, 139, 143, 151, 157–9
tradition, 1–3, 5, 8–9, 20–2, 24, 66, 70, 74–8, 80, 82, 87, 90–1, 93–4, 103, 128, 136, 140–1, 143–4, 146–8, 1 50–1, 158–9, 163–5
transition to democracy, 1, 4–9, 10, 11, 13, 16, 20, 22, 25, 41, 74–5, 77, 102, 130
Turtle March, 23

UCIDE (*Unión de Comunidades Islámicas de España*), 3, 82, 84–6, 98
UGT (*Unión General de Trabajadores*), 45, 56, 60–1, 66, 138
undocumented persons, 3, 5, 9, 12, 14–17, 23, 27–9, 31, 34, 37–8, 40, 43–4, 46–50, 53, 55–62, 64–9, 121, 124, 135, 159, 161–2
UNESCO, 115, 138, 158
United Left Party, 37, 45, 49, 66, 114, 129
United Nations, 11, 17, 22, 54, 59, 137–8
University of Valencia, 134, 145, 147

Valencia, 3, 44, 52, 54–5, 62, 69, 78, 90, 92, 95, 106, 128, 133–4, 139, 141–5, 147, 151–2, 154, 157–9, 163, 165
see also ICCV

Vatican II, 76, 165
veiling, 21, 93–5, 146
visibility, 8, 18, 58, 101–2, 105, 163
voice, 4, 5, 7,18, 29, 41–2, 45, 69, 70, 72, 89, 92, 101–2, 124, 161, 165

white flight, 52, 54–5, 126
Williams, Rosalind, 54, 134
see also racial profiling
women's rights, 5, 74, 87, 90, 105, 124
work permit, 1, 14, 48–9, 53, 57–8, 62, 68, 109
Worker's Commissions, 30, 45, 56, 58, 60, 66–7, 98

xenophobia, 53, 55, 107, 125